THE LEFT-ARMED CORPS

THE LEFT-ARMED CORPS

WRITINGS BY
AMPUTEE CIVIL WAR VETERANS

EDITED BY
ALLISON M. JOHNSON

LOUISIANA STATE UNIVERSITY PRESS
BATON ROUGE

Published with the assistance of a subsidy from the College of Humanities and the Arts at San José State University

Published by Louisiana State University Press
lsupress.org

DESIGNER: Mandy McDonald Scallan
TYPEFACE: Sentinel

COVER PHOTOGRAPH: Alonzo L. Mabbett. Courtesy Arthur Mabbett. Background: Sample of John Stewart's penmanship. Courtesy William Oland Bourne Papers, Manuscript Division, Library of Congress.

Cataloging-in-Publication Data are available from the Library of Congress.

ISBN 978-0-8071-7707-5 (cloth: alk. paper) — ISBN 978-0-8071-7746-4 (pbk: alk. paper) — ISBN 978-0-8071-7747-1 (pdf) — ISBN 978-0-8071-7748-8 (epub)

TO MY RIGHT-
(AND LEFT-)
HAND MAN,
BLAKE FREEMAN

CONTENTS

ACKNOWLEDGMENTS

I am extremely grateful to an amazing support system, comprising family, friends, and colleagues. They have supported me throughout this process, which started way back in 2011 in the reading room of the Library of Congress's Manuscript Division. The librarian who showed me Walt Whitman's walking stick and recommended I take a look at William Oland Bourne's papers has my eternal gratitude. When I first wrote about this amazing collection of left-handed accounts, I dreamed of one day fulfilling Bourne's goal of publishing a "memorial volume." James W. Long of Louisiana State University Press helped me make that dream a reality, as did an anonymous reader who aided me in strengthening the volume. During my research, I also encountered helpful descendants of the "Left-Armed Corps" and diligent preservers of Civil War memory. Many thanks to Karla Cook, Alan Ford, Tammy Jaeger, Robert Wayne Reynolds, Jane Sukow, and Donald Thompson. My colleagues at San José State University provided community and kind words, Dean Shannon Miller financially supported this endeavor, and Sara West helped out during the hard times (and provided a lot of fun times). My parents, Chris and Patti Johnson, tracked down census records (and also let me watch *Dances with Wolves* when I was little, which is partially to blame for my interest in amputation and the lives of Civil War soldiers). They, along with my in-laws, Mark and Joan Freeman, have been there when I needed them most. Thanks and eternal love to my husband, Blake, who puts up with all of my stories about Civil War veterans.

THE LEFT-ARMED CORPS

INTRODUCTION

On May 5, 1865, Burritt Stiles of the 14th Connecticut Volunteers, then a patient at New York's Central Park Hospital, added his name to a hospital chaplain's autograph book. The chaplain, an editor and poet named William Oland Bourne, labeled Stiles's entry "left hand writing," recognizing an important component of the one-armed veteran's recovery: learning to write with his left hand after losing his right hand as a result of military service during the Civil War. Bourne's interactions with men like Stiles inspired him to organize two left-handed penmanship contests. The resulting collection of sinister (derived from the Latin word for left) manuscripts provides invaluable insight into the ways in which former fighting men understood and commemorated their experience as Union soldiers, their bodily sacrifice, and their postwar positions; many also celebrated their membership in a brotherhood of similarly wounded men a cadre they called the Left-Armed Corps.

During his time as a hospital volunteer, Bourne met hundreds of recuperating veterans, many of whom had lost limbs. The three autograph books he passed around contain messages from grateful patients; next to at least twenty-two entries, Bourne wrote, "written with the left hand."[1] The annotations demonstrate his growing recognition of a unique subset of wounded veterans: men who lost their right arms or the use of their right arms or hands as a

1. Civil War Reminiscences by Soldiers and Sailors in Central Park Hospital, William Oland Bourne Papers.

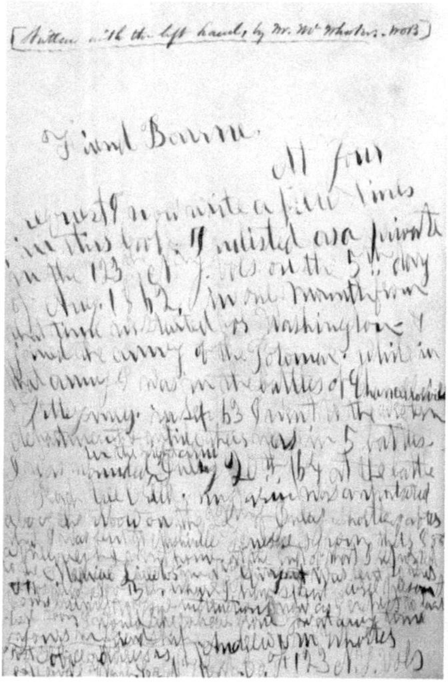

Left-hand writing in one of Bourne's reminiscence books from Central Park Hospital.
Courtesy William Oland Bourne Papers, Manuscript Division, Library of Congress.

result of the war. As a writer and editor, Bourne was well aware of the importance of telling, collecting, and sharing stories. He was also sincerely invested in supporting and rehabilitating the men he ministered to, especially those who wrote their names with shaky and tentative left hands. Of the newly left-handed men who signed Bourne's books, at least eight participated in the left-handed penmanship contests.

The Left Hand

The Union army recorded more than 16,000 arm-related amputations, and the resulting "empty-sleeves" were a common sight in the decades following the war.[2] Bourne did not hold right-handed penmanship contests for men who lost their left arms, obviously assuming that the vast majority who had lost

2. Figg and Farrell-Beck, "Amputation in the Civil War," 459. For more on amputation, see Nelson, *Ruin Nation,* 175–78, 186–227.

appendages were previously right-handed. In the 1860s, perhaps as little as 2 percent of the population was left-handed, in part due to stigmas associated with the sinister appendange.[3] Announcing the second penmanship contest, *The Brooklyn Union* acknowledged that "practicing left-hand writing . . . is an awkward business, and few would undertake it, or they would falter if they did, without bringing it to a successful issue, if it were not for some such inducement as Mr. Bourne offers."[4] By the time Bourne conceived of the contests, some members of the Left-Armed Corps had already brought left-handed writing "to a successful issue." Seth Sutherland, having returned from Shiloh minus an arm, was elected his county's auditor. Noting that observers frequently remarked "that it must be very awkward for [him] to write," he would reply: "Not at all sir, it is only the way you look at it. It was at first as a matter of course very awkward and tiresome, but now quite natural."[5] Judging by the varying levels of legibility among the contest entries, as well as the testaments of some of the contestants, not all men were as comfortable with or adept at their new skill.

Significantly, the contest called for entries penned with the left hand, not with an artificial hand. Bourne's newspaper, *The Soldier's Friend,* featured advertisements and endorsements for artificial arms and legs and in one instance printed an engraving of writing produced by an artificial hand; perhaps not surprisingly, the penmanship is noticeably sloppier than most of the left-hand specimens.[6] While Bourne praised the National Leg and Arm Company's prosthetics, noting that a man could "feed himself, take off his hat, hold the reins in driving, and even write a letter" with its artificial hand, fewer than twenty of the contestants referred to artificial limbs. These were obviously imperfect replacements, often ill fitting.[7] Neither James Henry Hunter nor William Jones could take advantage of federal funding for prosthetics since each lost an arm at the shoulder socket.[8] Henry Karsnitz lamented that

3. McManus, "History and Geography of Human Handedness," 37, 40.

4. "Interesting to One-Armed Soldiers," *Brooklyn Union,* Mar. 28, 1867, 2.

5. Seth Sutherland, Contest Entry, 1st ser., no. 1, Bourne Papers.

6. "Writing with Artificial Hands," *Soldier's Friend,* Sept 1865, 2.

7. Figg and Farrell-Beck, "Amputation in the Civil War," 464. For more on prosthetics, see Nelson, *Ruin Nation,* 211–20.

8. James Henry Hunter, Contest Entries, 1st ser., no. 70, and 2nd ser., no. 15, Bourne Papers; William Jones, Contest Entry, 1st ser., no. 132, ibid.

his replacement did not work, while George S. Warner praised his, noting it "look[ed] quite natural and [was] quite useful."[9] Marvin Burroughs obtained an artificial forearm in 1865 but only wore it "a few times" since "it was heavy and made the stump sore."[10] Despite his enthusiasm for prosthetics, Bourne was confident that the left hand could successfully replace the right and that ostensibly "crippled" men could, through perseverance and practice, make the left hand write and (almost) *right,* thus becoming fully functional members of society. Though some contestants participated in this rhetoric, others refused to cover over their wounds or narrate a seamless transition from right to left. Instead, they relied on the denigrated left hand to assert new forms of ability and bodily competence.[11]

Despite its potential awkwardness, left-handed penmanship did provide professional opportunities for men who could no longer engage in manual labor, and many of the contestants became government clerks or bookkeepers. Such employment was key to postwar rehabilitation, as mid-nineteenth-century notions of masculinity emphasized the ability to labor and provide.[12] Business schools and commercial colleges offered instruction in "business penmanship," so the contestants were not alone in their efforts to achieve maximum legibility and precision.[13] At the dedication of a business college in Syracuse, New York, in 1865, a speaker announced that the new institution's "course of instruction is pliable, and the managers have always shown a most laudable desire to adapt it to the exigencies of the public and the wants of meritorious classes. Hence, in favor of our maimed soldiers, the introduction in them of left-handed penmanship."[14] Bourne, then, was not alone in his belief that left-handed penmanship offered a way forward for disabled veterans.

9. Henry Karsnitz, Contest Entry, 2nd ser., no. 9, ibid.; George S. Warner, Contest Entry, 1st ser., no. 26, ibid.

10. *Medical and Surgical History of the War of the Rebellion,* 2(2):913.

11. See my discussion of the contestants' negotiations of disability, manhood, and identity in *Scars We Carve,* 90–120.

12. For disabled soldiers, gender identity, and labor, see Handley-Cousins, *Bodies in Blue,* 3–4, 20–22; Marten, *Sing Not War,* 77–78; and Nelson, *Ruin Nation,* 178–200.

13. "Lauden & DeFrance's National Business College, Portland, Oregon," *Corvallis (OR) Gazette Times,* June 11, 1870, 4.

14. "Great Educational Meeting!" *Buffalo (NY) Courier,* Nov. 18, 1865, 1.

William Oland Bourne

By the time Bourne organized the contests, he was already a well-known writer, editor, and advocate for Union soldiers. Born in Pennsylvania in 1819, he attended school in New Jersey and then entered an apprenticeship with a New York publisher.[15] He married Adelia Martin in 1844 (the union produced one daughter), edited a newspaper in upstate New York for two years, and in 1849 became registrar and assistant librarian for the New York Free Academy.[16] Beginning in the mid-1840s, Bourne was a contributor to various literary magazines, including *The Christian Parlor Magazine, The Columbian Lady's and Gentleman's Magazine, The Mother's Magazine,* and *The Union Magazine of Literature and Art.*[17] He published poems in northeastern and midwestern periodicals prior to the war and also appeared in southern newspapers following the conflict.[18] One critic described his ode for a celebration of Benjamin Franklin's birthday as "a beautifully worded, but rather vague, unmeaning affair. If the author thoroughly understands it himself, I fancy that he can accomplish more than most men."[19] His writings for children, including poetry collections and a volume of illustrated fables, were more successful; one of his books on education (most likely his history of New York public schools) was presented to the king of Siam in 1879.[20] Throughout his varied career, Bourne gave public lectures

15. "William O. Bourne," *New York Tribune,* June 7, 1901, 7.

16. "Married," *Brooklyn Weekly Eagle,* Dec. 11, 1844, 3; 1860 U.S. Census, New York Co., NY, pop. sched., New York City, p. 911 (stamped), dwelling 752, family 2197, William O. Bourne, NARA Record Group (RG) 29, M653, roll 795; Hough, *History of Lewis County, in the State of New York,* 287; "William O. Bourne," 7.

17. "The Christian Parlor Magazine," *Brooklyn Evening Star,* June 27, 1844, 2; "The Columbian Lady's and Gentleman's Magazine," *Alton (IL) Weekly Telegraph,* Apr. 2, 1847, 1; "The Mother's Magazine," *Vermont Chronicle* (Bellows Falls), Nov. 26, 1850, 3; "The Union Magazine of Literature and Art," *Carroll Free Press* (Carrollton, OH), May 19, 1848, 4.

18. For examples, see "The Press," *Brooklyn Daily Eagle,* June 7, 1844, 2; "The American Producer," *Winnsboro (SC) News and Herald,* Nov. 5, 1881, 4; and "The Teacher," *Sunday School* (London), Mar. 9, 1893, 7.

19. "The Celebration of Franklin's Birth by the Printers, Editors and Publishers of New York," *Hartford (CT) Courant,* Jan. 19, 1850, 2.

20. Bourne's works for children include *Gems from Fable-Land: A Collection of Fables Illustrated by Facts* (New York: Scribner, 1853) and *Little Silverstring; or, Tales and Poems for the Young* (New York: Charles Scriber, 1853). See also Bourne, *History of the Public School Society of the City of New York;* and "Education in Siam," *New York Times,* Aug. 14, 1879, 8.

on a variety of topics, edited at least three periodicals, acted as deputy clerk for the New York Board of Education, and served in the Municipal Reform Association of New York City.[21] According to the *Chattanooga Times,* he also found time to contribute to the origins of the Confederacy's unofficial anthem, "Dixie"; Daniel Decatur Emmett, the alleged composer, "cribbed the air from a piece that William Oland Bourne, a New Yorker, had cribbed from an old comic opera."[22]

Obituaries rightly proclaimed Bourne an "ardent Unionist," but his politics were more complicated than previous scholars have implied.[23] His father, a prolific writer and abolitionist named George Bourne, was born in England in 1780 and arrived in the United States in 1804.[24] A Dutch Reformed and Presbyterian minister, he left Virginia as a "result of his strong reaction to his direct contact with the institution of slavery" and moved to Pennsylvania, where his son William was born; the family later settled in New York.[25] The elder Bourne wrote multiple antislavery treatises, learning how to set type in order to wage war against the institution, and was one of the first advocates for immediate emancipation.[26] When William Oland Bourne died in 1901, the *New York Times* referred to his father as a "pioneer of immediate, unconditional emancipation."[27] Subsequent briefer obituaries in papers nationwide incorrectly applied the label to the son.[28]

William Oland Bourne was a vocal proponent of a gradual and peaceful end to the peculiar institution, a position that ran counter to the tenets of the Amer-

21. "Mr. William Oland Bourne," *N.J. Standard* (Middletown-Point), Feb. 22, 1854, 2; "Questions of Reform," *New-York Tribune,* Mar. 3, 1875, 12. Bourne also edited *The Iron Platform,* "a Democratic Republican Journal of Politics, Progress and Opinion." See "The Iron Platform," *Brooklyn Evening Star,* Dec. 27, 1862, 2.

22. "A Strolling Paragraph Says," *Chattanooga Sunday Times,* Aug. 14, 1898, 12.

23. See Jordan, *Marching Home,* 53. Jordan claims that Bourne followed in his father's footsteps as an abolitionist. Though Bourne was definitely an abolitionist, his views were quite different from his father's.

24. Theodore Bourne, "Rev. George Bourne, the Pioneer of American Antislavery," *Methodist Quarterly Review* 64 (Jan. 1882): 71–72.

25. *Dictionary of American Biography,* 485.

26. Ibid.; Bourne, "Rev. George Bourne," 74.

27. "Death List of a Day," *New York Times,* June 7, 1901, 9.

28. "William O. Bourne Dead," *Montgomery (AL) Advertiser,* June 8, 1901, 9; "The Death Record," *Janesville (WI) Daily Gazette,* June 8, 1901, 8; "William Orland [*sic*] Bourne," *Los Angeles Times,* June 8, 1901, 4.

ican Anti-Slavery Society.[29] Addressing "the people of the slave states" in 1851, he proposed that emancipation begin on the 100th anniversary of American independence, July 4, 1876.[30] In 1857, he articulated the founding principles of the Work-Men's Democratic Republican Iron Platform Association.[31] Appealing on behalf of northern workers and "white laborers of the Slave States," Bourne presented the Iron Platform: "The Gradual, Peaceful, and Patriotic Abolition of Slavery, by the Encouragement and Protection of Free Labor, in the Whole Union, North and South." His solution relied on the cultivation of "the splendid mechanical and manufacturing resources of the South," which would in turn "effect the quiet removal of slavery by the same influences that led to gradual abolition in the Northern States." Bourne believed such a platform would "extinguish the fires of Civil War."

Two years later, Bourne spoke in favor of the Anti-Slavery Colonization Society, an organization that supported sending free Black people to Africa.[32] In 1833, William Lloyd Garrison, articulating the beliefs of the American Anti-Slavery Convention, had labeled "delusive, cruel and dangerous, any scheme of expatriation which pretends to aid, either directly or indirectly, in the emancipation of slaves, or to be a substitute for the immediate and total abolition of slavery."[33] Bourne's conservatism continued in 1862, when, at a meeting of the New York City Republican Club, he rejected a resolution holding "that the wisest and quickest way to end the rebellion, and establish a permanent peace, is to proclaim immediate and unconditional emancipation."[34] Instead, he offered a series of resolutions, including one that supported "the gradual, peaceful, and profitable extinction of slavery, with the consent of the people, by the enlightened legislation of the States where it exists, and without discord, bloodshed, or disunion." An article in the *National Republican,* noting that Bourne's resolutions had failed, lambasted him, wondering "that the ghost of William's good old father did not rise from its grave and smite *him* to the earth for offering such a resolution."[35]

29. See Garrison, "Declaration of Sentiments of the American Anti-Slavery Convention," 66–71.

30. "1876," *Soldier's Friend,* Aug. 1865, 1.

31. "The Iron Platform," *Buffalo (NY) Advocate,* Dec. 23, 1858, 1.

32. "Domestic Summary," *National Era,* Mar. 24, 1859, 3.

33. Garrison, "Declaration of Sentiments of the American Anti-Slavery Convention," 69–70.

34. "New York City Republican Club," *National Republican,* Jan. 20, 1862, 2.

35. Ibid.

Nevertheless, Bourne was an early member of the Republican Party and a close friend of Horace Greeley, the progressive editor of the *New York Tribune*.[36] His wartime poem, "The New Reveille," called on the "well-tried sons of sorrow" of the South—formerly enslaved Black men—to join the Union cause, and later *The Soldier's Friend* published the narrative of William Hannibal Thomas (included in this collection), a left-armed veteran of the U.S. Colored Troops (USCT).[37] It seems Bourne, like Lincoln, recognized that Black military service should secure freedom and citizenship for African Americans and the franchise for Black men. By the time Bourne began publishing his newspaper, Lincoln had issued the Emancipation Proclamation, and abolition was firmly tied to the Union cause. *The Soldier's Friend* was nothing if not a Union paper, accused after the war of being "Radical" and, by one unhappy Democratic veteran, "to[o] BLACK."[38] The editor responded that the journal was "neither partisan nor politician in any narrow or sectarian sense," proclaiming, "The Declaration of Independence is our political creed, the Constitution is our platform, and the Union is our party."[39]

The Soldier's Friend

Most central to this collection, however, is Bourne's connection to the soldiers who fought what he called a "conservative war" to preserve the Union and usher in freedom.[40] Inspired by his time as a volunteer and chaplain at the Central Park Hospital, he began publishing *The Soldier's Friend* in December 1864.[41] "An experience of two years in connection with the Hospital service," Bourne told his readers, "has given us repeated evidence of the need of a NEWSPAPER FOR THE SOLDIER, which should present, as far as possible, all the important information which they will find valuable and essential relating to their interests, and the regulations and general orders issued from time to time by the [War]

36. "Death Record," 8.

37. Bourne, *Poems of the Republic*, 23; "A Wounded Soldier," *Soldier's Friend*, Feb. 1866, 2.

38. Untitled, *Perry County Democrat* (Bloomfield, PA), Nov. 4, 1868, 2; "Our Conservatism," *Soldier's Friend, and Grand Army of the Republic*, Feb. 13, 1869, 2.

39. "Our Conservatism," 2.

40. Ibid.

41. Civil War Reminiscences by Soldiers and Sailors in Central Park Hospital, Bourne Papers.

Department at Washington."[42] He claimed the publication would be "neither sectarian nor partisan, yet it [would] represent the purer and broader truths of a Christianity eminently catholic in its spirit, and practical in its application." The monthly journal, intended "for Ship and Shore, for the Parlor and the Camp, for the Hospital and the Fireside," would be "a medium of direct communication with the hundreds of thousands of brave men on land and sea who are striving to restore Union, Law, and the Constitution." It would also offer "a means of finding and furnishing employment for soldiers and sailors, and their families"; indeed, with the "single exception" of Bourne acting as editor, "the entire business of *The Soldier's Friend* [gave] constant employment to a corps of disabled men, or members of their families."[43]

Members of the Left-Armed Corps, including William M. DeCamp (who submitted to both contests), and other disabled soldiers worked as agents for the paper, selling subscriptions.[44] Articles contained advice for finding employment and argued that former soldiers, especially disabled ones, deserved preferential treatment when it came to government work: "vacancies should be filled by the men who suffered and bled for the Union."[45] The pages featured writings by left-armed soldiers like Phineas P. Whitehouse, John Bryson, and Philip K. Faulk (all included in this collection), as well as pieces attributed solely to "Left Arm" or "One of the Left-Armed Corps."[46] Bourne expressed confidence that his publication would "occupy a high and peculiar position as a literary journal of the war," in part due to contributions from "men who can use the pen as well as the sword, and who can engage in the conflict of mind as well as of arms."[47] Other contributors included the poet William Cullen Bryant, Rev. Henry W. Bellows (the president of the U.S. Sanitary Commission,

42. "To Our Readers," *Soldier's Friend*, Jan. 1865, 2.

43. "Prospectus of the Soldier's Friend," *Soldier's Friend, and Grand Army of the Republic*, undated extra edition, 2.

44. "Lieutenant William M. DeCamp," *Soldier's Friend, and Grand Army of the Republic*, July 1867, 2. In January 1870, the paper advertised that it no longer employed traveling agents.

45. "Employment for Soldiers," *Soldier's Friend*, Sept. 1866, 2.

46. Phineas P. Whitehouse, "A True Patriot," *Soldier's Friend, and Grand Army of the Republic*, Feb. 1867, 1; John Bryson, "Lines," ibid., July 1866, 1; Phil. K. Faulk, "Dacotah," ibid., July 1866, 1; "The Battle of the Wilderness," ibid., 4; "Soldiers of the Union Army—No. II," ibid., Mar. 1866, 4.

47. Untitled, *Soldier's Friend*, Aug. 1865, 2.

Office of the "SOLDIER'S FRIEND,"
No. 12 Centre Street, NEW YORK, February 7th, 1866.

Louis J. Boos, Esq

DEAR SIR,—A large number of the competitors for the premiums for LEFT HAND Penmanship having omitted to furnish the Committee with an attest of the genuineness of their productions, and the necessity of affording a guaranty of the good faith of the successful parties, for the satisfaction of the rest of the contributors, renders it requisite for competitors to make an affidavit of the facts before a Justice or Commissioner. You will please have this affidavit properly executed, and return it to my address IMMEDIATELY. Please state whether your arm is disabled or amputated. If *disabled* you must declare that you do not and cannot use your arm for writing.

Yours respectfully,

Wm Oland Bourne,
Clerk of the Committee.

State of Pennsylvania } S.S.
City of Philadelphia }

Personally appeared before me, an Alderman Louis J. Boos who being duly sworn, deposes and says that he enlisted in the service of the United States on the Nineteenth day of November 1861, and was a member of Company B., 6th Regiment, Penna Cavalry; that he was wounded in the service of the United States, on the seventh day of May 1864, at Tod's Tavern Virginia, and that his right arm, in consequence of said wound, is Amputated at lower third. He further deposes and says that he has learned to write with his left hand since the date of said wound, and that he did not write with his left hand previous to that time, and that the specimen of writing subscribed and presented by him to the Committee of Award for the distribution of premiums to soldiers and sailors who had lost their right hand, or the use thereof, during the late war, was written by him with his left hand, and that the contents thereof are true to the best of his knowledge and belief.

Sworn & Subscribed before me this ninth day of March A.D. 1866 Louis J. Boos.

Louis J. Boos affidavit. Courtesy William Oland Bourne Papers, Manuscript Division, Library of Congress.

a private organization providing services and supplies to Union soldiers), and reformer Mary C. Vaughan.[48]

In 1867, Bourne added "and Grand Army of the Republic" to the title and printed reports from state encampments of the veteran organization founded that year. By July, the monthly paper had 32,000 readers, which grew to 53,000 subscribers by September.[49] In June 1868, Bourne began publishing a weekly edition.[50] The November 1868 issue was one sheet rather than two, and the beleaguered editor called for new subscribers, adding, "we have furnished our paper more than a year at a *very heavy loss*"; reaching 100,000 subscribers, he

48. "Prospectus of the Soldier's Friend," 2; Mary C. Vaughan, "A Day with the State Agent," *Soldier's Friend, and Grand Army of the Republic,* Oct. 1867, 1.

49. "The Soldier's Friend," *Lancaster (OH) Gazette,* July 12, 1866, 3; "53,000," *Soldier's Friend,* Sept. 1866, 2.

50. *Soldier's Friend, and Grand Army of the Republic,* June 27, 1868.

explained, would enable the publication to double in size.[51] Unfortunately, it seems that additional subscriptions failed to materialize. Though a New Jersey paper reported in September 1869 that Bourne had stepped down as editor, he remained on the masthead until the periodical ceased publication; though the latest extant issue is from March 1870, a widely published 1887 article about the Grand Army of the Republic (GAR) reported that Bourne's paper had ceased publication in 1872.[52] The former editor, like many of the soldiers for whom he advocated, took a position as a records clerk in 1873.[53]

The First Contest

In its heyday, *The Soldier's Friend* was the official source of information regarding the left-handed penmanship contests. Bourne announced the first of these in the June 1865 edition; he reprinted the same article, "Premium $500 to the Left-Armed Soldiers of the Union," in subsequent issues.[54] "There are many men now in hospital, as well as at their homes," the article began, "who have lost their right arms, or whose right arm is so disabled that they cannot *write* with it. Penmanship is a necessary requisite to any man who wants a situation under the government, or in almost any business establishment." It then listed the premiums for the "best specimen[s] of left-hand penmanship" and stipulated that "in *all* cases the writer must give his name in full, his company, regiment, and rank, list of battles in which he was engaged, as complete as possible, the place where he lost his arm, with date, and his post-office address." Instructions called for the "literary part of the work," no more than seven pages but not less than two, to be original or selected (meaning that contestants could copy poems or sketches by other writers), although the committee preferred "brief essays on patriotic themes, and especially narratives of the writer's experience in the service of the country, incidents, or sketches of the war."

By October 1865, however, Bourne had removed the page limit and expressed the "desire that in every case the competitors shall furnish ORIGINAL ARTICLES,

51. "An Apology," *Soldier's Friend, and Grand Army of the Republic,* Nov. 1868, 2.

52. "Personal," *Monmouth Inquirer* (Freehold, NJ), Sept. 30, 1869, 2; "The Grand Army," *Racine (WI) Journal Times,* Sept. 17, 1887, 4.

53. "Board of Education," *New York Times,* Sept. 4, 1873, 2.

54. "Premium $500 to the Left-Armed Soldiers of the Union," *Soldier's Friend,* June 1865, 2

rather than selections." His reasoning reflected one of the main objects of the competition: to demonstrate that in "the contest of BRAIN VERSUS MUSCLE," brain would triumph, and that one-armed men could still find gainful employment.[55] "The man who has given *muscle* to his country," Bourne declared, "must now depend more upon his *brain.* If he be as true to himself and to society, in the relation of citizen, as he was to the country in the ranks of the army, he will develop his mental powers and resources, and if wisely done, he will, in the long run, *get better paid for his brain* than he did for his muscular or manual labor."[56] Expanding on the contest's goals, he noted: "Our purpose was to stimulate the courage, independence, self-reliance, and industry of the class of men selected. An intimate acquaintance of nearly three years with hundreds of wounded men in one of our large hospitals, had given us some opportunity of becoming acquainted with their circumstances, and their hopes and plans for the future."[57] Its "leading purpose," as the contest committee later explained, was "that of placing before the disabled men of the country incentives to a worthy ambition to become self-reliant, and to fit themselves for positions of honor and usefulness."[58]

The men selecting winners were well positioned to help veterans secure employment, and quite a few of the contestants explicitly asked for jobs. The committee consisted of seven "distinguished gentlemen" who had "given freely of their time, their labor, and their means, to advance, protect, and aid the soldiers at the front, and their families at home": William Cullen Bryant; Henry W. Bellows; Reuben E. Fenton, the governor of New York; George William Curtis, a writer and public speaker; and the three-man executive committee (including Theodore Roosevelt Sr.) of the New York Bureau of Employment, an organization dedicated to helping disabled veterans find work.[59] The high profile of each member would ostensibly help draw attention to the endeavor, as would the widespread reprinting of the contest instructions. Articles announcing the contest in *The Soldier's Friend* ended with requests that newspaper editors "throughout the country" republish the information. As a result, the

55. "Left-Hand Writing," *Soldier's Friend,* Oct. 1865, 2.

56. Ibid. (italics in the original).

57. "Left-Hand Writing," *Soldier's Friend,* Oct. 1865, 2.

58. Exhibition of Left-Hand Penmanship, Bourne Papers.

59. Ibid.

first contest began appearing in other publications in July 1865. The *Montpelier Daily Journal* announced "A Novel Premium," while papers in New York, Pennsylvania, Illinois, and Ohio published instructions.[60] In the months that followed, word reached Missouri, California, Kentucky, and Wisconsin.[61] The deadline for the first competition was initially October 1, 1865, but was extended to January 1, 1866, in order to allow sufficient time to those wounded in battles near the end of the war.[62]

Before the deadline, *The Soldier's Friend* printed and answered questions sent in regarding the contest and its rules. Some expressed concerns about the potential for "imposition" on the part of men who had not fought in the conflict or had already been left-handed prior to losing their right arms.[63] The response was clear: only men who had been right-handed soldiers of the Union army could compete. Answering a letter that suggested competitors take oaths verifying their disability, Bourne insisted that "any artifice" would be "promptly detected" upon the publishing of a list of competitors. But in February 1866 he mailed affidavits to competitors who had "omitted to furnish . . . an attest of the genuineness of their productions."[64]

Calling on readers to "make the matter known as far as possible," Bourne challenged the Left-Armed Corps: "Boys! One and All! You have stood before the rebel guns—do not be afraid of a steel pen and a bottle of ink!" Mailing their specimens to Bourne's New York office, 270 men answered the call. Many mentioned reading about the premiums in local newspapers, and several others expressed certainty that their penmanship would not stand up to much scrutiny. Nevertheless, the left-handed papers, as a whole, are remarkably legible and aesthetically pleasing; indeed, most of the specimens are far superior to

60. "A Novel Premium," *Daily Journal* (Montpelier, VT), July 19, 1865, 1; "A Premium to Disabled Veterans," *Buffalo (NY) Commercial*, July 21, 1865, 2; Untitled, *Lancaster (PA) Intelligencer Journal*, July 19, 1865, 2; "A Premium to Disabled Veterans," *Chicago Tribune*, July 26, 1865, 3; "A Premium to Disabled Veterans—Five Hundred Dollars to Left-Armed Soldiers," *Belmont Chronicle* (Saint Clairsville, OH), July 27, 1865, 2.

61. "A Premium to Disabled Veterans," *Howard Union* (Glasgow, MO), Aug. 10, 1865, 4; Untitled, *Sacramento Bee*, Sept. 7, 1865, 2; "Premium $500 to the Left-Armed Soldiers of the Union," *Louisville (KY) Courier-Journal*, Oct. 20, 1865, 3; *Mineral Point (WI) Weekly Tribune*, Oct. 25, 1865, 1.

62. "News Paragraphs," *Appleton (WI) Post*, Nov. 23, 1865, 3

63. "Left-Hand Writing," *Soldier's Friend*, Aug. 1865, 2.

64. Louis J. Boos, Contest Entry, 1st ser., no. 10, Bourne Papers.

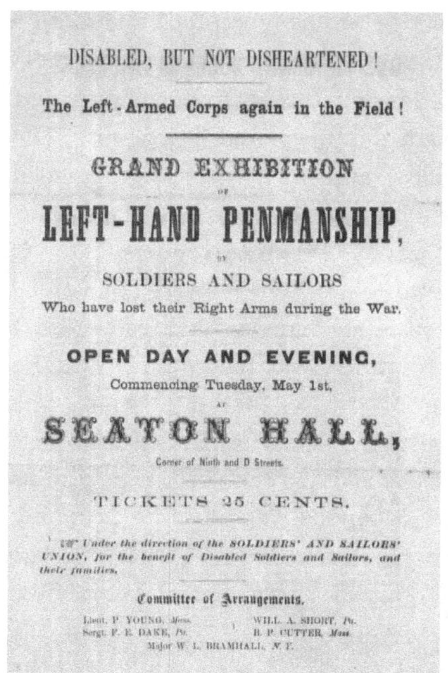

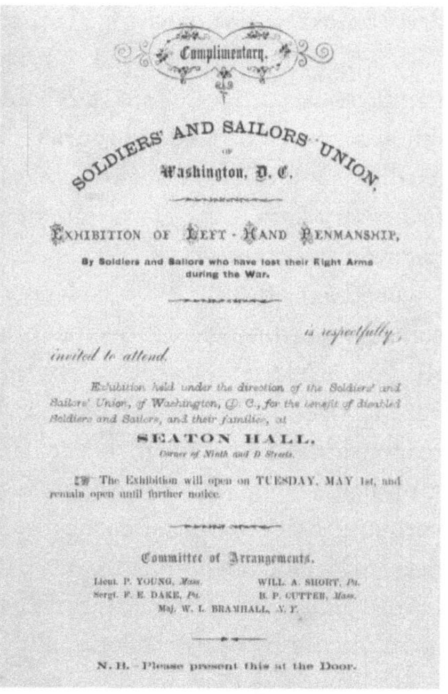

Broadside advertising the exhibition in Washington, D.C., and an invitation to the exhibition.
Courtesy William Oland Bourne Papers, Manuscript Division, Library of Congress.

twenty-first-century penmanship. There are exceptions, of course—Lewis A. Horton had lost part of his left thumb and two of his left fingers in addition to his right arm below the elbow; though not quite as legible as some of the other specimens, his submission won a twenty-dollar premium given his "exceptional circumstances."[65]

The award committee "disregarded" whether penmanship was "back slope," "vertical," or "forward slope"; they also made no distinctions based on "the length of time which the writers had for practice, their previous occupation, education, etc." Instead, they "decided impartially in favor of those manuscripts which possessed the best qualities of a legible, firm, business hand."[66] The committee awarded first ($200), second ($150), third ($100), and fourth ($50) prizes for best business penmanship and recognized a "second class"

65. Exhibition of Left-Hand Penmanship, Bourne Papers.

66. "What Our Left-Armed Soldiers Can Do with the Pen," 1.

of penmanship winners, adding additional premiums courtesy of the Sanitary Commission. Two contestants won $25 second-class prizes, while six, including Horton, received $20; four veterans earned $20 for their "ornamental penmanship," a popular art in the nineteenth century, especially among men who taught penmanship at business schools.[67] Two entries, both included in this collection, won $25 for "literary merit"; ten additional men received $20 for the same.[68] "The average degree of merit is high," the committee reported, "while many of the manuscripts are very fine specimens of chirographic excellence and artistic taste."[69] Newspapers from New York to Iowa, Connecticut to Kentucky, announced the awards, some highlighting local soldiers who had won prizes.[70] After reporting the winners, Bourne congratulated all of the contributors to "this interesting competition" via *The Soldier's Friend.* "It has demanded a vast amount of labor and time," he concluded, "which we have cheerfully given to it, but from which we would have been disposed to shrink could we have foreseen it all."[71]

The Exhibitions

"Should a sufficient number of specimens be sent in," Bourne had promised when announcing the first competition, "they will be placed on exhibition, and the proceeds, if sufficient, will be devoted to the publication of a memorial volume containing the prize essays, a list of contributors, etc., a copy of which will be sent to each competitor."[72] Though the volume was never published, he exhibited the collection twice—first in New York, and then in Washington, D.C. The New York exhibition opened in late February 1866 in the Union Central Committee hall and closed on March 1.[73] Ladies of the city's Union Relief Committee arranged and decorated the hall; gilded letters on the left

67. For penmanship in the nineteenth century, see Thornton, *Handwriting in America*, 42–71.

68. Exhibition of Left-Hand Penmanship, Bourne Papers; "Award of Prizes for Left-Hand Penmanship," *Daily Ohio Statesman* (Columbus), Mar. 7, 1866, 3.

69. Exhibition of Left-Hand Penmanship, Bourne Papers.

70. "Distribution of Prizes," *Buffalo (NY) Courier*, Mar. 7, 1866, 3; "From New York," *Davenport (IA) Morning Democrat*, Mar. 7, 1866, 1; "Personal and Political," *Hartford (CT) Courant*, Mar. 8, 1866, 2; "Premiums for Left Hand Writers," *Louisville (KY) Daily Courier*, Mar. 8, 1866, 3.

71. "What Our Left-Armed Soldiers Can Do with the Pen," 1.

72. "Premium $500 to the Left-Armed Soldiers of the Union," *Soldier's Friend*, Aug. 1865, 2.

73. "What Our Left-Armed Soldiers Can Do with the Pen," 1.

side of the room read, "The Left Hand," "The Empty Sleeve," and "All Americans Together/Not a Fetter in the Clime."[74] Evergreen boughs "mingled in happy harmony with the red, white, and blue of the flag of the Union"; the names of Union officers hung above the windows; and a portrait of Abraham Lincoln graced the upper end of the hall.[75] Many of the decorations would later travel to the nation's capital with the specimens, which rested on long tables covered with blue cloth; red tape held the white pages in place, completing a "very effective and truthful grouping of the national colors." Photographs of the contestants "brought the visitor into the presence of the honorable members of the Left-Armed Corps."[76] General Ulysses S. Grant visited the exhibition on February 24 and perused the collection for "nearly an hour." While leaving, he quietly remarked, "these boys write better with their left hand than I do with my right!"[77] The general would later attend the Washington exhibition along with "a large number of members of Congress."[78]

On April 28, 1866, the *National Republican* announced the opening of the Washington exhibition and proclaimed that the specimens produced by "left-handed heroes" would "astonish our citizens when they come examine them."[79] After all, the article claimed, "left-handed penmanship has been developed by the war to such an extent that it has become a matter of interest to the public." Not just the *American* public, the Soldier's and Sailor's Union of Washington decided two days later, when they passed a resolution that the Committee on the Exhibition of Left-Hand Penmanship should petition the secretary of state to send the penmanship manuscripts to the Paris Exhibition.[80] On the Tuesday before the exhibition opened, the same committee, accompanied by Bourne, met with President Andrew Johnson in the White House. After examining specimens of left-handed penmanship, Johnson "expressed a great interest in this novel enterprise, and gave the subject his hearty approval, stating that he would, if at all possible, visit the exhibition on the occasion of the opening."[81] Despite remarking "in substance that he was the soldiers' and sailors'

74. Ibid.

75. Ibid.

76. Ibid., 2.

77. Ibid., 1.

78. "Skill of Maimed Soldiers," *Philadelphia Inquirer,* May 5, 1866, 1.

79. "Sinister Chirography," *National Republican,* Apr. 28, 1866, 3.

80. "The Left-Hand Writing in Paris," *Soldier's Friend,* June 1866, 2.

81. "A Pleasant Interview," *National Republican,* Apr. 30, 1866, 3; "An Interview with the President," *Baltimore Daily Commercial,* May 1, 1866, 1.

best friend," the president did not attend, although a number of high-profile personages did, along with "large numbers of ladies and gentlemen from every part of the Union."[82]

The Grand Exhibition of Left-Hand Penmanship, by Soldiers and Sailors Who Have Lost Their Right Arms during the War opened on May 1 at 8 p.m. in Seaton Hall. Admission was twenty-five cents, with proceeds benefiting "Disabled Soldiers and Sailors, and their families."[83] By the time the event began, there was already a large crowd gathered in front of the building.[84] The 5th U.S. Cavalry's band played while attendees walked through a festooned hall, ornamented by "portraits of distinguished generals" and battle scenes, and admired the specimens, some accompanied by *carte-de-visite* portraits of the entrants, laid out on long tables covered in blue muslin.[85] The walls boasted "elegant mottoes and inscriptions" expressing "sentiments of patriotism and appeals for the brave defenders of the Union," among them, "The army and navy—the right and left arms of our nation's defense"; "Our disabled soldiers have kept the Union from being disabled"; and "We lost our right arm for our rights / And 'tis the left arm now that writes."[86] A U.S. flag hung above the stage, the blue portion emblazoned with "Peace"; nearby, a captured Confederate flag was displayed upside down. At the front of the gallery, a banner read:

The empty sleeve
Disabled but not disheartened
Union and liberty.[87]

Major General Nathaniel P. Banks gave the first address, invoking the weighty significance of the recently ended conflict and mentioning fears that veterans would turn to "insubordination, anarchy, and crime."[88] The general

82. "Call upon the President," *Chicago Tribune,* Apr. 30, 1866, 1; "Exhibition of Left-Hand Writing at Washington," *Soldier's Friend,* June 1866, 2.

83. "Grand Exhibition of Left-Hand Penmanship," *National Republican,* May 3, 1866, 2.

84. "Exhibition of Left-Hand Penmanship," reprinted from *Washington Chronicle* in *Louisville (KY) Courier-Journal,* May 8, 1866, 4.

85. "Exhibition of Left-Hand Penmanship," *Washington Evening Star,* May 1, 1866, 5; "Exhibition of Left-Hand Penmanship," reprinted in *Louisville (KY) Courier-Journal,* 4.

86. "Exhibition of Left-Hand Writing at Washington," 2.

87. Ibid.; "What Our Left-Armed Soldiers Can Do with the Pen."

88. "Exhibition of Left-Hand Writing at Washington," 2.

continued, "Yet, we behold the men who achieved these results . . . instead of throwing themselves upon the country for support, discard sympathy, and earnestly and industriously go to work to seek employment." Banks, like the contests and Bourne's hopes for them, emphasized self-reliance rather than dependence, adaptation rather than despondence—obviously oversimplifying the struggles many newly disabled men faced. Continually met with applause, he praised men "who were maimed in such a way as almost to preclude the possibility of their exerting themselves for their own support or that of their families," having "left their strong right arm upon the battlefield," but who now had "furnish[ed] to the number of nearly three hundred manuscripts which will challenge the admiration of the world." He asked, "What can we say that shall be too much in praise of these three hundred who, after losing their right hand, with the sinister agent have done that which we see tonight, and given an exhibition unparalleled in the history of the world?"

Speaker of the House Schuyler Colfax next addressed the attendees, receiving the "closest attention and the heartiest applause." He asserted that it was impossible to forget "an inexcusably wicked and parricidal rebellion," given the prevalence of "the empty sleeve, the weary crutch, the pallid face, [and] the wasted frame we meet so often on the streets."[89] The exhibition served as a further reminder of "the sacrifices so many had made for their country." Major General O. O. Howard, himself a member of the Left-Armed Corps, also gave a speech, as did Lucius Fairchild, the governor of Wisconsin, who had lost his left arm at Gettysburg. Though reporters failed to transcribe Howard's speech, *The Soldier's Friend* insisted it was "pointed, earnest, and full of sympathy," since the one-armed general "seemed to realize in a special manner that he was surrounded by a large body of his companions in arms."[90]

The second night of the exhibition was "well attended," and another slate of distinguished guests, including several members of the House of Representatives and the president of Iowa College, addressed the assembly; Representative William Higby of California "challenged the Old World to produce such an instance of literary and moral achievement on the part of its soldiers."[91]

89. "Address of Speaker Colfax," *Chicago Tribune,* May 3, 1866, 1.

90. "Left-Hand Penmanship," *National Republican,* May 2, 1866, 3; Ross, *Empty-Sleeve,* 217; "Exhibition of Left-Hand Writing at Washington," 2.

91. "Left-Hand Penmanship," 3; "Exhibition of Left-Hand Writing at Washington," 2.

Visitors could stop by during the day or the evening, and "many of the pupils of the public schools" passed through before the exhibition closed on the fifth.[92] Ira Broshears, whose writing is included in this collection, regretted that he could not attend: "How I should have enjoyed the display of them all . . . with autograph and photograph of each arranged beside the other, rank and file, as stood the authors in time past among the hosts of Liberty on the gory fields that were her altars—Then confronting the minions of slavery—now as resolutely seeking for chirographic excellence and mental conquest."[93]

Those who did attend recognized the uniqueness and significance of the exhibition and praised the Left-Armed Corps while expounding on its symbolic significance to the Union and its future. "It is at once a most impressive memento of the grandest struggle recorded in the world's annals," the *Washington Chronicle* proclaimed, "and a most striking illustration of the genius of the American people. We realize the vastness of the struggle as we think of the harsh fact that our left-armed soldiers are so numerous as to constitute by themselves a class large enough to arrest the attention of the nation."[94] Despite the "regretful feelings" attendant on recognizing the preponderance of maimed men, "we feel our pride stirred," the article continued, by proof "that whatever the physical loss our soldiers may have sustained through rebel bullet and surgeon's knife, they have at least brought home with them the same sturdy manhood which carried them to the field, and the unquenchable love of independence which was theirs by inheritance."

A Vermonter who visited the exhibition reported that among the 270 specimens "were all grades of hands," some "as fine as are often seen written with the right hand."[95] "W." particularly admired Thomas Perrine's "pretty little poem" and Phineas Whitehouse's "well written" essay; taken together, the penmanship specimens revealed "the determination and the fruitfulness of the American mind." W. asked, "With such soldiers, who can despair of the Republic? and with a nation of such opponents, what betrayer can succeed?" Fanny Fern, a well-known and widely read columnist and writer, declared: "As a moral lesson, I would have had every boy and girl in the land taken there to see the power of the

92. "Left-Hand Penmanship," 3.

93. Ira Broshears, Contest Entry, 1st ser., no. 64, Bourne Papers.

94. "Exhibition of Left-Hand Penmanship," reprinted in *Louisville (KY) Courier-Journal,* 4.

95. "Exhibition of Left-Hand Writing," *Green-Mountain Freeman* (Montpelier, VT), May 9, 1866, 2.

mind over the body. The potency of that one little phrase, 'I will try.'"[96] Believing the contest a "purely *American* idea," Fern expressed her gladness that the enlisted men of the army "had placed it on record that an American soldier is still wide awake and hopeful, though he may be so hacked and hewed to pieces that not half of his original proportions remain." Commentators and contestants alike insisted on the continued manliness of soldiers who had returned from the battlefield physically altered, thereby asserting a masculinity that depended not on physical wholeness but on perseverance and adaptability.

A *New York Tribune* article linked the Left-Armed Corps's newfound ability to write with the "sinister" hand to voting rights for formerly enslaved men.[97] The anonymous author argued that the exhibition "shows that any of us may become ambidextrous if we try, and that the most uncomfortable things in nature may become gifts, means of advancement and social progress." But "another class" of men was "neither permitted the dexter hand nor sinister hand" despite showing "devotion to freedom, nationality, manhood, [and] the flag, by valor in the field." While white disabled soldiers ask "that the world will forget their being cripples, and give them a day's wages for a day's work," the "other class" asks simply for the ballot. With the franchise, the article declared, they would be "freemen" indeed. Though somewhat convoluted, the linking of left-handedness and ambidexterity to political and social agency underscored the aims and significance of the contest and exhibitions; it also aligned left-handed soldiers with formerly enslaved people, both groups of people having to adjust to newfound identities and social positions after the war.

The Second Contest

In early 1867, Bourne announced a second contest "in compliance with the wishes of a number of the Left-Armed Corps," namely, veterans who had not submitted specimens to the first contest, "for want of the proper time and information," and petitioned Bourne for another opportunity.[98] In April and May, newspapers in the Northeast and Midwest announced the new competition and listed the Union officers who would lend their names to the premiums: Grant, Admiral David G. Farragut, Lieutenant General William T. Sherman,

96. "Left-Hand Manuscripts of Disabled Soldiers," reprinted from *New York Ledger* on exhibition brochure, Bourne Papers.

97. Untitled, *New-York Tribune,* May 17, 1866, 4.

98. "$500 in Premiums," *Soldier's Friend, and Grand Army of the Republic,* Nov. 1867, 2.

and Major Generals Philip H. Sheridan, Howard, George G. Meade, Winfield S. Hancock, Joseph Hooker, John W. Geary, and John A. Logan.[99] Contestants would compete for ten premiums of $50 each; winners would also receive a letter written and signed by the general who had selected their entry. In November 1867, *The Soldier's Friend* printed letters accepting their roles as contest judges from the "distinguished officers of the army and navy, who generously and cheerfully consented to pay this compliment to the brave boys who had suffered under their respective commands."[100] Grant's aide-de-camp wrote of the general's "complete sympathy for [Bourne's] efforts to ameliorate the condition of those who were wounded in the late war against rebellion." The other men wrote their own letters, expressing enthusiasm for the endeavor and praising Bourne's, to use Sherman's phrase, "purely charitable and worthy object."

The instructions for the second contest were more specific than those for the first. They required entrants to use only black ink to "furnish a sketch of their military history, from the date of their enlistment to their discharge, including company, regiment, rank, and a list of battles, date and place where wounded, etc." Contestants should send photographs "in every case where it is practicable to furnish one," while "original essays, poems, tales, incidents and anecdotes of the war may be added and are earnestly desired." Unlike the first contest, which initially relied on the honor system and the publication of contributors' names to prevent fraudulent submissions, the second required legal proof of disability and prior right-handedness: a "proper Affidavit must be made to the facts, to prevent imposition and injustice." Winners of the first contest were not eligible for premiums this time but were welcome to "contribute new specimens to the collection."[101] In response to inquiries, Bourne clarified that there was no bias against "back-slope" (penmanship that slants to the left instead of the right); indeed, "the majority of prizes distributed by the first committee were awarded to back-slope manuscripts. It is *excellence,* not the slope, which decides."[102]

The second series of premiums drew 115 submissions. *The Soldier's Friend*

99. For examples, see "To Left-Handed Soldiers," *Vermont Watchman and State Journal* (Montpelier), Apr. 3, 1867, 2; and "Soldiers Left-Hand Writing," *Piqua (OH) Democrat,* Apr. 17, 1867, 1.

100. "$500 in Premiums," 4; "Left-Hand Writing by Disabled Soldiers and Sailors of the War," *Soldier's Friend, and Grand Army of the Republic,* Jan. 1868, 4.

101. "To the Left-Armed Corps of the Union," *Soldier's Friend, and Grand Army of the Republic,* Mar. 1867, 2.

102. "The Left-Hand Premiums," *Soldier's Friend, and Grand Army of the Republic,* May 1867, 2.

announced the winners in January 1868, also printing transcriptions of the "autograph letter[s]" composed by the judging officers.[103] Grant wrote the shortest message, wishing Barnabas D. Palmer "prosperity and success." Meade congratulated Francis X. Burger, trusting that his "worthy example [would] serve to inspire others to greater exertions." Perhaps unsurprisingly, Admiral Farragut employed a nautical metaphor in his letter, informing 1st Lieutenant Selden C. Clobridge that "the voyager on the sea of life has storms to meet, and in some of his experiences he may find that the conflict of winds, and waves, and of enemies has disabled his craft, and he must reach the haven of rest under clearer skies and favoring winds, with his eye steadily turned to the true point." Howard, who had declined to participate himself in the contest due to his work as Freedmen's Bureau commissioner and his "inability to write a fair hand," selected George S. LaRue for his premium.[104] "I think we can demonstrate," he wrote to LaRue,

> that the right hand is not indispensable, though I confess the loss of it is often remarkably inconvenient; and with good feet and legs we surely can outstrip those who go on crutches or with wooden appendages in the *race* of life. If your crippled arm ever gives you trouble on account of changes in the weather, indigestion or from over-exercise or too much care, you must immediately begin by counting up your mercies to allay the first symptoms of discontent; putting your trust in that strong *arm*, which can supplement every weakness.

Like Howard, the other officers trusted in the potential of the Left-Armed Corps and the promise for future success evidenced by the contest, basing their faith on the men's service, sacrifice, and perseverance. As the following chapters demonstrate, however, the "race of life" was often difficult, the left arm was at times an imperfect replacement for the right, and some of the veterans struggled to reach "clearer skies."

103. "Left-Hand Writing by Disabled Soldiers and Sailors of the War," 4.

104. Exhibition of Left-Hand Penmanship, Bourne Papers.

The Contestants

The Left-Armed Corps consisted of men who willingly shared their stories, participating in contests shaped by rehabilitative and patriotic rhetoric. They are not representative of all men wounded or disabled during the Civil War; every wound was different, and every veteran was an individual. Though not a truly random sample, the corps still provides valuable insights into the types of men who volunteered to defend the Union.[105] Most enlisted in 1861, with thirty-four answering the first calls for troops in April 1861. Some fought in long lists of battles, while others were wounded in their first engagement. Twenty-four men lost their arms fighting in and around Petersburg, twenty-one at Cold Harbor, and twenty at Gettysburg. New York–based veterans sent the most entries (sixty-five) to the first contest, with veterans from Ohio (thirty-five) and Illinois (twenty-five) coming in second and third. New York contributed more men to the Union army than any other state, and Bourne's presence in New York most likely also accounted for the state's overrepresentation. Thirty commissioned officers, fifty-two noncommissioned officers (sergeants and corporals), and 185 privates composed the list of contributors.[106] Though around 179,000 Black men served in the Union army, only two submitted to the first contest and none to the second, perhaps reflecting lower literacy rates among formerly enslaved soldiers (though many became literate during and after the war).[107] Twenty-eight New Yorkers and twenty-four Pennsylvanians submitted to the second contest, with men from Massachusetts (twelve) and Ohio (ten) placing a distant third and fourth. Twenty-one commissioned and thirty-four noncommissioned officers competed. The youngest entrant was fifteen years old when he enlisted, and the oldest was fifty-two.[108] The majority were born

105. To the best of my knowledge, only Abellino S. Burt, John Bolen, Burritt Stiles, and Conrad Dippel were drafted. Trevor Baxter was a substitute.

106. "What Our Left-Armed Soldiers Can Do with the Pen," *Soldier's Friend,* Mar. 1866, 1.

107. For increased USCT literary rates, see Dora L. Costa and Matthew E. Kahn, "Forging a New Identity: The Costs and Benefits of Diversity in Civil War Combat Units for Black Slaves and Freemen," *Journal of Economic History* 66, no. 4 (Dec. 2006): 936–62.

108. I was unable to determine the exact birth years of two contestants and the death years of fifteen. As such, the numbers in this paragraph are not exact.

in the 1840s, the peak years being 1842 (thirty-eight) and 1840 (thirty-three). At least fifty-three were born abroad, accounting for 16 percent of the contestants and thus underrepresented relative to the makeup of the Federal army, 25 percent of which was foreign born.[109] The average age at enlistment was twenty-three, and the median was twenty-one, younger than the estimated age (twenty-six) of the average Civil War soldier.[110] As was typical of the Union army, the most common preenlistment occupation was farming or farm labor, and at least twenty-nine men lived on their father's farms. The second- and third-most-common professions were laborer and clerk.

At the time of the contest, twenty-seven men had served or were serving in the Veteran Reserve Corps (VRC), an organization unfortunately dubbed the Invalid Corps at its formation in 1863.[111] Intended to employ men too wounded or ill to fight, the corps enabled recuperating and disabled soldiers to continue to serve as guards and hospital workers; for men anxious to return to their regiments, the forced transfer and implication of inability (not to mention the unpopular sky-blue uniforms) caused frustration.[112] Nevertheless, some members of the Left-Armed Corps decided against accepting a discharge for disability (available to them since they had lost a limb) and remained in the service. After the war and the disbanding of the VRC, six men remained in the regular army, and two were longtime members of the same National Guard regiment; the vast majority, however, returned to civilian life.[113]

Postwar Lives

Though members of the Left-Armed Corps generally had more visible proof of their service than the average veteran, they were not alone in their struggles to adjust to civilian life.[114] An article about the GAR described the period

109. McPherson, *Battle Cry of Freedom,* 606.

110. These numbers are inexact because I did not take birth month into account. For average age, see McPherson, *For Cause and Comrades,* viii.

111. For the formation of the Invalid Corps, see Handley-Cousins, *Bodies in Blue,* 11–31.

112. Ibid., 22–28.

113. Selden C. Clobridge and Benjamin S. Steen served in New York's 14th Regiment. Howard, *Eagle and Brooklyn,* 823.

114. For Civil War veterans' postwar lives, see Jordan, *Marching Home;* Paul A. Cimbala, *Veterans North and South: The Transition from Soldier to Civilian after the American Civil War* (Santa

of demobilization that followed Union victory: "Out of the hundreds of thousands of old soldiers thrown suddenly into civil life in 1865 the majority were displaced from one cause and another. The farmer and the mechanic had lost their arts, the schoolboy had grown too old for the desk, and clerks and professional men had been superseded, and it became for a time a struggle for these men to adjust themselves."[115] The pension system, established before the end of the war to support soldiers who were no longer fit for service due to wounds or disease, was intended to help veterans adjust; legislation in 1862 granted pensions ranging from eight dollars to thirty dollars per month, depending on rank and level of disability.[116] Further legislation after the war designated different amounts for specific conditions, including fifteen dollars a month for men who had lost one hand or arm; the amount increased as decades passed, eventually reaching forty dollars for a hand and forty-six dollars for an arm above the elbow by 1903.[117] But amounts varied, and veterans, especially Black men who had served in the USCT, encountered difficulties when trying to secure payment.[118] The diligence with which members of the Left-Armed Corps went about obtaining employment reveals the insufficiency of pensions to support veterans and their families.

Massachusetts veteran John Frye Foster addressed "every man who will read these specimens of our left hand penmanship," calling on them to "give the soldier some employment to recompense him for his sacrifice; that he may still provide for the little ones dependent on him, and thus feel that he is remembered when his resources for maintenance are so limited without one's right arm."[119] Foster believed his back-slanted penmanship, combined with his military service and bodily loss, proved his worthiness, but he also highlighted the challenges of adjusting to life as a one-armed man. The rhetoric underpinning Bourne's contests argued that ostensibly disabled men could replace their right arms with their left arms. Yet the contestants and

---

Barbara, CA: Praeger, 2015); and Brian Matthew Jordan and Evan C. Rothera, *The War Went On: Reconsidering the Lives of Civil War Veterans* (Baton Rouge: Louisiana State University Press, 2020).

115. "Grand Army," 4.

116. Glasson, *Federal Military Pensions in the United States,* 126.

117. Ibid., 133.

118. See Logue and Blanck, *Race, Ethnicity, and Disability,* 41–82.

119. John F. Foster, Contest Entry, 1st ser., no. 242, Bourne Papers.

their entries presented visible evidence of the difficulties of adaptation and recovery. Many attested to the lingering physical effects of amputation and wounding as well as the emotional repercussions of returning home physically different than when they left.

While the majority of the contestants had visible proof of their service and sacrifice in the form of missing limbs, at least thirty-five veterans retained their right arms but lost partial or total use of them. Veterans whose disabilities were less visible or invisible often encountered difficulties obtaining pensions and proving their worth.[120] Though most of the contestants bore physical marks of valor, members of the Left-Armed Corps still confronted implications of diminished masculinity, sexual potency, and bodily competence.[121] Historian Megan Kate Nelson contends that "disembodied limbs and dismembered bodies . . . became sites on which Americans inscribed a range of social anxieties—including concerns about the impact of warfare on masculinity"; amputees had to contend with concerns about their ability to reintegrate and perform economically, romantically, and sexually.[122] Though almost all of the previously single men married and had children (the exceptions being a few confirmed bachelors), many of the entries reflected gendered anxieties, as contestants alluded to difficulties supporting themselves and their families, referred to sweethearts who might reject their remaining hand, or asserted their continued ability to face life's challenges. The "empty sleeve" became a badge of courage during and after the war, but it also simplified, sanitized, or elided the lived experiences of wounded and disabled men.[123] Bourne's contests not only promoted seamless rehabilitation through the substitution of the left hand for the right but also allowed veterans to negotiate and narrate new forms of ability and masculinity. If, as Nelson contends, Americans feared "incomplete men," then the personal testimonies of the Left-Armed Corps, grounded in a new form of ability, made the case for a new masculinity that did not depend on the presence of two arms or two hands.[124]

120. Handley-Cousins, *Bodies in Blue,* 86–92, 95–113.

121. For disability during and after the Civil War, see Marten, *Sing Not War,* 75–123; and Handley-Cousins, *Bodies in Blue.* For responses to amputation, see Nelson, *Ruin Nation,* 175–78, 186–200.

122. Nelson, *Ruin Nation,* 161, 191.

123. For "empty sleeve," see Johnson, *Scars We Carve,* 95–103; and Nelson, *Ruin Nation,* 179–200.

124. Nelson, *Ruin Nation,* 188.

In 1868, *Frank Leslie's Illustrated News* published examples of left-handed penmanship and told the story of Bourne's two contests.[125] Labeling the "collection of Left-Hand Papers" a "genuine testimony to the character of our volunteer soldiers," the article also commented on the plight of veterans whose "condition" was "made more embarrassing, and call[ed] for a firmer heroism, than when in the field." Though "unable to make detailed notices of the great beauty of some of these specimens, or to do justice to their literary and historic value," the newspaper did display three specimens of penmanship. Printed beneath General Howard's back-handed scrawl and Lieutenant Clobridge's "bold, handsome chirography" was the first-prize-winning penmanship of Franklin H. Durrah. Perhaps more than any other member of the Left-Armed Corps, Durrah undermines the optimistic rhetoric of the contests—namely, that the left hand could successfully replace the right so that one-armed men could seamlessly enter civilian society and the workforce. His "legible and superior business penmanship" would have served him well professionally, but his mother committed him to an insane asylum shortly after he won the contest; he spent the rest of his life institutionalized.[126]

Like Durrah, William S. Bergin, wounded when he was fifteen and the first contest's youngest entrant, used his left-handed penmanship to secure employment after the war, eventually working his way to a clerkship in the War Department. Unfortunately, he lost the position when the "gay life of the National Capital proved too much for the young clerk."[127] Back home in Ohio, Bergin became a "hard drinker and a rough citizen," traveling from place to place and at one point working as a clerk for an army quartermaster in Dakota Territory, where he witnessed the aftermath of the Battle of Little Bighorn.[128] Shortly thereafter, while "on a heavy debauch," Bergin shot and killed a hotel

125. "Left-Hand Penmanship," reprinted from *Frank Leslie's Illustrated News* in *Soldier's Friend*, Sept. 1868, 1.

126. Padilla, "Army of 'Cripples,'" 57–58; Clarke, *War Stories*, 169–70. The pages of the 1890 Census veteran schedules list Durrah on a page with six other men who were "too insane to give information." Durrah was apparently sane enough to provide some information. 1890 U.S. Census, Franklin H. Durrah, Special Schedules Enumerating Union Veterans and Widows of Union Veterans of the Civil War, Records of the Department of Veterans Affairs, NARA RG 15, M123.

127. William S. Bergin, Contest Entry, 1st ser., no. 109, Bourne Papers; "Deadly Drops," *Lima (OH) Times-Democrat*, Dec. 13, 1877, 2.

128. "Deadly Drops," 2.

employee; his defense cited a family history of insanity and his drinking, insisting that "when a boy he was gentle and tractable, but losing his arm in the army his nature became changed."[129] On December 7, 1877, he became the first person to be executed in Knox County, Ohio.[130] Though Durrah and Bergin are extreme cases, they do serve as important reminders that the contests did not tell the whole story; the rehabilitation Bourne promised did not always come to fruition.

Many members of the Left-Armed Corps *did* put their penmanship to good use, however, finding positions as government clerks, bookkeepers, and census enumerators. Information about the postwar lives of each veteran included in this collection derives from census and pension records, obituaries, and newspaper articles.[131] Surveying the employment histories of the contestants reveals significant patterns as well as the ways in which visible marks of service helped some veterans secure positions and political power. As historian James Marten asserts, "even less than other veterans—much less, in most cases—physically disabled men could not simply step back into their peacetime lives."[132] Losing a right arm surely required adaptations, but it clearly did not prevent some veterans from returning to their prewar occupations or engaging in manual labor. But of the ninety men who were previously farmers or farm laborers, only fifteen returned exclusively to farming, and fifteen others farmed while pursuing other occupations.[133] In total, twenty-eight of the veterans farmed after the war, and twenty-five others farmed in addition to other employment.[134] Sixteen were laborers, and six were carpenters. Others chose less physically taxing professions: nineteen worked as teachers, ten as salesmen, seventeen as attorneys, and twelve as merchants. Nineteen owned businesses, including Augustus Vignos, who founded Novelty Cutlery Company and was president of the American Mine Door Company, and Walter B. Shaw, who left his job as a Treasury Department clerk to cultivate water lilies and sell them at "enormous" profit.[135]

129. Ibid.

130. Ibid. The execution, attended by hundreds of people, was horribly botched.

131. My access to full pension and service records was limited due to the Covid-19 pandemic.

132. Marten, *Sing Not War,* 76–77.

133. Since around thirty men did not appear in the 1860 Census, these numbers are inexact.

134. I was unable to find postwar employment information for twelve men, so these numbers and those that follow are inexact.

135. "A. Vignos Dies," *Portsmouth (OH) Daily Times,* July 23, 1926, 12; "A Washington Man Who

Of the 333 contestants, 81 worked as clerks at some point in their professional lives. Before the advent of typewriters, such positions required legible penmanship.[136] Some men secured positions at the federal level, six clerking for the War Department and six others for the Treasury, including Jared D. Turrell, who celebrated fifty years of service as a law clerk in 1915.[137] Three men joined General Howard at the Freedmen's Bureau, and others worked at the Pension Office.[138] Allen B. Hayward, who lost his right arm at the shoulder, was a Pension Office clerk for over fifty years and built a famous "treetop house" in the woods near Washington.[139] Others were state, city, county, or court clerks. Left-armed veterans obviously took advantage of legislation passed in 1865 requiring that disabled soldiers "be preferred for appointments to civil offices."[140] Five were watchmen at government buildings, nine were tax collectors, and nine were customs officials. At least fifteen were letter carriers, a common postwar occupation for men who had lost hands or arms.[141] Smith S. Gilbert, known as "the one-armed mail clerk" during his time as an employee of the Central New England Railroad, "could sort mail as fast as many better equipped for the work."[142] At seventy, George F. Russ was still "one of the most nimble and efficient of Uncle Sam's railroad postal clerks, though possessing but one arm and thrice wounded in the Civil War."[143]

Prior to the Progressive Era, governmental bureaucracies were staffed

---

Farms the Water," *Washington Post,* Aug. 23, 1908, 8. Shaw's garden is now the Kenilworth Park and Aquatic Gardens. *Kenilworth Park & Aquatic Gardens,* www.nps.gov/keaq/index.htm.

136. Employment information compiled from the U.S. Census for the years 1870–1920. Since I was unable to find employment information for nine of the veterans, the numbers in this paragraph constitute educated guesses.

137. "City News in Brief," *Washington Post,* Apr. 9, 1915, 5.

138. Paul A. Cimbala notes that the Freedmen's Bureau employed a number of amputees. See *Under the Guardianship of the Nation,* 11, 104.

139. "Pension Clerk, 89, Gets High Honors," *Washington Evening Star,* July 27, 1920, 1; "This Man Lives in a Tree-Top House," *Brooklyn Daily Eagle,* Sept. 13, 1908, 40. Profiles of Hayward's treehouse appeared in papers countrywide. See, for example, "A Man Up a Tree," *Caldwell (KS) News,* July 30, 1889, 2; and "House in a Tree," *Huntsville (AL) Weekly Democrat,* Jan. 17, 1894, 1.

140. Quoted in Nelson, *Ruin Nation,* 205.

141. Ibid. 205.

142. "Veteran Mail Clerk Dies in Hospital," *Hartford (CT) Courant,* Mar. 10, 1911, 6.

143. "Well Known Mail Clerk Celebrates Birthday," *Arcanum (OH) Times,* Nov. 10, 1910, 5.

on the basis of political patronage, and many legislators clearly chose to reward men who had sacrificed limbs to preserve the Union. Even so, political fortunes could shift with new administrations.[144] In 1888, a Michigan newspaper reported that Turrell had been demoted to a "third-class clerkship" and replaced by a "Confederate soldier from Georgia"; the article claimed another one-armed clerk and a veteran who had lost his leg at Gettysburg suffered similar fates thanks to Democrat Grover Cleveland.[145] Nevertheless, by the time he retired, Turrell was chief clerk in his office; he was also appointed auditor of Cuba's temporary military government in 1901.[146] Other left-armed veterans were also able to retain their positions regardless of the party in power. John S. Fay was postmaster for forty-nine years, reappointed by each president after Andrew Johnson—even Democratic ones—despite his Republican politics. When Fay, who also served as junior vice commander of the GAR Department of Massachusetts, was up for reappointment in 1894, the *Boston Globe* explained, "the cause of his retention is the fact that he left an arm and a leg on a Virginia battle field"; his "unfortunate mutilated condition" apparently transcended political concerns, allowing him to avoid "the selfish and often cruel political methods of removal."[147]

Almost 30 contestants were appointed postmaster, a position usually dependent on political connections. President Grant made Andrew Denison postmaster of Baltimore in 1869. Breveted major general for "gallantry," Denison was also Maryland's first state GAR commander.[148] Upward mobility tended to coincide with political involvement and membership in the GAR, a national fraternal organization of Union veterans founded in 1866 that advocated for disabled veterans and fallen soldiers' dependents and helped secure pensions for them.[149]

144. See Samuel Kernell and Michael P. McDonald, "Congress and America's Political Development: The Transformation of the Post from Patronage to Service," *American Journal of Political Science* 43, no. 3 (July 1999): 792–811.

145. "How Union Soldiers Fare," *St. Joseph (MI) Herald,* June 16, 1888, 2.

146. "Jared D. Terrill Is Appointed Cuba's Auditor," *Buffalo (NY) Courier,* May 3, 1901, 1. Turrell spelled his name in his contest entry as I spell it here.

147. "Marlboro," *Boston Globe,* Dec. 17, 1874, 8; "Seeking a Reappointment," ibid., Dec. 15, 1894, 1; "Postmaster 49 Years," *Fall River (MA) Daily Evening News,* Feb. 18, 1914, 3.

148. "Death of Andrew W. Denison," *Baltimore Sun,* Feb. 26, 1877, 4.

149. For the Republican Party and the GAR, see Stuart McConnell, *Glorious Contentment: The Grand Army of the Republic, 1865–1900* (Chapel Hill: University of North Carolina Press, 1992).

Members attended meetings at local "posts," which belonged to statewide "departments," and national "encampments." There were no military ranks, but posts, named after officers and deceased soldiers, had commanders supported by other administrators, including adjutants, quartermasters, and chaplains. Left-armed veterans rose to positions of prominence at the local, state, and national levels. A tinsmith before the war, John E. Gilman was appointed statehouse messenger by Governor John A. Andrew in 1864 and later clerked for the Massachusetts State Board of Charities and the Public Institutions Office; he was Boston's soldiers' relief commissioner from 1901 until his death in 1921 and commander in chief of the GAR from 1910 to 1911.[150] Duane D. Stilwell was commander at J. H. Danseur Post 104 in La Grange, Indiana; Philo S. Fenton was senior vice commander of the Department of Wisconsin; and Peter G. Van Schaack was a charter member of the Lansing Hollister Post 27.[151] At least 206 of the contestants joined the GAR, a bastion of the GOP.[152]

Veterans who vied for local and state office ran almost exclusively as Republicans. When Martin Van Buren Keller ran for clerk of the Orphan's Court in Pennsylvania, the *Lancaster Intelligencer* announced he would "be the 'crippled soldier' candidate," indicating a larger trend of similarly maimed men who (purposefully or not) benefited from the political capital of being visibly marked by their military service. Another paper added that Keller was "poor, with a family to support," and his opponent was a financially secure, "able-bodied man," thus less deserving of votes.[153] At least ten veterans were city or county treasurers, though holding such a position seemed to be a mixed blessing; Sidney M. Hosier went to court to clear himself of charges that he misappropriated funds (the case was dismissed due to a decade having passed), Herman Baumhager was sentenced to six months in jail for embezzling $53.25,

150. "John E. Gilman Is Dead," *Boston Globe*, Feb. 21, 1921, 1, 6.

151. *Journal of Twenty-Sixth Annual Session of the Department of Indiana, Grand Army of the Republic*, 30; "Death of Philo S. Fenton," *Lake Geneva (WI) Herald*, July 26, 1907; New York Grand Army of the Republic Records, Post Descriptive Books, sub-ser. 11, ser. B1706, New York State Archives, Albany.

152. The number is potentially much higher but cannot be confirmed due to access restrictions on physical records due to the Covid-19 pandemic.

153. "The Republicans," *Lancaster (PA) Intelligencer*, Feb. 20, 1884, 6; "Fall In, Boys! Double Quick!!," *Lancaster (PA) New Era*, Apr. 11, 1884, 2.

and Robert James Dickinson was removed from office for defaulting.[154] Will Warren Jr. of Evansville, Indiana, was a county auditor and recorder as well as city controller and treasurer. When he died in 1937 at the age of ninety-four, he was still employed as a vault custodian.[155] Warren's obituary noted he was Evansville's last surviving GAR member and declared him "always a Republican." Anthony Beaver was appointed postmaster in 1869 and successfully ran as a Republican for associate judge, serving two terms.[156] The political cachet of losing an arm for the Union survived Beaver himself; one year after his death in 1924, an article announcing his son's candidacy for county sheriff reported Beaver had been "a brave soldier of the War of the Rebellion, who, in one of the battles lost an arm."[157]

Twelve entrants relocated to Kansas after their service, following thousands of other veterans taking advantage of the Homestead Act of 1862, and three of them served in that state's legislature. Benjamin C. Cook served four terms as a Republican state representative and was commander of his local GAR post; he is credited with originating the idea of decorating veterans' graves (both Union and Confederate) with flags.[158] Benjamin Franklin Hogg was a Democratic-Populist state senator, and Ira Day Brougher was a Republican representative. As commander of the Pap Thomas GAR post, Brougher erected a bronze soldier monument that stands to this day in Great Bend, Kansas; he also served as state-wide commander in 1914.[159] After fighting for the 43rd New York, Roswell P. Bishop moved to Michigan to take advantage of that state's offer of free tuition and land grants to veterans. A farm laborer before the war, he was a county attorney prior to being elected to the Michigan house of representa-

154. "Case Dismissed in Which Official Was Defendant," *Buffalo (NY) Courier,* July 29, 1900, 11; "The Scott County Treasurers," *Saint Paul (MN) Globe,* Feb. 21, 1881, 1; "Illinois," *Chicago Tribune,* Feb. 16, 1872, 2.

155. "Civil War Soldier Pneumonia Victim," *Indianapolis News,* Jan. 2, 1937, 5.

156. "Pennsylvania Postmasters," *Philadelphia Inquirer,* Apr. 20, 1898, 12; "Services Today for Former Judge Beaver," *Altoona (PA) Tribune,* Nov. 5, 1924, 12.

157. "Another Has Entered Lists for Sheriff," *Altoona (PA) Tribune,* June 23, 1925, 8.

158. "An Old Kansan Is Gone," *Harper (KS) Advocate,* Mar. 16, 1906, 8. A historical marker in Mottville, New York, honors his suggestion. See wgpfoundation.org/historic-markers/benjamin-c-cook.

159. "Ex-Senator Hogg Dead," *Weir (KS) Weekly Tribune,* Nov. 17, 1896, 1; "Unveil Monument in Park Today," *Great Bend (KS) Tribune,* Nov. 19, 1915, 1.

tives and remained active in the GAR.[160] From 1898 to 1910, he represented the state's Ninth District in the U.S. House of Representatives as a Republican and was appointed chairman of the Spanish Treaty Claims Commission by Theodore Roosevelt.[161] Like Hogg, a few other veterans bucked the Republican trend: David O. Mull ran for clerk on the Democratic ticket in 1868, and attorney Silas M. Shepard switched from the GOP to the Populist Party in the 1890s, acting as secretary for the party's Indiana state committee and running for mayor of Indianapolis and state supreme-court judge on "the people's" ticket.[162]

When members of the Left-Armed Corps passed away, their obituaries regularly mentioned their service, their missing or disabled arms, their membership in the GAR, and their upstanding citizenship. Not all received such glowing tributes, however, and at least two men died by suicide.[163] Josiah Phillips spent time in Sing-Sing after knifing a man who attempted to steal his $90 pension payment and later was killed by his wife after a drunken quarrel over yet another pension payment.[164] Like Bergin and Durrah, Phillips is unique, though a few others had run-ins with the law. Some of the veterans were "pensioners" by the end of their lives, but most were financially secure—indeed, Edwin A. Brooks left behind a $75,000 fortune.[165] Twenty-seven of the left-handed veterans died

160. Rose D. Hawley, "Recalls When Bishop Family Resided on Harrison Street," *Ludington (MI) Daily News,* Aug. 6, 1953, 3; 1860 U.S. Census, Ostego Co., NY, pop. sched., Ostego, p. 34, dwelling 306, family 306, Roswell Bishop, NARA RG 29, M653, roll 875; "Roswell P. Bishop Chosen," *Washington Post,* Nov. 3, 1907, 10.

161. Hawley, "Recalls When Bishop Family Resided on Harrison Street," 3; "Roswell P. Bishop Chosen," 10.

162. "Franklin Township Democratic Nominations," *Daily Ohio Statesman* (Columbus), Mar. 23, 1868, 3; "District and County Meetings," *Columbus (IN) Republican,* Jan. 3, 1896, 1; "Populist City Convention," *Indianapolis News,* Sept. 5, 1895, 7; "The Ballots and How to Vote Them on Election Day," ibid., Oct. 14, 1892, 6.

163. Dorus E. Bates and Marvin Burroughs, "Captain D. E. Bates," *Woodstock (IL) Sentinel,* Aug. 26, 1880, 2; "Wealthy Seneca Falls Politician Hangs Himself," *Rochester (NY) Democrat and Chronicle,* Jan. 11, 1918, 5.

164. "Veteran Phillips Uses a Knife," *New York Sun,* Mar. 7, 1891, 5; "Wife Kills Her Husband," *Buffalo (NY) Times,* Nov. 16, 1900, 1.

165. Joseph Egolf shot a man he accused of writing a slanderous article about his employer, and Charles Presley served time in Sing-Sing for burglary. "Court of General Sessions," *New York Daily Herald,* Mar. 21, 1868, 5; "General Carr's Son Shot," *Brooklyn Daily Eagle,* Apr. 26, 1885, 1; "The Late Edwin A. Brooks," *New Haven (CT) Morning Journal-Courier,* Feb. 6, 1893, 4.

before 1875, at least 7 from tuberculosis, and 113 did not live to see the twentieth century. Some succumbed to their wounds, sometimes decades after receiving them. Frederick L. Sanderson lost control of his horses and perished after being dragged behind a farm roller, while Frederick M. Platt was thrown from a carriage. Newspapers blamed the accidents primarily on the veterans' missing limbs: Sanderson's horses "became unmanageable to a one-armed driver," while Platt, "having only one arm, fell head foremost on to a sharp stone."[166] Most of the veterans (77) died between 1910 and 1919, 62 others died in the 1920s, and 15 lived until the 1930s. William B. Hutchinson, who worked as a bookkeeper for a transit company, was the longest living member of the Left-Armed Corps; he died in 1937 at the age of ninety-seven.[167] Though it is impossible to summarize or generalize the sentiments of 333 men, it is clear that many of the veterans lived their lives as proud members of the Left-Armed Corps, carrying their experiences and changed bodies into futures shaped by their time as soldiers.

Left-Handed Legacies

The Soldier's Friend regularly advertised "an attractive book" to be titled "Battle Memories of the Left-Armed Corps."[168] Comprising "the sketches, tales, poems, and war narratives of the Left-Armed Corps," the "octavo volume" would feature an introduction by William Cullen Bryant and ample illustrations. For three dollars, subscribers could secure a copy of what would "be one of the best literary contributions to the history of the war, as well as the memorial of an entirely new feature in literature—the united production of several hundred left-armed veterans of the battle-field." Though he had received "a number of additional letters from various sources in regard to the volume," Bourne explained that he would not "undertake" the project until three thousand subscribers signed up. Apparently, they did not. Printing the results of the second contest, Bourne expressed his "hearty thanks" to all of the competitors "for their appreciation

166. "Petersham," *Fitchburg (MA) Sentinel,* May 12, 1886, 3; "Portchester," *Yonkers (NY) Statesman,* May 25, 1871, 1.

167. "W. B. Hutchinson, Canton's Oldest Civil War Veteran, Is Dead at Age 97," *Ogdensburg (NY) Journal,* Feb. 16, 1937, 12.

168. "An Attractive Book," *Soldier's Friend,* Sept. 1866, 2.

of our efforts and our purposes." He continued, "in due time it will appear that *they* are not forgotten." *The Soldier's Friend* "would be glad to send them all a substantial token of our friendship, but we must be patient of our desires if they will be of our inability to do more than we have done."[169] Bourne apparently refers here to the unrealized memorial volume.

For more than a century, the left-handed papers remained unpublished, aside from a few selections in Bourne's newspaper. Until the recent digitization of the collection, only scholars interested in the writings of Civil War veterans with access to the Library of Congress's manuscript reading room experienced the unique and "united production" of amputee veterans.[170] Literary scholar Benjamin Cooper argues that the contestants' "personal impressions represented . . . the diverse wartime experiences of hundreds of veterans from multiple regions across the Union, yet their full significance within the literary history of Civil War narrative will remain forever obscure and incomplete."[171] Nevertheless, this volume allows members of the Left-Armed Corps to speak for themselves and insert their stories into the literary record of the Civil War. Consciously participating in a collective act of testifying to national trauma, they presented their reconfigured bodies and lives to the public. In so doing, they created not only what Bourne called a "rich literary entertainment . . . for the public" but also a powerful archive of suffering, recovery, and survival.

This archive exists because 333 men were willing to remember their time as soldiers, relive moments of trauma, undertake the sometimes difficult task of shaping letters with their left hands, and tell their stories. Some of the competitors in the first contest wrote in the months immediately following Appomattox, their wounds still healing. Nelson argues that northern amputees were expected to suffer "pain in manly silence," and some of the veterans mentioned their wounding and surgeries only in passing.[172] The contest rules required that

169. "Left-Hand Writing by Disabled Soldiers and Sailors of the War," 4.

170. See Clarke, *War Stories,* 144–70; Cooper, *Veteran Americans,* 140–44; Johnson, *Scars We Carve,* 90–120; Jordan, *Marching Home,* 105–8, 111–24; and Padilla, "Army of 'Cripples,'" 20–59. To view the digitized papers, see Civil War Soldiers: "Disabled but Not Disheartened," By the People Campaign, Library of Congress, https://crowd.loc.gov/campaigns/civil-war-soldiers-disabled-but-not-disheartened.

171. Cooper, *Veteran Americans,* 144.

172. Nelson, *Ruin Nation,* 185.

entrants provide the date and place of their wounding, but many also included graphic descriptions of their ordeals, explaining the specifics of the injuries they suffered and the surgeries they underwent. Viewed as a "united production," the writings of the Left-Armed Corps do much to complicate and revise our understanding of what historian Gerald Linderman has referred to as "the Hibernation"—the reticence and willful forgetfulness of Civil War veterans in the years immediately following the conflict.[173] According to Linderman, returned soldiers "turn[ed] rapidly from the war" and focused on the present, adjusting to life as civilians. "Their perception of what they had done from one day of battle to the next," he argues, "shifted, overlapped, and merged, leaving them with blurred memories and blunted emotions."[174] Though a few contestants admitted to being uncertain about particulars—one because he lost his wartime diary—many were able to present meticulous and detailed narratives of their time as soldiers; some also expressed a vested interest in the course of Reconstruction and the cause of Black citizenship and suffrage.

Not until the 1880s, Linderman contends, did public interest inspire an outpouring of regimental histories and autobiographies.[175] Yet the Left-Armed Corps was obviously invested in helping shape the larger narrative of the war and the reasons it was fought shortly after Appomattox. Aiming to establish the significance of their personal sacrifice and bodily transformation, they also commemorated the collective efforts of their comrades. These men bore the physical and emotional legacies of the conflict and were thus uniquely qualified to attend to its presentation to posterity. Two members, Corporal James R. Burns and Colonel W. W. H. Davis, went beyond submitting to the contests, publishing a reminiscence of the Battle of Williamsburg in 1865 and a regimental history in 1866, respectively.[176] As early postwar reflections, the

173. Linderman, *Embattled Courage,* 266–75. I am not alone in revising Linderman's "hibernation" argument. See Jordan and Rothera, *The War Went On.*

174. Linderman, *Embattled Courage,* 268, 267.

175. Ibid. 275.

176. See James R. Burns, *Battle of Williamsburgh, with Reminiscences of the Campaign* (New York: James R. Burns, 1865); and W. W. H. Davis, *History of the 104th Pennsylvania Regiment* (Philadelphia: Jas. B. Rogers, 1866). Burns and Davis were not alone—Peter C. Luebke notes that veterans published around fifty regimental histories between 1865 and 1866, providing accounts "from the perspective of immediate retrospective." Luebke, "'To Transmit and Perpetuate the Fruits of This Victory,'" 186.

left-handed papers constitute a valuable addition to the archive of Civil War soldier writings, primarily comprising letters and diaries written during the conflict.[177] Describing the mundanities of military service, the horror and fervor of battle, the agony of wounding and amputation, and the aftermath of bodily loss, the contestants added their personal stories and their reconfigured bodies to the vast corpus of Civil War literature.

The men who sent penmanship specimens to Bourne's contests recognized their membership in a unique group of veterans and enthusiastically participated in what Colonel Davis called the "Left-Handed Literature movement."[178] Eagerly awaiting a collected edition of these writings, W. Augustus MacNulty wrote to Bourne, "I look forward to the publication of such a book with joyful anticipation as it will embrace the history of many of my brave comrades with whom I have fought for the establishment of our national existence upon a basis which I trust will be as lasting as it is secure; truly such a book will be prized next to the Bible itself." MacNulty perhaps exaggerated, but he was not alone in recognizing the literary significance of the personal testimonies of left-armed veterans. According to Ohio veteran William Johnson, "these individual incidents constitute a great part of the unwritten history of the rebellion."

Editing the Left-Armed Corps

The members of the Left-Armed Corps were individuals, each with unique ways of expressing themselves, different levels of education, and syntactical tics some wrote fluently and grammatically, while others struggled with spelling and punctuation. If a contest entry was nearly error free, I silently corrected the occasional misplaced comma. When editing would have significantly influenced the flavor or feeling of a veteran's writing, I preserved the original spelling, grammar, and punctuation errors. Some entries required minor editing for clarity and are labeled (in footnotes) as such. Footnotes also identify less familiar places and names that are unique to individual entries, while Appendix B provides information about repeatedly mentioned battles. Using census records, death and marriage certificates, regimental rosters and histories pension indexes, obituaries, newspaper articles, and—in a few instances—

177. See Bonner, *Soldier's Pen,* 10–11.

178. W. W. H. Davis, Contest Entry, 1st ser., no. 268, Bourne Papers.

information from direct descendants of the contestants, I have done my best to piece together the pre- and postwar lives of the men featured in this volume. Due to the Covid-19 pandemic, I was unable to access pension records, which could provide valuable insights into how the veterans dealt with their injuries over time and how they presented their lives and bodies to representatives of the government they fought to preserve. Using the biographical information provided in the full list of contestants (Appendix A), future scholars may wish to compare contest entries to pension applications and supporting documents; doing so could reveal medical or personal details contestants chose to omit as well as provide insight into the ways in which aging veterans advocated for themselves and understood the continued significance of their service. Census pages and obituaries do not tell the whole story, around fifteen entries are missing from Bourne's papers, and a few contestants do not even appear on official regimental rosters; as such, I welcome input from anyone who recognizes one of their ancestors in the pages that follow.

Though Bourne hoped to publish every entry, the resulting tome would have comprised thousands of pages. In the interest of including as many veterans as possible and organizing the material thematically, I have pruned passages and summarized lengthy descriptions of troop movements (indicated by italics). All of the entries are worthy of publication, but the ones I include here speak to the commonalities of the writings as an archive. Narrating their transition from citizens to soldiers, providing anecdotes of life in camp, realistically reporting the sensations of battle and the agony of wounding, asserting their loyalty to their adopted country, poeticizing loss, philosophizing, or describing their new lives, the Left-Armed Corps adds their voices to the literary record of the Civil War. In August 1865, Ora D. Walbridge sat down with pen in left hand to produce a specimen of his best business penmanship; he did not expect to win a prize but instead wrote in recognition of the award committee's support of "the unfortunate soldier."[179] "Such men are remembered by me," he wrote, "I, for one, always extend the only hand I have left to greet such men." In the pages that follow, Walbridge's comrades extend their left hands, offering their stories and asking for recognition.

179. Ora D. Walbridge, Contest Entry, 1st ser., no. 24, ibid.

1.

MUSTERING AND MARCHING

Instructions for both contests required official information from entrants: full personal name, company and regiment details, a list of battles experienced, and "the place where he lost his arm."[1] The second contest asked writers to "furnish a sketch of their military history, from the date of their enlistment to their discharge."[2] As a result, many of the entries begin with the date of enlistment and provide insight into the experience of signing up, mustering, and marching during the Civil War. Contestants discuss their reasons for volunteering and the journeys they took to do so. As historian James M. McPherson notes in his study of why men fought in the Civil War, old veterans looking back on their time as soldiers and writing for the public about their motivations might be tempted to "put the best face on [their] motives and behavior, to highlight noble and courageous actions and to gloss over the ignoble and cowardly."[3] Though the Left-Armed Corps wrote with the possibility of publi-

1. "Premium $500 to the Left-Armed Soldiers of the Union," *Soldier's Friend*, Oct. 1865, 2.
2. "Honor to the Brave," William Oland Bourne Papers.
3. McPherson, *For Cause and Comrades*, 10.

cation and ostensibly to make a good impression on the contest judges, they did so in the immediate aftermath of their military service—indeed, some had wounds not fully healed while they wrote. Enthusiasm for reconciliation with the South and gatherings between the boys in blue and the boys in gray were future phenomena; the "romance of reunion" would come later.[4] With fresh memories and pride in defeating traitorous southerners and ending slavery, the veterans aligned themselves on the side of Union, loyalty, and freedom.[5] McPherson draws primarily on letters and diaries to determine the often ideological motivations for military service, and it is clear that many contestants relied on similar materials when composing their narratives.[6] As such, these writings constitute a hybrid form that provides insights into veterans' understandings of their service and its significance in the months and years immediately following Appomattox.

Their memories intact, the contestants relate in painstaking detail their transformation from citizen to soldier. For most, the period after enlistment entailed monotonous training, disorienting travel, and nervous anticipation. Marches, in particular, fill the left-handed pages, revealing the geographical components of soldiering as well as the mobility required of, at times, bedraggled and exhausted troops. Many of the men mention both their enlistment date and their date of muster; by emphasizing their enlistment, the veterans underscore their status as volunteers—men who chose to serve—rather than as compelled draftees or paid substitutes. In the first years of the war, men enlisted in companies as they were being organized. Those companies then were mustered into service in the Federal army; subsequently, recruits enlisted with an established unit and then traveled to camps or to join their regiments in the field. In the selections that follow, veterans make their individual military histories official and detail the events that led to their joining the Left-Armed Corps.

4. See Nina Silber, *The Romance of Reunion: Northerners and the South, 1865–1900* (Chapel Hill: University of North Carolina Press, 1993).

5. For a discussion of Union soldiers' relationship to the Union cause, see Gary W. Gallagher, *The Union War* (Cambridge, MA: Harvard University Press, 2011).

6. McPherson, *For Cause and Comrades*, 11–12. A few contestants lamented the loss of wartime diaries, which made it difficult for them to provide exact dates for some of their experiences.

ROBERT A. PINN

First Sergeant, Co. I, 5th United States Colored Infantry

Robert A. Pinn.
Courtesy Library of Congress, Prints and Photographs Division, LC-USZ62-118551.

Pinn, one of two members of the USCT to compete in Bourne's contests, was born in 1843, the son of a formerly enslaved man.[7] The 1890 Veterans Schedule notes that he could not enlist earlier than 1862 "because colored"; instead, he signed on as an aide to a surgeon for the 19th Ohio Infantry and first shouldered arms at Shiloh.[8] He enlisted in 1863 and earned the rank of first sergeant in September 1864.[9] As a result of his service at the Battle of Chaffin's Farm, Virginia (September 29–30, 1864), he received the Medal of Honor for taking "command of his company after all the officers had been killed or wounded and gallantly [leading] it in battle."[10] Pinn married in 1867 and owned a business. After selling it, he attended Oberlin College and studied law, eventually joining the Stark County Bar and practicing as a pension attorney.[11] Pinn became junior vice commander of his local post of the GAR in 1888 and died in 1911.[12] An Akron newspaper noted that he was "a respected colored citizen and attorney" who "loved to tell of his thrilling experiences during the war."[13] W. E. B. Du Bois included the above portrait of Pinn in a collection of photographs of notable African Americans presented at the 1900 Paris Exposition.

7. Robert A. Pinn, Contest Entry, 1st ser., no. 29, Bourne Papers (punctuation edited); Hanna, *African American Recipients of the Medal of Honor,* 46–48.

8. 1890 U.S. Census, Stark Co., OH, vet. sched., Massillon, Robert A. Pinn, Special Schedules Enumerating Union Veterans and Widows of Union Veterans of the Civil War, NARA RG 15, M123; Hanna, *African American Recipients of the Medal of Honor,* 47.

9. Compiled Military Service Records of Volunteer Union Soldiers Who Served with the United States Colored Troops, Robert A. Pinn, NARA RG 94, M1820, roll 61.

10. Hanna, *African American Recipients of the Medal of Honor,* 47.

11. Ibid., 47–48.

12. "Grand Army of the Republic," *Summit County Beacon* (Akron, OH), Feb. 29, 1888, 1; "Lawyer L. L. Pinn Dies at Massillon," *Akron (OH) Beacon Journal,* Jan. 3, 1911, 3. The article title incorrectly refers to Pinn's brother, who attended the funeral.

13. "Lawyer L. L. Pinn Dies at Massillon," 3.

September 15, 1865

I was born in the town of Massillon, Stark County, State of Ohio, where I experienced all the disadvantages peculiar to my *proscribed* race. Being born to labor I was not permitted to enjoy the blessings of a common School education. It is hardly necessary to say that very little can be expected of me, so far as correct composition is concerned.

In '61, when the whole of the Loyal North was aroused by reason of the cowardly assault upon Fort Sumter, I was very eager to become a Soldier, in order to prove by my feeble efforts the black man's wrights to untrammeled manhood. I was denied admission to the ranks of the loyalists, on account of my color not being of that kind which is considered a standard in this country.

In '63, however, when the Rebellion which burst out at Sumter had assumed higher proportions it was deamed expedient to the government to enroal the able bodied black man among its defenders.

The Gov. of Ohio[14] was very slow in acknoledging this Change in public affairs. The Gov. of Massachusetts,[15] being of a more humane tem[pera]ment, enlisted and equipped two regiments before Ohio's Gov. became interested in the matter.

On the 19th day of June 1863—long may it be remembered—a camp was opened near the town of Delaware, Ohio, for the purpose of forming a Colored regiment. In September of the same year at the age of twenty I enlisted and joined the regt. then forming at Delaware and designated as the 5th U.S. Col'd Troops.

In October I was apointed a Sergt. in Company I. My regt. soon after moved to Norfolk, VA, whe[re] I had my first experience in active Military life. We left Norfolk, VA, on the 3rd of December on a scouting expedition through North Carolina, and after a long march having been engaged in several skirmishes returned on the 23rd of the same monthe. Cold weather having set in, the next duty assigned was the building of quarters. But we had scarcely compleated them when on the 18th of January we were ordered to Yorktown, VA. Arriving there on the 20th we were Brigaded with the 4th and 6th

14. David Tod, governor of Ohio (1862–64), resisted enlisting Blacks. See Gerber, *Black Ohio and the Color Line*, 33–34.

15. John Andrew, governor of Massachusetts (1861–66), advocated for enlisting Blacks and organized the 54th Massachusetts. See Pearson, *Life of John A. Andrew*, 71–91.

Regiments of U.S. Col'd Troops. Here as at Norfolk, we built winter quarters. During our stay at Yorktown under the direction of General Wister[16] we made several marches up the eninsular.[17] A march into King and Quean county in search of the murderers of Colonel Dalghrun[18] nearly completed our duties for the winter. Preparations had already began for the historic campaign of '64, when my regiment was ordered to Old Point Comfort.[19]

In the course of three or four weeks under the direction of [Major] General [Benjamin] Butler there was assembled at this place nearly fifteen thousand Colored soldiers, these constituted the brave and justly celebrated 3rd Division of the 18th Army Corps.

On the 15th of June '64, we went into battle before Petersburg, VA. Of the successes of that day the country is well informed. I have participated in nearly all of the battles in which my regiment has been engaged, and was wounded before Richmond on the 29th of September 1864, from which I am now a sufferer, having lost the use of my wright arm.

CHARLES R. POST

Private, Co. F, 173rd New York Volunteer Infantry

Post was born in Westbrook, Connecticut, in 1842 and moved with his parents to New York City in 1845.[20] He enlisted when he was nineteen in response to the second call for volunteers. Discharged in 1864, he was appointed government clerk at Fort Hamilton, New York; became a clerk at the Brooklyn Navy Yard in 1871; and married in 1876.[21] In 1919, a laudatory article

16. Brevet Brigadier General Langhorne Wister (1834–91).

17. Pinn's spelling of "Peninsula." King and Queen County is located in Virginia's Middle Peninsula.

18. Union colonel Ulric Dahlgren (1842–64) was killed in an ambush during a raid on Richmond. Papers allegedly found on his body ordered the assassination of Confederate president Jefferson Davis. The so-called "Dahlgren Affair" resulted. See "Colonel Ulric Dahlgren," *Harper's Weekly* 8, no. 378 (Mar. 26, 1864): 1; and Duane Schultz, *The Dahlgren Affair: Terror and Conspiracy in the Civil War* (New York: Norton, 1998).

19. The tip of the Virginia Peninsula and site of Fort Monroe.

20. Charles R. Post, Contest Entries, 1st ser., no. 89, and 2nd ser., no. 110, Bourne Papers; "42 Years in Service of Tax Office Here," *Brooklyn Daily Eagle,* Oct. 12, 1919, 19.

21. "42 Years in Service of Tax Office Here," 19.

Charles R. Post.
Courtesy William Oland Bourne Papers, Manuscript Division, Library of Congress.

reported that Post had retired after forty-two years of service at the Brooklyn Tax Office.[22] The piece described his gallantry while leading a charge, his presidency of the Fully Disabled Veterans Association, and "one of the most extraordinary achievements of Mr. Post," his playing the organ with one hand for a local lodge of the Independent Order of Odd Fellows "for one whole year." It also mentioned his winning of the Hooker Premium. The general chose Post's second submission for the prize, writing, "I express my sincere wish that the sacrifice you have made as a soldier, may be more than equaled by your future prosperity." After retiring, Post looked forward to enjoying "his porch and garden"; he died in 1922.[23] His first entry, excerpted below, received honorable mention.[24]

First Entry: December 28, 1865

We were encamped on Rikers Island[25] while recruiting. When we had our complement of men, and had been on the Island about six weeks, rations were dealt out to us, and we were put aboard of two small steamers. I took one more look (perhaps the last, I then thought) at the old barracks where we had spent so many lonely days.

At last we were off amid the weeping of mothers, the crying of wives and children, the sobs of sweethearts, and the waving of handkerchiefs.

As we steamed down the East River many were the anxious gazes and wishful looks cast at the familiar houses and places along the route.

We were next put aboard of the large propeller "Continental" then anchored opposite the Battery, where we remained four or five days. Finally we got up steam and started, and many were the conjectures as to our destination.

After a very rough voyage of fifteen days we anchored off of the city of New

22. Ibid.

23. "Chas. R. Post Died; Tax Clerk 42 Years," *Brooklyn Daily Eagle,* Sept. 19, 1922, 2.

24. Exhibition of Left-Hand Penmanship, Bourne Papers.

25. An island in New York's East River between the Bronx and Queens.

Orleans. Next morning we started up the Mississippi river and nearly everybody aboard felt and spoke of the difference in the climate, it was so warm and mild. On our way up the river we saw beautiful orange trees loaded with oranges, and some of the men on shore tried to throw some of them on board, but were not quite successful, for the oranges would just reach the side of the vessel and drop into the water, which was very aggravating to us. At last we reached Baton Rouge, and were immediately put ashore. I for one, was glad to get once more on terra firma. After forming we marched up through the city with our colors flying. How beautiful those colors looked then. How faded and torn they are now!

We pitched our camp just outside of the city. The citizens did not greet us kindly, but rather the reverse. What few stores were open in the place charged enormous prices for anything they knew we wanted and would have, such as butter, cheese, tobacco, fruit, pies, etc.

We were allowed the privilege of going to church every Sunday morning, and after a while we had religious services in our own camp by the chaplain of my own regiment, which I usually attended. During the week-days, four hours a day were devoted to drilling us, and very awkward work we made of it at first, for we did not receive our arms until we reached Baton Rouge.

Four were in my tent, and I generally done the cooking, when we had anything to cook, but seldom could we forage, for [Major] General [Nathaniel] Banks—in command of the Department [of the Gulf]—issued an order prohibiting all foraging. After remaining in Baton Rouge about two months we struck tents and prepared for a long campaign.

After marching up through the Teche country[26] we found the rebels strongly intrenched at a place called Camp Bisland. . . .

Pushing forward to within about one hundred and twenty yards of the rebel works under a heavy fire, we laid down in a narrow ditch. Our artillery coming up in the meantime and getting into position opened on them, but the rebels maintained a stubborn silence until we got our heavier artillery to bear on them. They then answered with shot and shell. I recollect distinctly the feeling I then had. It was a feeling of fear. I trembled all over during the first day's battle, but the second day, I did not mind it so much.

26. The region along Bayou Teche, in south-central Louisiana.

This battle[27] commenced on the 12th of April 1863. In the afternoon we were ordered to charge the works, but the order was immediately countermanded, and we fell back into our former position. Night coming on we posted a heavy picket. Next morning—the 13th—at about seven o'clock, fire was opened on the enemy, but with the same result as before, until our firing became pretty brisk. They then replied almost shot for shot, and in this way, with a few short intervals, the firing was kept up nearly all day. At night the pickets exchanged shots every little while.

On the morning of the 14th we found the place evacuated, thin pickets remaining until the very last. After we had marched inside of the works, we saw the dead men and horses strewn all around, also a number of dismounted cannon.

The loss in my regiment amounted to only thirty. It was remarkably small owing to our being somewhat sheltered, and the rebels firing too high. From here we followed the rebels, marching sometimes thirty miles a day, starting in the morning at five, and camping at eight at night, until we reached the suburbs of Port Hudson (May 27th, 1863) in which I also took part. We drove them through the woods slowly, the rebels keeping themselves sheltered behind trees and logs. They fired with more accuracy and effect than in the previous battle. In the afternoon my regiment was ordered to support a battery that were posted somewhat in the advance. Here we could plainly see the rebels slowly falling back, until they were compelled to get inside of their fortification.

We immediately laid siege to the place, throwing up breastworks of cotton, and digging intrenchments (mostly at night). We placed two logs on top of the breastwork—one on top of the other—with places cut into them shaped like a diamond when put together, thus forming a very convenient, as well as safe, port-hole to shoot through. We remained here until the 14th of June 1863 (Sunday morning) just before daybreak, when a grand charge was made. Moving forward with as little noise as possible we reached within twenty

27. The Battle of Fort Bisland, Louisiana. Attempting to move toward Alexandria, Louisiana, and Port Hudson, Major General Nathaniel P. Banks's XIX Army Corps confronted Major General Richard Taylor's Army of Western Louisiana at the fort. Fighting ended after Union gunboats joined the assault on the thirteenth. Taylor ordered an evacuation when he found out a Union division was in position to block his retreat.

yards of the works, when they opened on us. Our artillery in the rear then belched forth, but fired pretty high to avoid us.

Our progress was necessarily quite slow, crawling on our hands and knees through the ravines up to the works, a number reaching the top of the parapet, but only to be shot down, for the moment any of our men showed their heads above the top of the work, they would drop like chunks of lead. Corporal Robertson of my company got on the top of the breastwork with his hands and knees and dug a place in the top of the work to shelter him. He was about to get up—raising his head to look inside, when several of us remonstrated with him about being so indiscreet, but he did not heed us. Only a few seconds afterwards a bullet struck him over the left eye, coming out at the back of his head, killing him instantly.

We remained in the ditch until evening and then retired, but not until the wounded were taken care of. A flag of truce was raised the next morning to give us an opportunity of burying our dead.

My regiment lost in killed and wounded one hundred and twenty, including several commissioned officers. My company were quite fortunate, six being our total loss. . . .

We remained in our intrenchments until the 9th of July 1863, when the fort was formally surrendered and taken possession of. Shortly after we had camped inside[,] ten days rations of flour were issued to us. Then came my first real experience in using it. I bought some baking soda from the sutler,[28] which helped me considerably. I could then make biscuit[s] very well. But my first efforts in this direction did not end well—the biscuit[s] were very heavy and nearly as hard as very hard, "hard tack."[29]

Post engaged in fighting at Vermillion, Louisiana, before participating in the Battle of Sabine Cross Roads on April 8, 1864, as he describes below.

The first of the three battles of the ill-fated Red River Expedition,[30] it was fought in the afternoon about four o'clock. The Thirteenth Corps were about

28. A seller of provisions to soldiers.

29. The name soldiers used for a very hard and unappetizing "flour-and-water biscuit" issued as part of their rations. For a veteran's description, see Billings, *Hardtack and Coffee*, 113–19.

30. General Banks's attempt to take Shreveport, Louisiana, in the spring of 1864.

seven miles in advance of us, when they were attacked by a large body of rebels. After receiving rations of hard bread we marched forward between a double quick[31] and a walk until we got within two miles of them, when, the firing becoming more rapid, we quickened our pace until we were on a full double quick, reaching the battle ground just in time (for the Thirteenth Corps had about used up all of their ammunition) and filing into line we gave the rebels several good volleys, which had the desired effect: they retired. About midnight we retired also, for the rebels had decidedly the advantage in numbers. The Thirteenth Corps suffered a great deal more than the Nineteenth, to which I belonged. The loss of the rebels must have been as great, if not greater, than ours.[32]

After marching all night long—almost without a halt—we camped at Pleasant Hill,[33] and after posting a heavy picket, rations of fresh raw beef were given us. We were cooking it when the rebels advanced on us, yelling in their peculiar style. We could not get a good shot at them owing to a rise in the ground right in front of us. They came on in overwhelming numbers, a battery of ours right in rear of us cutting great gaps in their ranks with grape and cannister.[34] They finally succeeded in breaking our line, and capturing eighteen of my company. Soon after the rebels broke our line I fell back to the next one, which was somewhat sheltered by small piles of rails.

The rebels came on until they reached this line, when they received a terrific volley, which staggered them; at the same time getting orders to

31. Rapid marching speed, equivalent to 180 paces per minute in modern usage. An 1862 tactic manual equates it with a run. See Silas Casey, *Infantry Tactics for the Instruction, Exercise, and Maneuvers of the Soldier, a Company, Line of Skirmishers, Battalion, Brigade, or Corps d'Armée,* vol. 1 (New York: D. Van Nostrand, 1862), 243.

32. Confederate forces had 1,200 killed or wounded, with 426 taken prisoner, during the fighting at Sabine Cross Roads, while Union forces had 994 men killed or wounded, with 375 missing. Kennedy, *Civil War Battlefield Guide,* 170.

33. The Battle of Pleasant Hill, April 9, 1864. Part of General Banks's Red River Campaign. Following a Confederate victory at the Battle of Mansfield, Louisiana, on April 8, Banks withdrew his troops to Pleasant Hill and forced a Confederate retreat on April 9 after heavy losses on both sides. Given his concerns about water supply and his incorrect belief that General Taylor, the Confederate commander, had superior numbers, Banks abandoned his plans to capture Shreveport. See John D. Winters, *The Civil War in Louisiana* (Baton Rouge: Louisiana State University Press, 1991), 340–56.

34. Grape refers to an artillery round consisting of iron balls separated by iron plates. Canister is a short-range round consisting of a tin can containing iron or lead balls.

charge, we did so and were successful in driving them and taking a number [of] prisoners. The number of our killed and wounded amounted to about one hundred. They were taken care of the same night.

Post's division marched along the Red River as Banks retreated toward Alexandria, fording the Cane River on April 23, 1864.

As soon as we gained the other side [of Cane River] and got formed, we marched through the woods until we could see the rebels posted on a bluff. This we afterwards found was called Monet's Bluff. Our line was formed along a rail fence. The 128th New York were detailed as skirmishers[35] on our left. When they had got some distance in advance of us, a staff officer advanced a short distance in front of us and said, "It is General Birge's[36] orders to charge that bluff," and then unsheathing his sword and waving it over his head, said, "Men follow me."

We were instantly in motion, and tearing down the rail fence, went across the field on a double quick, with a yell. On the way I saw quite a number wounded and shot dead. As I neared the foot of the bluff I saw a rebel on the top, lying down and aiming at me. At the same instant I felt a very slight twinge near my right shoulder but did not know I was shot until I felt my arm powerless and drop to my side, some seconds afterwards. Looking at my arm, I saw a bullet hole through it. I immediately caught up my arm and let me rifle drop, for the bone was entirely severed and the arm hung by the flesh.

I walked to the rear, I could not go faster. It seemed as though my arm would shake off. I took another look at the rebel as I left and thought, if I could only have the privilege of firing one more shot it would give me a great deal of satisfaction.

I did not go back in the same direction that I came. I reached the fence, but could not get over it. I felt weak from the loss of blood. I finally got a soldier to help me, and with his assistance, reached the other side. I walked through the woods until I saw a lieutenant with a squad of men; I told him I had a handkerchief in my pocket and asked him to tie up my arm. He did so,

35. Troops dispersed in front of an advancing force to make contact with the enemy or to provide early warning of an enemy attack.

36. Henry Warner Birge (1825–88), brigadier general during the Red River Campaign.

tying it just above where I was wounded, thus stopping a great deal of the blood. I then sat down by a tree (I could stand no longer) and shortly after was taken on a stretcher to the surgeons, where I remained two hours. I was then taken to a little cotton gin about a mile off. I laid here until about half past eight—five hours after being wounded—when my arm was amputated about two inches from the shoulder.

I was next put into an ambulance, in which I rode for two days. About ninety miles above Alexandria I was transferred to a hospital ship. I finally reached Alexandria, LA, where I remained a week in the hospital. From here I was sent to New Orleans. I was quartered in the Barracks Hospital, which is situated about four miles from the city of New Orleans, where I remained two months. After being in the hospital two weeks, I wrote a letter home to my parents and every word I wrote made me sweat. I abbreviated the letter as much as possible, but it was read quite easily. During the time I was in the hospital, I wrote no less than ten letters, as much to see how I could write as anything else.

I was discharged from the Barracks Hospital June 1864 and went to the "Soldiers Home" in New Orleans where I was very kindly treated. I was paid in full and Mr. Seaton, the pension agent, made out my pension papers, which I received from Washington, two months after coming home. I took passage on the transport *United States* and arrived in New York July 5th 1864.

Before leaving New Orleans, I bought some lemons and sugar and a corporal—belonging to a Maine regiment, who was shot in the same battle that I was, who also lost his right arm close up to the shoulder, and with whom I became acquainted while in hospital, and who was discharged and put aboard of the same vessel with me—helped me make lemonade. He held the lemon, while I cut it up, and in this way we got along very well. He supplied my right arm when I wanted to do anything, and I done the same for him.

About eight months after coming home, I determined to seek employment and earn my own living. Accordingly I collected recommendations from persons who were well acquainted with me. I also applied to my colonel for one. In reply, he sent me an excellent letter, enumerating the battles I was in, and stating how I conducted myself while serving under his command. I went to Major F. E. Prime, Corps of Engineers, and applied for a situation. He was very kind to me, and gave me the position of Clerk of the Works, at the New Battery at Fort Hamilton, which I still hold. I have been employed here during the last nine months. When I first came here I experienced a little difficulty in regard to my writing, duties, etc., but through the kindness of the Superintendent—Mr. Bryson—I overcome [*sic*] it all, and can now get along very well.

I did not commence practicing with my left hand until about five months after coming home. It is fourteen months since I have tried to write. I was always right handed. I never wrote with my left until after I lost my arm. I can write either way—the natural slope or backhanded, but find the latter the handiest.[37] When not employed by the Government, I am allowed eight dollars a month pension. It was stopped as soon as I obtained this situation.

~~~

GEORGE S. WARNER

Private, Co. F, 13th Ohio Volunteer Cavalry

Warner was born in Ohio around 1846.[38] Though an obituary labeled him "Colonel," Warner remained a private throughout the war.[39] In 1880, he was working as a clerk in a "notion store" and would later own a harness store. According to the obituary, "having a generous heart, he didn't collect many bills and in this manner lost much money."[40] Fortunately, he had an "independent income," though he put his penmanship to good use as a bookkeeper in later years.[41] Warner was a member of GAR Post Hazlett No. 81 and died in 1911.[42]

37. Post used the "natural slope" to list the battles he participated in and backhand to write the rest of his narrative.

38. George S. Warner, Contest Entry, 1st ser., no. 260, Bourne Papers (punctuation edited); 1880 U.S. Census, Muskingum Co., OH, pop. sched., Zanesville, p. 384D (stamped), dwelling 179, family 179, George S. Warner, NARA RG 29, ser. T9, roll 1054.

39. "Arranged for Brother's Funeral, but Died First," *Zanesville (OH) Times Recorder*, Jan. 25, 1911, 1.

40. 1880 U.S. Census, Muskingum Co., OH, pop. sched., Zanesville, p. 384D (stamped), dwelling 179, family 179, George S. Warner; "Arranged for Brother's Funeral, but Died First," 1.

41. "Arranged for Brother's Funeral, but Died First," 1.

42. Ibid.
~~~

January 30, 1866

From the beginning of the War I took a lively interest in the movements of the army and had a strong desire to enlist, but being only 16 years of age my parents thought me too young and would not consent to let me go until I would be 18 which seemed a long while to wait, but it came at last and a few days after I was enrolled as Saddler[43] for Co. B 5th Independent Battalion O.V. Cav. and was sworn in March 3rd 1864 to serve three years.

Warner's company arrived in Washington, D.C., on May 13. They took a steamship to Belle Plain Landing, then proceeded on to Port Royal, Virginia.

Five companies of our regiment were mounted here but I belonged to the company that went "foot back"[44] and carried our traps.[45] We left this place together with 10,000 or 12,000 troops and moved in the direction of the main army passing through Bowling Green[46] and next day forded the Pamunkey river reaching Hanover C.H.[47] at dark. Here we found we were in pretty close quarters so we started off again and marched until about daylight through rain and mud. Having two hours rest we then moved on again reaching the main army about noon near Baltimore crossroads where the troops were engaged. The musketry could be heard very distinctly. We were immediately drawn up in line of battle and remained so all night. Next morning we moved toward White House Landing where we stopped at noon and pitched tents in a field in which we stayed three days without rations except what we foraged. We then moved to the landing where we remained until the base of supplies was changed to City Point.[48]

43. This was the soldier in charge of caring for and repairing saddles, harnesses, and other horse-related equipment in cavalry and artillery units.

44. To march on foot rather than to ride a horse.

45. Equipment.

46. Town in northeast Virginia.

47. Hanover Court House (now Hanover), Virginia. The Pamunkey River runs north of it.

48. This town in Virginia at the confluence of the James and Appomattox Rivers was the site of Lieutenant General Ulysses Grant's headquarters and principal supply depot during the Petersburg siege.

On the morning of the 20th of June our pickets were driven in and we went into the rifle pits to await the attack. In a few moments their forces could be seen forming in line on the crest of a hill some distance off. Our artillery soon opened on them and annoyed them considerably. In the meantime the wagon train was crossing the river on the pontoon bridge and succeeded in getting over before the enemy commenced shelling us. About 9 o'clock the artillery firing became very sharp and continued until about 4 p.m., when a shot from one of our guns struck their caisson[49] causing it to explode. We stayed in the pits all night expecting them but they did not attack us. In the morning [Major General Philip H.] Sheridan's troops crossed the river and started in pursuit of them while we remained to come through with the wagon train. We left on the night of the 22nd and had a slight skirmish with the enemy next day and routed them. We had rather a tedious march as the weather was very warm and water was scarce. Several of our regiment were sun struck before we reached the James river. We camped near the river a day or two and then marched on to Petersburg.... On July 10th we were ordered into the rifle pits and stayed until the morning of the 30th when we were ordered out and moved along the line to Gen. Potter's[50] Hd. Qtrs.

Here we formed in line of battle and lay down until the explosion of the mine.[51] Then the charge [was] ordered and one regiment after another went over the works with a yell, taking their first line of works, and planted the Stars and Stripes on the fort. Here we were ordered to lie down as the enemy had a cross fire on us from a fort on each side and while lying I received a flesh wound in my right arm causing me to leave the field. Our 1st Lieut. [Clayton G. Jewell] was mortally wounded and died. Several others of our company were killed and a number wounded. I was sent to the hospital.

I returned to the regiment Sept. 1st and found them in camp on the Weldon R. R. near the place where the battle had been fought in August. On the 29th of Sept. we moved to the left, the 5th Corps taking the advance. They drove the enemy out of a strong line of works capturing two guns and

49. Cart for carrying artillery ammunition.

50. Brigadier General Robert Brown Potter (1829–87), division commander under Major General Ambrose E. Burnside during the Petersburg Campaign.

51. Intended to create an opening in Confederate entrenchments, this explosion led to a Union defeat at the Battle of the Crater on July 30, 1864.

a number of prisoners. Next day we met them at Pegram farm[52] and fought until dark. We worked all night throwing up works and next morning the firing commenced again but did not last very long.

The day following we made a reconnaissance in force toward the left of the enemy's line and found them strongly intrenched. We then fell back to our old position and went to work strengthening the fortifications. Oct. 28th at 2 o'clock AM we broke camp and started toward the South Side R.R. together with the 2nd and 5th Corps and Gregg's[53] Div. of cavalry. We met the enemy's pickets and drove them back until 2 p.m. when the firing became very heavy in the direction of the 2nd Corps. We advanced within 200 yards of the enemy's works, and threw up a temporary line in case they should come out and attack us. The firing continued until dark and opened early next morning very briskly and continued until noon when we were ordered to fall back as the 2nd Corps had been overpowered by numbers and had to give way. The enemy followed us nearly to our strong works but would not venture to come within range of our guns.

All remained quiet here until Nov. 29th when we exchanged positions with the 2nd Corps, our regiment being placed on picket along the Appomattox river where we were relieved on the 12th of December and ordered to, dismounted, camp near City Point where we turned over our infantry arms and accoutrements and received cavalry equipments and horses. Jan. 1st 1865 we found the 2nd Brig. 2nd Div. of cavalry commanded by Gen. Gregg and went into winter quarters. . . .

Warner's unit fought at Hatcher's Run on February 5–7, 1865, and gradually moved toward Richmond, skirmishing along the way.

We arrived there [Jetersville, Virginia] on the evening of the 3rd of April. 100 men of our regiment were detailed to go below Burkeville Junction[54] and

52. The fighting that occurred at Pegram's Farm near Petersburg on October 2, 1864, was part of a series of engagements (usually referred to as the Battle of Poplar Springs Church) fought south of Petersburg, which were all part of Lieutenant General Grant's Fifth Offensive against the city. See Richard J. Sommers and Frank E. Vandiver, *Richmond Redeemed: The Siege at Petersburg* (Garden City, NY: Doubleday, 1981).

53. Major General David McMurtrie Gregg (1833–1916).

54. Junction of the Southside and Richmond & Danville Railroads.

tear up the R.R. When we got to the Junction we found that a good many of their wounded had been sent there to the hospital from Richmond. We accomplished our work by daylight, captured a mail[55] at the Junction, and returned to the command with a few prisoners and some fine horses we captured on our way. Our Div. had made a dash on the enemy capturing 5 headquarter flags belonging to Lee's army. Also 5 pieces of artillery, a large part of their wagon train and many prisoners. From here we started on the morning of the 6th of April in pursuit of the rebel wagon train. We had a skirmish with the rear guard and drove them until 3 p.m. when our regiment was ordered to charge on the train which we did with a yell and set fire to the wagons. We captured a number of prisoners and mules, then returned to the Div. which was ready for a charge as the enemy were in strong force. The 6th Corps were in line on our right and as soon as the order was given the whole line advanced driving the enemy back and capturing several of their battle flags and a great many prisoners. Among the officers captured were Generals Ewell, Corse, Lee, and many other prominent officers.[56]

Our loss was not very heavy. Next morning we started after them again. Our Div. kept the center and the 2nd Corps on the right and the 24th on the left. We marched four or five miles before we caught up to them. Skirmishing soon became very brisk and continued so until we reached High Bridge[57] where our Regiment was ordered to make a charge and drive them out of their works. The charge had to be made up a very steep hill and just as we reached their works, which were made of rails, I received a very bad wound in my right arm while in the act of firing. I rode back to our brigade Surg. and had my arm bound up, which relieved me [a] great deal. I then walked back to a large white house where two or three Surgeons of the 24th Corps were dressing the wounds of our soldiers. They examined it and told me it could not be saved as the bones were too badly shattered. I then gave it up willingly, for I had the assurance that it could not be given for a nobler or better cause.

55. Wagon carrying Confederate correspondence.

56. The generals—Richard S. Ewell (1817–72), Montgomery Dent Corse (1816–95), and George Washington Custis Lee (1832–1913)—were all taken prisoner after the Battle of Sailor's (sometimes Sayler's) Creek, April 6, 1865.

57. A railroad bridge over the Appomattox River. The battle there occurred on April 6–7, 1865.

The day that Lee surrendered I was sent to Burkeville to the hospital and remained there until after the boys came back with the captured battle flags and other trophies. It was a very pleasant sight to all of us that could see them as they passed the hospital. From here I was sent to City Point on the second train that left Burkeville arriving there in the night, after a tedious and painful ride, remained there two days and then was sent north with a great many other wounded to Annapolis where we landed on the morning of the 15th just as the news came that our Noble President was assassinated, news which made every true soldier feel sad. I remained in the hospital where I received kind treatment until July 27th when I received my discharge and returned home where I found most all of our company already, but there were some faces I missed and they are lying in their peaceful graves around Petersburg where they fell yielding up their lives for our Glorious Union.

Since my return I have received the [prosthetic] arm allowed by the Government. It looks quite natural and is very useful.

I am now attending Nelson's Commercial College, Cincinnati, Ohio.[58] My first attempt at writing with my left hand was just before I left the hospital. I tried to write a letter and succeeded in writing one that could be read. I commenced practicing writing about the middle of Sept. and this is a fair specimen of my penmanship at present.

HEMAN S. ROCKWOOD

Private, Co. E, 106th New York Volunteer Infantry

Leaving a farm in Hopkinton, New York, behind, Rockwood enlisted in August 1862 when he was eighteen years old.[59] After the war, he attended the University of Vermont, graduating with an MD in 1871, and became a "well-known practitioner of Franklin and St. Lawrence Counties, N.Y."[60] Rockwood married twice and had at least two children; he died in 1915.[61]

58. Also known as Nelson's Union Business College, the institution was founded in 1856 and trained students "in business by its actual transaction." *Thirteenth Annual Report of the State Commissioner of Common Schools to the Governor of Ohio* (Columbus: L. D. Myers & Bro., 1867), 135.

59. Heman Rockwood, Contest Entry, 1st ser., no. 265, Bourne Papers (punctuation edited).

60. "Deaths," *Journal of the American Medical Association* 65, no. 1 (July 3, 1915): 446.

61. New York State Marriage Index, Heman S. Rockwood, New York State Department of Health,

January 31, 1866

Dear Sir,

Your favor of Dec. 24th 1865 containing a request that I would send you a specimen of my penmanship with a promised reward providing my specimen excelled others submitted to your judgment, has been received. But considering myself deficient, in this respect, I have deferred complying with your request until now and even at the present I am persuaded to do so by the reception of another request desiring me to furnish you a brief history of my military life, which I do with much hesitancy lest I may be called a boaster.

I am but one among many who have played an active part in securing our country from the hands of traitors, and although maimed for life I am not worthy of any more glory than my more fortunate comrades. . . .

Shortly after mustering, Rockwood's regiment reported to the Department of West Virginia.

We remained in this department until June 1863 when we suddenly were aroused from our peaceful slumbers by the approach of the rebel army on their way to Maryland and Pennsylvania. It was a time long to be remembered by the members of the 106th N.Y. Vols, for every available man was called upon to perform a duty which he had long anticipated and for which he had impatiently awaited. But a single duty was enough to satisfy our longings for costly was our initiation. In attempting to repel the rebel hosts we were driven hastily to Harpers Ferry[62] and much to our expense as sore feet and empty stomachs were all we had to comfort us. From Harpers Ferry we were ordered to join the army of the Potomac, which we succeeding in doing July 8th soon after the battle of Gettysburg, and were immediately joined to the 3rd Div. 3rd Army Corps with which we remained until the spring of 1864 when we were transferred to the 6th Army Corps with which we served until the close of the war. I remained with my regiment until May 6, 1864, ever trying to perform the duties enjoined upon me as a private soldier. May 4th 1864 the

---

Albany; 1880 U.S. Census, Franklin Co., NY, pop. sched., Bombay, p. 453A (stamped), dwelling 12, family 13, Heman S. Rockwood, NARA RG 29, ser. T9, roll 833; "Deaths," 446.

62. This town in what is now West Virginia is located where the Potomac and Shenandoah Rivers meet. It was the site of a U.S. armory, famously attacked by a group led by John Brown in 1859.

Army of the Potomac with Gen. Grant at its head crossed the Rapidan river[63] and began their march towards the city of Richmond. May 5th we met the enemy in their entrenchments, where we always found them, and at the cost of many a life tried to force them from their strongholds but in vain as night found us holding the same ground as at noon, our numbers being thinned by the enemy's missiles of death. Through the entire night a continuous roar of musketry sounded along our line, darkness seemingly increasing its fury. The shrieking shells performing their mission of death, the groans of the wounded and the dying and the expectations of the coming morrow made the place anything but a desirable one.

During the night the enemy brought his artillery into position and when light broke in upon us he sent into our midst shot and shell grape and cannister which killed and wounded many. Well do I remember the death-like sound of a single shell as it came howling through the air, striking a pine tree just in front of me, busting and scattering its fragments among our number, killing and wounding sixteen. Among the number was myself. A piece of shell entered my right shoulder fracturing the bone and mangling the flesh in a horrid manner. I was sent to Fredericksburg and from thence to Washington where I remained for three months and then returned to my regiment under Sheridan in the Shenandoah valley. From place to place we were ordered often in great haste, frequently meeting the enemy with whom we would contend the points, sometimes being victors and at others being compelled to yield.

No battle of any great moment took place until September 19th which is known as the Winchester fight.[64] We had been encamped some two weeks at Summit Point a distance of twelve miles from Winchester. At one o'clock on the morning of the fight we were called up to prepare our breakfast and ordered to be ready to march at moment's notice. But before coffee could be prepared we were hastily commanded to sling knapsack and gun and in less time than I am relating this we were on the road to Winchester. Steadily we moved forward, each breast being filled with mirth and sport, little expecting that before night some would sleep their last, long sleep.

63. A principal tributary of the Rappahannock River.

64. The Third Battle of Winchester.

To our surprise when but two miles from Winchester our advance guard was fired upon. Then came moments of haste. We double-quicked for one mile [and] hastily formed our line of battle on the crest of a hill, where we lay down and waited for the signal to advance. We rested until nearly noon when the command was given to advance and drive the enemy from his position at the point of the bayonet. And here let me remark that this was a moment of deep interest. In the countenance of every soldier could be seen the fear of death depicted accompanied with the spirit of earnestness. We moved forward under a heavy shower of shot and shell until within some fifty rods of the enemies [*sic*] entrenchments, where I was struck in the right arm by a bullet from the foe and forced to leave the field. With my crippled arm hanging at my side I followed in the train of wounded about two miles when I came where were the physicians and nurses administering to the wants of the wounded. Here they pitched their tents and at once established a field hospital.

I was immediately cared for by the physician who relieved me of my ever remembered friend, the strong right arm. I remained in the field hospital for two weeks, was then transferred to General Hospital Philadelphia where I remained until discharged.

~~~

ELISHA R. WISE

Co. A, 7th, Pennsylvania Volunteers
First Sergeant, Co. F, 11th Pennsylvania Volunteers
First Sergeant, Co. 109, 2nd Batallion Veteran Reserve Corps

Wise was born in 1838 in Pennsylvania.[65] After his discharge, the citizens of Warren, Ohio, elected him alderman. According to Wise, "they [had] not forgotten the soldier here, placing many of them in good positions." He remained in Warren for the rest of his life and was a member of GAR Bell Harmon Post No. 36.[66] Appointed postmaster there in 1871 and reap-

65. Elisha R. Wise, Contest Entry, 2nd ser., no. 34, Bourne Papers (punctuation edited).

66. *Journal of Proceedings of the Forty-First Annual Encampment of the Department of Ohio, Grand Army of the Republic*, 103.
~~~

pointed in 1879, he also worked as a bookkeeper.[67] By 1910, Wise had been married for forty-five years; he died in 1924.[68]

June 1867
Memoirs of One of the Left Arm Corps

It will be necessary for me before giving any details to state that my business called me frequently to visit the southern cities. It was at this time in company with others we proceeded down the Mississippi river. All nature was beginning to break forth in its beauty, the farther we proceeded on our journey. From indications we concluded to go no farther than Memphis. The air was becoming rife with rebellious sentiments, and loud were anathemas heaped upon those who dared vindicate their rights. Northerners were fleeing to their homes and Southerners returning to their soil, all to take part in the great rebellion that followed. We turned our course homeward, but not to find peace and friendship hand in hand as when we left it. All was commotion when we landed in Pittsburg.

> There was mounting in hot haste the steed,
> The mustering squadron and the clattering car
> went pouring forth with impetuous speed.
> And swiftly forming in the ranks of war.[69]

Sumter had been fired upon. The ardor of loyal men was aroused, regiments were forming and moving to the tented field. I bade farewell to my companions; and on the twentieth of April 1861, enlisted in Company A Seventh Regiment Pennsylvania Volunteers for the period of three months. On the following morning we took our departure for Harrisburg, and were

67. Record of Appointment of Postmasters, 1832–1971, NARA RG 28, M841, vol. 25A; "The World's Work," *Watertown (WI) News*, Feb. 26, 1879, 2; 1870 U.S. Census, Trumbull Co., OH, pop. sched., Warren, p. 401B (stamped), dwelling 38, family 37, Elisha R. Wise, NARA RG 29, M593, roll 1272; 1900 U.S. Census, Trumbull Co., OH, pop. sched., Warren, p. 18, dwelling 387, family 407, Elisha R. Wise, ibid., T623, roll 1330.

68. 1910 U.S. Census, Trumbull Co., OH, pop. sched., Warren, p. 9B, dwelling 200, family 222, Elisha R. Wise, NARA RG 29, T624, roll 1235; Ohio Department of Health, Death Records, 1908–1932, p. 8355, Ohio Historical Society.

69. Lord Byron, *Childe Harold's Pilgrimage*, canto 3, st. 25.

placed under command of Colonel William H. Irving. We were immediately ordered to Chambersburg.[70] At this point we donned our first "suit of blue." Then began the duties of the Soldier.

From here we moved to Greencastle[71] and remained about a week and received orders to report at Williamsport, [Maryland,] on the Potomac, which was accomplished after several days marching. After performing the ordinary camp duties, we were ordered to have three days' rations in our haversacks, and be ready to move at any moment. On the 2nd of July we broke camp, and were in line, and crossed the Potomac and took up positions on the South Side. It was a bright and beautiful morning, all of the soldiers being in the best of spirits, and were reviewed by [Major] General [Robert] Patterson as they passed by. A force of rebels were on the range of hills on the Virginia side under [Brigadier] General [Thomas J. "Stonewall"] Jackson, who upon the approach of our troops fell back and took up position near Hainesville,[72] where the[y] were dislodged by our advance, throwing away in their flight knapsacks, canteens, etc. etc., which our men gathered as trophies.

A short distance from here we went into camp for the night, moving on the following morning to Martinsburg.[73] At this place great destruction was done the Baltimore and Ohio R.R. The inhabitants seemed quite loyal, presenting a stand of colors to the Eleventh Penn. Vols. We remained here quite a while, being often aroused by the long roll.[74] Here we spent our first fourth of July in the service of the United States. An oration was delivered and the articles of war read to us. . . .

Our term of enlistment was fast expiring and with some it had expired. Requests were made of the men to give their services but a short time longer, but with no avail. From here we were sent to Hagerstown[75] and thence to Harrisburg and from the latter place to Pittsburg, where we were mustered out.

On the 14th of October, 1861, [I] again enlisted at Greensburg, Westmoreland County, Pennsylvania, in Company F eleventh regiment Penn.

70. City in south-central Pennsylvania.

71. City in south-central Pennsylvania.

72. Town near the western bank of the Potomac River in what is now West Virginia.

73. City in what is now West Virginia.

74. Drum beat instructing troops to ready for action.

75. Town in Washington County, Maryland.

Vols., for the period of three years. The regiment was then in Camp Curtin,[76] near Harrisburg. On my arrival was appointed Sergeant. Here we had to perform considerable drilling and soon after was ordered to Annapolis, Maryland. . . .

While we were here, General Burnside was fitting out an expedition,[77] and details were made heavily upon us for fatigue duty. After the departure of the expedition, we were placed on duty on the Annapolis Junction R. R. but were soon ordered to report at Washington. While there [we] marched to the President's mansion, and listened to a few encouraging remarks from him. . . .

In response to Jackson's maneuverings in the Shenandoah Valley in the summer of 1862, Wise's division was ordered to Manassas Junction, Virginia, eventually arriving in Front Royal. Heavy rain delayed supply trains, and rations soon ran out. The Union troops moved first to Waterloo, then on to Warrenton Springs and Culpeper.

The enemy soon developed a strong force and on the 9th of August, 1862, took up position on Cedar Mountain. General Banks advanced to the attack, but the engagement did not fairly open until near 6 o'clock p.m. Our division pushed forward and occupied the right of Gen. Banks, taking the place of his right wing which he had massed on his center; but before this could be effected it became quite dark and the musketry firing had ceased. We rested on our arms for the night in line of battle. During the night a constant cannonading was kept up between the enemy's batteries and ours. On the next morning the enemy had fallen back and soon our whole force pushed forward as far as the Rapidan.

Moving to the rear, Wise's division went to Rappahannock Station on the eighteenth before falling back to Warrenton Junction. Jackson's forces, located a few miles from Manassas in Gainesville, now separated the Union troops from Washington, D.C.

76. A major Union training camp, named after the state's governor, throughout the Civil War.

77. Burnside led an expedition in early 1862 along the North Carolina coast, targeting Roanoke Island and New Bern.

We were ordered to Gainesville but it was countermanded by an order to proceed to Thoroughfare Gap[78] and hold it to prevent any reinforcements from reaching [Major General] Jackson. At about 2 o'clock we reached the Gap and pressed back [Major General James] Longstreet's advance and compelled him to desist; he after finding he could effect no passage here moved to Hopewell Gap, and succeeded in coming to the support of Jackson.

We then received orders to retire. In this engagement we lost heavily. That night we rested on our arms near Gainesville and before daylight moved to Bristoe Station[79] where after a few hours rest [we] marched to Manassas Junction.

On the next morning we were in line and all was in readiness for battle. The enemy had been strongly reinforced and already had an engagement with some of our forces.[80]

On the morning of the 29th of August the second battle of Bull Run commenced. Our men hotly contested the field. At this time we were placed on the right and after several attempts to take a battery that we had unmasked fell back in disorder.

While lending a hand to a wounded man, I did not get along as rapidly as some of the rest; thus I became a prisoner in the enemy's hands and was taken to their rear near Gainesville, and from my knowledge of the country, concluded to make my escape which I accomplished that night striking for the Potomac, and after some days reached Leesburg[81] where I found an old negro woman, who furnished me with something to eat, having subsisted on green corn and apples since I made my escape. Her husband that night piloted me towards the river, and placed me in the hands of another negro who ferried me across the river before daylight, and directed me on my way to Washington, and at Rockville,[82] met some of our troops who were moving to meet a force of rebels who already had crossed the river.

I was then sent to my regiment where I obtained a furlough being in a

78. A pass through the Bull Run Mountains east of the Shenandoah Valley. Hopewell Gap is another pass north of Thoroughfare.

79. Now Bristow, Virginia.

80. The Battle of Groveton, August 28, 1862.

81. Virginia town northwest of Washington, D.C.

82. Maryland town north of Washington, D.C.

condition not fit to keep up [with] them. At the expiration of my furlough I rejoined my regiment near Stafford Court House.[83]

Here we remained until about the 10th of December when we proceeded to Fredericksburg and on the 12th crossed the river. On the 13th were in line of battle. We then were in [Maj.] Gen. [William B.] Franklin's left grand division. Quite early in the firing commenced on the right until it became general. The 16th Maine relieved us and here let me say never did a regiment going on a field keep up a front as they, not a waver when their comrades would fall but closed up in their places. This was the battle of Fredericksburg. On being relieved by the 16th Maine we fell to the rear and in the evening moved to the left of the line going on outpost duty for the night. On the next day Sunday the 14th both armies remained comparatively quiet. On Monday night the 15th our forces recrossed the river and moved to our old camp where we remained for the winter.

In April 1863, Wise's division took up position two miles south of Fredericksburg.

Some sharp skirmishing here took place between the enemy and those of our men who already had crossed. That night the remaining portion of our corps lay to the side of the road that runs parallel with the river. During the evening our bands commenced playing and as the sound wafted across the river the rebel bands took it up playing alternately their favorite pieces and both concluding at the same with "Home Sweet Home." The sounds of "Home Sweet Home" still rang in our ears when our weary eyes refused longer to keep open. The next morning we [were] early on the move to the right where [Major General Joseph] Hooker was then engaged at Chancellorsville. It was late when we arrived crossing at United States ford[84] and took position on the right when we set to work vigorously entrenching ourselves, using tin plates, bayonets, and jack knives, and in the morning had quite strong breastworks.

The contest raged fiercely on our left. It had already commenced to rain

83. Virginia town north of Fredericksburg.

84. Ford of the Rappahannock River near Chancellorsville.

quite heavily. At about 3 o'clock a.m. the next morning we were called in, having been on picket, and the recrossing commenced. It is difficult to say what our fate would have been as the river then was running bank high.

We again encamped near our old quarters but not long to remain as the enemy were again on the move and some of their forces were in Pennsylvania. On Sunday, June the 14th, again [we] were on the move. Our march was rapid and sometimes disorderly. The men, choked with dust, straggled into the fields in search of water. All night of Sunday we marched and on Monday about noon went into camp in the neighborhood of Centreville.[85] . . .

Wise's unit crossed the Potomac and arrived in Frederick, Maryland, moving to Emmitsburg the next day.

While we were here the rebels were concentrating their force in the vicinity of Gettysburg, Pennsylvania. Early on the morning of the 1st day of July we moved to Gettysburg to open that memorable battle. When at the line between the two states,[86] our colonel made a few remarks, and the men [showed] their approval of it by loud cheers and a determination to drive the rebels from their native state. We had proceeded but a few miles when our ears caught the sounds of guns. The battle of Gettysburg had commenced. [Major] General [George G.] Meade had taken command. [Major] General [John F.] Reynolds while reconnoitering in force was wounded and shortly after died, compelling his advance cavalry to fall back.

At this time our corps appeared; the first division under General Wadsworth[87] was in the advance; the division of Gen. Doubleday[88] formed on the left while that of Gen. Robinson's[89] (ours) on the right. I at this time being Orderly Sergeant was ordered to call the roll and of all reported for duty there was not one absent.

85. Virginia town just north of Bull Run and near Washington, D.C.

86. Maryland and Pennsylvania.

87. Brigadier General James S. Wadsworth (1807–64), division commander, I Corps, Army of the Potomac (AOTP).

88. Brigadier General Abner Doubleday (1819–93), division commander, I Corps, AOTP. After Reynolds's death, Doubleday took command of I Corps.

89. Brigadier General John C. Robinson (1817–97), division commander, I Corps, AOTP.

The position occupied was a ridge northwest of town which sloped to the west into an open valley of ploughed fields and meadows. Across these fields we advanced and here it was I received a wound in my right arm and was compelled to go to the rear and was sent to one of the churches where I received attention.

Our men did not long hold their position and fell back and took positions on Cemetery Hill,[90] the rebels taking possession of the town. Our knapsacks that we were ordered to leave on the outside of the building were sacked of their contents and my diary that I highly prized fell into their hands which I hope may account for my absence of dates. Suffering from the pain of my wound I had an examination made on the 3rd by the surgeons of the brigade, they making incisions in my arm to see the nature of it, and after consultation concluded that amputation was necessary to preserve life.

The amputation was performed by Drs. [William B.] Chambers of 97th New York, Chase of 13th Massachusetts, and [J. W.] Anawalt of our regiment.[91] It was a gunshot fracture through the elbow joint requiring amputation above leaving about five inches of the stump.

During the afternoon I succeeded in getting up into the belfry of the church and witnessed some of the desperate charges of the rebels but each time [they] were hurled back with great slaughter.

On the 4th we were ordered to the rear of Cemetery Hill and there was placed in a barn. The enemy had commenced to fall back and many were the sufferers they left behind. How long we remained here [I] cannot say. We were well taken care of by the members of that noble organization the Christian and Sanitary commissions. God bless them one and all. In the latter part of August [I] was furloughed and at its expiration ordered to report to U. S. General Hospital at Pittsburg and here remained during the winter of 1863. In the Spring of 1864 [we] were formed into a detachment of the Veteran Reserve Corps and sent to Washington.

After remaining here awhile a detail was made of an hundred men including myself and placed on board the transport Connecticut in charge of Dr.

90. Northern portion of the "fish-hook" line of the Union defensive position at Gettysburg.

91. A surgeon named Chase is not listed as part of the 13th Massachusetts. Albert A. Chase was an assistant surgeon for the 28th Massachusetts. N. A. Strait, *Roster of All Regimental Surgeons and Assistant Surgeons in the Late War* (n.p., 1882), 101.

Wood who assigned to the men their duties such as ward masters, attendants, cooks, etc. and to myself the general superintendence over all. General Grant had taken command of the army and was fast affecting his purpose. Our duties was for transporting the sick and wounded of his army to Hospitals throughout the north. Suffice it to say the duties were not of the most agreeable kind but all our energies were exerted to alleviate the sufferings of these brave boys. We could sympathize with them. . . .

From the beginning of Grant's campaign in Virginia till I left, which was about the 1st of September, we carried about fifty-six thousand sick and wounded. The *Connecticut* was one of about ten transports.

At my request I was discharged [from] the Service of the United States the 5th of September 1864.

WALLACE MORDECAI MOORE

Private, Co. E, 13th Pennsylvania Reserves / 1st Pennsylvania Rifles ("The Bucktails")
Corporal, Co. E, 190th Pennsylvania Volunteer Infantry

By the time of his death, Pennsylvania-born Moore was one of the few surviving members of "The Bucktails." He married in 1866 and remained so until his wife died in 1920.[92] After a brief stay in a home for disabled veterans in 1871, Moore moved his family from Pennsylvania to Iowa, where he was elected auditor in 1872 amid cheers for "One-Armed Moore," serving until 1883.[93] According to Moore's great-grandson, Moore and his wife built a sod house on land granted to them through the Homestead Act; their nearest neighbor was nine miles away. The veteran also served as postmaster of Mount Vernon, Iowa.[94] Moore died in 1932 at the ripe old age of ninety, survived by three children and nine grandchildren.[95] For his accounts of battle, see chapter 3.

92. Wallace M. Moore, Contest Entry, 2nd ser., no. 114, Bourne Papers; "W. M. Moore, G.A.R., Former Mt. Vernon Postmaster, Dead," *Cedar Rapid (IA) Gazette,* Jan. 11, 1932, 4.

93. Historical Register of National Homes for Disabled Volunteer Soldiers, 1866–1938, Wallace M. Moore, NARA RG 15, M1749, roll 160; "W. M. Moore, G.A.R., Former Mt. Vernon Postmaster, Dead," 4; Perkins, *History of Osceola County, Iowa,* 176. I am indebted to Alan Ford, one of Moore's descendants, for the anecdote about "One-Armed Moore."

94. "Wallace Moore, Civil War Veteran, Is Dead," *Mason City (IA) Globe-Gazette,* Jan. 12, 1932, 2.

95. "W. M. Moore," *Wellsboro (PA) Gazette,* Jan. 27, 1932, 1.

Wallace M. Moore with his daughter, Katherine Ford, and grandchild.
Courtesy Alan R. Ford.

April 27, 1868

No loyal man has yet forgotten the eagerness with which the people responded to President Lincoln's call for 70,000 volunteers[96] in the spring of '61. So great was the rush to the various points of rendezvous that the call for three months men was mainly filled by those living nearest to those points, those living in more remote sections not being able to organize and report before the quotas were filled. And in no state was this more remarkably the case than in Pennsylvania. "The infected District"—intensely loyal and bitterly opposed to secession—poured out its fighting men with a prodigality not surpassed in the annals of the war: but this District is composed in great part of the mountainous regions of the northern countries, where the mails are tardy and means of transportation slow; and thence it happens, that before these hardy Lumbermen, Hunters, miners, farmers, etc., could report at Harrisburg, the quota of Pennsylvania was filled, and the Governor was sending dispatches to different points, to the effect that no more men were wanted, and advising the companies already formed to stay at home, and keep up their organizations, and drill, in anticipation of another call. They would not and did not understand it, but kept pouring into Harrisburg, company after company, until there were enough volunteers for twelve or fifteen regiments over and above the State's quota. Nor would they be put off, but insisted on having a chance in with those who happened to get into camp a little earlier through living nearer the great arteries of transportation. It seemed hard to send these men home again, especially as many of them were personal, and most of them political

96. Lincoln in fact called for 75,000 volunteers.

friends of Gov. Curtin;[97] so, an extra session of the Legislature was called, and a bill hastily passed which provided for the organization of fifteen regiments of state troops, to be called a reserve, but subject to the call of the general Government at any time. They were to be enlisted for three years, and were to be on the same footing in every respect as the other volunteers: and this was the starting point of the "Pa. Reserves"

I enlisted on the 22nd of April 1861, at Wellsboro, Tioga Co., under Capt. A. E. Niles. The company was formed on the call for three months volunteers, but, before reaching Camp Curtin the call was answered without us, and we waited in idleness about camp for two or three weeks, until the legislature passed the act above mentioned, when we had the choice of enlisting for three years or returning home. About one half of the company went in for three years, the rest returned. One of the fifteen regiments comprising the "Reserves" was organized as a rifle regiment under the name of the "1st Pa. Rifles," and it was this that afterward became justly celebrated as a skirmish regiment, by the name of "Bucktails." Fully one half [of] the men in the regiment were deerstalkers, and a large majority were sharp shots with the rifle. It was my fortune to go through the war as a member of this rifle regiment, until the affair of the Weldon R.R., at which time and place I was compelled to lay down—at least one of my arms. At the time of my enlistment I was twenty years old, and in excellent health—had never been sick a day since my infancy. At Camp Curtin I first came to realize what it was to be sick away from home and friends. The measles broke out in camp, and I took them in malignant form,[98] but, through good treatment and good nursing, soon got well, although several, who were sick at the same time, died. During my sickness the regiment had been ordered to West Virginia, but, on becoming convalescent, I hastened to join it in company with about forty others who had been left behind. We found the Bucktails with the 5th Infantry and a section artillery encamped about six miles from Cumberland, MD while Col. [Lew] Wallace with [the] 11th Indiana occupied the camp ground at Cumberland. The 11th had some sharp skirmishes with the famous "Black

97. Andrew Gregg Curtin (1817–94), governor of Pennsylvania, 1861–67.

98. Medical texts from the nineteenth century differentiate between "benign" and "malignant" measles, the latter characterized by a rash and cold-like symptoms. See Moore, *Textbook of the Eruptive and Continued Fevers,* 142–48.

Horse" band[99] which then infested that region, in which the aforesaid horsemen got handled in [a] manner rather calculated to astonish than please them, and they were jubilant when Col. Wallace and his men—their three months having expired—vacated Camp McGinnis.[100] They had small cause for rejoicing: the camp was vacated by Col. Wallace one afternoon, and before daylight the next morning the 5th Infantry and the inevitable Bucktails were quietly settled on it. Col. [Thomas L.] Kane with some 200 scouts went after this gang of lawless riders, and, after some skirmishing, in which their leader and several of his men lost their lives, succeeded in driving them back to the rebel army—much to the relief of the inhabitants about Cumberland and New Creek. Having relieved the people of these plunderers, and rebuilt a bridge over the Potomac which they had destroyed, we received marching orders for Harpers Ferry. It was in the month of July, and the weather was fine, but the nights were cold among the mountains of the upper Potomac, and my clothes were decidedly of the shoddy[101] order: I caught a severe cold; and what with lying on the damp earth, coupled with the lingering effects of previous illness, took a fever which brought me to death's door. I kept up, however, until we reached Harpers Ferry, when I was obliged to go into hospital, where I was reduced so low that few of my comrades ever expected to see me in the ranks again. To Asst. Surgeon Humphrey,[102] who stuck to me and brought me around after I had been given over to die by the 1st Surgeon, I owe a debt of gratitude, which I take pleasure in acknowledging here. He is one of the few Army Surgeons within my observation, who never shirked his duty through fear, drunkenness, or laziness, and he was also one of the most skillful surgeons in the army. From Harpers Ferry the Regt. was ordered to Darnestown;[103] and I, being unable to march, was sent to the General Hospital at Baltimore. The regulations and treatment at this Hospital were excellent, and I improved so rapidly that in about a month I was able to join my company at Darnestown, where I found the Regiment under marching orders, and the next day we marched to Tennelytown,[104] a distance of thirty

99. Company H, 4th Virginia Cavalry, Army of Northern Virginia.

100. The camp was located near Cumberland, Maryland.

101. Slang for cheap wool fabric.

102. Potentially Wesley Humphrey of the 52nd Illinois. Strait, *Roster of All Regimental Surgeons*, 25.

103. Maryland town near the Potomac River and Virginia border.

104. Now Tenleytown, Maryland, a Washington, D.C., neighborhood.

miles! And this in a dusty road, under a hot sun. The march was needlessly forced, and here I will take occasion to say that the way the "Bucktails" were marched on any slight occasion or no occasion, as might be, was not only *heartless*, but what is more in a military point of view, *headless*. No man is fit to command a regiment, who will drive men into aimless, useless hardships, just to show that *his* regiment can *march*. Scores of strong, able men were thrown out of service by this nonsense, who might have done yeoman's service under proper management.

At Tennelytown we joined the Reserve Corps under Genl. Meade, and after a month in camp, marched over into Virginia via the Chain Bridge,[105] and went into winter quarters about ten miles from Washington. We named our camp Camp Pierpont[106] and, in it, the winter passed very pleasantly. On the 20th of Dec. however, the monotony of camp life was broken by an order, the carrying out of which brought on the Battle of Dranesville[107]—the first action in which I bore a part. It was a smart little affair, in which the rebels suffered severely, and in which the tide of battle—which had seemed to be against us for months previously—turned decidedly in our favor. Capt. [Alanson E.] Niles was shot through the body in the early part of the fight, and the wound was supposed to be mortal. He recovered, and is now in the regular army—having been through the war from first to last, and several times wounded. We lost a few men in this battle, but inflicted severe punishment on the enemy, whose loss was out of all proportion to ours. A young man by the name of Geo. Cook, who was a member of our company, happened to be on guard duty when we marched out to Dranesville. He was anxious to be along with the regiment, and hired another man to do duty for him in his absence. He was able thus to be in the fight, but was shot through the head, almost at the first fire.

In the spring we were ordered to Manassas—to look after the wooden guns,[108] I suppose, as there was little else there at the time of a military char-

105. This spanned the Potomac River between Washington, D.C., and Virginia.

106. The name most likely honored Francis H. Pierpont (1814–99), a Unionist Virginian who was instrumental in the founding of West Virginia. See Charles H. Ambler, *Francis H. Pierpont: Union War Governor and Father of West Virginia* (Chapel Hill: University of North Carolina Press, 1937).

107. The fighting occurred near this Virginia town northwest of Washington, D.C.

108. These were the "Quaker Guns," made of wood, used by Confederate forces to create the appearance of strong fortifications and large numbers of defending troops.

acter. We marched out in a cold rain, and before arriving at our destination received orders to countermarch, and back we went in the cold March rain, to Alexandria, where we stayed about two weeks, seeing troops constantly en route for the Peninsula,[109] and in daily expectation of orders to join them. Our destination, however, proved to be Fredericksburg, whither we were sent with the first Corps under Genl. Meade.

Genl. Bayard[110] with a Brigade of cavalry had preceded us, driving the rebels who remained about Fredericksburg back on their main army, so that we met with no serious opposition, and about the first of May we encamped at Falmouth on the Rappahannock, where we remained about a month, when we received orders to join the army under McClellan on the Peninsula. We took [a] boat a few miles below Falmouth, landed at the White House, marched up the line of the main army some ten miles, and camped in rear of the centre. Things began to look pugnacious. Every day there was more or less fighting, we were never out of sound of artillery, and while we lay here, Stuart made his famous raid in the rear of our main army.[111] He crossed the R.R. at Tunstall's Station about six miles below us, and our Brigade was sent after him; it was infantry after cavalry, and we were too late to do more than see the fires the raiders had kindled. Picked up several dead men, buried them, and returned to camp. . . .

Moore's company dug rifle pits in view of Richmond. They were left behind on the battlefield on June 26, the second day of the Seven Days' Battles, and eluded capture by flanking Confederate troops.

Following the road, still at double quick, we came in sight of a large body of men, and Capt. Niles, taking it for granted that they were Union Soldiers, halted us to reform and report in soldierly shape. We had just formed, when we saw the rebel flag hoisted by these fellows, and we quickly deployed by the left flank, and again started on the double quick, for a cornfield, which we

109. The Virginia Peninsula, the southernmost of three major peninsulas in eastern Virginia, surrounded by the James River (south), York River (north), and Chesapeake Bay (east). Site of Major General George B. McClellan's March–June 1862 campaign to take Richmond.

110. Brigadier General George Dashiell Bayard (1835–62).

111. Brigadier General J. E. B. Stuart (1833–64) led his Confederate cavalry on a reconnaissance mission, riding all the way around the AOTP.

succeeded in reaching without the loss of a man, although the rebels took the hint before we got out of range, and sent a shower of bullets after us. Across the cornfield, across lots, anywhere, to get away from the rebel army, and we came to a large swamp which lay directly in our route; across this, mid-deep in mud we waded, came out on the other side, and—alas, that I should have to record it, stumbled directly onto Stonewall Jackson's Corps—and it was up with us of course. Some of the boys who were a little behind took the hint and hid in the swamp, but were taken all the same, either that day or the next, and Co. E of the Bucktails went down to Richmond, almost in a body. The ghastly horrors of Andersonville have made the tobacco house of Richmond[112] seem trifling hardships, to many readers, and doubtless, in comparison they were. Nevertheless, I can testify that the old tobacco house by the river—in which were confined 900 prisoners—was not such a place as any civilized nation in Christendom would be allowed to hold prisoners of war captive in, nor was the food given to the prisoners such as any man could subsist on and retain his health or strength. Two weeks in the tobacco house, during which we had about half enough sour bread and maggoty soup to satisfy the cravings of hunger,—and then I was transferred to Belle Isle,[113] where I stayed a little over two weeks, and was then lucky enough, to be included in an exchange of 3000 prisoners which took place at that time.

We had to march about 15 miles to Aiken's Landing,[114] where we took boat for Harrison's Landing, at which place we joined the Regiment once more. A fortnight's rest, and we were en route for another battle field: this time by Fortress Monroe, and Aquia Landing[115] to Falmouth, thence by marching to Rappahannock Station, where the rebels were trying to make a crossing. At this time the army under [Maj.] Genl. [John] Pope was falling back, and we joined it in time for the three days battle of Bull Run. I am not going to describe that battle; it has all been done already by abler pens than mine: besides, this is merely a personal sketch, and although I was a good deal interested [in] Bull Run the second, I was not wounded. Our company, however, suffered fearfully. I never saw such suffering on any battle field

112. Former tobacco warehouses in Richmond were converted to prisons for captured Union soldiers during 1862.

113. An island in the James River at Richmond, used as a prison during the war.

114. An access point and settlement on the James River.

115. Boat landing on Aquia Creek where it meets the Potomac River.

for the want of water, and the little we did get was like mud. On the 31st of August Company E could only muster seven privates for the battle which was fought on the afternoon of that day.

From Bull Run we retreated, falling back on Arlington Heights,[116] where we rested for a few days; and then, away once more, in search of another battle field. This time it was the Maryland Campaign, and the battle ground was South Mountain, where we arrived at noon on Sept. 14th, and immediately went in. We fought the battle that afternoon and evening. Being a Rifle Regt., it devolved on us as usual to commence the ball by "skirmising up," which we did to the satisfaction of the Genl. commanding. I had a man killed on each side of me that afternoon; the Regiment suffered pretty severely in killed and wounded in this affair. The next day we marched to Antietam, opened the battle on the right under "Fighting Joe"[117] just before sundown, and had our Colonel (McNeal)[118] killed about dark, as we were driving a rebel skirmish line out of a piece [of] woods.

Commenced fighting again next morning at daylight, and fought till noon, when we got out of ammunition and were relieved. As we were falling back, I was hit on the shoulder by a spent ball, which left a black and blue mark, but did not disable me. At the end of this battle we had only seven men fit for duty; the rest were killed, wounded, or sick in hospital.

After the battle of Antietam we had a resting spell in which to recruit in health and numbers, for about six weeks, when we went after them again. This time the battle ground was at Fredericksburg, and it was a right lively affair: it came off on the thirteenth of December, and the Bucktails caught it some on that day. Our company had been gaining in numbers until we mustered 31 good men on the day of battle. Twenty one of these were killed or wounded, leaving us ten men for duty. I received a flesh wound on the thigh which disabled me for a time; but it gave me a furlough, and I came home for a few weeks.

When I next joined the Regiment it was at Fairfax Court House.[119] Here we lay for some time, doing guard duty there and at Fairfax Station, but on

116. Site of Robert E. Lee's home in Virginia, along the Potomac River near Washington, D.C., occupied by Union troops in May 1861.

117. Nickname for General Hooker.

118. Colonel Hugh W. McNeil (1830–62), 1st Pennsylvania Rifles.

119. Town and seat of government for Fairfax County, Virginia.

the retreat of the army after the disastrous battle of Chancellorsville, we joined it, and away we went, up through Maryland to Gettysburg, where we arrived at 10 a.m. on the 2nd of July, having marched all the previous night, and being weary and travel worn. There was no time for rest however. . . .

From Gettysburg we followed the retreating rebels to Williamsport, MD where we waited three or four days to give our Generals a chance to make up their minds about attacking. By this time the rebel army was safely over the river and on the "sacred soil" of Virginia. We went down the river to Berlin,[120] where we crossed, went down Loudon Valley, and followed them to Rappahannock Station, where we had a little fight, but nothing decisive. Soon after we had the Mine Run battle, in which our Regiment suffered but slightly, and from Mine Run we fell back to Rappahannock Station. . . . A soldier's life in winter quarters is too well known to need description, and too monotonous and tame to interest the general reader. The ball opened for us in the spring, quite lively. We joined the main Army at Culpeper Court House, marched to the Wilderness, went into battle, and were in for three days: it got a little thick occasionally, but I came through without being hit.

From the wilderness we marched to Spottsylvania Court House. . . .

We were immediately ordered into action, and Co. E was ordered out on the skirmish line. Somehow we seemed to be in hard luck that morning; either the rebs were more numerous, better posted, or they were shooting better than usual, for, hardly had we got deployed when our men began to fall rapidly. We had hardly been fighting fifteen minutes, and had already suffered severely, when, as I was taking aim at a rebel from behind an oak tree, a ball tore through the muscle of my right arm, and my part of the battle was played. It was a severe wound, and bled badly. I went back about half a mile, but was failing and fainting from loss of blood, when two men from the 62nd PA came to me, took off my accoutrements, bound a ligature tightly above the wound, and helped me to the temporary field hospital, where my arm was properly dressed. After three or four days in the field hospital, an order came for all who could be moved to report at the Capitol, and those who were wounded in the arms, but strong otherwise were to go on foot, owing to the scarcity of ambulances. So a lot of us who were crippled in the

120. Now Brunswick, Maryland, this town sat along the north side of the Potomac River in Frederick County, around six miles east of Harpers Ferry.

arms walked to Aquia Landing, where we took boat for Washington. I was put into Campbell Hospital, where I received the very best of treatment, and where my wound was thoroughly examined by competent Surgeons, who pronounced the bone unhurt and amputation unnecessary. This was a relief to me, as I had feared the loss of my arm.

In about three weeks I was able to avail myself of the wounded soldier's reward—a furlough Home! For thirty days I was a free man: free to visit, free to go and come as I pleased, free to revisit old scenes, and old friends: feted, treated—Oh well! *that* thirty days just traveled with a speed that would have astonished McClellan; and on the first of July I was back again, in Washington.

About this time the rebel Genl. Early[121] was threatening the Capitol, and every convalescent who could by any possibility handle a gun was detailed for duty in the fortifications around the City. I went with the rest and did duty for some two weeks, when I was sent to Camp Distribution,[122] stayed there three or four weeks, and then—my arm being pretty strong again—joined my Regiment, in front of Petersburg. I had been with the Regiment about a week when our Corps (the 5th), was ordered down on the Weldon R.R, and on the afternoon of August 18th, we had a sharp skirmish with the enemy. It came off in a piece of woods, and we held the ground, forming our picket line on the right of the R.R, just where our skirmish line left off fighting in the evening. The next morning saw the fighting renewed where darkness left it, but *my* fighting was nearly done. While attempting to get my shots in as tellingly as possible, I was again hit in that unlucky right arm, and this time there was no salvation for it. The ball struck me squarely on the elbow, shattering the bone to fragments, and rendering amputation unavoidable.

It is a remarkable fact, that, within four hours after I received my wound, our Regiment was "gobbled up," almost entire, by a superior force. The men were taken to Salisbury prison,[123] where [a] portion of them died miserably through starvation and ill treatment. Few of the original members of the "Bucktail" Regiment are left alive: For those who went down on the field of

121. Lieutenant General Jubal Early (1816–94). His "Washington Raid" threatened the capital in July 1864.

122. Hospital camp in Alexandria, Virginia.

123. This prisoner-of-war camp was in North Carolina.

battle, or who perished by the ordinary vicissitudes of a soldier's life, I shall say nothing—Their lives are woven into the history of the Republic. And the wrongs of those who were fiendishly and systematically frozen, starved, and rotted, in Southern prisons,—"God shall requite."

Politicians may forget—Soldiers will remember.

Written with the left hand—the right having been accidentally left—near the Weldon R. Road.

2.

THE SOLDIERING LIFE

"The literary part of the work," instructions for the first contest read, "may be original or selected."[1] Most entrants chose to write original pieces, responding to Bourne's request for "narratives of the writer's experience in the service of the country, incidents, or sketches of the war."[2] In telling the story of their military experience, many veterans detailed what Charles T. Coleman calls in his submission the "pleasures of a soldier's life." Interspersed between descriptions of marching and details of battle are anecdotes that reveal the human aspects of war and the vicissitudes of life in the army. Individual veterans focused on disparate facets of military service; some highlighted particularly meaningful events, some commemorated fallen comrades, and others recounted humorous incidents. As Coleman explains in his entry, "to show the pleasures more plainly it is necessary to bring in strong contrast some of the horrors."

Writing between 1865 and 1867, left-armed veterans recorded their recollections while memories were still fresh, well before the outpouring of regi-

1. "Premium $500 to the Left-Armed Soldiers of the Union," *Soldier's Friend,* Oct. 1865, 2.

2. Ibid.

mental histories and memoirs in the latter part of the nineteenth century. Most Union soldiers had ample practice recounting their wartime lives in letters written to those they left behind; as literary scholar Christopher Hager has noted, Civil War Americans sent and received around half a billion letters between 1861 and 1865, many of which focused not on battle formations but instead on emotional ties and everyday life.[3] Many of the contestants presented their submissions as letters to Bourne, not only addressing him respectfully but also sharing their thoughts and feelings as well as the less celebrated but more commonplace aspects of military service. Though literacy levels differed (some men admit to having little schooling), the desire to write down and thus preserve their experiences united the contestants, just as much as their missing or disabled limbs did.

EZRA DAYTON HILTS

Corporal, Battery D, 1st New York Volunteer Light Artillery

Hilts was born in New York in 1839.[4] He was a farmer when he enlisted in August 1861 and served at the Siege of Yorktown in late April and early May of 1862 before losing his arm a few days afterward at Williamsburg; he was discharged the following September. In 1869, he graduated with a law degree from Union University's Albany Law School and was admitted to the New York Bar.[5] He served as postmaster of Cape Vincent, New York, for seven years and was twice elected justice of the peace.[6] Married in 1873, he had two daughters; he died in 1908.[7] Hilts sent his reminiscence of the evacuation of Yorktown to both contests, receiving honorable mention for his first submission.[8] Angle brackets indicate selections from his slightly edited second entry.

3. Hager, *I Remain Yours*, 3.

4. Ezra D. Hilts, Contest Entries, 1st ser., no. 14, and 2nd ser., no. 50, William Oland Bourne Papers; 1900 U.S. Census, Jefferson Co., NY, pop. sched., Cape Vincent, p. 10, dwelling 227, family 227, Ezra Hilts, NARA RG 29, T623, roll 1041.

5. *Catalogue of the Alumni of the Albany Law School*, 38.

6. "Ezra D. Hilts—A Native of Herkimer," *Ilion (NY) Citizen*, Dec. 3, 1908.

7. 1900 U.S. Census, Jefferson Co., NY, pop. sched., Cape Vincent, p. 10; Goodhue, *Lineage Book*, 146.

8. Exhibition of Left-Hand Penmanship, Bourne Papers.

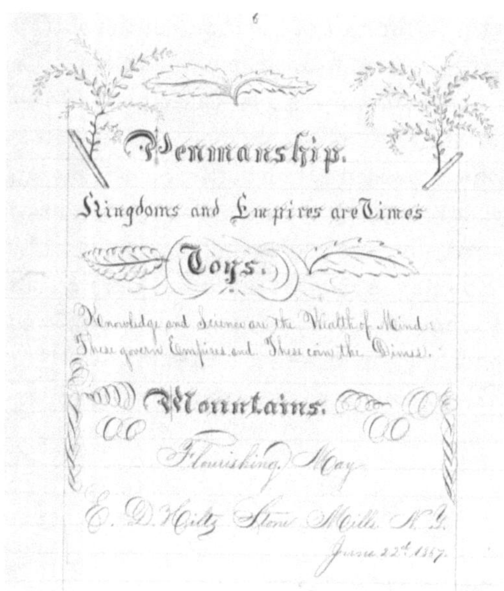

Title page of Ezra D. Hilt's entry for the second contest. Courtesy William Oland Bourne Papers, Manuscript Division, Library of Congress.

First Entry: **December 16, 1865**
Second Entry: **June 20, 1867**

I was in action but a short time, perhaps 3/4 of an hour, when I was wounded accidentally by premature discharge of cannon. I was in the act of ramming down the cartridge when, owing to the vent not being properly closed, the gun went off shattering my right hand and wrist very badly. It was amputated in the evening of the same day. . . . I saw but one battle and saw but little of the hardships of weary campaigns and long marches, and although I have met with a serious loss, yet there are thousands worse off than I am, and I have abundance of reason to be thankful that it is as well with me as it is; and that I am in the enjoyment of health and strength and that I have lived to see peace restored to our beloved country. Slavery is no more, and Providence again smiles graciously upon our fair land.

EVACUATION OF YORKTOWN

It was past the hour of mid-night and all was still in Camp Winfield Scott,[9] save now and then the sharp crack [of] a rifle on the picket line would ring out on the still night air and reverberate amid the surrounding forests, followed by a volley in quick succession, and then all was still again. Suddenly footsteps and the light tinkle of a sword was heard in front of our tents, then came the command from the Major in low, but distinct tones, "Battery turn out," and as if by magic the men were out—horses were harnessed and attached to the guns,

9. Field camp near Yorktown, Virginia.

and "Battery D" was on the move towards the "Picket line." Many were the conjectures as to the cause of this sudden alarm, if there really was any cause, but no one <save the commanding officer> knew. We had proceeded but a short distance from Camp when we halted to await further orders. A light was seen in our front and we knew by the direction that the fire must be in or near Yorktown.

There was a balloon a few rods to our right in which two men made an ascent to learn, if they could, what was up among the rebels, for it was evident that something unusual was taking place, which we "Yankees" were very desirous of knowing.[10] <In the meantime frequent explosions were heard.>

The balloon descended in a short time and we heard the words "Yorktown is evacuated." Those were magical words which caused many a brave heart to beat quick with emotions of joy. It was now growing light and we returned to our camp for breakfast. The news spread with lightning rapidity. We soon received marching orders, and were informed that our army would make a "forced march"[11] towards Richmond.

The whole army was now in commotion, and as I stood upon a place more elevated than the surrounding camps I paused involuntarily <in utter admiration as I contemplated the scene around me>.

That scene, and the <thoughts and> feelings that came over me at the time I will not attempt describe. I thought of the surrender of Lord Cornwallis to General Washington in 1781, which took place but a short distance from where I was standing, and contrasted the circumstances which brought about the Revolution with those which brought about this wicked Rebellion. How striking the contrast!

Again I gazed on the scene around me, <officers hurried to and fro—orders were given—tents disappeared and all was bustle and confusion. But by and by, regiment after regiment formed in line and marched off in regular order to the tune of "Yankee Doodle."> We soon passed the immense fortifications and I found myself in the renowned city of Yorktown. I was not so much impressed with the immensity of the fortifications as with the insignificance of the "city." I thought the place was greater in renown than reality. Here and there in the roads and paths where our soldiers would be most likely to walk,

10. Thaddeus Lowe and the Balloon Corps of the AOTP used hot-air balloons for reconnaissance. See Eugene Block, *Above the Civil War: The Story of Thaddeus Lowe, Balloonist, Inventor, Railway Builder* (Berkeley, CA: Howell-North Books, 1966).

11. A longer and/or more rapid march than usual.

the rebels had maliciously planted infernal torpedoes,[12] nicely concealed, and woe to the luckless ones who chanced to step on one of them. We soon left here and marched slowly along, halting occasionally till the "shades of night gathered over us,"[13] when our halts were longer and more frequent, and to make it still worse a drizzling rain set in. We moved slowly along through mud and rain, till after midnight when we received orders to halt and rest till morning. I wandered away from the rest of the company and had the good fortune to find a comparatively good place in which to lay myself away, among the ruins of an old building, where I was sheltered from the rain, and wrapping my blanket around me I was soon in the land of dreams, little dreaming of what was in store for me on the morrow.

~~~

CHARLES T. COLEMAN

Corporal, Co. B, 75th New York Volunteer Infantry

Coleman was born in New York in 1840 but spent his postwar life in Illinois, working as a bank clerk before becoming an insurance agent.[14] In 1893, he was commander of his local GAR post and was elected senior vice president of the Illinois GAR in 1895.[15] When he married for a second time at the age of sixty-seven, Coleman was still engaged in "insurance and real estate."[16] He had two children. Coleman died in 1915.[17]

September 18, 1865
The pleasures of a soldier's life.

12. The term then used for what now are called mines (or land mines).

13. From Eliot Warburton, *Reginald Hastings; or, A Tale of the Troubles in 164–* (London: Henry Colburn, 1850), 264.

14. Charles T. Coleman, Contest Entry, 1st ser., no. 49, Bourne Papers (punctuation edited); 1900 U.S. Census, Fulton Co., IL, pop. sched., Canton, p. 10, dwelling 243, family 254, Charles T. Coleman, NARA RG 29, T623, roll 302; 1870 U.S. Census, Fulton Co., IL, pop. sched., Canton, p. 388A (stamped), dwelling 25, family 24, Charles T. Coleman, ibid., M593, roll 222.

15. "In Illinois," *Chicago Inter Ocean,* May 6, 1893, 12; "Powell Is Chosen," *Streator (IL) Times,* May 16, 1895, 1.

16. Iowa Department of Health, Marriage Records, 1880–1922, Charles T. Coleman, RG 048, State Historical Society of Iowa, Des Moines, Iowa.

17. Charles T. Coleman, Pension File, application 1047531, certificate 23002, NARA RG 15, T288; 1880 U.S. Census, Fulton Co., IL, pop. sched., Canton, p. 123B (stamped), dwelling 231, family 241, Thomas Coleman, NARA RG 29, T9, roll 207.
~~~

Aside from the great principle of love of country (which actuated us in leaving our pleasant and happy homes, our many friends, kind brothers and sisters and loving parents, which buoyed us up in the trials and hardships consequent upon the life of a soldier) there are many little incidents that occur to brighten our lives as soldiers and make time pass almost as pleasantly as when under the home roof.

To enumerate some of the bright scenes that occurred in my own personal experience is my present intent. I enlisted at Auburn, Cayuga Co., NY, on the 16th day of Sept. 1861 in the 75th infantry regt. as a private soldier. We were in a camp of instruction at Camp Cayuga one mile from the city of Auburn for nearly two months before we were ordered into active duties. While here, we were made acquainted with battalions, maneuvers, the manual of arms somewhat, but our instructions were more particularly in regard to guard duty. Many laughable scenes occurred to brighten the days spent in a camp at home but one which was often rehearsed amid peals of merry laughter was the following: the officer of the day had been drilling the guard in respect to receiving the grand rounds.[18] He had visited each sentinel at his post and if each did know his duty it was not the officer's fault certainly. He thought the work had [been] done so thoroughly it would be a fine opportunity to ask some of his friends to witness his success. Accordingly in making the rounds several accompanied him. All passed off finely until they neared the post of a poor tired German in the second relief who imagined he had stood full his two hours. He was on the alert however and presently the sharp concussion of his musket was heard as he brought it to an "arms port"[19] and loud rang upon the air the challenge, "Who goes there." "Grand rounds" was answered. "Got for tam,[20] I taut t'was de tird relief," answered the dutchman[21] as he shouldered his piece, turned about, and walked to the other end

18. A military routine in which the commanding officer visits guards on duty. The guard, after acknowledging the officer, asks for the "countersign," or password. Upon receiving it, the guard "presents arms." See *Regulations Established for the Organization and Government of the Military Academy,* 116–17.

19. Position in which the soldier brings his firearm in front of his body diagonally, with the muzzle pointing past the left shoulder

20. Coleman's rendition of the German term *gottverdammt,* which translates as "God damn" in English. The soldier mistakenly believed the next guard on duty had arrived.

21. An Anglicization of *Deutscher Mann,* or "German," often used as a derogatory term for a German American in the nineteenth century.

of his beat. The captain was completely nonplussed, but was soon himself again and it was the last time he took any of his friends to visit the post of a raw recruit to show his powers in military training.

It was a pleasant trip to us from Auburn to Albany by railway thence to NY by water. The pleasant scenery along the Hudson [River] drove away the dull thoughts engendered by the inconveniences of a crowded steamboat, and [the] view such as we had of the metropolis of the western world would well repay at any time the hard toil of a month's guard duty or tiresome drill. Probably many of us would never have had this pleasant sight had it not have been at the expense of our country and possibly none of us would ever have taken a trip of seven days length on [the] "old ocean" but from this same cause. A splendid trip we had and how many such pleasant journeys have been taken at the expense of government that could never have been taken except by its agency and what makes all these things the more pleasant is the fact that at the same time we conferred a blessing we received one.

At last we reached our destination (Santa Rosa Island, Fla). It is true this is a barren white sand island, but the few birds and flowers we did see gave the more pleasure as they were very rare, and the excitement we experienced at sundry times relieved the monotony of our every day camp life. Rumors of our speedy return home were often afloat, then would come the thrilling news that the rebels were on the island and were coming down upon us, all of which would die away in due time and we would be left still upon the white sand which glared in the Sun by day and sent out its million[s] of fleas by night. The first shot we ever saw fired by the enemies was on the first day of January 1862. A rebel steamer ran into forbidden waters and we fired upon her; the fire was returned by the guns in the batteries along the coast and by Forts Barrancas and McCree.[22] The bombardment was kept up all day and most of the night. Our shell burned the old US barracks and we had one man killed. . . . While here we were destined to witness one of the grandest exhibitions ever beheld by man in the line of fireworks. The rebels evacuated Warrenton[23] and all their works on the opposite coast from us and set fire to all U.S. property. As soon as the first fire was discovered we opened fire from Fort Pickens[24]

22. Confederate-occupied forts guarding the passage to Pensacola Bay, Florida.

23. Warrington, Florida, southwest of Pensacola.

24. U.S. Fort on Santa Rosa Island near the entrance to Pensacola Bay.

and the batteries on the island hastened the enemy's movements in evacuating as much as possible. The sight of these fires was grand indeed, and when they were at their height, the small revenue cutter[25] *Maria Wood* unfurled her canvas, put boldly down the coast, crossed the channel, ran her prow nearly into old Ft. McCree, then changed her course and ran up the channel between the fires and us making one of the grandest sights ever beheld by man. Proudly she floated in waters which for months had not been pressed by the weight of any vessel. Up! Up the channel she passed into the dense blackness and there cast anchor and lay until daylight undisturbed and quiet as an infant on its mother's breast, a happy finale to a night of intense excitement. The next day we crossed the channel and took possession of the city of Pensacola and the adjoining coast. Our regt. was encamped within the limits of the city. A laughable circumstance occurred here to one of my best friends and which ought not to be told but it is to[o] good to keep. We had been six weeks without any mail and were getting gloomy enough when one afternoon the *Rhode Island* hove in sight and brought us a very large mail and also the news that McClellan had taken Richmond. Our regt. was called out in undress uniform[26] in front of the Col's headquarters and the news published officially. Cheer after cheer rang out upon the air hearty and loud and everybody was wild with joy. We were dismissed after a half hour and broke ranks and passed to our tents in squads as we chose. My bunkmate and I were walking side by side with others when he spoke and said, "this is glorious news. I am so happy, I am, I feel as though I could shout" and suiting the action to the word he seized his pants in that part covered by the coat tails (when he had one on which he had not) and leaped into the air, gave one hearty soul inspiring shout, "hurrah," and came down but alas! Alas! Those were days when shoddy had not entirely disappeared and he came down with the torn fragments of what had been the seat of his best pants in his hands, and he was left a living specimen of the brutality of the early contractors for soldiers' clothing in the state of NY. He and I concluded at once that Richmond could not have been taken; it must have been a mistake.[27]

While at this place we used often to make little expeditions up the Black-

25. The Revenue Cutter Service was the predecessor of the Coast Guard.

26. Regular, everyday uniform.

27. Of course, it was a rumor only. Richmond did not fall until April 2, 1865.

water and Escambia rivers[28] which the boys used to call picnics gotten up expressly for our enjoyment, but more truthfully for the purpose of getting cattle and wood for Military purposes. We always went by steamboats, which made it pleasant indeed. Our next trip for pleasure was across the gulf of Mexico to New Orleans and for two months we were encamped in the suburbs and had ample opportunity to visit all the sight[s] worth seeing in the Crescent City, the metropolis of the South. To one as fond of travel as myself these frequent changes of localities afforded infinite pleasure. We here formed a part of the first Brigade ever commanded by Genl. Godfrey Weitzel[29] and soon went on the expedition down the bayou Lafourche,[30] which we enjoyed hugely as we were allowed to forage on our own account and we proved ourselves good soldiers in this respect. When we halted for the night there was hardly a knapsack to be found that did not have two or three chickens or ducks dangling from the straps.

We were constantly kept in good humor while on this march by the appearances of the new accessions to our train which by the time we reached Thibodeaux[31] amounted to about four thousand persons of all ages, sizes, and colors and speaking a mongrel of all kinds of languages.[32] As we passed each plantation on the route expressions like the following would meet our ears from the purely loyal people of the South as they flocked to the fence along the road: "Oh! bless de good Lord, the day of Jubilee hab come. May de good Lord bress yous all, wheres yous all gwine to?" "Oh! de whole North hab come down to us."[33] Immediately they would bestir themselves and a mule and cart or mule and horse before a cart or some kind of a turnout would be loaded with the sparse effects of each negro family and they would join our force and march along. We defeated the rebels at Labadaville[34] and encamped one mile below the village of Thibodeaux.

The most of our pleasures now consisted in the real romance of a soldier's life, plenty of guard duty with an occasional march and fight thrown in. An expe-

28. Rivers in the Florida Panhandle feeding into Pensacola Bay.

29. Brigadier General Godfrey Weitzel (1835–84), later promoted to major general.

30. Louisiana waterway southwest of New Orleans.

31. A principal town along Bayou Lafourche.

32. Coleman refers to formerly enslaved people who followed the army as refugees.

33. Coleman uses dialect typical of contemporary depictions of enslaved people and other African Americans in the South.

34. This skirmish at Labadieville occurred on October 27, 1862.

dition was soon fitted out to start from Brashear City[35] to go up the bayou Teche and destroy the rebel gunboat *Cotton*. We were ordered to join and took an active part in the fight in fact took the front and brunt of it and came off with laurels. Eighty of our men volunteered as sharpshooters to pick the gunners from the *Cotton* and well they done their work. Although we did not get the Steamer that night they swung her across the bayou as an obstruction and burned her to the water's edge. In the morning our work being accomplished we retraced our steps a happy body of men for we had gained the favor of our General and had won what is the dearest boon to a true soldier: a name for bravery and strict obedience to orders as we had before won praise for our good discipline and perfection in the drill and we now stood among the first regiments in the department. . . .

The 75th New York remained in bayou country, eventually becoming part of the army under General Banks that confronted the Confederate garrison at Port Hudson.

We landed and marched to the rear of Port Hudson, and on the 27th day of May 1863 made a combined assault on the works and were not successful in capturing them but held our ground and drove the enemy completely inside their fortifications and soon formed rifle pits and planted artillery and commenced the siege in earnest. On Sunday the 14th of June everything being ready we were ordered to make an assault at one point supposed to be the weakest.

General Weitzel had command of a division in this fight. The 12th Conn. Regt. and ours were deployed as skirmishers and were the attacking force. We had just reached the rebel works at daylight. I stood at the edge of the ditch a little in advance of the main line and had my gun raised at an aim and was almost ready to fire when a bullet sped through my right arm and eventually left me a one armed man for life. Some persons might think this ought not be mentioned in connection with the pleasures of a soldier's life but to show the pleasures more plainly it is necessary to bring in strong contrast some of the horrors. The pleasures now follow. All was done to save my arm that could be done by kind surgeons and tender nurses but after keeping it on for eight weeks it was found necessary to take it off to save my life. Everything was procured for my comfort that could be under the circumstances and all persons were kind to me.

35. Now Morgan City, Louisiana, along the Atchafalaya River.

As soon as I recovered sufficiently I was sent home free of expense, in the spring of 64. I went to New York and thence to Boston, was fitted with an artificial arm, came back to New York and thence home. The government paid my board, my transportation, and for my arm, and is now paying me eight doll[ar]s per month. The pleasure in all this consists in knowing that my feeble efforts for the benefit of our common country are remembered and appreciated and when I see the many little comforts that this eight doll[ar]s per month procures for my wife and child, I cannot but feel happy to think that I lost my arm in so good a cause and for so just a government.

I have said much and written a long tiresome history of "I" and yet after all the happiness of a true soldier may be summed up in these words: plenty to eat, plenty of marching and plenty of fighting.

FRANK GEORGE OTIS

Commissary Sergeant, Co. B, 10th Connecticut Volunteer Infantry
Second Lieutenant, Co. G, 10th Connecticut Volunteer Infantry

Otis, born in 1842, served as "Soldier and Officer" for three years and eighth months.[36] Wounded in April 1865, he married in 1867 and had three children.[37] In 1867, *The Soldier's Friend* listed him as an authorized traveling agent for the paper.[38] When he died in 1878 at the age of thirty-five, Otis was serving as the commander of the Connecticut Department of the GAR.[39] The following excerpt combines the two entries he submitted, since they are for the most part very similar; his age changes, however, as does his initial enthusiasm for joining up. Selections from his second entry are indicated by angle brackets. Otis received a twenty-dollar prize for literary merit.[40]

36. Frank G. Otis, Contest Entries, 1st ser., no. 62, and 2nd ser., 107, Bourne Papers (punctuation edited); 1860 U.S. Census, New London Co., CT, pop. sched., Colchester, p. 64, dwelling 470, family 549, G. F. Otis, NARA RG 29, M653, roll 90.

37. Smith, *Mack Genealogy,* 1454.

38. "Travelling Agents," *Soldier's Friend, and Grand Army of the Republic,* Nov. 1867, 4.

39. "Obituary," *Boston Post,* Aug. 12, 1878, 2.

40. Exhibition of Left-Hand Penmanship, Bourne Papers.

Frank G. Otis.
Courtesy Karla K. Cook.

First Entry: **December 28, 1865**
Second Entry: **September 23, 1865**

I take pleasure in preparing this short sketch of my Army life, not alone because I wish for the premium so kindly offered, but also to acknowledge the kindness of the donor, and if possible to add a little to the book, which I understand you propose to publish, containing the different specimens of left-hand writing. Probably there will be but few of the many competitors, who have had less time to practice writing and prepare their samples, than myself; still I am resolved to try, as I am sure it cannot do me any injury.

<I deem it the duty of every member of the left-arm'd corps, who can write at all, to add something to the collection of specimens, if it is only to express their thanks, to you, and the many others, who have so kindly and generously, contributed aid to the unfortunate left-arm'd Soldiers of our Army.>

When I first lost my right arm, it seemed as though my left was made in vain, it was so awkward, and I presume scores of others have thought the same, but not while they had the right one to use, however I am gradually becoming accustomed to using my left and every day am more and more convinced that a left-hand is better than none, and if "trained up in the way it should go"[41] may sometime become quite useful—or as the saying goes, a handy thing in the family. . . .

<When the War broke out, I was young (only seventeen) a farmer's Son, and but little acquainted with, or interested in, the affairs of our Government, and thought, as did many others, that Uncle Sam had ample means to

41. A reference to Proverbs 22:6, which reads: "Train up a child in the way he should go: and when he is old, he will not depart from it."

suppress the rising Rebellion, and that the trouble would soon be settled. But we were mistaken. . . . >

During the summer of 1861 I could not feel contented at home, for it seemed to me that my country needed my services, but as my Father owned a large farm, and had no-one beside myself and a younger brother only twelve years old (I was eighteen) to help improve it, it did not seem best that I should leave him; accordingly, I stayed at home through the summer. After the reverse of our arms at Bull Run, and in other minor battles, I could plainly distinguish the voice of Uncle Sam calling his boys to rally round the flag above my Father's to rally in the corn field, and concluded at once, that the old flag must be protected, farm or no farm. Accordingly, on the 18th of September I went to Manchester, a town twenty miles distant, and enlisted as a private in a company then organizing there, from that, and adjoining towns. . . .

During the afternoon our tents arrived, and we were soon engaged [in] constructing our new quarters. Pitching tents was new business to the most of us, and awkward work we made of it, I assure you, but with the aid of our Captain, and a few others who were in the three months service,[42] and had had some experience in the art, we succeeded admirably and by sunset were ready to receive calls. After supper, we might have been seen gathered in groups, some jumping, others wrestling, others telling stories. Still later in the evening imagine us about eighty in number, assembled around the camp fire, singing the Red White and Blue, Star Spangled Banner, John Brown chorus, and many other camp songs too numerous to mention. After which we retired, but how much we slept I will leave you to guess; perhaps it is enough to say that even the soft side of those boards seemed hard to us that night, but how many times since think you, would we have willingly accepted of even the hard side?

<Our time passed swiftly and pleasantly here in camp. A little exercise by way of company drill was just sufficient to keep our appetite good, not only for our regular rations, but also for the beautiful Apples with which the neighboring Orchards were laden. Of course we didn't steal them, for Soldiers never steal. We just confiscated them for Government use, you see,

42. The volunteers who had signed up in response to Lincoln's initial call for 75,000 men to serve for three months after the bombardment of Fort Sumter.

and I might relate several amusing incidents connected with our exploits in this line, but time and space forbid.

Many of our friends visited us here in Camp, which made it very pleasant for us, and we really enjoyed this kind of soldiering.>

October 5th we received our uniforms, and a few days later commenced a regular routine of camp duty. It was not until now that we began to realize that we were Soldiers. Standing guard in a dark night, with an old musket, minus lock, stock, and I almost said barrel, was to us exciting if not dangerous business, however we were never attacked except by Sir Candy, Gingerbread, or Yankey [*sic*] notion peddlers, and these we could generally repulse by the free use of our money.

By the middle of the month the companies which were to compose the 10th Regiment had all arrived, field and staff Officers were appointed, and we commenced a daily battalion drill. . . .

We left Hartford amid the shouts and cheers, waving of flags and handkerchiefs, the goodbyes and farewells of thousands. It was a trying time indeed to us as we stepped on board the Steamer *Granite State* which was so soon to separate us from loved ones, perhaps too forever. Sad indeed it seemed to see Wives and Sisters, Fathers and Mothers, Daughters and Sons as they pressed eagerly forward through the crowd on either side, to exchange one more parting word and kiss with a dear friend, and bid him Godspeed. <Many were the silent, but earnest prayers, then and there, offered for our success, and safe return. *Success we had*, but of those who left Hartford that day, as members of the 10th Regiment, less than half ever returned.>

We arrived at Annapolis November 4th, and went into Camp a little out of the city as a part of Genl. Burnside's coast expedition.[43] Here was a magnificent sight, the fields for miles around were dotted here and there with encampments. It seemed to us that there were more troops here already than would be necessary to sweep the Confederates into the Gulf of Mexico. The months of November and December were spent in drills, parades, reviews, inspections, etc. The weather here was quite comfortable, we had camp stoves which we could use if desired, and which we found quite convenient

43. Burnside's "coast expedition" was part of the Anaconda Plan and took place in coastal North Carolina from February to June 1862, establishing a strong Union presence in Pamlico Sound for the rest of the war. To read the general's account of this operation, see Burnside, *The Burnside Expedition* (Providence, RI: N. Bangs Williams, 1882).

during some of the long evenings in December. We had a daily mail, and the daily papers, and I venture to say that these two months were spent as pleasantly as any two, either before or after.

<New Regiments and Batteries arrived every few days. Steamers were being loaded with provision and ammunition, and we considered our prospect for spending the winter in Maryland not very flattering, though when we left Hartford, the general opinion was, that before we should get thoroughly drilled, and organized, the South would be subdued and peace restored. How little did we then know of what was before us.>

January 7th 1862 the Burnside expedition sailed from Annapolis. Our destination, which proved to be Roanoke Island, NC, was reached after long weeks of exposure, and suffering, on crowded transports, which I will not here attempt to describe: those only who were with us off Hatteras[44] during those long and awful storms, can realize, or begin to form any conception of our situation.

Several vessels were driven on shore, and nearly all on board lost, several schooners loaded with horses were wrecked and the most of them lost, several boats loaded with provision, also went to the bottom, and the cargoes all lost, and the consequence was we were short of rations. Mail too was seldom sent, or received; under these circumstances, you will not be surprised when I tell you that there was some murmuring, or if you choose, growling, among the men, and I presume I did my share. February 7th we arrived off Roanoke Island, and on the 9th took possession after two days hard fighting. I will not attempt to give any particulars of this, our first engagement, for I must hasten on with my story as it is some ways home yet. . . .

Otis and his unit campaigned in North Carolina, fighting in a series of battles and skirmishes, before being transferred to South Carolina.

Of our campaign in South Carolina, during the spring and summer of 1863, I have not time to give particulars. In the battles of Seabrook, James and Morris Islands,[45] and also in the Siege of Forts Wagner, Gregg,[46] and

44. Cape Hatteras, North Carolina, a notoriously treacherous area of the Atlantic Coast in winter.

45. Engagements on the Sea Islands near Charleston, fought between March and July 1863.

46. Fort (or Battery) Gregg was a rebel stronghold on the northern tip of Morris Island. Confederates abandoned it on September 6, 1863.

Sumter, the 10th Conn. proved itself as brave and efficient, as it had before in North Carolina; and in more than one instance, were we selected to perform some important, and hazardous duty, as for instance, the night attack on Fort Sumter,[47] and always received from Generals [Quincy Adams] Gillmore, [Alfred] Terry, and others, the highest praise. But, as was the case with many other regiments, constant campaigning, in the malarious swamps,[48] and scorching suns of South Carolina proved too much for us, and during the months of August and September over twenty of our number were consigned to the sands of Morris Island, while the majority of those remaining were so prostrated with chronic diarrhea, that they were unfit for any duty whatever.

October 18th we were examined by the brigade surgeon, and pronounced entirely unfit for field service; and on the 25th were ordered to St. Augustine, Florida, to recruit our health. We found this a very pleasant and healthy situation. With fresh fish and oysters, and plenty of wild game, and always a fresh sea breeze, we soon began to regain our health, and the commissary found it necessary to increase our rations. Oranges, Lemons, Figs, Melons, and several other kinds of fruit were found in abundance, flower gardens were in full bloom, and we could hardly believe that it could be winter. During the month of January 1864 the majority of the Men reenlisted for three years more, myself among the number, and in February came home on our veteran furloughs of thirty days. It was the first time I had been home since I enlisted, and the days hardly seemed as many hours. At the expiration of our furlough we reported at Washington, and were assigned to the Department of Virginia Army of the James.[49] That portion of our regiment which did not reenlist, and which we left in Florida, joined us here, which, with the recruits we brought back with us, filled us up to about eight hundred strong.

In the campaigns before Richmond and Petersburg from May 8th 1864 to April 9th 1865, the old 10th was always found ready, whether with shovel or musket, and was among the number to receive the surrender of the Rebel

47. Otis most likely refers to Major General Quincy A. Gilmore's planned attack on the night of September 8–9. That same night, marines and sailors launched an unsuccessful amphibious assault on the fort.

48. The marshy and swampy terrain around Charleston provided a perfect home for malaria-carrying mosquitoes, which plagued the soldiers.

49. The Army of the James was established under General Butler in April 1864. It fought in Virginia and North Carolina.

Army under Lee, April 9th 1865. They were then sent to Richmond where they remained, doing provost and picket duty, until the last of August, when they were ordered to Connecticut to be mustered out of the service. They arrived in Hartford August 30th with only one commissioned officer, and less than one hundred enlisted men of the original thousand. By one commissioned officer I mean only one who went out as such. The regiment was in the U.S. Service just three years and eleven months.

I have stated that I enlisted as a private, I served in that capacity, until January 1st 1864, when I was made Corporal. September 10th 1864, I was promoted to Commissary Sergeant of the regiment. February 6th 1865 I was commissioned second Lieutenant and assigned to company G (I was formerly a member of Co. B).

<. . . [I]n the desperate, and hand to hand encounter at Fort Gregg,[50] I lost my right arm. This of course deprived me of the pleasure of being present at the surrender of Lee's Army. . . . >

I was in Hospital at Point of Rocks, VA, until May 28th when I received a leave of absence for thirty days, but before it had expired I was honorably discharged the United States service by official order from the War Department, on account of my wound.

<But the War was over, our Government again restored to peace, and I was ready to leave the service, feeling that the sacrifice I had made was but little, in comparison to the honors, the rights, and the power we have gained as a Nation, for the old flag floats today, triumphantly over North, South, East, West, *and long may she wave over* the land of the free and the home of the brave.

The future sometimes looks dark before me, as I think that I must work my way through life, with this awkward, and almost obstinate left-hand; yet I can truly say, that I do not regret that I gave my right to my Country, and should the South again rise in rebellion against us, I stand ready with my left, to defend our rights, and if necessary, shall say to it "Go thou and do likewise."[51]>

~~~

50. This fortification was part of the Confederate siege lines near Petersburg, Virginia. Fighting occurred there on April 2, 1865.

51. Luke 10:37.
~~~

JOHN W. REYNOLDS

Private, Co. G, 15th Ohio Volunteer Infantry
Sergeant, Co. G, 49th Ohio Volunteer Infantry

John W. Reynolds in 1897.
Courtesy Robert Wayne Reynolds.

Reynolds was born in Centre County, Pennsylvania, in 1834. In 1858, he moved to Sycamore, Ohio, where he worked as a blacksmith.[52] Responding to Lincoln's call for 75,000 volunteers to "suppress the then infant rebellion," Reynolds was the first man from his township to enlist. He was serving as postmaster and justice of the peace when he submitted his contest entries. After the death of his first wife, Reynolds moved his family to Trego County, Kansas, in 1877, and remarried in 1880.[53] His first marriage produced four children, while his second produced eight. Reynolds died of heart failure at the age of sixty-four.[54] Upon his death, the Trego post of the GAR passed a resolution recognizing him as "an earnest and worthy member," a "good citizen . . . , faithful husband . . . , [and] a kind and indulgent father."[55] Selections from his second entry are indicated by angle brackets.

First Entry: **January 23, 1866**
Second Entry: **April 22, 1867**

I served in Co. G 15th Ohio Volunteers during the three months for which we had engaged, doing duty along the R.R. in and about Grafton, VA. At the

52. John W. Reynolds, Contest Entries, 1st ser., no. 240, and 2nd ser., no. 31, Bourne Papers (punctuation and spelling edited).

53. "Answered the Last Roll Call," *Western Kansas World* (WaKeeney), Nov. 19, 1898, 4.

54. Family information courtesy of Robert Wayne Reynolds, John W. Reynolds's great-grandson.

55. "Resolutions of Respect," *Western Kansas World* (WaKeeney), Nov. 26, 1898, 1.

expiration of our time of enlistment we came to Columbus, and turned over our arms and accoutrements to the proper authorities, then [were] sent home without pay or discharges. Things remained in this condition until the 28th of August, where we were paid at Upper Sandusky in gold, something we have not seen since. We received our discharges also at the same time and place, but two days after we came home from Columbus, I was taken sick with fever. I thought my time had come, but owing to a good constitution, I recovered and when I got well enough I enlisted in the 49th Ohio Vols. . . .

Reynolds's new regiment was sent to Louisville, Kentucky, in September 1861.

Ours was the first organized regiment from the north of the river to enter the city. They received us with cheers and shouts of joy. At the cars we had to wait sometime and here the union citizens brought up lots of good things to eat; we were very hungry and done full justice to them. From here we went to Lebanon Junction, got off of the cars. The Johnnies had destroyed the R.R. bridge over the Rolling Fork of Salt River.[56] Here was a trial which we had never experienced, viz. wading the river. The water was very cold. We stripped to the buff, and went for it. The bottom was rough and the boys done some tall swearing. We had a good deal of sport; some would fall and lose guns and all. Our first Lieut. Hartsough had stripped to wade but got a chance to ride and after he got off the horse, he was congratulating himself upon his good luck, when, the bank being very slippery from so many going out of the water, his feet slipped and down he come on his butt leaving a very fair imprint upon the soft mud. He was a fine fellow and it was good fun all around. . . .

Reynolds's company stayed at Camp Nevin near Elizabethtown, Kentucky, before marching to Nashville and then on toward Savannah, Tennessee.

Nothing of moment occurred until we arrived within about twenty five miles of Savannah, when we could hear the report of artillery; it was Grant and [General P. G. T.] Beauregard at Pittsburg Landing. This was on the sixth of April 1862. We stacked our knapsacks, and marched in light order.

56. The Rolling Fork flows into the Salt River about twenty miles south of Louisville. The ruined bridge was about thirty miles south of the city.

We arrived in Savannah at ten o'clock at night when it rained torrents. We all got a ducking. I laid four rails on the ground and stretched my bones on them. All the night long we could hear the boom, boom of the gun boats shelling the rebs in the woods. The town was full of our wounded and dying. Our first duty in the morning was to put our arms in order for the last night's rain had wet them. About ten a.m. we embarked on board the *John J. Ray* for Pittsburg Landing. In the meantime all kinds of reports reached us, but we landed at noon and such a crowd of demoralized soldiers I never saw before nor since. Some begged us for God's sake to not go on to the field for we would be all killed. Others were more hopeful, but as soon as [we] landed we were marched onto the field. Here our Lieut. Col. [Albert M. Blackman] made us a speech in which he exhorted us to stand by our colors and win for ourselves and our posterity immortal glory. For my part I felt like going right for them. We could hear the musketry in the front, and could see the wounded coming back to the rear. These men were without exception in good spirits and told us to go in, that we were driving the Johnnies here and there in our advance. We would pass either dead or wounded men. That looked heavy to us new soldiers, but we marched in line through the woods in the direction of the battle. <Our army had reinforced Grant the night before and this morning old Nelson[57] had opened the ball himself, and forced the rebels back about three miles. We went into the battle in good style and there was some hot work. I came out unhurt although a ball struck my belt, doing no damage however.> The battle was receding and we knew our men had the advantage. We lay down at the edge of a field. Whilst here a ball passed over my head five or six feet. I thought that was pretty close. But we did not stop here long. We were ordered forward and soon were receiving their compliments in the shape of minnie balls. They had a cross fire on our left. Co. B. suffered severely having several men killed and wounded. Our Co. had but one man hit. John Wise, or as we called him the governor, was wounded in the side and fell. We advanced a mile, when the Johnnies being out of sight and hearing, we were ordered to return to our camping ground near the landing.

<After the rebels had retreated we could pick up any quantity of Bowie

57. Brigadier General William "Bull" Nelson (1824–62), division commander in Major General Don Carlos Buell's Army of the Ohio at Shiloh.

knives on the field. They had an idea that they could come to close quarters and then tickle our ribs with them, but that played out. Our regiment stacked arms close by where Gen. Sherman had his headquarters. Before the battle, his tents was riddled with balls. Some of our wounded men had crept into them to keep out of the rain and shelter them from our balls, for they were right between our fires for some time. Our boys went into Sherman's tents and helped themselves to his sugar. Our adjutant[58] told the General. He said "roll it out to them." We also went for his molasses. It was all right with old "Billy" as the boys called him. I picked up a very nice sabre and as the General came riding along I showed it to him. He said it belonged to some officer he knew but I have forgotten his name. The General had his hand tied up. He was wounded. I had seen him in Kentucky and knew him as soon as I saw him.>

That night the rain came down in a perfect deluge. I laid down to sleep on the ground but sleep was impossible. All the hollows and ravines were full of water. Next morning we were marched over the battlefield and camped at the outer edge. <I have been in many fields but this was the most horrible. Two days fighting over the same ground had strewn the ground with dead and wounded, horse, cannon, caissons, and arms of all descriptions.> The sights that met our gaze were awful but we soon become [*sic*] accustomed to them. A week after the battle we were engaged in burying the dead, and waiting for our baggage.[59] At length we moved towards Corinth, Miss., where Beauregard was fortifying his position. Our army lay a long time before the works without accomplishing much; after we had got ready to go for them they quietly left, and we captured the city of Corinth. . . .

The Ohioans marched east and stopped in South Florence, Mississippi.

While here I played a trick on an officer. Most of our regiment lay in a ravine, while our teams were on the bank of the Tennessee [River]. I came down one day to our Co. team. When Sergeant Weber told me my fish was done, I knew there that something was up. I inquired and they told [me] that a negro had come out of a house close by, and told him that officer's fish was done. I understood it now. I called for a large white plate we had. I went in by the guard and told the darkey the officer had sent me for his fish. His woman

58. An administrative assistant to a commanding officer.

59. In his second entry, Reynolds explains that it took a full week to "bury the dead and to collect arms."

dished it up. I paid her thirty cents for cooking it, and went out to our boys. It was a feast fit for a king. I'll bet that shoulder strap[60] was disappointed. . . .

We arrived at Battle Creek[61] about the last of July. <We encamped on the Tennessee. We on one side and the enemy on the other. No firing was allowed. We could talk to them over the river. We stayed here until the 20th day of August when we began our retreat toward the north.>

The Federals passed through Jasper, Tennessee, and encountered a superior enemy force under General Braxton Bragg. They marched back to Battle Creek, then crossed the Cumberland range at Altamont, descending into a valley.

<We were now in a nice valley with plenty of corn for bread. The rebel cavalry had cut the railroad and stopped our supplies before we left Battle Creek. Every other man carried a grater made by melting open a canteen and punching each half full of holes with the point of a bayonet. We would grate down the corn on the ear and make pancakes and mush. The next day after going down the mountain we marched into Manchester.[62] In two days after that we made Murfreesboro, and right glad I was too for my shoes were worn out, and besides the weather was so very hot.>

Reynolds's division continued to follow Bragg's army as it moved north, the Federals stopping in West Point, Kentucky, and Louisville.

We arrived at Louisville towards the last of September. Here we refitted and some of the troops were paid off but our regiment was not and we were mad certain. The bulk of the army marched to Bardstown[63] where the rebel army lay. Our division marched to Middletown[64] the first day and was paid early the next morning about three o'clock. . . .

60. A reference to the rectangular strap or board on each shoulder of a Union officer's uniform that displays his rank insignia.

61. A waterway in Marion County, Tennessee, near the eastern end of the border with Alabama.

62. A town northeast of Jasper and thirty-two miles southwest of Murfreesboro, a Tennessee city southeast of Nashville.

63. Town forty miles southwest of Louisville.

64. Town fourteen miles west of Louisville.

Reynolds's unit later in October pursued Bragg to East Tennessee before returning to Nashville.

We encamped close to the Lunatic Asylum until the last of December when our army under [Maj.] Gen. [William S.] Rosecrans moved towards Murfreesboro where the rebel army under Bragg was waiting for us. Our regiment was on the extreme right of the whole army on the morning of the thirty-first December [18]62. They attacked us at break of day.[65] That was a sad day for us. We lost half of our Co. in killed, wounded, and prisoners. The force of the onset scattered us like chaff. When the regiment rallied more than half of our number was gone. Things looked blue. They still advanced and we were driven to the [Nashville] pike. Here the artillery was massed and only here were they checked. We were marched to the rear to protect our trains from the rebel cavalry, which was pressing towards the pike. <On the evening of the first day we were ordered to Rosecrans' headquarters. As we passed by the General and his staff he spoke to [us] and said, "Never mind boys, we'll fire them yet." Some of our boys who heard him, not knowing who he was, said, "there is another damned officer drunk again." Our second sergeant asked us if we knew who that was that spoke and told him it was Rosecrans.> We were on this duty until the second of January when we were [sent] to the front and there we lay in reserve until evening when a grand charge was ordered, and as we were advancing up a hill I felt a blow on my left shoulder. <I received a ball in my left breast ranging diagonally under my left shoulder joint.> I fell out of ranks and went to the rear. <The blood flowed freely and I felt something hard in my sleeve. I shook it out and the ball rolled into my hand. As I passed on I became very weak and thirsty. I lay down at the foot of a tree and thought I would faint.> A little boy came along with his shoulder strung full of canteens. I took one and about emptied it. A cavalry man put me on his horse and took me back to the ambulances. They took me to the Brick house east of the bridge over Alls creek. It commenced raining before morning and as we had to lay out it was very disagreeable. I tried to have my wound dressed but could not get it done. I had saved all my traps but now I left my gun, cartridge box, and dog tent[66] and struck out for another Hospital. I went to one six miles from town.

65. Reynolds refers to the Battle of Stones River.

66. Basic enlisted man's tent similar to a pup tent.

There I got a drink of good wine and waited for several hours. Then I went in and took a good drink of whiskey. Four surgeons now took charge of me, cutting off my shirt the first thing. They dressed my wound and I left and then I was to go to Nashville that night, but it got cold and windy so I would not go, but next morning struck out alone for Nashville. I travelled twelve miles that day and stayed in a negro shanty, had cornbread and milk for breakfast. I arrived in the city before noon and was put in the convalescent camp of our division. I stayed here until the eleventh day of April [1863] when I was sent to my regiment. I did my duty along as usual. . . .

Reynolds was promoted to sergeant and, after recruiting duties and a furlough, rejoined the 49th Ohio in Tennessee in March 1864.

On the third of May we took up our line of march for Tunnel Hill[67] where the rebels under [General] J.E. Johnston were camped. On the fifth of May we came in contact with the enemy driving him from Tunnel Hill to his stronghold on Rocky Face Ridge. Our regiment did its full share of duty in all the battles and marches in this long and severe campaign from Dalton to Lovejoy Station.[68] On the twenty seventh of May in a charge we made on the rebels at Picketts Mills[69] I was wounded in the middle finger of my right hand <the ball having passed through Joseph Whiteman. My finger became very sore and as they would not send me back to the hospital, I kept with the regiment doing no duty except drawing rations for the Company. . . . > I was off duty just two months and had a crooked finger at that. . . .

After the capture of Atlanta, Reynolds's unit marched to the city and camped there. General John Bell Hood, having assumed command of Confederate forces from General Johnston a few months earlier, now attempted to push the Federals out of Georgia. Sherman detached substantial forces to deal with Hood, and they followed the rebels into Alabama before falling back into Tennessee, eventually to Franklin. Hood attacked them there on November 30, 1864.

67. Georgia town twenty-five miles southeast of Chattanooga, site of the first major combat of Sherman's Atlanta Campaign.

68. Engagements in Georgia in February and August 1864 during Sherman's Atlanta Campaign.

69. Pickett's Mill, site of an intense battle in Paulding County, northwest of Atlanta.

As soon as they came in sight they formed their lines and charged. This was a tremendous battle. The rebels were repulsed time and again. They captured part of our line, but were soon forced out. We captured a large number of prisoners. Our troops fell back to Nashville, thirty miles. Our lines were formed around the city when in the distance could be seen the rebel skirmishers advancing. They advanced to within about seven hundred yards when they halted and threw up a line of works. Things remained in this way until the fifteenth of Dec[ember], when Gen. Thomas[70] being ready, he went for Hood right straight. We drove him out of his works, capturing lots of prisoners. Just before night the fifteenth Ohio Vols. of our brigade captured five brass [artillery] pieces. It was a glorious day. That night we spent in building works. I was very tired that night. The next morning we advanced and found the Johnnies well posted on a range of low hills, which they had strengthened with works. Our men shelled them a long time, but that did not do much. Towards evening we were ordered to charge. Now came the tug of war. We advanced over a knoll and came in full sight of the rebels. They had four pieces of artillery trained upon us. The grape and canister whistled through the air, the minnie balls flew thick and fast, we advanced to within twenty feet of the works when we encountered a line of abatis formed of felled trees with the tops sharpened. <The black troops had charged first and been repulsed. Their dead strewed the ground.> This was too much. Our men were falling fast, and what was left was finding cover behind logs, tree stumps, and so forth. I stepped behind a tree and paid my respects to the artillery men in front of us. <The fire from the works was all this time very severe. I stood firing as fast as I could when a ball struck me on the outside of the left leg at the knee. I thought my leg was broke for a minute, but on examination found no damage done more than a little skin knocked off. I stepped behind a tree and kept firing.> I had just loaded my gun and lowered my right hand to cap my gun when I was shot through my elbow. I immediately about faced and moved to the rear, got into an ambulance and was taken to the hospital. At about ten that night my arm was amputated about two inches above the elbow. I was moved to hospital number two in Nashville. I got along very well. I stayed here until the fourth of January, when they put me aboard the hospital boat *Gen. Wood* and I was taken to Jeffersonville, Indiana, which

70. Major General George Thomas (1816–70), commander of the Army of the Cumberland.

we reached on the ninth. I left here on special transfer for Columbus, Ohio, on the twenty-seventh. I arrived on the twenty-eighth and was received at Tripler hospital. I was discharged on the twenty-ninth of May 1865.

<I am now at home. I am Postmaster in the town of Sycamore, Ohio, also Justice of the peace, my fellow citizens thinking me worthy of their confidence.>

~~~

MARTIN DOUGLASS HAMILTON

First Sergeant, Co. G, 17th Indiana Volunteer Infantry

Hamilton enlisted in 1861 when he was seventeen years old and farming.[71] After the war, he attended Indiana University.[72] An obituary referred to Hamilton as a "pioneer resident" of San Diego, California, where he had relocated by 1880 and worked as an assessor and county clerk.[73] By the time of his death in 1926, he was again farming and a member of GAR Heintzelman Post No. 33. Hamilton married at least three times and was survived by three children.[74] For his appeal on behalf of "one-armed soldiers," see chapter 7.

January 23, 1866

After fighting at Chickamauga in September 1863, Hamilton's regiment marched through Tennessee and Kentucky, eventually following Confederate cavalry under Brigadier General John Hunt Morgan into the Blue Grass State. Colonel John T. Wilder commanded Hamilton's brigade.

Wilder being a wonderful man for adventures of diferent kinds he tells the Division comander (this was on new years or knight rather before

71. Martin D. Hamilton, Contest Entry, 1st ser., no. 243, Bourne Papers.

72. *Annual Report of Indiana University,* 15.

73. "Pioneer Citizen of S.D. Succumbs," *San Diego (CA) Evening Tribune,* Aug. 5, 1926, 5.

74. 1920 U.S. Census, San Diego Co., CA, pop. sched., San Diego, p. 3A, dwelling 54, family 55, Martin D. Hamilton, NARA RG 29, T625, roll 130; "Pioneer Citizen of S.D. Succumbs," 5; 1880 U.S. Census, San Diego Co., CA, pop. sched., San Diego, p. 557C (stamped), dwelling 437, family 447, M. D. Hamilton, NARA RG 29, T9, roll 72; 1900 U.S. Census, San Diego Co., CA, pop. sched., San Diego, p. 2, dwelling 30, family 30, Martin D. Hamilton, ibid., T623, roll 99.
~~~

new-years) that if he would let him have enough mules out of the Division train to mount his men he would inshore him that he would capture Morgan so by 11 o'clock that knight all was ready and orders come for evry man to take his partner[75] or mule it turned out to be. So hear we went for the mule no sadeles as you may supose and wild mules to[o]. You can guess we had high times for an hour or t[w]o. Mules balling men falling laughing holloring, crying curseing preying and every other manoever you can picture out. O but if I only had a phiz[76] of it to put in some public place. So I will just say that we did not go any[where] nor did we get any Morgan. But enough fun to last till now eaven through life. I must hasten now. I will not say anything more untill our noted Col. Wilder got to teasing Gen. Rosecrans to give us the Spincer gun[77] and mount us. Now fun of soldiering set in. We had to press our horses mules Jacks[78] or any thing that would ride a man as we ust to say amongst ourselves etc. Gay times these were finding the fine horses in the parlor and then the fair damsull of the south come and beg with tears in her eyes to leave her riding hors. It looked hard to do but our orders were insperation and must be obeyed and so it went untill we were mounted.[79] Then we spent a very pleasant 2 months in scenting the enemy around about Lebanon (not in the old country but in Tenn.) and very often come in contact with a bunch of Johneys. . . .

On the 1st day of April 1865 I received my wound in my right arm just above the elbow. When wounded I was in the Rebels' lines. After geting the natural [illegible] of abuse taking my clothing they left me. Thankful I was too. Hear Our company lost 20 men out of 60 captain included. I was then left in the Rebs hands at Selma AL while the comand went on this being [the] next to the last fight our Regt. was in. I will hasten to a close. Any way this was near the focus[?] of the Rebellion and not much more time. I will begin to wind up my poorly composed contribution. After my arm got so I could be

75. Hamilton jokingly refers to getting on his mount as taking a dance partner.

76. The word generally refers to a facial expression, but Hamilton most likely means a photographic image.

77. A Spencer rifled carbine, an early breech-loading repeating shoulder arm.

78. Jack mule, or male mule.

79. In converting infantry troops into cavalry, Wilder commanded his men to obtain horses from the surrounding countryside. See Eric J. Wittenberg, *Holding the Line on the River of Death: Union Mounted Forces at Chickamauga, September 18, 1863* (El Dorado Hills, CA: Savas Beatie, 2018), 20–21.

moved the war being over I was shiped west with some more livestock. . . . Now summing all up and acording to our Col's report we have been in 84 diferent engagements besides skirmishes that no account was kept. Well I was a member of the 17 Ind. and was Discharged as 1st Segt Co G 17 Ind with my Regt. the 29 of Aug 1865. Since that time I have been goin to school at Clear Spring[80] as regular as circumstances would permit. But for what I am going to be fit for I cannot say but hoping I with the rest of the Left-armed Corps may be of some use to ourselves and others. But hear I am and say God help us. Leaveing this with you asking you Mr Editor to curect mistakes if published for this is my first atemp and send along one of the volumes if you please.

80. Village in Indiana.

3.

EXPERIENCING BATTLE

As soon as (and even before) the Civil War ended, regimental histories and official battle reports began to appear, though the heyday of such publications would arrive in the 1880s.[1] Members of the Left-Armed Corps recognized that the major events leading up to momentous battles and the troop movements during these campaigns and engagements had for the most part already been recorded; in response, they focus in their writings on their individual experiences of what Philip K. Faulk calls "the bloody drama" of war. While some describe their part in multiple battles, others relate particularly significant engagements, including their first and last battles, or the fighting in which they received life-changing injuries. With stark realism and evocative detail, their personal accounts of Gettysburg and Antietam reveal the human side of crucial battles and participate in an ongoing reckoning with the meaning of the war and the ways in which it fundamentally shaped the future of the United States. Walt Whitman famously intoned, "the real war will never get in the books," but traces of this "real war" abound in the left-handed papers, revealing the sincere efforts of veterans to document their service and understand its significance.

Though scholars have identified silence and patriotic forgetfulness as the primary response to the widespread bloodshed of the conflict, the veterans

1. Linderman, *Embattled Courage*, 275.

included here (along with other contestants) attested to the difficulties of communicating but tried all the same to present in surprising and sometimes graphic detail what they saw, heard, and felt during battle.[2] The resulting texts are important counterpoints to claims that Civil War Americans prioritized reunification over acknowledging loss and the physical and emotional costs of internecine war. Ostensibly writing for an audience who had not been to war, the contestants employed different methods to recreate the scene of battle. Some accounts begin by establishing the natural setting, describing a peaceful sunrise or a beautiful morning; familiar to readers of fiction, this technique enabled veteran writers to juxtapose relative tranquility with the sudden arrival of artillery fire or a surprise attack. Joseph F. Smith shifts from the past to present tense at a "critical moment," transporting his readers to the field as a rebel company descends. Other contestants memorialize fallen comrades, praising them as martyrs for freedom and Union. Though the 1870s would bring reconciliation and reunions of the blue and the grey, the Left-Armed Corps' writings express vehement dislike for the "Johnnies" and disdain for the Confederate cause.[3] The memories of the men who fell at their sides remain palpable, the pain in their bodies still present; with their narratives, they add those memories and their bodies to the larger record of the conflict.

JOSEPH F. SMITH

Private, Co. H, 37th Illinois Volunteer Infantry

Born in Rock Island, Illinois, in 1844, Smith enlisted when he was a seventeen-year-old laborer.[4] Discharged in March 1862 after losing his arm in his only battle, he worked as a flagman at a railroad crossing and married in 1880.[5] In 1900, Smith was a landlord, and by

2. For silence and forgetting in the interest of reconciliation, see Nudelman, *John Brown's Body*, 2; and Sweet, *Traces of War*, 110.

3. Blight, "Decoration Days," 104–5.

4. Joseph F. Smith, Contest Entry, 1st ser., no. 48, William Oland Bourne Papers (punctuation edited); "Funeral Held for Civil War Veteran," *Rock Island (IL) Argus*, July 28, 1931, 2.

5. 1880 U.S. Census, Rock Island Co., IL, pop. sched., South Moline, p. 432D (stamped), dwelling 76, family 77, Joseph F. Smith, NARA RG 29, T9, roll 246; "Funeral Services for Joseph Smith Conducted Today," *Moline (IL) Dispatch*, July 28, 1931, 11.

1910 he was living on his own income.[6] After a five-month illness, Smith passed away at the age of eighty-six in 1931; he was survived by two children, seven grandchildren, and four great-grandchildren.[7]

September 25, 1865

The 7 day of March 1862 will long live in the annals of our Country and the day will be remembered by thousands painfully and sorrowfully as one amongst the first of the bloody battles of Pea Ridge.[8] That Friday morning broke splendidly beautifull. The sun rose up grandly in a clear sky. All nature was smilling and peaceful. The reble masses suddently fell like an avalanche upon our rear which was commanded by the gallant [Brigadier General Franz] Sigel. Although not exactly surprised, the Union troops were almost entirely unprepared for the attack. The enemy soon reached our camp and almost before we were aware of them they had us surrounded.

Our pickets, unable to hold their position against a vastly superior force, were compelled to fall back. Encouraged by their success the furious rebles swept on like a whirlwind pressing hard upon our right and center untill they were checked by the determined stand made by our gallant Regiment. My regiment was advanced on the left to meet the attack of the enemy but after severe fighting we had been unable to stand before their overwhelming onset and were compelled to fall back.

Our regiment were soon formed in the cover of the thick woods and as the enemy came on in formidable lines of seven deep yelling and shouting like demons they were met by a continual volley after volley which throwed them in confusion. They were speedily rallied however and with reckless audacity precipitated upon our regiment once more, which caused it to waver before this determined onslaught.

At this critical moment we were ordered to hold our ground if possible

6. 1900 U.S. Census, Whiteside Co., IL, pop. sched., Rock Falls, p. 16, dwelling 355, family 368, Joseph F. Smith, NARA RG 29, T623, roll, 352; 1910 U.S. Census, Whiteside Co., IL, pop. sched., Rock Falls, p. 7A, dwelling 156, family 158, Joseph F. Smith, ibid., T624, roll 331.

7. "Funeral Services for Joseph Smith Conducted Today," 11.

8. Battle of Pea Ridge, Arkansas, March 7–8, 1862.

in order to give the artillery men a chance to draw of[f] their pieces. Consequently almost all of their horses were killed and what few did remain were severely wounded and unfit to render them any service whatever in drawing the artillery back to the rear.

Our regiment, unable to hold its position under the terrible fire of the enemy, we were once more ordered to fall back and this movement brought us in the rear of our battery. On comes the enemy. They have now emerged into the open field and have caught sight of our artillery which is speedily worked by our men who is trying to drive them back.

Halt is plainly heard to ring along the enemy's lines, fix bayonets, and prepare for the charge. "Charge, my brave Texas rangers," is repeated and those words are eagerly catched by our boys as they ring out in the still calm air. On they come double quick with the determination of capturing the artillery. They are compelled to charge across the open field under our raking fires. We are coolly laying within close supporting distance of the artillery watching their movements with close attention. The enemy have almost reached the cannon's mouth, which is charged heavily with grape and canister.

The brave men have fired their pieces for the last time and some of the brave men unwilling to forsake their noble artillery was also captured in the field. This throwed us in confusion but we were soon rallied and was standing once more in line of battle. It was hard for us to give up our artillery but we were compelled to do so as our small force only contained about seven hundred men and one third of them had fallen in action while that of the enemy was estimated to [be] about 5000 and therefore it was impossible for us to retake the artillery.

Consequently reinforcements were soon sent to our aid and with a shout that was rather a yell of rage than a cheer the brigade rushed forward and so impetuous was our attack that the lately victorious antagonists fell back in disarray.

It was in this charge that I had the misfortune of losing my right arm. And there the second day's fight is ended.

~~~
~~~

WILLIAM HENRY DOUGAL

Private, Co. E, 6th Connecticut Volunteer Infantry

A native of Naugatuck, Connecticut, Dougal was a student when he enlisted in August 1861.[9] He served in South Carolina at Port Royal, Morris Island, and Fort Wagner, where he was wounded. Discharged in November 1863, he set about "trying to learn something" and "succeeded very well in Telegraphy." At the time of his submission, he had worked for nine months as a telegraph operator in Tennessee for the Cumberland Department of the U.S. Military Telegraph Corps; he continued as a telegrapher until August 31, 1865.[10] Dougal married for the first time in 1865 (he remarried in 1881), was a traveling agent for *The Soldier's Friend,* and worked in a Philadelphia post office from 1867 to 1868; after that, he was a trial magistrate for twenty years in Connecticut.[11] Elected to the Connecticut House of Representatives as a Republican in 1908, he served until 1910.[12] Dougal was very active in the GAR and, in 1912, while serving as justice of the peace for New Preston, was elected commander of the Connecticut department.[13] Apparently a man of many talents, he was also a "mechanic of considerable ability," a house painter, and a phonograph merchant.[14] He died in 1924. Dougal wrote the following essay for *The Soldier's Friend.*[15]

My Presentiment

The Old 6th C.V. or rather what is left of them will never forget the disastrous assault upon Fort Wagner Morris Island July 18th 1863 in which we lost many of our brave comrades and with them our noble true hearted Colonel John L. Chatfield whose favorite command was "come on my Brave Boys

9. William H. Dougal, Contest Entry, 1st ser., no. 98, Bourne Papers (punctuation edited).

10. "A Remarkable Record," *Bridgeport (CT) Times and Evening Farmer,* Apr. 9, 1909, 6.

11. Marquis, *Who's Who in New England,* 342; Church Records, 1767–1970, W. H. Dougal, 1881, Episcopal Diocese of New York, New York City; "Travelling Agents," *Soldier's Friend, and Grand Army of the Republic,* Nov. 1867, 4.

12. "Representatives Elected," *Hartford (CT) Courant,* Nov. 5, 1908, 14.

13. "New Preston Man Elected G.A.R. Head," *Bridgeport (CT) Times and Evening Farmer,* Apr. 20, 1912, 2.

14. *Connecticut Legislative History and Souvenir,* 151; 1900 U.S. Census, Litchfield Co., CT, pop. sched., Washington, p. 17, dwelling 362, family 385, William H. Dougal, NARA RG 29, T623, roll 141; 1910 U.S. Census, Litchfield Co., CT, pop. sched., Washington, p. 17B, dwelling 377, family 399, William H. Dougal, ibid., T624, roll 135.

15. Will, "My Presentiment," *Soldier's Friend and Grand Army of the Republic,* Mar. 1869, 1.

follow me," which command was never disobeyed by his boys when given by him. He fell there a martyr to the cause of freedom and right and a sacrifice upon the Nation's altar. Those of his old regiment who yet survive him to tell the stories of many hard fought battles will never forget but even cherish his memory, for he was a Christian Gentlemen, a good soldier and an officer well worthy of our love and esteem but now

> He sleeps his last sleep
> He has fought his last Battle
> No sound can awake him to glory again.[16]

We had worked night and day with scarcely any intermission for some fifteen days before the battle and were pretty well played out when the time for the Battle came round. We with other regiments had built what was then known as Gillmore's Advance Batteries, with others including that world-renowned Single Gun Battery known as the "Swamp Angel"[17] which spit fire rather to the discomfort of the Johnnies in Charleston and well might that colored individual exclaim upon seeing a shell from it burst and the destruction immediately after, "Hell hab laid an egg"[18]—About 5 o'clock p.m. on the 18th the order "Co E. fall into line!" was given and into line we fell. The regiment formed into line and took our line of march toward the Fort. Since morning I had felt rather curious and as the day advanced I felt more and more as if something was going to happen to me. Yet I cannot describe the feeling and when the order came to fall in to line my heart beat as fast as it ever did in my courting days. It seemed as if I was in an awful hurry and could not hurry fast enough and must get my equipments on and get into line as soon if not before anyone else. To be sure there was some excitement but that was not all. Something seemed to hurry me up

16. Lyman Heath, "The Grave of Bonaparte" (Boston: Oliver Ditson, 1843). This song circulated as a broadside.

17. A famous 8-inch Parrott rifle deployed on Morris Island to bombard Charleston in 1863.

18. A formerly enslaved man's alleged response to "the first Greek-fire [incendiary] shell from Gillmore's batteries." Untitled, *North Carolina Times* (New Berne), Feb. 6, 1864, 1. The incident was widely reprinted after the war, even as late as 1924. See, for example, "History from *The Gazette Times* Files," *Pittsburgh Post-Gazette*, Jan. 20, 1924, 44.

yet I knew not what for nor could I help it or account for it. My hurrying was a very little like "falling in for pay" on pay day, especially when one has loved ones at home waiting for the money to keep them from hunger and cold.

As we marched nearer and nearer our station to be in readiness for the coming Battle that presentiment grew stronger and as we lay down in front of our batteries while they were firing over us and the shot and shell shrieking over our heads as they passed I turned to a comrade and said, "H— if I am killed in this battle please write home and tell my mother and tell her all about it, will you?" Said he, "yes I will, but you don't expect to get hit do you?" "Yes," said I. "I expect to be killed or wounded and in fact I feel sure of it. I have felt so all day and now more than ever." Several of the boys looked at me as much as to say that's a whim. I told them to wait until after the Battle and then look for me. It had now grown nearly dark, say 8 p.m., yet we could discover objects a few rods off. The Batteries ceased firing and the order, Forward!! was given. Up we jumped, formed in mass. Guns right shoulder shift,[19] and marched forward. I was about the third man from the colors. Between myself and the color bearer was a man who was called by the name of Granny, owing to his notions and grannyfied way of doing some things. When in camp he had from some quarter got some of the "Darling stuff"[20] and had during the day taken so much that it required rather more room than the tactics allowed to march in; his underpinning was also rather unwieldly. His mouth and eyes were wide open, looking straight towards the fighting which had then commenced, his Gun loped over his shoulder, the bayonet in rather too close proximity to his rear neighbor's cranium to make him feel comfortable, an expression of wonder, surprise, and I-don't-want-to could be seen up on his countenance. He was somewhat in the rear of his place and I said to him, "Come Granny, come up here into your place. You are not going to get hit." Whereupon he stepped into his place. Aside from his peculiarity he was a good whole souled fellow such as we soldiers call a "Bully fellow" or "Hunky Boy." He did not get hurt in that battle or any other that I know of. To my right there was a vacancy which was immediately filled by a comrade by the name of Peck who was afterwards wounded in one hand I believe.

We were now near the fort with a good solid front, but not destined to remain so long for "zip" "whizzz" came and went a minnie ball entering my

19. Drill command instructing soldiers to rest their guns on their right shoulders.

20. Dougal most likely means whiskey or some other form of alcoholic drink.

right arm near the wrist on the underside, breaking the small bone and passing out through the elbow joint. I bled quite freely and was soon carried off the field. I walked part way myself but soon became faint and weak. Through neglect on the part of nurses and surgeons my arm became inflamed and soon after arriving at Ft. Schuyler[21] it became so severe that mortification set in and I had it taken off above the elbow.

I am not a believer in Ghosts, Goblins, or Witchery, or Dreams, but I do believe I had a presentiment of what did really happen to me on the 18th day of July 1863.

PHINEAS P. WHITEHOUSE

Corporal, Co. C, 6th New Hampshire Volunteer Infantry

Whitehouse, one of the most prolific contestants, submitted to both contests and published original poems and sketches in *The Soldier's Friend.* His poem "My Crippled Arm" earned him twenty-five dollars for "literary merit."[22] He was twenty years old when he enlisted in 1862. His regiment served in "Virginia, Louisiana and Mississippi, and was engaged in the battles of Fredericksburg, Jackson, Miss., the Wilderness, and Spotsylvania." At the latter, he suffered a gunshot wound in his wrist, resulting in an excision that left his "fingers stiff . . . and the hand . . . of no use to him as regards labor"; *The Medical and Surgical History of the War of the Rebellion* includes an illustration of a plaster cast of Whitehouse's forearm and reports that his hand had not improved by 1873.[23] Having traveled to Central Park Hospital to obtain an apparatus "designed to promote mobility of the hand," he added his name and an original poem to Bourne's autograph book on May 22, 1865; seven days later he added a philosophical sketch.[24] After the war, Whitehouse continued to write; the *Boston Globe* referred to him as a "soldier-poet" in 1898.[25] He married in 1869 and had three children.[26] Farming

21. Located in the Bronx, it was the site of a military hospital during the war.

22. Phineas P. Whitehouse, Contest Entries, 1st ser., no. 136, and 2nd ser., no. 8, Bourne Papers; Exhibition of Left-Hand Penmanship, Bourne Papers.

23. *Medical and Surgical History of the War of the Rebellion*, 2(2):938.

24. Ibid.; Civil War Reminiscences by Soldiers and Sailors in Central Park Hospital, Bourne Papers.

25. "Letter from Phineas T. [*sic*] Whitehouse," *Boston Globe*, Nov. 18, 1898, 6.

26. New Hampshire Marriage Records Index, 1659–1947, Phineas P. Whitehouse, New Hampshire Bureau of Vital Records, Concord; 1880 U.S. Census, Rockingham Country, NH, pop. sched., South Hampton, p. 183A (stamped), dwelling 3, family 3, Phineas P. Whitehouse, NARA RG 29, T9, roll 763.

Phineas P. Whitehouse.
Courtesy William Oland Bourne Papers, Manuscript Division, Library of Congress.

in 1880, twenty years later he was a widower and a journalist.[27] Acting as "presiding officer of the day," Whitehouse read an original poem as part of an Old Home Day celebration in his hometown of Southampton, New Hampshire, in 1902.[28] A member of GAR Wallace Post No. 122, he died while summering in South Carolina in 1910.[29]

Second Entry: August 1866
My First Battle

I had been nearly three months a soldier, before I knew from experience the full meaning of the term battle. At an earlier period I was initiated into the mysteries of the manual of arms; was taught how to maneuver in the various company, battalion, division, and skirmish drills; was carefully instructed in the science of military aesthetics, or the art of making a fine appearance at inspections and reviews; and was shown how to guard the camp, how to bivouac,[30] and how to march with a loaded knapsack. All this had become quite familiar when, in that little city on the storied Rappahannock, I was brought for the first time to witness sterner scenes, and to listen to harsher sounds.

The great battle of Fredericksburg was fought, as is well remembered, on the thirteenth of December, 1862. Having for weeks lain quietly encamped among the oak and vines, near the little old village of Falmouth, the troops composing the great army in Virginia were glad of anything to break the

27. 1880 U.S. Census, Rockingham Country, NH, pop. sched., South Hampton, p. 183A; 1900 U.S. Census, Rockingham Co., NH, pop. sched., South Hampton, p. 13, dwelling 301, family 321, Phineas P. Whitehouse, NARA RG 29, T623, roll 950.

28. *Reports to the Legislature of the State of New Hampshire,* 162.

29. *Journal of the Forty-Fifth Annual Encampment Department of Massachusetts, Grand Army of the Republic,* 101; "P.P. Whitehouse Dead," *Boston Globe,* Nov. 22, 1910, 11.

30. Set up temporary camp while on the march or otherwise in the field.

weary monotony, and when, on the morning of Thursday, the eleventh, the Union batteries opened on the city over the river, all good soldiers were ready, with clean musket or shining sabre, for the first forward signal of the bugle and the drum.

Our regiment, the Sixth New Hampshire Volunteers, was called out early on Friday, and forward in light marching order, was soon the instruction given to the several commanding officers. Directly to the river in front of the town, we marched, where our pontoons[31] were ready to receive us. A few troops had gone over before us driving the enemy from his outer entrenchments on the bank of the river, and we were permitted to cross with little molestation. A great battle was expected that day, but none came. The rebels gave us a few shells now and then, but they did little harm. One burst in front of a regiment, and spoiled a Yankee Doodle which a band was playing while passing a very conspicuous position. "Too impudent!" doubtless thought the enemy; "if you are coming over, you must come more quietly!" And they did come with less music afterwards, and it proved to be the best policy.

As no regular fighting was done that day, our regiment, with many others, made it their home in the streets of the city, and the curious were busy picking up relics and looking into the deserted houses. A glance inside of some of the best dwellings gave evidence of a most precipitate flight on the part of the citizens. Rich carpets covered some of the floors, elegant easy-chairs and sofas were in their places, gilded mirrors and beautiful pictures adorned the walls, and in some instances choice libraries were unremoved. In one handsome apartment I saw a fine piano, with a Yankee soldier sitting before it and playing as unconcernedly as though he were in his own quiet New England home. His thoughts must have wandered to that loved spot, as he rendered some familiar tune, often sung by the dear ones far away.

The next morning after a fair night's rest in the street, we were wakened by the thundering noise of our batteries across the river, which had opened on the heights in rear of the town, behind which the enemy lay strongly fortified. A return fire was soon commenced, and we now began to realize that the battle day had arrived, and that, before the setting of the sun, many a brave soldier boy must sleep in death. To those of our number who were now about to experience their first actual engagement, the whizzing

31. Referring to a temporary bridge made of floats or boats.

of shells over our heads and through the buildings, gave anything but an agreeable sensation. Our regiment was partially protected by a large hotel, before which we were standing, awaiting the order to advance. The Irish Brigade,[32] wearing their sprigs of evergreen, were passing along before us, when one of the noisy messengers from the enemy burst in front of a regiment, scattering the men in every direction. A groan in one place, and a faint cry in another, told us that the iron monster had not been sent altogether in vain. Our own regiment was also occasionally visited. As I was standing in the garden, near the Colonel—now Major General Griffin[33]—a savage looking piece of shell struck the fence about three feet in front of my face, and not much farther from the person of our commander. The colonel smiled and quietly remarked, "If they come no nearer than that, I don't care."

Soon after this, as the shells were coming uncomfortably near, two of our men were seen to crawl through a small window in the basement of a house. The Colonel soon found it out, and called them back. They came out with a rather sheepish air, and when the Colonel asked them their names and company, could hardly hold up their heads to answer. "Pretty boys, you are," said the Colonel, "to crawl in there! What would your mother say if she could see you! Watch these boys," said he, turning to an officer of their company. I was glad they did not belong to the company of which I was a member.

Very briskly, all the morning, the shelling was kept up, and about noon the sharp crack of musketry was heard in the direction of the fortifications occupied by the enemy. The battle had begun. We were immediately hurried into line, to be ready for our turn to take part in the great contest. Slowly at first came the sounds of the rifle shots, but gradually increased in rapidity, till we could hear only a confused rattle, like the rattle of a box of fire-crackers when all ignited at once. We saw regiment after regiment move forward, and finally, at one o'clock, we were ordered to advance.

Marching a short distance through two or three streets, we were soon in rear of the town, and within the sound of the flying bullets. Scenes pitiful and shocking met our gaze, as we neared the field of battle. The returning wounded,

32. The popular nickname of the Second Brigade, First Division, II Corps in the AOTP. It consisted of regiments from New York, Massachusetts, and Pennsylvania whose soldiers were mostly Irish or Irish American.

33. Simon Goodell Griffin (1824–1902), breveted major general at the end of the war.

with powerless arms, shattered legs, or bloody and fearfully disfigured faces, were objects so dreadful to look upon, as to cause the bravest soldier to tremble, the stoutest heart to flutter, as, with floating banners, we hastened to the front. Halting a few moments behind a fence and high woodpile, to dress our files,[34] we marched out into the open plain, in full view of the enemy's works. Here quickly facing to the front and moving in line of battle, we met with so terrible a fire, it seemed that our whole regiment must be cut down.

A shell burst among our men on the right, doing much damage. The man next to me on my right fell dead. These death-messengers often broke our ranks, but our brave Colonel, on foot and on the double-quick, was leading us and we hastily closed up to fill the places made vacant by our fallen comrades, and made our way as rapidly as possible over that bloody plain, where so many had fallen before me. Across the plain—some three hundred yards wide—was a little ridge occupied by our advance, who had been fighting bravely. These troops, whose ammunition was nearly exhausted, it was now our object to relieve. We gained the ridge at last, and commenced firing at the rebel infantry, who were seen swarming the heights beyond.

Our position now slightly favoring us, we were not subject to quite so galling a fire as when marching up over the plain. We were permitted to lie down in line of battle, and load and fire at will. We were thus protected, for two-thirds of the time or more, by the ridge before us. When standing or sitting up to fire, however, we found the zipping visitors more plentiful than was either safe or agreeable. Sometimes they would come so near that we could almost feel them graze the hair about our ears, and we would dodge back involuntarily, forgetting, for the instant, that that peculiar sound was ample proof that the ball could not harm us.

Some of the men were too proud, or foolish—the latter is perhaps the better term—to accept the privilege afforded, of lying down to load their muskets. They preferred to remain on their feet, and were, in many instances, sorely punished for their foolhardiness. Some would place themselves several yards ahead of the line, to be counted braver than their comrades, when the stern order of the Captain would send them back in the ranks. Others, under the influence of a poison more fatal than the dreaded bullets of the enemy, were

34. Realigning a unit's soldiers into straight and properly spaced battle lines after a movement or combat.

heard to utter the most fearful oaths, and to throw out the most shocking curses, that it is possible for human lips to pronounce.

But there were some, on the contrary, who could not conceal their fear and trepidation, in the heat of such a conflict. The scenes of death around them were more than their hearts and their nerves could bear. Some trembled from head to foot, and could hardly control their muscles long enough to load their muskets. Some would get half a dozen cartridges one above the other, and think each had been discharged. Some would aim their muskets high in the air, thinking, perhaps, that the bullets might drop down on the heads of their foes. Some were so overcome while marching to the front that they fainted by the way, and had no opportunity of seeing the gray uniforms.

There were others—would that their number had been greater—who seemed to realize the solemnity of the work in which they were engaged; who appeared to understand their duty and to desire to perform their part, and yet to feel the danger to which they were exposed. Such were seen always in their places, calm and steady, never noisy, never boasting, ever ready to do the bidding of their superiors.

We fought an hour and a half or more at the ridge, receiving no order to charge on the enemy's works. By this time our ammunition was nearly expended, and a rear line moved forward to our relief. Our regiment ceased firing, and lay down close to the ground, where the musket shots were not so liable to annoy us; but even then the Miniés came so near, at times, that it seemed a miracle one could escape without a scratch. We lay a long time listening to the continuous cracking of muskets, the whistling of bullets, and the bursting of shells, till the approach of night quieted, in a measure, the contending armies, and we were ordered back to the city. The revolting scenes I witnessed in marching back over the field of blood, I will not attempt to describe. It is sad enough to think of them. They were scenes which, as long as memory lives, can never be forgotten.

That night we made our beds in the same street which we occupied on the night previous. But all were not there. Our regiment, which had long been small in numbers, counted seventy men among its killed, wounded, and missing. Some of those who lay down with us the night before, were suffering in the hospital, from amputated limb, or from wounds more serious; a few from sickness were unable to be with us; and others, sleeping in silence their last sleep, lay scattered over the bloody plain.

Thus ended my first experience in actual warfare. A kind and merciful Providence watched over and protected me during that fearful conflict, and I came out unscarred. The noisy shells, which sometimes burst so near, were not intended for me, and the singing bullets all passed harmlessly by. But in many a household among the pines of Maine, the granite peaks of New Hampshire, the green fields of Vermont, the busy villages of Massachusetts, the beautiful farms of the Empire [State], and the fertile prairies of the West, the battle-field of Fredericksburg will long be remembered as the place where a loved one lay down to die!

~ ~ ~

PHILIP KEPPEL FAULK

Private, Co. F, 11th Pennsylvania Volunteer Infantry
Second Lieutenant, Co. C, 54th Pennsylvania Volunteer Militia
Second Corporal, Co. F, 11th Pennsylvania Volunteer Infantry

Faulk, "by trade and profession a printer," informed Bourne that he enlisted for three months in April 1861 and reenlisted in November 1861 for three years; discharged in January 1863 due to sickness, he once again reenlisted for three months' service in June and was commissioned second lieutenant.[35] He returned home in the fall of 1863 before rejoining his old regiment in February 1864 as second corporal. Three months later he fought in his last battle, described below. When he submitted his first contest entry, Faulk was working as a messenger in the Surveyor General's Office in Yankton, Dakota Territory; he was also the "Dakota correspondent" for the *Brookville Republican,* a Pennsylvania newspaper that announced his $20 prize for literary merit and wished "that all our maimed soldiers could so readily see their left arm thus taking the place of the good right arm they gave to their country."[36] By 1869, Faulk was a clerk in the General Land Office, earning $1,100 annually.[37] He was admitted to the bar that year and set up practice in 1871; he married nine years later at the age of thirty-nine.[38] When

35. Philip K. Faulk, Contest Entries, 1st ser., no. 142, and 2nd ser., no. 91, Bourne Papers. Faulk reported that he enlisted for three months in April 1861 in Westmoreland County, but his name does not appear on any of the three-month regiments organized there. Official records list his enlistment as November 9, 1861.

36. "Home News," *Brookville (PA) Republican,* May 23, 1866, 3.

37. *Register of Officers and Agents, Civil, Military, and Naval, . . . 1869,* 158.

38. *Biographical Directory of the South Dakota Legislature,* 309; 1880 U.S. Census, Yankton Co., SD, pop. sched., Yankton, p. 246D (stamped), dwelling 95, family 109, P. K. Faulk, NARA RG 29, T9, roll 1[illegible].

he died of a paralytic stroke in 1900, Faulk was "one of the oldest and best known lawyers in the southeastern part" of South Dakota.[39] His half-brother was the third governor of Dakota Territory.[40] For his address to comrades, see chapter 7.

***First Entry:* December 16, 1865**
My Last Battle

In attempting a brief sketch of the great Battle of the Wilderness where the "fortunes of war" deprived me of my right arm, I shall not enter into a lengthy detail of the events preceding the battle, but relate "my own true tale" at once by commencing with the advance, which began at midnight May 3rd 1864, and which ultimately resulted so gloriously to our arms.

The veteran, battle scarred Army of the Potomac, occupied, as is well known, the North bank of the Rapidan, and there, during the long, dreary Winter, like a tiger couchant,[41] was watching the rebel hosts confronting it on the opposite bank. Spring at last came, and with it came blood and tears. The widow's sighs and orphan's cries, the dying soldier's groans, and the victor's shout of exaltation. But to my story. The morning of the 4th saw long blue lines of infantry whose bristling burnished steel gleamed in the sunlight, debouching into various roads leading to the fords of the Rapidan. Before noon, almost the entire Army had effected a crossing without meeting resistance or firing a shot. Here I beheld a most magnificent sight. More than 70,000 men were in line and in full view, only awaiting the orders that should lead them forth to conflict. This "terribly stern army" slowly began to press Southward, and as the sun sank behind the distant peaks of the Blue Ridge, the entire army had bivouacked for the night. Our brigade camped upon the banks of a clear gurgling brook, whose pellucid waters were as yet unsullied by the grime and gore of battle.

Early on the morning of the 5th while the dew yet lingered on the tender leaflet, we were advancing, momentarily expecting to meet again the misguided impetuous sons of the South who had so often dyed the soil of their native hills and valleys with blood in fierce conflict with the legions that fought under the brave old "Banner of the Stars." All day the sultry rays

39. "Phil. K. Faulk," *Black Hills Weekly Journal* (Rapid City, SD), Apr. 6, 1900, 2.

40. "Dakota Pioneer Gone," *Dakota Farmers' Leader* (Canton, SD), Apr. 6, 1900, 6.

41. In heraldry, a tiger at rest with its head raised.

of the sun beat down pitilessly upon friend and foe alike. Suddenly about 4 o'clock the familiar boom boom of artillery, mingled with spiteful volleys of musketry on our right told plainly that the bloody drama was enacting. Our brigade of the 2nd Div. 5th A.C.[42] was immediately ordered to the support of the forces engaged. Moving forward on the "double-quick" we reluctantly caught glimpses of the maimed and dying as they hurried and were borne to the rear. I shall not attempt to describe the emotions I experienced as I beheld these scenes and heard again the fearful noise of battle. I can only say that such proximity to the "King of Terrors"[43] in his awful work of destruction is enough to draw deep, hard lines upon the features of the most youthful and harden the most sensitive into utter callousness and disregard of death. But I am digressing.

In the face of the shrieking shell and hissing shot we advanced until a position was gained that arrested the tide of success on the part of the foe. The roar of battle died away, but 'twas only a lull in the tempest. A number of rebel prisoners were here captured. They exhibited the utmost nonchalance, calmly smoking their pipes and apparently unconcerned and careless. All was now quiet: The fight had not lasted an hour, but was the precursor of the impending conflict that was to rage unchecked until the soil should drink the blood of thousands. The evening twilight was deepening into darker shades and the air was calm but marred by clouds of sulphurous smoke and dust. This silence, was, however, of brief continuance; for again, far to the left, the hoarse rattle of musketry, loud and deep, smote upon the startled ear. In a few moments our division was ordered into line, and "forward" rang out in loud and clear notes from rank to rank. How simultaneously beats the heart when marching forward apparently into the jaws of death. Who can describe it? But this was no time to falter or turn pale. Excitement soon eclipses every other feeling, and even cowards become brave.

We enter the dark forest, break through the burning underbrush while a long, loud cheer bursts from every part of the line. The roll of musketry is deafening, the hurtling minie is doing its bloody work, and many of our boys are falling dead and wounded from their places in the ranks. We hold back the leaden storm of death and continue to advance until the somber curtain of night puts an end to this mimicry of hell—this fearful slaughter of brave

42. Army Corps.

43. A phrase from Job 18:14 referring to personified Death.

men. In the darkness of the gathering night we lay down upon our arms to await a revival of the conflict upon the morrow.

The night was one of comparative quiet, broken only by the stifled groan of the dying, or an occasional rifle shot on the skirmish line. I slept sound, for my physical as well as mental system was wearied. Ere the first grey of dawn was visible we were again in line. How I realized as I stood chilled with cold, amid the dry leaves of that grim old forest, the fearful work before us. I knew that hearts beat there that would soon cease their pulsations forever. It is surely a fearful thing to go into battle with that vague presentiment pervading your very being, that perhaps your lithe and active body may suddenly, violently be banished into the veiled mysterious world beyond the grave. No wonder that the bravest hearts recoil as they contemplate these things during the awful suspense that precedes every battle. But in less time than is required to write these facts, our column again advanced, and as the startled picket's alarm told of the night attack, with wild excited cheers we burst upon the foe, and sweeping over the breastworks soon had possession, but with heavy loss. Our onslaught was so sudden and unexpected that the rebels were surprised, but only yielded after a desperate struggle. The welcome light of the sun was now peering through the pointed [painted?] foliage of the forest. The ground was strewn with the dead, cold and stark, and bloody. We again advanced under a withering fire towards the enemy's second line of works. We finally reached a point where we were ordered to lie down. We did so. While in this position two minie balls grazed my head, occasioning rather unpleasant cogitations. Suddenly the rebels made a furious attack and as the entire line rose to stem the fiery, surging storm, I received a ball through the right elbow while in the act of firing, and at the same moment my left hand comrade sank dead at my side. Dropping my undischarged musket, I turned to leave the field. As I did so our line was faltering under a murderous fire, and the ground was cumbered with the dead and dying. I hurried from the dread scene while a stream of blood spattered from my shattered elbow, dyeing red the wild flowers and grass at every step. I remember distinctly how I passed over the dead of friend and foe, scattered all through that dark wood reeking with blood, and choking hot with fire and smoke; and how I at length reached an ambulance which carried me back to one of the field hospitals where my arm was amputated by Surgeon John Jamison, 86th NY. I remember vividly all this, and more besides than I have space to relate. I might tell of other incidents connected with this fight, but this must suffice.

I now realize that my arm was not given to my country in vain, and though I may never again mingle in mortal conflict with any foe, I am proud in the consciousness that I strove to do my duty in my last battle.

~ ~ ~

ALONZO L. MABBETT

Captain, Co. I, 24th Connecticut Volunteer Infantry

A native of New York, Mabbett enlisted in September 1862.[44] Prior to the war, his Quaker parents were conductors on the underground railroad; an obituary reported that Mabbett "had interesting stories to tell his friends about the times when he as little more than a lad assisted his father in helping fugitive slaves to escape."[45] He served under General Banks in western Louisiana, receiving the wound that ended his military career at Port Hudson. He required two amputation surgeries and was unwell for two years as a result.[46] A formerly enslaved man named Lafayette Hoag cared for the wounded Mabbett and accompanied him home.[47] Mabbett's varied career included stints as county clerk, clerk of the superior court, superintendent of schools, and manager of an oil refinery's shipping department, working at the last for twenty-five years; he was also a member of the GAR.[48] He and his first wife, Cora, had three children, none of whom survived to adulthood, and one adopted child.[49] She died in 1897, and Mabbett remarried in 1900, dying seventeen years later.[50] His submission won a second-class-penmanship prize of twenty-five dollars.[51]

44. Alonzo L. Mabbett, Contest Entry, 1st ser., no. 176, Bourne Papers (punctuation edited).

45. Rod Leith, "Civil War Friendship Broke Barriers Here," *South Bergenite* (Rutherford, NJ), Feb. 16, 2012, A9; "Death Takes Alonzo Mabbett, a Veteran," *Rochester (NY) Democrat and Chronicle*, Feb. 15, 1917, 16.

46. *Medical and Surgical History of the War of the Rebellion*, 2(2):765.

47. Rod Leith, "History Chest: Rutherford's Part in Post–Civil War America," *South Bergenite* (Rutherford, NJ), Feb. 2, 2017, E2.

48. "O.T. Stacy Will Admitted," *Rochester (NY) Democrat and Chronicle*, Mar. 23, 1917, 19; 1880 U.S. Census, Monroe Co., NY, pop. sched., Rochester, p. 100C, dwelling 180, family 210, Alonzo L. Mabbett, NARA RG 29, T9, roll 862; 1910 U.S. Census, Monroe Co., NY, pop. sched., Rochester, p. 2B, dwelling 32, family 42, Alonzo L. Mabbett, ibid., T624, roll 989; "Death Takes Alonzo Mabbett," 16.

49. I am indebted to Mabbett's great-grandson, Arthur Mabbett, for this information.

50. "An Active Woman," *Rochester (NY) Democrat and Chronicle*, Jan. 4, 1897, 10; 1900 U.S. Census, Monroe Co., NY, pop. sched., Rochester, p. 3, dwelling 41, family 50, Alonzo L. Mabbett, NARA RG 29, T623, roll 1073; "Died," *Rochester (NY) Democrat and Chronicle*, Feb. 16, 1917, 19.

51. Exhibition of Left-Hand Penmanship, Bourne Papers.

Alonzo L. Mabbett.
Courtesy Arthur Mabbett.

December 29, 1865
An Incident at the Siege of Port Hudson

It was after that final terrific assault of the 14th of June 1863,—made simultaneously at every point along the vast semicircle of works which constituted that almost invulnerable Fortress, whose adamantine wall of fire we had, from dawn till past midday, with desperate charges, repeatedly yet vainly endeavored to scale. Before each struggling Division or Storming column, when evening came, the ground for hundreds of yards around threw back unchanged the hue of Heaven, from the blue robed corpses of the martyred heroes, where from sheer exhaustion the battle rested—each foeman, with sullen jealousy guarding the field.

Since the hard fought battle of the 27th of May there had been no combined attack of our forces, or general engagement; the period having been mostly occupied in getting heavy siege pieces and land mortars into position, after which our Batteries, and the Navy,—whose mortar fleet was slowly but regularly belching forth its terrible messengers of destruction,—would for days at a time pour an incessant shower of shell upon their fated works, which must certainly have annihilated almost every living creature within them, had it not been for their numerous bomb-proofs.

The inhuman foe had during the day not only fired upon our Ambulance Corps, and in every instance prevented any assistance reaching our wounded, but in many cases they had wantonly fired upon the poor fellows themselves; deliberately shooting any who should attempt even to change their position to one of more comfort; and thus many a noble fellow whose wound would not have proved mortal, or perhaps very serious, was brutally murdered by those dastardly fiends, who, safely covered, were coolly firing through their sand-bag embrasures. During the night our fatigue parties were continually fired upon while attempting to remove the wounded, the friendly darkness alone enabling us to accomplish the rescue of any.

Many, very many were not reached; and upon the following morning we could see, scattered among the dead bodies of their comrades, quite a number whom death had not yet relieved.

From the position held by our regiment, where we had partially entrenched ourselves—within 40 or 50 yards of the rebel embankment—we could easily overlook most of the ground, and though we could see many who still showed signs of life, for some cause we became more deeply interested in the fate of one who lay out upon an open plain, at the left, about 40 yards from and in full view of the enemy's works. With his handkerchief or cap he tried to fan himself and draw away the flies, or to shield his upturned face from the burning rays of the sun. We watched every movement, guessed the extent of his injuries, and speculated upon his chances of holding out till an armistice for the burial of the dead should relieve him; when sympathy overcame discretion, I resolved at least to attempt to render him assistance.

Taking one of my most trusty men who volunteered to accompany me, and providing a canteen of water and bottle of whiskey, we commenced our perilous undertaking. Going back into a slight ravine, we followed it down towards the open plain; cautiously creeping by some of the exposed places and running quickly by others, we met a soldier upon the same errand as ourselves. He had been down still farther, and finding it impossible to render any assistance to the wounded man, had turned back, but upon our decision to at least make an attempt, he volunteered to accompany us.

We pressed forward until we reached the last sheltered position, and were directly opposite the poor fellow. In order to reconnoiter, my companion laid down and slowly worked himself out close to the ground, and succeeded in getting six or eight yards before attracting attention: but then a shot was fired, plowing into the ground close by his head; then another, passing over his back and striking the ground just beyond.

Deeming the undertaking too hazardous, I called for him to return, which he quickly did, under fire so rapid as almost to cover him with dust. Thinking we must return without accomplishing our object, I called to the wounded man, and getting his attention told him to try and keep up courage until night, when we would take him from the field. "O, for God's sake," he replied, "get me some water!" I told him that we had attempted to, but had been driven back; that we could not help him then, but would come to his rescue at night.

Still he cried to us most beseechingly for water; "Just one drop of water!" I told him to roll over towards us, which he attempted, but uttered a painful groan and fell back.

He said he belonged to the 114th New York, and was wounded, "here," placing his hand upon his chest. His piteous pleadings for us not to leave him longer without water were too heart-rending for endurance, and hastily laying off my coat, hat, and accoutrements, I had thrown myself upon the ground, resolved to get as near as possible and throw him the canteen; but ere I could proceed, the soldier who had joined us pulled me back, insisting that if any one made the attempt, it must be he, for being smaller than I, he would not be as easily seen. Placing the canteen around his neck and giving him the bottle of whiskey, I yielded to his wish; first telling him to leave his cap, as it would more readily expose his movements; he hesitated, saying if he was wounded he should need it to shield his face. I assured him that if wounded we would in some way rescue him, and giving me his cap he began slowly and cautiously to crawl towards the wounded man. We watched his progress with breathless anxiety; he had accomplished two thirds of the distance safely; not a shot had been fired and we were just congratulating ourselves that he was certainly escaping the notice of the enemy, when a voice from their works called out: "Halloo there!" Our man hugged the ground in silence. "Halloo there, I say!" Again no answer, but a closer hugging of the ground. "Halloo there! answer, or we'll shoot you!" This time the soldier turned his head slightly, and observing the half dozen guns surely aimed at him, thought it useless longer to attempt concealment, and raising his head, feebly answered: "What?" "Are you wounded?" shouted the rebel; "Yes," was his reply (which was doubtless true, of *the state of his feelings*). "Well, what are you trying to do?" "Getting some water to a wounded comrade," answered our man; "Get up then and give it to him, and *then come in here*." The soldier rose up, limped along to the wounded man, raised him to a sitting posture, held the canteen to his lips, and then the whiskey, which seemed greatly to revive him; the rebels, meanwhile, graciously waiting for him thus to minister to the poor fellow's wants. "There, now come in here!"

was then shouted; he hesitated; "Come in here, I say, or we'll put a dozen bullets through you!" The noble fellow raised his eyes imploringly to us, but we were powerless to help him. Again they shouted; he cast a quick glance over the space between us, as if carefully measuring the length of the fearful gauntlet, and then looked towards the rebel embankment, where every embrasure for hundreds of yards was bristling with its deadly aimed rifle; as he looked again towards me, I shook my head sadly, and waved my hand to tell him that he must give himself up; 'twas his only hope of life.

Slowly he turned, and walking up to their works, surrendered himself;—as noble and brave a sacrifice as was ever offered in behalf of the life of a fellow man.

During the following night we made every attempt to reach the wounded soldier, but were driven back by repeated volleys of musketry, fired from the immediate vicinity of where he lay. As the rebels could easily hear my promise to rescue him at night, they evidently had thrown out a force in the darkness to guard the field.

When morning came, his still form told us that death had finally done what we had failed to do,—come to his relief. A few hours later, and I was wounded by a sharp-shooter, resulting in the loss of my right arm, and in long weary months of fearful sickness, during which time I left the Department, and then the service,—never learning the fate of the noble fellow who was taken prisoner. I only heard that he was a Corporal in Company B of the 12th Maine Volunteers.

~~~

EDWARD HAYES

Lieutenant Colonel, 29th Ohio Volunteer Infantry

A distant relative of President Rutherford B. Hayes, Edward Hayes was born in Ohio in 1829; he married in 1856 and had three children.[52] A farmer, he enlisted in August 1861 as a captain, spent four months as a prisoner of war, was promoted to major after Chancellorsville, fought at Gettysburg, was promoted to lieutenant colonel, fought at Lookout Mountain, and then participated in the Atlanta Campaign. After the war, he was a county treasurer and govern-

52. Edward Hayes, Contest Entry, 1st ser., no. 220, Bourne Papers; Carpenter, *Genealogical History of the Rehoboth Branch of the Carpenter Family in America*, 842.
~~~

ment clerk, working for the postal service for twenty years.[53] Hayes died suddenly in 1899 while attending the 29th Ohio's reunion.[54] In a letter to Bourne acknowledging a twenty-five-dollar prize for literary merit, he expressed his belief that "there is really no reason why the human race should not use the left hand equally well with the right" and his surprise that his sketch, which was "nothing extra," should win recognition; the general quality of the submissions, he concluded, "must be full average."

December 29, 1865

In the first action of the campaign at Dug Gap, Georgia,[55] I was very severely wounded in the right shoulder, and compelled to submit to a resection[56] of the whole of the shoulder joint, together with portions of the humerus and scapula. I am not and never shall again be able to write with my right hand. . . .

My wound was nearly a year in getting well, and as I have never since been able to ride I was honorably discharged. In the article accompanying this letter, I have not given names from a wish to avoid undue publicity.

MY LAST BATTLE

I do not propose in the following sketch to relate any dashing actions done on the "perilous edge of battle"[57] or to bore the readers of the "Soldiers Friend" with strategy; but only to give, as simply as may be, my own personal experience in the last action in which I had the honor to fight for the Union.

On the second day of May 1864 I left Bridgeport, Alabama, as Second in command in a regiment which in itself was second to no other in the service. . . . Sherman had spoken and one hundred thousand men had moved as one man.

The 8th of May found this army in front of Rocky-face Ridge with the

53. 1870 U.S. Census, Trumbull Co., OH, pop. sched., Hartford, p. 151B (stamped), dwelling 29, family 29, Edward Hayes, NARA RG 29, M593, roll 1271; 1880 U.S. Census, Trumbull Co., OH, pop. sched., Hartford, p. 140B (stamped), family 149, Edward Hayes, ibid., T9, roll 1070; "Col. Hayes' Funeral," *Akron (OH) Daily Democrat*, Aug. 22, 1899, 2.

54. "Col. Hayes Dies," *Chillicothe (OH) Gazette*, Aug. 18, 1899, 1.

55. The fighting there occurred on May 8, 1864, as Sherman began moving his forces south.

56. A surgical removal or excision of tissue or bone.

57. John Milton, *Paradise Lost*, bk. 1, line 275.

enemy confronting it at every pass. The ridge, perhaps 20 miles long and from eight to twelve hundred feet high, stood wall-like, a granite fact, the key to the heart of Georgia.

We could not get around and therefore *must* get over it; a little after noon on the 8th our division (the 2nd of the 20th corps) debouched from a wooded ravine, upon gently rolling fields, sloping away to a small creek from which similar ground stretched away to the base of the ridge, perhaps half a mile distant. We were in front of the Dug-Gap crossing and the enemy were supposed to be in force. Our few preparations were soon made. Two batteries went into position on the best ground they could get, but it needed no practiced eye to see that with the enemy one thousand feet above our guns they could be of very little use to us.

Our brigade deployed and while the next one was forming I with the aid of a good glass took a look at the position. The sides of the ridge were seamed and scarred with fissures and ravines, but it looked as innocent of human occupation as if the creation of the world had only been finished that morning. The field officers dismounted and the command preceded by a thin line of skirmishers swept down to the creek which had been rapidly bridged in half a dozen places, crossed the rolling ground beyond it and began to climb the ridge.

The work was so severe that frequent halts were necessary. Our regiment had the extreme left of our line, and before we were half way out, a few shattering shots far away to our right, followed by a volley, told that the enemy had succeeded in drawing the fire of that part of our line. I felt somewhat nervous, for we had in our regiment one hundred recruits who had never been under fire, but I might have spared myself the trouble for men never behaved better.

As we advanced, we gained ground to the left by direction of the general commanding and the skirmish line was too short to cover us. Twenty minutes more of climbing and the enemy opened fire with a few dropping shots intended to draw our fire. Some of the recruits brought their pieces to "ready," but a word from their officers checked them and we still pushed upward and in five minutes more a gleam of fire ran along the crest of the ridge and the minies came slashing through the brush all about us. We had drawn the enemy's fire and although it had cost us something it "counted us one for gain [game?]." There, and not 'till there did our Colonel order the fire returned which was promptly done, by division, and hardly checked our advance. A few moments more and we could fairly see the nature of the position we were trying to storm.

The ridge was capped by a palisade of perpendicular rock from ten to thirty feet high with only two or three breaks in its fortress-like line. The thing looked hopeless and our men, taking in the situation at a glance, instantly availed themselves of such cover as could be had, but still worked forward until we were within forty or fifty yards of the crest. And now began a singular fight. No foolish volley firing, but sharp, close, and for us at least, terribly deadly work.

Our artillery now sent in a few shots, but as the chances of hitting us and the enemy were about equal, soon desisted. It may be asked why we did not withdraw. For several reasons. There was a deep ravine on our right, and as we could not see how the rest of our line were making it, we hoped they might find better ground and possibly carry the position, if we could only keep the enemy in our front so busy as to prevent his doubling on our right. There was another reason. It was our boast that in nearly three years' service we had never "limbered to the rear" without orders.

Our regiment had stood like a rock amid crowds of fugitives at Chancellorsville, had rolled back charge after charge at Gettysburg, and without orders it *could not* go back.

It was equally certain that we could not stay where we were, and we therefore decided to make an attempt to carry the ridge at points where the breaks in the palisade of rock suggested the possibility of doing so. I had just gone to the left to give the order, when a blinding flash before my eyes, a sensation as if an hundred pound rock had struck my right shoulder, followed by a tumble down hill, admonished me that my share in that fight was over.

With no very clear idea of what had happened I attempted to get up; finding that my right arm would not respond, I took a look in that direction and seeing a hole in my coat between the strap and the collar, began to think I was hit. Then, feeling myself bleeding I passed my hand inside my vest and drew out a handful of blood to see the color, and remember saying to myself that it was venous blood.

Two men stepped out to pick me up, but just as they raised me from the ground a dozen balls whistled by and one of the men pitched headlong down the hill. I had afterwards the pleasure of knowing that he was not killed, although very severely wounded. Of the next ten minutes I have no distinct recollection, but afterwards learned that I passed along to the center of the regiment, reported to the Colonel that I was hit, and requested him to send another officer to the left.

I only mention this to show the value of discipline. Under certain circumstances it is a very good thing for a soldier to be a machine. Getting a little out of range, our assistant surgeon adjusted a temporary bandage for me, and then as a stretcher could not be used on such steep ground, I began to work my way down the mountain as best I could. Ah me, but it was weary work that mile and a half, but I reached the field hospital at last, and was at once shocked and astonished at the crowd of wounded I found there. Those at the foot of the mountain could hardly understand where all the wounded came from. The number seemed so out of all proportion to the firing.

My turn came at last and I awoke from the chloroform sleep to find that I was a cripple for life and that my military career was ended. Of the after horrors of the ambulance ride to Ringold,[58] and the trip by rail to Nashville, I have no disposition to speak. I am writing for soldiers and the bare mention is enough.

Before closing I ought to say a word for the regiment. It did not carry the ridge, for the Colonel and Adjutant were both hit severely ten minutes after I was wounded, but it got a position that enabled our men to seriously annoy the enemy and keep him busy. Our men maintained the fight until dark, and then were withdrawn carrying with them their wounded.

One third of our number had fallen but when the roll was called (the regiment being halted for that purpose as soon as it was out of range) every man, not killed or wounded, was there to answer to his name. There were no skulkers. Anyone who has been in rear of a battle and witnessed the crowds of this class which, on one pretext or another manage to get to the rear, will appreciate this fact.

Although the fight was not a victory, it was not barren of results, for our attack was so persistent as to convince the enemy that Sherman's whole right wing was there, and they accordingly withdrew from Snake-Creek Gap (ten miles to our right) leaving it open for Gen. McPherson[59] whose Corps poured through it, and by the next morning was thundering on their flank, and the key of central Georgia was won.

Far away to our left at Rocky-face crossing our troops (the 4th corps) either better handled or encountering less opposition, carried the pass.

Taken altogether the battle of Dug Gap is not likely to live in song or story, although a harder fight than many more noted engagements. Neither

58. A town in Catoosa County, Georgia, on the Western & Atlantic Railroad.

59. Major General James B. McPherson (1828–64), commander of the Army of the Tennessee.

did it ever figure very largely in reports for no general liked to father the loss caused by shoving troops against such a position. Particularly as the same results could have been attained with far less loss of life.

~~~

JOSIAH QUINCY CROSBY

Sergeant, Co. G, 13th Massachusetts Volunteer Infantry

Born in New Hampshire, Crosby was a shoemaker before he enlisted at Stoneham, Massachusetts, in April 1861.[60] He remained in Washington, D.C., following the war, working as a clerk for the Treasury Department for forty-three years.[61] A charter member of GAR Burnside Post No. 8, he married in 1871 and had one son.[62] When he died in 1908 at age seventy-eight, an obituary noted that he was "highly esteemed by his fellow-clerks, and was regarded as a man of pronounced integrity."[63] Crosby competed in both contests, submitting nearly identical pieces, though the handwriting in his first was noticeably more back slanted. His second submission won the fifty-dollar Hancock Premium. The general wrote to Crosby, "May the honorable badge you wear—an Empty Sleeve—be the passport to an honorable triumph in the future."

***First Submission:* December 26, 1865**
***Second Submission:* June 29, 1867**

Crosby's regiment left Boston in July 1861 and arrived in Maryland in August. In March 1862, they crossed the Potomac and entered Virginia. "First under fire, though not engaged" at Cedar Mountain, they participated in the Second Battle of Bull Run.

60. Josiah Q. Crosby, Contest Entries, 1st ser., no. 222, and 2nd ser., 95, Bourne Papers; *Massachusetts Soldiers, Sailors, and Marines in the Civil* War, 2:108.

61. "Funeral of Mr. Crosby," *Washington Post,* Feb. 12, 1908, 14; "Funeral of Josiah Q. Crosby," ibid., Feb. 13, 1908, 14.

62. "Funeral of Mr. Crosby," 14; Massachusetts Marriage Records, 1840–1915, Josiah Q. Crosby, New England Historic Genealogical Society; "Josiah Q. Crosby," *Washington Evening Star,* Feb. 12, 1908, 15.

63. "Josiah Q. Crosby," 15.
~~~

We were held in reserve during the early part of the day, frequently changing position in the rear of our line of battle, till about 3 o'clock p.m. when the enemy massed their force and made a furious attack upon the left. We were immediately ordered to reinforce that point, and we advanced under cover of a ridge along which our line of battle extended, making a desperate effort to hold its position against a vastly superior force. We had just deployed in line at the foot of the ridge, when the line in front, now terribly thinned and exposed to a murderous fire—wavered, then broke, and a large number of the men rushed down headlong through our ranks. This caused some disorder in our line. We advanced, however, up the slope, but had scarcely reached the position when the enemy swung a brigade around on our left, and poured in a galling fire on our flank. Just then a battery opened on us from some heights beyond in the same direction, thus enfilading[64] our line with both artillery and infantry. It was impossible to withstand such an assault, and we were forced to retire with severe loss. We were next under fire at Chantilly,[65] also in the second line of battle at South Mountain. At Antietam we were posted on the right, under Genl. Hooker. We were exposed to a severe shelling on moving into position the night before the battle, and advanced on the enemy's lines the next morning at daylight. We found them strongly intrenched and they received us with a volley when we had arrived within short range. We were hotly engaged for about two hours when we were withdrawn and sent to support batteries.

Our Brigade lost more than half its number, and our company which went in with thirty men had twenty-two killed and wounded. I was one of the eight that came out uninjured. . . . We were recruited and next engaged at the battle of Fredericksburg on Dec. 13th. We were attached to [Brigadier General John] Gibbon's Division, Reynold's [*sic*] Corps (1st) and Franklin's Grand Division, which formed the left wing of the Army. This battle was fought under great disadvantages. The enemy occupied a very formidable position which they had had time to fortify and render nearly impregnable to any assault on their front. The attack was made, however, and with great vigor and determination, but our men were terribly slaughtered and were

64. Firing from a position on the opponent's flank (end) to rake the enemy line lengthwise.

65. A battle occurring in Fairfax County, Virginia, September 1, 1862, as Union forces retreated to Washington.

repulsed at every point. Our Brigade was badly cut up, but our Regiment, being engaged as skirmishers, suffered less severely. . . .

Crosby and the 13th Massachusetts remained in camp for the winter. In May 1863, they marched to Chancellorsville.

After a toilsome march we crossed the river about sun-down at United States Ford, and were preparing to bivouac for the night near the river, when we were ordered to fall in and proceed to the front. We soon learned that during the engagement of the afternoon the enemy had made a vigorous assault upon the right wing and had turned it. We moved forward, and, after some delay, our Corps was posted on the right: the whole length of our line extending into a wood and along a narrow road.

It was after midnight when our lines were formed: skirmishers were then thrown out, and we were busily engaged during the remainder of the night in entrenching and preparing for the expected attack in the morning. The attack, however, was not made upon the right, but near the center, on that part of the line formed by the 2nd and 3rd Corps. It began at daylight. The enemy gave a hideous yell and charged furiously upon a point of our lines at some distance to our left. Our position did not afford us a view of the battle but the firing was very heavy and rapid. It continued for about three hours, and a brisk cannonade was kept up at intervals during the day. This was on Sunday May 3rd. . . .

After Chancellorsville, Lee mounted his second invasion of the North, moving into Pennsylvania. Union forces pursued and soon faced the Confederates. Crosby and his regiment arrived at Gettysburg on July 1.

While on the way the sound of rapid artillery firing convinced us that we had warm work to encounter. When within a short distance of the town we left the main road, and filed off to the left toward Seminary Ridge[66] and halted near the Seminary. We then learned with great sorrow that Genl. Reynolds, our Corps commander, had been killed.

Our 1st Division which had preceded us was hotly engaged on another

66. Ridge just west of Gettysburg, home to a Lutheran seminary.

ridge further from the town, and running nearly parallel to the one we were on. It was soon found that they were getting outflanked, and our Division was moved forward and formed on their right, with our Brigade on the extreme right which was posted perpendicular to the main line and extending towards the 11th Corps, but leaving an interval of several hundred yards between the two Corps. We had scarcely formed when the enemy commenced the attack.

They had advanced their lines to within a hundred yards, and for a short time the carnage was terrible on both sides at this short range. We finally charged and captured a number of prisoners, then changed front forward to the left to meet another attack from that direction. We were engaged in receiving and repelling the attacks of the enemy, frequently changing position under a galling fire, from noon till about 4 o'clock when we were ordered to withdraw. This we did gradually and in a good order, being closely pressed, but in attempting to pass through the town we found the main street blocked up with the 11th Corps which was passing at the same time; this caused us a heavy loss in prisoners.

We finally got into position (or what remained of us) on the high ground a short distance west of the Cemetery. The loss in our Division of killed, wounded and prisoners, amounted to nearly three fourths. . . . We fought against great odds. We had some advantage in position, but there were no reserves to reinforce us while the enemy which greatly outflanked us was constantly deploying fresh troops. The other Corps were coming up during the night, and at daylight our Army had nearly all arrived. Our Division lost slightly in the battles of the two succeeding days: we were principally engaged in supporting batteries, and in changing position at double quick from right to left in order to reinforce threatened points. When it was found that the enemy had retreated we followed up and prepared for battle near Hagerstown, but no attack was made. . . .

On the 4th of May [1864] we again crossed the Rapidan at Germanna Ford and entered the Wilderness. The battle began about noon next day and continued till after dark. We were engaged on the right and met with considerable loss. The fight was resumed early in the morning, and, during the greater part of the day, there was a continual roar of musketry, the dense wood rendering artillery service nearly impracticable. We were held in reserve, but towards dark formed on the line near the left, where we intrenched ourselves and remained the next day, all being quiet in our vicinity. When the enemy fell back our Division was the first of the Infantry to follow them. After marching all night towards Spotsylvania, early in the morning we heard brisk skirmishing ahead, and we knew our Cavalry which had preceded us were engaged. We soon deployed, advanced in line and encountered the enemy in a wood. They fell back after a sharp fight, but the trees and brushwood prevented our pressing them very closely or advancing in any kind of order. As soon as our lines could be closed up we again advanced, and, after clearing the wood found them drawn up in the open field with a battery directly in our front. We were ordered to charge this battery and were moving forward at double quick to execute the command when they opened on us with grape and canister.

I was struck with a grape-shot which shattered my right arm above the elbow and nearly tore it off. This was on Sunday May 8th and within a few weeks of the expiration of my term of service. My arm was amputated on the field, and I was conveyed to Finley Hospital, Washington, and was finally discharged with my Regiment at Boston on August 1st, '64.

~~~

ULYSSES S. EATON

Private, 19th Battery, Indiana Volunteer Light Artillery

Eaton was born in Indiana in 1842 and was a farmer prior to enlisting.[67] A front-page article published one year before his death began with a description of the then eighty-eight-year-old: "'U.S.' Eaton, slowly plodding about the streets of Cambridge City, with an empty sleeve dangling at his right side, and a cane lending support to his somewhat hesitating step, is one of the city's most familiar figures."[68] According to the article, the night before he lost his arm, Eaton "wondered if he might be able to write his name with his left hand." The profile reported that his lack of a right arm did not prevent him from splitting wood for railroad ties or punishing two men who called him "One-Arm Lass." He married twice and was father to

67. Ulysses S. Eaton, Contest Entry, 1st ser., no. 262, Bourne Papers (periods added); "Cambridge Man Is Last Survivor of Famous 19th Ind. Volunteers," *Richmond (IN) Palladium-Item,* Dec. 20, 1930, 11.

68. "Cambridge Man Is Last Survivor of Famous 19th Ind. Volunteers," 11.
~~~

nine children, grandfather to thirty-three, and, before his death, great-grandfather to fifteen.[69] In addition to farming, Eaton also "operated both baking and grocery stores."[70] When he died in 1931, he was the last surviving member of Indiana's 19th Battery.[71]

February 3, 1866

Dear sir excuse my writing for I am trying to farm and have been gitting out railroad ties this winter.

On the 3 day of August 1862 I was enrolled or volunteered to serv as private in the 19th Battery of Indiana volunteers fore the tirm of three years or during the war.

On the 11th day of August I bid adieu to all my friends and Relatives at Camebridge City Indiana and with a sorrowfull but Patriotic Heart started for the field of Battle to shear with my felows soldiers the fortunes of war in sustaining the honor of the stars and stripes. We started about two weeks at Indianapolis the Capital of the state from thence we wear moved in hast to Luisville Kentucky to meet the Rebbels under old Brag[g] that was threating that town. We scouted round there near a month and followed Him to Perryville. There we first smelt powder. Mind I tell you we had quite a scrape there the Rebbles charged on us we drove them back they massed there force came on us again throwing a perfect sheet of fire and led. We stood it sir like salamanders till the Infantry fell back and the Rebs was nearly on us. We fell back and brought off all of all our guns but two.

Next morning we got our guns and took through the Battle field after them hardly taken time to eat or sleep we run them over mountins and Hills scurmishing a long till they came to Palahomy.[72] There they made a small stand but we soon started them again and they made for the south. Oh you aught to have seen how the greybacks run.

Then we took a real fox chase after Morgan and this racing through the states of Tenissee and Kentucky. Finally we gave them up and took the train for Nashville rested there some two or three days from thence to Murphres-

69. Ibid.

70. Ibid.

71. Indiana Death Certificates, 1931, Ulysses S. Eaton, Indiana Archives and Records Administration, Indianapolis, roll 11; "Only Cambridge City Civil War Vet Dead," *Indianapolis Star,* Oct. 27, 1931, 4.

72. I am unable to identify this location.

boro into winter quarters. Some sixteen or twenty of us took a couple of our Bull dogs and went a forageing. On our return Morgon got after us and commenced fireing. We fell back to a Hill near Milton Tennessee.[73] There many a brave fellow fell to rise no more. Shells were bursting all around and over my Hedd a canon ball struck a lim and fell close by me an other went through an oak tree about three feet over on the other side of me and thousand of small bullets scremed all around then you ought to have herd our Bull dogs roared. I sprang to one of them and sighted to the smoke of ther guns which seemed to silence them at once. The most of the Rebs took to there heels but over three hundred wear left behind in dead wounded an prisoners. Next morning we returned to camp with corn, Potato and chickens without further molestation. You had beter think we feasted then.

Next we met the Enemy at Hoovers gap[74] and tronced them soundly in mud and water nearly knee deep. I never Heard such Canonnading roar with peal after peal that shuck the earth far and wide. We chased to the Tennessee River. We crossed the River and got in the rear of Chickamauga. There is whare Chickamauga opened on us. On the 19th of September 1863 this memoberable Battle commenced. Our Battery was ordered to the front and we took our position on a hill prepared and waited for the enemy. They came on to us in about an hour and charged upon our Battery. A perfect host of them. The balls sang zip zip in every direction. We stood our ground as long as we could then we limbered up to start out our ammuniton being spent. I mounted the wheel horse[75] and called to lead driver to mount. Others told him to mount but still he failed. By this time the Rebbels wear close enough to call to us to halt but no halt. A fellow mounted the lead hors[e] and a way we went through the woods over trees and logs. We struck an old tree tore it down across the Casin [caisson] with a perfect crash. I thought half the Casin was shot off but the tree broke into [in two] and we made safe our retreat.

We got amunitian and returned to the front again and laid in line of battle all night. Next day at 8 o'clock they appeard on us again. We faught

73. An engagement also known as the Battle of Vaught's Hill, March 20, 1863.

74. Fought on June 24, 1863, it was part of the Tullahoma Campaign in Middle Tennessee.

75. The horse harnessed nearest the wheels of a wagon.

for hours and hours and many wear the widows and orphans made that day.

They charged upon our battery again and again for many a long hour we foght in sight of each other till the support on our left first gave way and we was entirly surounded as in a bull pen. Many of our brave solders and officers fell this day. Some of the officers proposed to surrender but the Brigadiear commander swore he would take them out of that. Our Brigadiear commander King was shot dead while in that pen we tuck him on the ca[is]son and cut our way out and tuck servel of the johnneys with us and when we got to Chattanooga our guns was so disableed there was but one fit for use.

There we lay for [a] month with the enemy all a round us nearly out of provision and but little else to feed our horses but pipe stems. Many of them starved to death they eate each others mane and tales off and the enemy keep shelling us near all the time....

The next Battle we had was on lookout mountain. There we gave them gass again. From thence to Ringgold. Here we comenced fighting from day to day driven the enemy before us. At Tunnel Hill they made a stand and we foght them a fuw hours and again at Buzard Roost[76] but we forsted them on till they came to Resaca gea. There we fought too days hard fighting. In the morning on the 15th of May 1864 while I was a throwing up [an] embankment a Rifle ball struck my right arm above the elbow. I started to the rear a telling the boys it would hafto come off. I walked about twenty five yards and srank down. They put me on a blanket and took me whare the doctor war and he examined it. He bound it up a little and put me in the ambulence and then I went to the field Hospital. My side of my pants was stiff with cloded Blood. We soon got to the Hospital which was not more then a mile then I was taken out and I set down on an table. I told them to save it if they could. He said it must come off.

And after my Right Arm was ampitated I woak up and I cant tell my feeling. I can feel my fingers and Hand. They feel like they was sore but they are not Hear.

I took the chills and fever. I had a long and serius time of it so that my life was dispered of but after several pieces of bones coming out I got well.

~ ~ ~

76. The fighting at Buzzard Roost, in Whitfield County, Georgia, on May 9, 1864, was part of the Battle of Rocky Face Ridge.

WILLIAM FITHIAN MOORE

Corporal, Co. K, 12th New Jersey Volunteer Infantry

Moore, born in 1836, enlisted in Bridgeton, New Jersey, in August 1862.[77] At Spotsylvania Court House, he suffered a gunshot wound that disabled his right arm and hand. Despite his injuries, after his discharge, he continued his prewar work as a tinsmith and married in 1870.[78] Moore died in 1908.[79]

[undated]

After mustering into service, Moore's company headed first to Baltimore and then to Ellicott's Mills, Maryland, along the Patapsco River in Baltimore County.

Our Military Duty now became Active as well as instructive Duty. Such as Picketing, Scouting, Arresting Deserters, etc. Here we remained until two days before the Fredericksburg Battle when we broke Camp again for the Front. After arriving at Washington had our Arms inspected: was found to be so Defective that we were dealt out new Guns. . . .

Marched for Falmouth, VA. Things had the appearance of real war. Constantly passing camps and Hospitals. Here we see for the first the realities of war. The Dead, Dying, and Wounded. Arrived at our camp ground about Dusk. Built fires, cooked Supper, and made ourselves as comfortable as we could for the Night. Next day had a permanent Camp Ground assigned us. Went to Work clearing ground. . . . Remained in this camp doing the usual camp Duties. Lost during the Winter 80 men from Sickness. . . .

The New Jersey soldiers built a pontoon bridge at Chancellorsville and fought Jackson's troops during the subsequent battle. Remaining in camp until June 10, they then headed to Gettysburg, arriving on July 1.

77. William F. Moore, Contest Entry, 2nd ser., no. 83, Bourne Papers (punctuation edited).

78. 1860 U.S. Census, Cumberland Co., NJ, pop. sched., Bridgeton, p. 400 (stamped), dwelling 389, family 389, William Moore, NARA RG 29, M653, roll 687; 1870 U.S. Census, Cumberland Co., NJ, pop. sched., Bridgeton, p. 132A (stamped), dwelling 320, family 364, William Moore, ibid., M593, roll 859; Clara Dare Ettinger, *Genealogy of the Dare Family* (Chicago, 1901), 111.

79. William F. Moore, Pension File, application 887844, certificate 666872, NARA RG 15, T288, roll 334.

Was Ordered up on the Field at daylight of July 2nd connecting on to the Left of the 12th corps. Line extending from the Baltimore Pike to the Base of Cemetery Ridge.[80] Remained so until 10 o'clock when [the] whole Division deployed as skirmishers relieving parts of 11th and 12th Corps. Was Relieved by other troops that night. Took position with our corps (2nd) which we found in line of Battle, Right on base of Cemetery Hill facing Gettysburg. . . .

During the morning of the 3rd charged a Brick Barn, capturing 90 Johns. Setting Fire to the Building, Fell back to our line of Battle in good Order although under a heavy Skirmish Fire, bringing all our Prisoners in safe with a loss of 3 killed and 5 wounded from our Co. Lay still until about 1 o'clock when all at once the Johns opened a tremendous Artillery Fire on us which they kept up without the least Slacking of Fire until about 2 o'clock. The Smoke had hardly cleared away when we see a heavy line of Battle unmask from the woods in the rear of their Skirmish-line. This was followed by two more lines of battle extending as far as the Eyes could see Right and Left. Such Determination I never before see in any Engagement as were here evinced by our men. Such cool Preparations for Battle. It seemed as though every Soldier thought this the Turning Point of the War and So I believed it was and so it has proved to be. On they came but what a Reception. It only lasted about 30 minutes but what Death and Distruction in those few minutes after we repulsed them and then they commenced Sk[ed]addling.

Then came grape and Canister at short range, at which they fell in great numbers. Thousands came into our lines and gave themselves up as Prisoners. We held the key to the Position and it was nothing but Clean-Fighting wot enabled us to do it having no Support of any kind—but in fact the Support of all the Artillery in the Center of the Army.

How Sweetly I slept that night knowing as I did that they have the worst Repulse they could have. July 4th woke up to see the Sun of another 4th alive, but feeling verry sencibly the pangs of hunger having bin without anything to eat all day of the 3rd. Went out from the line of Battle far enough to find a heavy ladened Haversack which I returned to the Co. with sharing its contents with my tent-mates—but hardly had we got to Eating when up to our lines drove Wagon after Wagon loaded with Commisary Stores just the verry things we Wanted, Hungry as we was.

80. This rise was the shank of the "fish-hook" line of the Union defensive position at Gettysburg.

Was employed until 5 o'clock of the 4th of July in helping to clear up the Battle Field. At dark started on the March after the Johns, moving by the Left as far as Two Taverns[81] where we halted for the night. Continued our march until we struck the Potomac to the Left of Williamsport. Here we stayed several days awaiting an attack "but got none."

~ ~ ~

CALEB B. FISHER

Sergeant, Co. A, 143rd Pennsylvania Volunteers

Caleb B. Fisher.
Courtesy William Oland Bourne Papers, Manuscript Division, Library of Congress.

Fisher was born in Wilkes-Barre, Pennsylvania, in 1844.[82] After the war, he lived in Illinois, was a member of the GAR, and worked as a merchant and pension agent.[83] Fisher's winning of the Sherman Premium was a badge of honor for the rest of his life, continually referenced by newspapers. When he visited an old comrade in Scranton, Pennsylvania, in 1901, a local paper announced his arrival and (incorrectly) noted he had competed against 1,300 entrants.[84] In 1914, a Los Angeles newspaper announced that Fisher, a "champion left-handed writer of the United States . . . has come from Peoria, Ill., to Santa Monica to make his home."[85] When he relocated, Fisher brought Sherman's letter, which noted the general was influ-

81. Town five miles southeast of Gettysburg.

82. Caleb B. Fisher, Contest Entry, 2nd ser., no. 111, Bourne Papers; 1860 U.S. Census, Luzerne Co., PA, pop. sched., Wilkes-Barre, p. 960 (stamped), dwelling 95, family 94, Caleb B. Fisher, NARA RG 29, M653, roll 1133.

83. 1870 U.S. Census, Henry Co., IL, pop. sched., Geneseo, p. 486A (stamped), dwelling 666, family 665, Caleb Fisher, NARA RG 29, M593, roll 229; *Illustrated Roster of the Department of Illinois Grand Army of the Republic,* 82; 1910 U.S. Census, Kane Co., IL, pop. sched., Aurora, p. 1A, dwelling 15, family 16, C. B. Fisher, NARA RG 29, T624, roll 296.

84. "Personals," *Scranton (PA) Times-Tribune,* Sept. 7, 1901, 3.

85. "Left-Handed Writer Has Sherman's Letter Naming Him Champ," *Los Angeles Evening Express,* Sept. 2, 1914, 5.

enced in his decision "by the plain and legible nature of [Fisher's] manuscript." The article quoted the letter in full, including the following: "Whilst we have been accustomed to regard the loss of the right arm as almost fatal to a useful and consequently happy life, these samples show how nature substitutes wisely and well our other arm; and I hope and trust that you may enjoy a long life, crowned by the contentment which the sacrifice of the best part of your body to your country's flag and safety is calculated to give." A retired widower by the time he arrived in California, Fisher died in 1931.[86]

June 1867

When the Rebellion broke out, I was too young to enter the Army but joined the home guards, a company recruited for defending my native State, Pennsylvania. On the 6th day of August, 1862, I reenlisted as a private . . . to serve three years.

Fisher's regiment fought at Pollock's Mills (April 29–May 2, 1863) and at Chancellorsville. The unit arrived in Gettysburg on July 1.

Our Regiment doubledquicked the last four miles. Our company was the first on the skirmish line. We made a charge and drove the Rebel skirmish line from behind the fence where they were consealed and took possession with the loss of six brave men.

We were in a position that was difficult to get out of without some loss but were well protected by the fence and high grass; could lie down and load our Rifles, and onley expose ourselves when fireing. After remaining in this position about two hours the Rebel battle line was seene mooving forward through the field and over fences. The Rebel skirmish line was aware that we would soon have to fall back to our line of battle. They then could take the advantage.

Remaining in this position and fireing at the rebel skirmish line until the line of battle was within fireing distance, we started back to join our Regiment. Volley after Volley was poured into our ranks as we fell back.

With the loss of a few brave men among them our Captain and Lieutenant

86. 1920 U.S. Census, Los Angeles Co., CA, pop. sched., Santa Monica, p. 18B, dwelling 440, family 597, Caleb B. Fisher, NARA RG 29, T625, roll 116; California Death Index, 1905–39, Caleb B. Fisher, California Department of Health and Welfare, Sacramento, 2169.

the only Officers of the company, we were safe again with the Regiment but only for a short time. The 1st Army Corps was small. The rebels had four times our number and our only hope was to give them battle. Which we did, and after seven long hours of steady fighting, we fell back stubbornly.

The loss of the rebels on the first of July was two to our one. When the infantry was falling back one of our Batteries kept its position. The officer commanding called for support. I with others remained with the Battery until most of the pieces was taken off the field. Before we could get away we [were] taken prisoners.

I was in the last campaign with General Grant. . . . It was in the charge upon Petersburg June the eighteenth that I lost my right arm. It was amputated above the elbow, the same evening. From that time on I was confined to the Hospital most of the time at Philadelphia PA where I was discharged the 16th day of December 1864.

~ ~ ~

WALLACE MORDECAI MOORE

Private, Co. E, 13th Pennsylvania Reserves / 1st Pennsylvania Rifles ("The Bucktails")
Corporal, Co. E, 190th Pennsylvania Volunteer Infantry

For Moore's soldiering life and a biography, see chapter 2.

April 27, 1868

Seven Days

Soon we were ordered the extreme right, where we dug rifle pits and did picket duty, our pickets being on the bank of the Chickahominy[87] and the Johnnies on the other. When on picket, we could plainly see the rebel capitol, and we felt that the crisis must soon come. In this paper, I can hardly be expected to do more than briefly glance at the events more immediately connected with my own share of the seven days fight before Richmond.

87. Sluggish, swampy river flowing north and east of Richmond through the Peninsula to the James River.

The expected attack was made on the 26th of June. My company (E) was on picket duty at the time, and we retreated to our rifle pits, where we had just time to get nicely ready for them when the Johnnies came down on us, charging across an open field.[88] The particulars of what followed have never been told in print, and I will try to convey a faint idea of what transpired in that part of the field, referring to all the surviving witnesses of the events, for the accuracy of my description. We were, as I have said, in rifle pits, we were also supported by artillery. In front of us was a swamp or marsh—nearly or quite impassable—and across this was a road, over which it was necessary for a hostile force to pass in order to charge us out of our pits. Beyond the swamp with its narrow road, lay the field, over which a large rebel force was charging. When they had charged up in easy range the artillery opened on them with grape and canister, mowing them down in heaps, making long gaps in their ranks, which were instantly closed up, however, on and on they came. On, almost to the swamp. But the swamp looked impassable, and they closed up to cross by the road: then we opened on them with Spencers and Sharps rifles, pouring a steady rain of conical balls into that mass of crowding, hungering, writhing humanity, clogging the road with dead and wounded, and actually cutting them down faster than they could come on. Few lived to reach the center of the crossing—not one got over, so far as I saw.

In vain the officers yelled and used their swords to drive them on to certain death. The officers themselves fell as fast as the smoke allowed us to distinguish them. In vain their cavalry drove their Infantry on to the fatal crossing—that bit of road was a "dead line" over which no rebel passed. The cavalry attempted to cross the marsh, but their horses got mired, and they turned and sought the opposite bank, which few, either horses or men, reached alive. Charge after charge was made with a recklessness that looked like insanity, or drunkenness, but in vain: and night came down on us, murky and lurid, before the attempt was abandoned.

It seems the rebel general had given orders to carry this point at *any cost*, which was the cause of this ill conceived attack. The point was not carried, but they found the "cost" all right. What looked strange to us was the part, that, by deploying their left around the swamp they could have flanked us

88. Moore does not specify his company's exact position, but it was most likely part of the Union defenses along Beaver Dam Creek.

out of the pits with a tenth of the loss, and in a quarter of the time, but a rebel told us that the order had been to carry the pits "by assault." We were only two regiments,—5th infantry and the Bucktails—with a small detachment of Berdan's Sharp Shooters,[89] but I speak within bounds when I say that we killed and wounded more than twice our own number. A long time afterward some of our men were over that battle ground, and the bones of horses and men were bleaching where they fell. When night had fairly closed on us, and the noise of battle had subsided, it was pitiful to hear the chorus of agonized groans from the wounded men who lay at the crossing, in the marsh, and on the field beyond. Ever and anon some poor fellow would sing out, "Yank! come and get me—come and give us some water, D–n it! What['s] the use—fight's all over—come an git us," etc. But we had orders not to leave the pits, and many a wounded man died that night, raving for water with such thirst as man in health has no conception of. The war was getting sufficiently real to satisfy the most rabid. Tired with the battle, we rested in the pits that night, oblivious of the fact that the Army of the Potomac was falling back during the night, and that our own Regiment had gone along with the rest, leaving a part of three companies in the pits, to be captured.

We were partially aroused to these facts by a lively little shelling, with which the rebels saluted our camp on the morning of the 27th just at daylight. We made the best of it and waited, expecting either to be reinforced or ordered to fall back; but neither happened, and this is how Company E came to be captured.

We had waited hour after hour for orders, information, or something to act on, convinced that the army was gone and we were unaccountably left behind, when we saw, far to the right, a constant line of bayonets passing a low spot that flanked the distant road, and we were not slow to infer that the rebels had flanked us and were already in our rear. Sergeant Ludlow was sent to reconnoiter, and immediately reported a brigade of rebels forming in our rear, evidently with the intention of charging; there was no time for talk: crouching low, we double quicked by the left flank along the trenches, which luckily were intersected by a ravine, got out of the pits without being seen, followed the ravine, got out of view of the pits, and came out on the road

89. 1st and 2nd U.S. Sharpshooters, organized by Colonel Hiram Berdan (1824–93).

just as the rebels charged into and over the works with their well known yell. They captured a few old knapsacks and two or three dead bodies, but we had escaped—for the time. . . .

Gettysburg

It really seemed as though the life of the nation trembled in the scale of battle, and I never saw more willingness to face danger and death than was exhibited by all ranks. We went into battle about 2 p.m. of the 2nd, and were kept in until the 4th without being relieved. We lost our brave Colonel (C.F. Taylor) on the first day. He was shot through the heart while cheering on his men. We were in a narrow piece of woods, and we made lively work of it until dark, when, the firing having ceased, we fell back a few rods. Colonel Taylor being killed, and the Lieut. Col. Niles severely wounded, the command devolved on Maj. Hartshorn, as brave a little fellow as ever drew a sword: He formed the Regiment in line a little after dark, and called for twenty volunteers, who were soon forthcoming. I was one of the number. An officer led us (the volunteers) to the place we had just left in the wood, and posted us as pickets. . . . I was not wounded in this battle, though I had my coat collar cut in halves at the back of my neck by a musket ball. . . .

4.

WOUNDING, AMPUTATION, AND RECOVERY

Though some contestants only briefly mention the moments that made them one-armed men, many focus on the sensations of being wounded, the particulars of their surgery, and the process of their recovery. They describe the means of wounding—shot, Minié, shell—and the location at which wounding or amputation occurred—upper third, elbow, shoulder. Some clarify whether surgeons left a flap of skin to cover the stump or instead used the circular method, leaving the stump uncovered.[1] Contestants foreground the fundamentally life-altering significance of wounding and amputation—the sudden transition from being in the prime of life to dealing with suppurating wounds, ragged stumps, and phantom pains. In providing granular details of their wounding, amputation, and convalescence, the veterans underscore the bodily aspects and physical costs of military service. Despite scholarly arguments that Civil War writers covered over unwieldy or fragmented bodies in the interest of reconciliation and recovery, many left-armed veterans refused to conceal

1. See Chisolm, *Manual of Military Surgery*, 374–76.

their injuries or ignore the horrors of going under the knife.[2] Veterans describe consenting to (or, in a few instances, declining) surgery and remember the soporific influences of chloroform and the disorientation attendant upon awaking to find oneself minus a limb. Some number their wounds and others report on maggots and gangrene, refusing to suffer in silence or sanitize their experiences.

As the full contestant list below indicates, not all amputations occurred immediately after wounding, and some contestants underwent multiple surgeries. Surgeons in tents at the rear of the action or in division hospitals operated with and without anesthetic, and a number of them receive high praise from contestants.[3] Men who mention "resections" (excisions) retained their limbs but lost portions of bone and tissue. Others lost all use of their arm, even though it remained intact. Some contestants suffered from their wounds for years, dying decades later as a result. As historian Sarah Handley-Cousins notes, "amputation became the most powerful symbol of the conflict's destructive power" but accounted for "a small fraction of Civil War wounds."[4] Nevertheless, the contestants were not alone in their predicament. Abellino S. Burt sent his entry "by request of [his] friends . . . being the only left-handed man in town."[5] He explained, "in my little town there are four beside myself with one arm gone, but more fortunate than myself have lost their left, instead of right arm." Seth Sutherland mentioned "three or four other men in this county minus the right arm."[6] As men whose bodies were fundamentally changed by the war, the veterans included here narrate their trauma and connect their bodily sacrifice to the preservation of the Union. Charles W. Dodge claims that the average civilian was "less inclined to raise the blazing cross of honor, which he has generously granted—to gaze upon the wound that won it." Dodge and others like him uncover what lies beneath the empty sleeve, baring to the public their wounds and the means by which they received them.

2. See Long, *Rehabilitating Bodies*, 7.

3. For Civil War medicine and hospitals, see Margaret Humphreys, *Marrow of Tragedy: The Health Crisis of the American Civil War* (Baltimore: Johns Hopkins University Press, 2013); and Shauna Devine, *Learning for the Wounded: The Civil War and the Rise of American Medical Science* (Chapel Hill: University of North Carolina Press, 2014).

4. Handley-Cousins, *Bodies in Blue*, 2.

5. Abellino S. Burt, Contest Entry, 1st ser., no. 63, William Oland Bourne Papers.

6. Seth Sutherland, Contest Entry, 1st ser., no. 1, Bourne Papers.

ROBERT JAMES DICKINSON

Private, Co. B, 127th Illinois Volunteer Infantry

A married carpenter prior to the war, Dickinson enlisted in August 1862.[7] He continued as a carpenter after the war, also teaching and serving as county treasurer from 1865 to 1872 before being removed from office as a "defaulter."[8] In 1880, he put his penmanship to good use as a census enumerator.[9] By 1900, only three of his eight children were still living; he himself died sixteen years later at the age of eighty.[10] Dickinson sent two manuscripts to the first competition, the second one devoted to describing his time in hospitals and defending them from criticism.

September 11, 1865

On the 22nd at 10 AM another charge was ordered.[11] We were standing in line (our Brigade) the troops on our right was moveing, and the "Balls" flying thick. Our "Colonel" gave the order "shoulder arms," and at that minute, whiz went a ball through my right-hand. The next minute "forward march" and the Regt moves off and I retire to safer quarters, have my hand bandaged up and then go to the "Hospital" where it was properly dressed. The sights I saw that day I hope never to see again. Men mangled and torn in evry concievable shape. Oh! the horrors of war. The next day I with others was sent across the county to the "Yazoo" River,[12] thence to the floating "Hospital" *Nashville* laying in "Pawpaw Shoot,"[13] from there to Memphis, Tennessee, where I remained one month. Then to St. Louis, MO, my hand steadily getting worse, though the "Surgeons" all tell me it will get well, until I got to St. Louis. The Surgeon in

7. Robert J. Dickinson, Contest Entry, 1st ser., no. 25, Bourne Papers (punctuation edited); 1860 U.S. Census, Stark Co., IL, pop. sched., Goshen, p. 815, dwelling 311, family 311, Robert J. Dickinson, NARA RG 29, M653, roll 229; *Report of the Adjutant General of the State of Illinois,* 6:496.

8. Hall, *History of Stark County, Illinois,* 313; 1880 U.S. Census, Stark Co., IL, pop. sched., Toulon, p. 426B (stamped), dwelling 133, family 135, R. J. Dickinson, NARA RG 29, T9, roll 252; "Illinois," *Chicago Tribune,* Feb. 16, 1872, 2.

9. 1880 U.S. Census, Stark Co., IL, pop. sched., Toulon, p. 426B.

10. 1900 U.S. Census, Stark Co., IL, pop. sched., Toulon, p. 7, dwelling 152, family 154, Robert J. Dickinson, NARA RG 29, T623, roll 345; Robert J. Dickinson, Pension File, application 1090389, certificate 826389, NARA RG 15, T288, roll 122.

11. This was on May 22, 1863, at Vicksburg.

12. Navigable river in Mississippi that enters the Mississippi River just north of Vicksburg.

13. Pawpaw Chute near the Yazoo River, north of Vicksburg.

charge says, "Sir, your hand will have to come off," and on the 29th of July, 1863, my right arm was amputated midway, between the wrist and elbow joints. After the amputation, it healed so rapidly, that on the 24th of September following I was discharged, at St. Louis, MO, and arrived home on the 27th "crippled for life."

December 22, 1865
About Hospitals

Ever since the breaking out of the "Rebelion," both before and since I entered the service, I have heard a great deal of fault-finding with "Government Hospitals," and have always thought that to a great extent it was uncalled for, and not knowing of a better subject have decided to say a few words in favor of those Institutions. I was wounded on the memoriable twenty-second day of May AD 1863 in the assault upon the enemies works in the rear of "Vicksburg." I was sent to the field Hospital which consisted of tents, Negro huts, and one quite respectable house, all on a Plantation, about a mile back of the Battle-ground. Here of course all was confusion as the wounded were constantly coming in, but notwithstanding this, everyone received proper attention, and I began to think that if all I had heard about Hospitals was true surely this one must be an exception. . . . I noticed that those who scolded the most, never stopped to co[n]sider whether everything was as good as circumstances would admit but if all was not as good as they thought it ought to be went off in a fit about the treatment soldiers received at "Hospitals." Now I dont pretend to say that everything at all times is just what it should be, or would be, under more favorable circumstances, but I do think, that everything considered, there is little room for fault-finding. One great cause of complaint is the limited supply of "Rations" at times or that the quality of food is not good enough. As for the first cause it is sometimes true that the "Rations" are scant, but is there no reason for this? I think there is, for instance, suppose that some day after the "Rations" are drawn a boat load of Patients are sent in. Of course they must have something to eat, and the result is that what was provided for few is divided among many. This is frequently the case, and ought rational men to find fault with these things? I think not. In regard to the quality of food I can say that I have been in four "Hospitals" and in each of them the Patients were served with better victuals than I ever expected to see in the army, and better I verily believe than those who found so much fault were in the habit of having at home. It seemed that some entertained the idea, that it was the special business of the "Government" to administer to their wants, and see that their every wish was gratified.

From "floating Hospital" I was sent to "Union Hospital" at Memphis, Tenn. This was a fine large Building well arranged and in perfect order, enough to eat, drink, and wear. (I will say here that there never was any lack clothing, of good quality) everything clean, and, even tasty, and yet there were those that could see nothing right, constantly grumbling.

Next I came to St. Louis, MO, and it is but just to say that the "New House of Refuge" Hospital was modle in every respect. The Building is a large Brick Structure five stories high including Basement. There were two wards on each floor, above the Basement, all tasteily arranged, and beautifully decorated with "Red White and Blue."

Our meals were ready at the regular times and gotten up in good style. The Surgeons, Stewards, and attendants were always kind and obligeing, the rooms clean and neat, and it did seem to me that all were made as comfortable as possible under the circumstances, and yet there were those who thought themselves dreadfully abused, and even went so far as to write to the Governors of their own States, to have their wrongs adjusted, when in reality there was no wrong, only in their fault-finding.

Perhaps I am scolding to[o] much about others scolding, but it does seem to me, that men, who are brave enough to enlist and fight, as our soldiers have done, ought not to magnify these little inconveniences, as some have done in regard to these "institutions."

~~~

LEWIS E. KLINE

Private, Co. C, 33rd Missouri Volunteer Infantry

Born to German immigrants in 1843, Kline enlisted in 1862 when he was nineteen years old; two years later, he received the wounds that would eventually lead to his death.[14] Having refused amputation, he remained in a barracks hospital for a year, serving as a librarian and sexton, before being discharged.[15] According to a biography of Kline in an 1883 history

14. Lewis Kline, Contest Entries, 1st ser., no. 41, and 2nd ser., no. 25, Bourne Papers.

15. Scharf, *History of Saint Louis City and County*, 1673.
~~~

Lewis E. Kline.
From Scharf, *History of Saint Louis City and County, from the Earliest Periods to the Present Day (1883).*

of Saint Louis, he entered the care of "the best surgeons in the West," who told him "he was a badly mutilated man, almost beyond the help of medical skill, and that his only hope lay in his own force of will."[16] For the next two years, Kline "submitted . . . twice each day, to surgical treatment, and finally saved both his life and his arm."[17] After his discharge, he "went with his arm in a sling from store to store and from street to street in search of employment. But no one seemed desirous of having a man without the use of his right arm."[18] Kline studied telegraphy and bookkeeping, earning a position at the "largest religious publishing house and bookstore in the city" in 1866, eventually becoming chief clerk and bookkeeper.[19] For twenty-seven years, he managed the Saint Louis branch of the American Baptist Publication Society.[20] Kline and his wife moved to San Francisco in 1897 in the hopes of improving his health.[21] The *St. Louis Post-Dispatch* reported that his "wound always gave him trouble, and sepsis resulted from an operation," leading to his death fifteen months later; interestingly, the paper incorrectly identified his left arm as the wounded appendage.[22] Another newspaper explained that the operation was "intended to relieve the effects of wounds received in the Civil War."[23] The glowing 1883 biography concludes with the following: "Mr. Kline is in the best sense of the term a self-made man, and one who, having risen from the lowest round of the ladder by his own rare determination, is both sympathetic in helping those who are working their own way up in life, and worthy of the highest confidence and regard of all who reverence honest merit and genuine success."[24]

16. Ibid.
17. Ibid.
18. Ibid., 1674.
19. Ibid.
20. "Kline Burial Here," *St. Louis Post-Dispatch,* Dec. 19, 1905, 13.
21. Ibid.
22. Ibid.
23. "Lewis Kline's Death Due to Civil War Wounds," *St. Louis Republic,* Dec. 9, 1905, 1.
24. Scharf, *History of Saint Louis City and County,* 1673.

***First Submission:* December 15, 1865**

Seeing in your columns of the generous inducement you hold forth to such soldiers that have lost their right arms (or have lost the use of their right arms), I concluded that I would compete, not altogether however as a competitor, but also from a sense of duty, thinking that some soldier who may have been so unfortunate as to have lost his right arm may hear of the numerous specimens of left hand penmanship that have [been] sent to you for investigation, and the premiums have been awarded, may thereby take heart and go to work body and soul; and if nothing else he can write, he must make up his mind that he can do so, and he will gain his end. For where there is a will, there is always a way.

But this is not what you demand of a competitor, and so I will at once comply with your agreement. I enlisted as a private in company C 33rd Regiment, Missouri Volunteer Infantry in [*sic*] August 11th 1862. I had been in active service two years minus two months, when I was wounded. I was wounded on June 6th 1864 at Old River Lake, Chicot County, Arkansas, in a charge on a Rebel Battery, then blockading the Mississippi River.[25] The ball struck my right arm a little above the elbow joint shattering the bone, and passing through the shoulder blade, lodging in my back. My arm bone was so fearfully fractured that the Doctors pronounced amputation of the arm necessary to save my life, but I remonstrated too severe and so I retain my arm, but minus nearly 5 inches of the arm bone, and some of the shoulder blade. The ball was extracted five days after I was wounded and is in my possession as a memento, however the effects of it (the Ball) are memento enough. I was prostrated for 12 months and at present writing I still retain 10 open holes, but I can be about. The Doctors in the hospitals seeming to fail in curing me, I have taken my Discharge and have my Doctor on my own expense. I have had a long and serious time of it, but I presume that patience and time will at last effect a cure!

***Second Submission:* June 12, 1867**

Although not a one armed man, yet, I have so lost the use of my right arm so that I am classified with the left arm department. Nor am I ashamed to acknowledge it. I am not ashamed to own the cause. Nor through what means

25. Also known as the Battle of Ditch Bayou.

I was made what I am. Being afflicted as I am three years and six days to day, I can with gratification to myself (and without any egotism) defy the world at large of anyone who has ever heard me complain of my misfortune. I like the Apostle Paul have striven that in whatsoever situation I am placed therewith to make myself content and have found it to be more benefit in my situation than all the Doctors put together. It is to this that the doctors and myself attribute my present existence. But too many of my comrades who were wounded with me and by no means so severe, have died in consequence of giving up to despondency. There is nothing for a wounded or sick man that is of more benefit to him than to put and keep on a bold front. Here allow me to give you a brief synopsis of my military career....

I will not go into the details of the skirmishes and marches, because it would take more time and patience than I have to devote to this at present. As it is I almost was afraid I should not have the pleasure of writing on [account] of business. I somehow do not possess the taste for telling or reviewing my Soldier life, as they customarily are, not having given my own relations a full history of my military life....

On the evening of June 5th 1864 we disembarked from the steamers and on the morning of June 6th 1864 we started in our line of march to conquer our foe. We had not proceeded far when the report of a musket gave us to understand that there was warm work ahead. Our regiment being in advance we soon came to where the cannon and musket balls sounded rather unpleasant, slaying a comrade now on the right and now on the left. The command for a charge was given, and in which I participated until a stray ball found its way in my arm and shoulder, naturally putting a stop to my further operations.... The ball struck my right arm a little above the elbow, passing through the entire arm and shoulder. The ball lodging in the back, where it was not found till the fifth day after being wounded, but then extracted and which I still have, not as memento, but relic. The medical faculty held a consultation of my case and decided that to save my life I must lose my arm. But I did not look at it in that light and protested all such proceedings. They seemed to wish it for my best, and yet I remonstrated contending that it could be amputated any time, but not replaced after once gone. My remonstrances were finally acceded to, and to do the best they could for me, I found that I was taken off the operating table with about five inches of the arm bone and some of the shoulder blade minus. But I heeded this not, rather congratulating myself that it was not worse than it was. Although as I afterwards was informed by the doctors that I did or could not begin to realize the perilous condition my life was in. The doctors despaired of my recovery, but as I said previously, that trying to make myself contented in whatever situation I was placed and by the kindness of a Lady (who I will never forget) I had the satisfaction of seeing my arm and shoulder doing as nicely as could be expected. Here I beg leave to say a word in favor of the Ladies who have so nobly stood up for their country, and although not carrying a gun they did more than many who did! Leaving home, friends, plenty and peace, for toil hunger and the disgust of demoralizing Army life. They were ever ready to give a helping hand, depriving themselves of their comforts and bestowing them on some not as worthy as themselves. Many are the soldiers that are indebted for their lives to these noble women. I for one know that I am in part! God bless them all. If not in this life, the promise is that the cup of cold water shall not go without its reward. Honor to whom Honor is due and these women truly deserve it.

My condition in the Hospital was varied. At times critical, and then again favorable. Having at one time had eleven open cavities in the arm and shoulder I remained in the Hospital up to Dec 11th 1865, when I despaired of a cure in the hospital and concluded to try citizen life again and a change of a doctor. I then could be about without any inconvenience to my wounds and therefore tried to find something I could do. Carrying my arm in a sling, and which had to be dressed daily, I was considered foolish for any such undertaking. But being of a very independent disposition I cared but little for the compliment. I studied the Telegraphing by Sound, but found all offices supplied with operators. Last December I then went in a bookstore as cashier and bookkeeper, but was not over 10 days there when I met with the accident of rebreaking my right arm which I could leave out of the sling. It was just about the same time of day that I had it first broken. This was December 23rd 1866, 10 a.m. as I was going to church where in crossing the street I fell and rebroke the arm. This was a hard blow. But all shall be for our best. Thus suddenly were my bright air castles crushed. But not forever, for two weeks after the accident, I found myself back at my post.

My advantage was that I was not necessitated to relearn to write with my left hand and so with right in sling my left plied the pen. The Pen is mightier than the Sword and so comrades, cheer up. We know what the Sword has done. Now let us try and see what the "Pen" can do. I now have my hands full of work for both day and night and so much so that I almost despaired of getting time to write and it is only by leaving the other aside that I hastily scratch a few lines on this paper. I have not the time, I am very sorry to say, to write my best. At present writing (although 3 years and 6 days since I am wounded) I still have six open cavities and which need dressing daily. But I do not mind all this. If I would not be under the painful necessity of having someone to dress me I could paddle my own canoe.

And now a word to those who have made such a liberal proposition. Too much cannot be said to your credit in thus placing that class of men who were so unfortunate in the war to bestir themselves to new life, which undoubtedly it has done, giving them new ideas, determinations and resolutions to work out their own Salvation.

CHARLES W. DODGE

Corporal, Co. B, 13th New Hampshire Volunteer Infantry
First Lieutenant, Co. B, 22nd Regt. United States Colored Troops
Second Lieutenant, Co. E, 24th Regt. Veteran Reserve Corps

Prior to the war, Dodge worked on his father's farm and attended Appleton Academy in Mont Vernon, New Hampshire.[26] He enlisted in August 1862 at the age of eighteen, was mustered in September, and traveled with his regiment to Falmouth, Virginia, where it joined the Army of the Potomac. Dodge was mustered out of the VRC in 1868.[27] Married and working as a store clerk, he died in 1880 at the age of thirty-seven.[28]

26. Charles W. Dodge, Contest Entry, 1st ser., no. 47, Bourne Papers; 1860 U.S. Census, Hillsborough Co., NH, pop. sched., Mont Vernon, p. 724 (stamped), dwelling 87, family 87, Charles Dodge, NARA RG 29, M6563, roll 673; *Catalogue of Officers and Students of the Appleton Academy*, 4.

27. "Honorably Discharged," *Buffalo (NY) Morning Express and Illustrated Buffalo Express*, Aug. 31, 1868, 1.

28. U.S. Census, Philadelphia Co., PA, pop. sched., Philadelphia, p. 499B (stamped), dwelling 178, family 197, Charles Dodge, NARA RG 29, T9, roll 1185; "Died," *Philadelphia Times*, Aug. 31, 1880, 3.

How I Came to Lose My Arm

In telling how it was that I lost my right arm, I purport to give neither any very startling incidents nor novel circumstances. Many, aye, thousands of brave boys have met the same—misfortune I cannot call it—let me say then, the same glory and in the same manner. Secure in his home, and far from the scene of danger, the civilian is prone to regard the mingled horrors of a battlefield, much as he would some brilliant spectacular drama.

At the startling incidents he applauds. The more sublime episodes he hangs over, perhaps, in mute admiration; but he is less inclined to raise the blazing cross of honor, which he has generously granted—to gaze upon the wound that won it.

I will endeavor to do this. I shall try to show the dark rolling clouds of battle as well as the flashing fires which are thought to illumine and glorify them,—but which are in fact, but the glittering heralds of that Death, of which the dark clouds form the merciful shroud.

To give my little history, understandingly, necessitates a short digression of rather uninteresting datas which will, however, be passed over as rapidly, as possible. . . .

After fighting at Fredericksburg, Dodge's regiment defended Suffolk, Virginia, against Longstreet. In December 1863, Dodge was commissioned second lieutenant in the 22nd Regiment, USCT. Newly organized and equipped, the regiment traveled to Fort Monroe. Dodge was promoted to first lieutenant in March 1864.

But to return to my subject. On the 15th of June, 1864, a day memorable to me, upon which the 18th Corps, to which my regiment was attached, was to make an advance on the city of Petersburg, we crossed the Appomattox river the evening before, and came upon the enemy's skirmishers about daybreak.—Never shall I forget that morning. Fresh and lovely each object animate and inanimate, breathing an audible thanksgiving, as it were.—It seemed impossible that the sulpherous smoke of battle should so soon pollute that atmosphere of peace and beauty; yet within five hundred rods lay the rebel artillerists, safely ensconced behind heavy works, and only awaiting our nearer approach to hurl death and destruction through our ranks.

A small belt of woods had thus far concealed them from our sight and after pushing through this, our progress being somewhat impeded by a heavy undergrowth of tangled brush and vines, we came full upon the rebel works.

The fire that now opened upon us was terrific, for from that short distance, the rebel riflemen poured in a continuous rain of leaden messengers which was scarcely less fatal than the well-directed fire of their artillery The small bit of woods was swept through and through by shot and shell, and many brave men fell on every side. A malediction almost sprang to my lips, as I beheld the rebel banner flaunting before us. The black smoke of battle circling it as though it was wreathed by the Shades of Tartarus.

But little time was given me for thought, for the next instant a fearful pain, agonizing beyond expression, ran through my frame.—A cannonball had severed my right arm just below the elbow; but as I fell the glorious flag of my country was planted in triumph upon the enemy's works, and the hated banner of treason torn down and debased. Ah! in spite of the agony I suffered a thrill of extacy ran through me to know that victory was won, and a feeling of exultation and pride filled my heart, which made my sufferings seem immeasurably less.

But my wound demanded attention; the pain was something terrible, so I endeavored to find my way to the rear, where the Surgeons were in waiting. There I found it necessary to have a second amputation performed, this time by the knife in the hands of a skillful surgeon.[29] Upon this I will not dwell, nor upon the long weary hours subsequently passed in hospital. "This bravery of strong patience, which untried/ Waits calmly, while the tedious months fulfill/ Their work of good or ill."[30]

It was a trying period, but thank Heaven, I am here to tell of it and to add, that I am still in the service of my country, and still shielded by her glorious stars and stripes!

~~~

29. Lemon Barnes performed the surgical amputation of Dodge's mangled arm.

30. From "Wounded," by Florence Percy (pen name for Elizabeth Akers Allen). See George Bancroft Griffith, *The Poets of Maine* (Portland, ME: Elwell, Pickard, 1888), 471–72.
~~~

WILLIAM H. RICHARDSON

Private, Co. F, 69th New York State Militia / 182nd New York Volunteers

Richardson enlisted in September 1862.[31] After spending three months as a prisoner of war, he was paroled; sent first to Annapolis, he eventually arrived in New York. Richardson signed his name in Bourne's reminiscence book while a patient at Central Park Hospital, expressing his gratitude for the "great many favors" he received.[32] Unfortunately, further information about his postwar life is unavailable.

William H. Richardson.
Courtesy William Oland Bourne Papers, Manuscript Division, Library of Congress.

[undated]

It was on the third day of June 1864 at the Battle of "Coal Harbor"[33] that I was wounded. . . . On the morning of the 3rd, we had charged upon the enemy's works and were repulsed. Had rallied again, when as I was in the act of priming my rifle, being upon my right knee, at the time, when I was struck by a minie ball. The ball having entered the inner side of my right arm, three inches above the elbow, it having so badly shattered my arm, that it was amputated a few hours afterwards, leaving but one inch of the bone from the joint. In going to the rear of our lines I became so exhausted, caused by the loss of blood and intense pain which I experienced from my wound, that I fell insensible. I must have lain about an hour, when I came to, and upon seeing one of my comrades who was connected with the 69th to whom I called. He turned around and upon seeing me exclaimed "Halloa Will! What's the matter!" "I am wounded in the arm, Mac," I exclaimed (his name being MacCormack). I then asked him if he had any water. He sat down, saying that he would get me some as soon as he had rested himself, he being out of breath at the time as he had run to get out of the reach of the Rebs. And would also help me off the field. He had received

31. William Richardson, Contest Entry, 1st ser., no. 77, Bourne Papers (punctuation and spelling edited).

32. Civil War Reminiscences by Soldiers and Sailors in Central Park Hospital, Bourne Papers.

33. Richardson's spelling of Cold Harbor.

a wound himself, in the right side. He then got me some water for which God knows I was thankful. He finally took hold of the trunk of the tree, by which we were laying, when he received a ball in the left hand. He sunk back exclaiming, "My God! they have hit me again. That is twice today." I told him to come around to the other side of the tree or he would be killed. Scarcely had I uttered the words, when he received a ball in the brain. He turned his eyes on me and feebly uttered, "good bye, Will!" then fell a corpse. Never will I forget that last sentence. Peace to his departed Soul.

I was soon startled by hearing the yells of the enemy, and cries of "come over here you d—d Yank, and surrender, or we'll shoot you." "There is no use of shooting me," I exclaimed, "I am shot already." "Then come with us." "Come and lift me up," said I. They then made a motion as if to get hold of my right arm, which was twisted in a lot of brush. I told them that my arm was broken when they came around to my left side and lifted me up, telling me to stoop low for if I did not some of the Yank sharpshooters might hit me again. They hurried me through the woods, which we got through about daylight. We there met a Reb Lieut. who asked me to what Regt. I belonged. I told him. He then asked a Brig. Gen. who was sitting by the works with his men if he wanted to see me?

The Gen. asked if I was wounded? He told him that I was. Then he ordered me to be taken to an hospital. On the road there, the guard told me that it was the 27th Georgia Infantry which had taken me prisoner. After having walked about half a mile, we came to the hospital. The surgeon examined my arm, shook his head saying that he could do nothing with the exception of putting it in splint, on account of having so many of their own wounded to attend to. The guard then started me to another hospital, about a mile and a half from there. After a while the surgeon examined my wound, telling me to get upon the table; he then probed the wound by inserting his fore finger and thumb. I told him to take them out: that an ounce of lead was enough without his fingers. He then had me put upon the "Execution Block"; I asked him if the arm would have to come off, but got no answer. He then gave me about half a pint of whiskey, which made me feel very strong, then etherized me. At the same time an attendant held my left hand. He gave me so much ether that I thought he would suffocate me. I tried in vain to free my hand from his grasp. Finally I pretended to sleep, then he loosened his hold. Suddenly I gave my arm a wrench, and knocked the bottle from my face. The Surgeon exclaimed "here, here, that will not do, Yank," and instantly replaced it. Finally I became conscious, and upon inquiring where my arm was, he told me to look over the side of the table. I did as he directed me and beheld the forsaken member laying upon a number of amputated limbs. I then turned over and said that the sight was more than I could endure. I told him that I was very weak when he then brought me some stimulant. After a while he returned and with the assistance of another man carried me a short distance to a fly tent.[34] I laid there three days in that place. On the morning of the fourth day the Surgeon came and told us that we were to be sent to a hospital in Richmond, and that we would be soon paroled and sent to our own hospitals. An amb[u]lance drove up to the tent. We was put into it. We had rode about two miles when we were stopped and put upon the ground until the train arrived which was to take us to Richmond. We were then put into baggage cars and started for Richmond. We got there and were conveyed to the Sïgdon Factory Hospital, where our wounds were dressed. Finally a Reb came along and asked me if I wanted anything to eat and threw me a piece of corn bread about four inches square. Two days after our arrival at the hospital the surgeon came around and looked at our wounds, asked us a few questions, then walked away. In a few weeks, we began to gain strength and I assure you our thoughts and conversations were of home and the dear ones there. Every flag that was seen floating from the masts of the vessels which were seen sailing on the river James, we eagerly scanned to see if it were the flag of truce. At last, one day, just as we had given up all hopes of ever seeing home again, the surgeon in charge said to us, "I think that I will send you Yanks home in the morning." I saw men that never flinched in battle cry like so many children when they heard the glad tidings. The same night the officers came in with the parole lists and took our names. The next morning, about ten o'clock, the ambulance drove up and those who could not walk were put into them. The rest of us, one of whom was myself, had to walk about a mile to the navy yard where we were put upon the parole boat and taken to "Aiken's Landing" upon the James River. Our feelings can be bettered imagined than described on beholding the glorious old Flag floating to the winds of heaven in defiance of the dastard foe whom had struck at the fabric of American Love and Liberty. Such a cheer as ascended from the throats of that three hundred living martyrs, I never heard, and never expect to hear again. . . . When we got on board the steamer, *New York*, rations of bread and warm coffee were served out

34. This was a basic tent, usually without walls, just a canopy.

to us: Which seemed like a feast, although the bread was a week old. The next morning we steamed down the river for Annapolis, where we arrived on the 14th of August, just 71 days from the date of my being wounded and captured. So, that you see, my Dear Sir, ended my experience in a Rebel prison.

~~~

EDWARD AMES EDWARDS

Private, Co. K, 15th Indiana Volunteer Infantry

Edward A. Edwards in 1922.
Courtesy Tammy Jaeger and Jane Sukow.

Edwards, born in Indiana in 1840, was a student when he enlisted and fought at Shiloh, Corinth, and Stones River, among other battles and skirmishes.[35] He was working as a librarian at the Saint Paul Circulating Library when he sent his submission; by 1870, he had returned to Indiana and found work as a teacher.[36] In 1880, he was a farmer in Kansas, living with his wife and children; three of his neighbors also bore visible scars from the "late rebellion," as the census taker reported, including a missing leg.[37] By 1900, Edwards was a sewing-machine agent. In 1910, by then a widower, he was an office clerk in Los Angeles, living with his daughter and son on Sunset Boulevard.[38] Edwards died in 1927.[39]

35. Edward A. Edwards, Contest Entry, 1st ser., no. 178, Bourne Papers.

36. 1870 U.S. Census, Tippecanoe Co., IN, pop. sched., Jackson, p. 33B (stamped), dwelling 53 family 56, E. A. Edwards, NARA RG 29, M593, roll 362.

37. 1880 U.S. Census, Anderson Co., KS, pop. sched., Rich, p. 207A, dwelling 72, family 76 Edward A. Edwards, NARA Record 29, T9, roll 372.

38. 1900 U.S. Census, Shawnee Co., KS, pop. sched., Shawnee, p. 4A, dwelling 67, family 6[?] Edward A. Edwards, NARA RG 29, T623, roll 500; 1910 U.S. Census, Los Angeles Co., CA, pop. sched. Los Angeles, p. 21B, dwelling 393, family 413, Edward A. Edwards, ibid., T624, roll 84.

39. California Death Index, 1905–29, Edward A. Edwards, California Department of Health and Welfare, Sacramento, 3059.
~~~

[undated]

I was a member of the 15th Regiment Indiana Volunteer Infantry from June 14th, 1861 to March 20th, 1863. My history was simply that of the regiment up to the 31st day of December, 1862, when at the battle of Stones River, my right arm was torn, mangled, and rendered powerless forever, but [to] proceed to my sketch, which will be short and simple. . . .

The morning of the 31st, the last day of the year, we were in position on the extreme left of our army and on the very bank of Stones River. Here we were directed to remain, to hold our position at all hazards; we were flanked by artillery in the enemy's works across the river, and compelled to fight a superior force in front; we made one charge in which we captured 175 men besides killed, but our loss was severe. In one hour's time 30 of our men were killed and 100 wounded, but we cleared the field that time; but they were coming to the attack again, and we were lying down waiting their close approach, when all at once a shell burst over me. As I lay with my right hand on the gun, it was suddenly paralyzed, and I drew it up to see the blood streaming and the hand a mangled mass of flesh bones and blood.

I was then sent to the rear, to make my way to one of the field hospitals; across the open field for the distance of half a mile, a perfect storm of shot and shell was sweeping, but finally I succeeded in getting out of range of artillery and found my way into an ambulance; after twenty hours had passed my hand was dressed, the thumb and index finger being split off, and taken off from the wrist joint; two small pieces of shell had entered into the back part of that portion of the hand remaining which has rendered all the remaining fingers and wrist powerless. I was as soon as able to ride in a wagon sent to Nashville, where I took passage on a steamboat for Louisville, had gone as far as Harpeth Shoals on the Cumberland river, when a crash through the boat, and the sound of a cannon told us we were again at the mercy of the enemy, being now in a more helpless condition than ever. We were paroled; a number of other boats were burned; ours was allowed to go on, after we had been thoroughly robbed. We then went on to Louisville; from there I was sent to the Marine Hospital Cincinnati, from which place I was discharged.

~~~
~~~

JOHN BRYCE

Private, Co. H, 1st New York Volunteer Infantry

Born in Glasgow, Scotland, Bryce was a forty-year-old barber when he enlisted in May 1861; he was discharged for disability in November 1862.[40] Bryce sent his penmanship specimen from a hospital on Davids' Island in the Long Island Sound; Bourne was familiar with this institution and, in July 1866, treated the disabled soldiers there to "a considerable quantity of refreshments."[41] Unfortunately, further information about Bryce's postwar life is unavailable. As for his entry, the penmanship is noticeably sloppier than that of the majority of contestants; he apparently wrote his submission while acting as a sentry at the hospital. In addition to a few barely legible and brief poetic attempts and his reflections on chloroform included below, Bryce quotes President Millard Fillmore and relates a story from his sailing days (neither of which is included here).[42]

December 2, 1865
How I felt under Chloroform

I was laid on the table about 5 1/2 p.m. past on 6 September '62. Armory Hospital 7th street Washington D.C. Professor Bliss M.D. I thought Sergt. Gunn of 5th Michigan shook hands with me of whom I was acquainted. I then set sail as a vessel sailing through the air. I had a narrow river to cross which seemed very deep. I got to the top of the embankment and who jumps up before me but general [Joseph K. F.] Mansfield. I shouted out the general's name. I felt no pain during the cutting of my arm. It seemed pleasant while in the stupor.

~~~

40. John Bryce, Contest Entry, 1st ser., no. 199, Bourne Papers (edited for clarity); New York Civil War Muster Roll Abstracts, 1861–1900, John Bryce, New York State Archives, Collection 13775-83, box 1, roll 838; *Annual Report of the Adjutant General of the State of New York for the Year 1898,* 14.

41. "The Fourth of July," *New York Times,* July 4, 1866, 8.

42. Due to the scant personal details he provided, I am unable to confirm the details of Bryce's postwar life, though it is possible he eventually settled in Minneapolis and lived until at least 1910. 1910 U.S. Census, Hennepin Co., MN, pop. sched., Minneapolis, p. 13A, dwelling 80, family 104, John Bryce, NARA RG 29, T624, roll 702.
~~~

FREDERICK R. CUTLER

Private, Co. K, 72nd Pennsylvania Volunteer Infantry
Co. 55, 2nd Battallion Veteran Reserve Corps

With two years of an apprenticeship left to serve, Cutler enlisted in August 1861 to battle "for right and humanity."[43] He sent his contest submission from Chester, Pennsylvania, having served in the VRC after his amputation.[44] Cutler worked as a recorder of deeds for Delaware County before dying there in 1873 at the age of twenty-nine, leaving behind a wife and daughter.[45]

January 27, 1866

. . . having fully made my [mind] up to go knowing that I would lose my trade and perhaps some of my limbs, I went to abide by the consequence and like the soldier with his head carried away by a cannon ball never to regret it. I served all through the Peninsula Campaign from the beginning until the ending. . . .

Cutler fought in the Battles of Yorktown, Fair Oaks, and throughout the Seven Days.

I was fortunate enough to escape unhurt through all these, but at the battle of Antietam I was not fortunate. I just had time to fire my peice and was in the act of reloading when I was struck in the right arm just below the shoulder. My peice rested on my left wrist. In [my] left hand I held the cartridge in the act of tearing the paper off the ball with [my] right hand when I was struck. I seised my peice with my right hand and for two minutes or more I could not release my hold and my peice kept twisting around while in my hand and as soon as my hold was released my wound commence to bleed very freely which was alarming to me as I did not know how to stop it,

43. Frederick R. Cutler, Contest Entry, 1st ser., no. 241, Bourne Papers (punctuation edited).

44. Bates, *History of Pennsylvania Volunteers,* 2:860.

45. Pennsylvania Veterans Burial Cards, 1777–2012, ser. 1, Frederick R. Cutler, Bureau of Archives and History, Pennsylvania Historical and Museum Commission, Harrisburg; Wiley, *Biographical and Historical Cyclopedia of Delaware County, Pennsylvania,* 94.

it being so close to shoulder and the bone being badly shattered I suffered severely. I dragged my peice as far as I was able to to prevent it falling into the hands of the rebels. I now looked to myself for I was bleeding freely now for the Doctor to have my wound bandaged to prevent its bleeding and the thought [of] this ran quickly through my mind and I made all haste for the rear going about a mile and a half to the hospital only to be disappointed in not finding a Doctor but at last a hospital steward dressed my wound and I felt considerable releived. I endured my sufferings patiently knowing that I would be properly attended to in time besides there were others who were worse than I who had to be attended to first. Here [I] lay at this hospital until the following morning when I was removed to our own division hospital. They put two of us in an ambulance and drove us through the woods over an [*sic*] newly made road and our sufferings were severely felt by the jar of the ambulance in going over stumps and stones. My comrade being wounded in the right lung it caused him to spit blood. At the division hospital I lay three days without anything to eat excepting a few crackers and some green apples. The fourth day some of the members of the Sanitary Commission made their appearance and then I was comfortably carried [*sic,* cared] for, my wound properly dressed, and myself clad in clean clothes. Many thanks to the Sanitary Commission. Here at this I lay two weeks then I was removed to Frederick City to the Convent hospital, I suffered severely come over the mountains in the Ambulance. The road was so rough that it caused the ambulance to jar my fractured limb so that my sufferings were intense, and during all this time I had nothing done for [my] wound except simple cerate[46] dressing. While at this hospital a regular Army surgeon took charge of the ward I was in and the nurse called his attention to my case. Now this was the first time that I had had a regular surgical examination of my arm since the battle, it being in a sling ever since the day that I [was] wounded. The Doctor took a hold of my arm and drew it from my body in a hurried manner, which caused me much pain. Now I am not in the habit of swearing but on this occassion I said something which I ought not to have said for which the Doctor in reproving [me] for said that I was a brave young man [and] ought not to swear. I then beg[ged] his pardon, he told me to beg God

46. An ointment made of wax, lard, and/or oil.

pardon and not his. And he then told me that I would I have to loose my arm. Now this seem hard but as I made up my mind to abide by the consequence I did not give away to feelings knowing that I had been wounded in an honorable and just cause. My arm was amputated at the shoulder joint on account of mortification setting in, the Doctors deeming it necessary. For three days I lay insensible and on comming to my senses I was told that I could not live twenty four hours and advised to send for my Friends. I was very weak from the loss of blood. The main artery had come untied and the blood from it had soak[ed] through three matresses before discovered. But never the less I did not feel discouraged and I live contrary to the predictions of the Doctors although I was six months in recovering and my stump did not heal entirely until the 25th day of May 1863. My treatment while in the hospital was good and my case had all the attention it required and thanks to Him who hold[s] our destinies in his hands and to the skill of my Doctor,[47] also to the Sister of Charity who acted the part of the good Samaritan towards me, who when the nurses could not come near me on account of my stump smelling so offensive assisted the Doctor in dressing it, but enough of this. I have been asked how I felt on going into battle well to [tell] the truth I felt badly scared but on becoming engaged with the Enemy all fear vanished and whenever I would see a comrade fall felt as if I could take two lives for one for I felt bounded to my comrades as so they were my Kindred relations. Here the writer would beg to be excused from any further on account of the awkwardness and the tediousome labor of this left hand writing.

ANDREW J. FRIES

Corporal, Co. E, 100th Illinois Volunteer Infantry

Fries was born in 1836 and worked as a farm laborer before enlisting; he continued that work when he returned home.[48] "Can drive team on the mower and reaper and plough and drag

47. H. S. Hewit performed the amputation, but it is unclear if he attended to Cutler after the surgery.

48. Andrew J. Fries, Contest Entries, 1st ser., no. 256, and 2nd ser., no. 103, Bourne Papers (punctuation edited); 1860 U.S. Census, Will Co., IL, pop. sched., Plainfield, p. 128, dwelling 1035, family 961, Andrew Fries, NARA RG 29, M653, roll 238.

and many kinds of work equal to a man with two hands," Fries explained. "The only thing I ever failed in was trying to get an office from the Government." Nevertheless, he eventually served as treasurer for Will County and taught school.[49] Married in 1869, he and his wife had three daughters.[50] In 1874, the *Chicago Tribune* noted that Fries's herd of cattle was one of the "finest on exhibition" at the county fair.[51] Fries died in 1881, leaving his farm and "considerable property" to his widow.[52]

***First Submission:* January 27, 1866**

I received your circular the 24th inst.[53] but could not write before today as I have to teach a district School for a living and all the time I have to write is Saturdays. I write not with the expectation of receiving a prise as I have seen much better left-handed writers than I am. I always have had a desire to know how many there is of us and if I can learn by writing I shall feel well paid. . . .

I was on the march from Murfreesborough to Chattanooga and our Brigade was the first to go in the town. The next day we drove the Rebs acrost the Chickamauga River and watched them till the 18th of Sept. when they took the offensive and the battle of Chickamauga was fought.

I was wounded on Saturday the 19th. Our Regt. made a charge three p.m. drove the Johnies fifty roods[54] and held them thirty minuts. We lost one hundred and sixty men in that charge, most of them were killed. I was hit after the Regt. had fell back. I heard the order to fall back but saw such good marks that I could not resist the temtation. Was right in the open field about twenty roods from the enemy. While loading my gun a miny

49. "Will County (Ill.) Republican Convention," *Chicago Tribune,* Sept. 13, 1871, 1; "Blood on the Moon," *Bloomington (IL) Pantagraph,* May 28, 1890, 1.

50. Illinois Marriage Index, 1860–1920, Andrew J. Fries, accessed via Ancestry.com, 2015; 1880 U.S. Census, Will Co., IL, pop. sched., Joliet, p. 287B (stamped), dwelling 204, family 226, Andrew Fries, NARA RG 29, T9, roll 260.

51. "Fairs," *Chicago Tribune,* Sept. 12, 1874, 12.

52. Fries's widow, Charlotte, later married an attorney named David Gilmore, who tried to control her property and was abusive. She left him, and another lawyer aided her; Gilmore attempted to murder the lawyer. "War of the Lawyers," *Chicago Inter Ocean,* May 28, 1890, 11.

53. Short for *instante mense,* meaning the current month.

54. A linear measurement, one rood equals between seven and eight yards.

ball struck me between the elbow and sholder. My ramrod flew six paces from me. I went to pick it up but could not, saw that our men had fell back. I walked about ten roods when a Johny requested me to stop. I told him I could not think of it. I walked a few roods farther and found it imposible to get into our lines as our men had opened on the Rebels. I laid down on the ground and remained there probaly thirty minuts when our boys drove the Johnies back, gave me a swallow of water helped me up. I walked three miles to our hospital, had the mother earth to lie on and the sky for a shelter. The next day the Hospital was surrendered. About sundown my arm was dressed and I felt better. Dr. Woodruff[55] Assistant Surgeon of the 100th cut out a piece of ball about the shape of the bowl of a teaspoon. Oct 1st I was paroled and sent into our lines.

The 20th inst. Surgeon McMan[56] took the balance of the ball out of my arm. Oct 30th the main artery slushed off and I lost considerably blood before the surgeon could get a compress on. The 31st just as the sun was going down Surgeon McMan of the 65th Ohio Regt. amputated my arm. . . .

November 8th the ligature came off. I bled considrable before it could be taken up. On the night of the 9th the ligature sliped off again. Had a hard time in getting it taken up. But after an hour's hard work the artery was tied and it stade. The next morning I felt pretty week but soon felt better. I never for a moment was sorry that I enlisted. I was satisfied that I had searved my Country faithful and was willing to leave the rest to him that ruleth all things well. I was discharged Aprill 18th 1864. My stump did not heal till last Spring. I never was in the hospital a day till I was wounded then I got my discharge as soon as I found that I could be of no use to the Government. I was always treated as well as I could wish. I am a grate home boy but I think that the way our hospitals are conducted a wounded man can be better treated than at home unless a man gets homesick then he had better be sent home. . . . I have written about all that I can fine time to spend. I have written it just as I would write anything else. The misstakes are numerous but I need not tell you. You will see them soon enough.

~~~

55. Acting Assistant Surgeon E. Woodruff.

56. Surgeon Abraham McMahon of the 64th Ohio Infantry. Fries notes that McMahon was acting as division surgeon at the field hospital in Chattanooga at the time of his operation.
~~~

GEORGE C. BUCKNAM

Private, 3rd Independent Battery, Massachusetts Volunteer Light Artillery

George C. Bucknam.
Courtesy William Oland Bourne Papers. Manuscript Division, Library of Congress.

Bucknam was working as a teamster when he enlisted in 1862. He fought at Antietam, Fredericksburg, Chancellorsville, Gettysburg, Second Rappahannock Station, Mine Run, and the Wilderness, then was wounded at Laurel Hill near Spotsylvania Court House.[57] Following the war, he worked as a laborer and an inspector for Ward 2 of Melrose, Massachusetts, and was a member of the GAR.[58] Bucknam was also a breeder of Dark Brahma chickens and competed at poultry shows; he won first prize in 1895.[59] By 1910, he had been married for fifty-one years; not all of those years were happy, apparently, given the suit his wife brought against him for spousal support in 1900 (despite the fact that the couple continued to live together).[60] Six of their eight children were living in 1910.[61] That same year, the *Boston Globe* published an editorial by Bucknam critiquing federal pension legislation; despite being owed $100 a month, he received only $72.[62] He ended the editorial with an appeal: "While we boys of 1861 to '65 considered and have proved that we were the flower of the country, have we deteriorated so since that we cannot understand the justice of our cause?" In 1912, he petitioned Congress for his full pension. Bucknam died in 1915 at the age of eighty.[63]

57. George C. Bucknam, Contest Entry, 2nd ser., no. 47, Bourne Papers; *Massachusetts Soldiers, Sailors, and Marines in the Civil War,* 5:374.

58. 1870 U.S. Census, Middlesex Co., MA, pop. sched., Charlestown, p. 192A (stamped), dwelling 658, family 983, George C. Bucknam, NARA RG 29, M593, roll 625; *Reports of the Town Officers of Melrose,* 64.

59. "Cackle, Gabble, Squawk," *Boston Globe,* Feb. 11, 1890, 4; "Stoneham Fanciers' Club," ibid., Jan. 4, 1895, 6.

60. 1910 U.S. Census, Middlesex Co., MA, pop. sched., Melrose, p. 4A, dwelling 80, family 86, George C. Bucknam, NARA RG 29, T624, roll 602; *Northeastern Reporter,* 343.

61. 1910 U.S. Census, Middlesex Co., MA, pop. sched., Melrose, p. 4A.

62. "Age Pension Bill before Congress," *Boston Globe,* Dec. 29, 1910, 12.

63. *Statutes at Large of the United States,* 1279; "Deaths," *Boston Globe,* Mar. 13, 1915, 12.

June 19, 1867

May 8th Battle of Laurel Hill, VA. Started out where we lay in park (part of the night) at 7 a.m., and went double quick about 2 miles, and went into Battery. We advanced with the 1st Brigade of the 2nd Div. of the 5th Corps, and went into action. The Rebs broke our lines, and we retired back about three hundred yards, and held them in check. The 2nd Brigade of the 2nd Div. our Corps came to our support, when we drove the Rebs back into their works again (for they had works all prepared to fall back into). In this engagement our Captain (A. P. Martin) was wounded, also several Privates and Noncommissioned officers, included in the privates was myself, through the carlessness of one of our own men, my gun Prematured, as I was drawing out my sponge staff after ramming a 12-lb shot in the gun, and blowed my Right hand off above the wrist, and three fingers of my Left hand, and burst the drum of my Left ear, and burnt my face, and knocked me down, and jarred me considerable, but left me sensible, so I got up and walked off the field 1 1/2 miles to the rear, for I couldn't wait for a stretcher, and I knew I had no occasion to stay and let the Rebs gobble me up. As soon as I got back to the rear the Doctors began their butchering, the same as they were used to, and I was soon a man with a few hands and less fingers than I had 2 hours before.

Perhaps you can imagine my feelings for the first Twenty Four hours after I was wounded thinking I should have to part with the remaining thumbs and finger. And then began the splendid accommodations that our Army afforded. I laid in this place until the 10th of May. During that time I had a big biscuit as big as a Bull's eye, they made them in the field and that was all I had to eat for 5 days, it wasnt the Governments fault, but they thought the nigger would be good to take care of the wounded but the white trash was beneath the niggers notice but they thought something of me for they took a pair of stockings off my feet when I was riding in the Ambulance. They were courageous when they were to the rear and they knew that I couldnt help myself. I was transported from the battle field to a place called Belle Plain on the Potomac River, in an ambulance through a place called Fredericksburg and thence to Washington DC in the Steamer *Nellie Baker*, arriving there at 8 p.m. about tired out, and took up my summer quarters in the Stanton Hospital, situated on the corner of J Street and New York Avenue. My wounds not having been dressed for four days, they were full of vermin so they very near frightened some of them Milk & Water Doctors, they was there they said they was no use to dress my wounds, but on my prevailing them I would live until morning, they went to work and it took three Drs three hours, to get the vermin all off. I then had something to eat and then some sleep, the first for four nights, so you may judge I was pretty tired and sleepy. The Sanitary Commission Ladies (thanks be to them) gave me some brandy, on the boat at Belle Plain, which done me good and help revive me a great deal. I got along very slowly in the hospital it being warm weather, and the Drs knife being so handy that he kept cutting a little every day so he almost ruined what I have left but by keeping up good courage and having a good constitution I got along very slowly so I started for home the 2nd day of August arriving in Boston on the 6th where I recruited up very fast with my cripple thumb and finger. This ends my Spring and Summer Campaign of 1864.

~ ~ ~

DARIUS HINDS

Private, Co. A, 3rd Michigan Volunteer Infantry
Private, Co. 137, 2nd Battalion Veteran Reserve Corps

Hinds, a farm laborer before the war, enlisted in May 1861 at the age of twenty-seven; he fought at Blackburn's Ford (July 18, 1861), First Bull Run, Yorktown, Williamsburg, and Second Bull Run.[64] When he sent his submission, he was in Washington, D.C., working as a "watchman in the Interior department." He later clerked in the Pension Office.[65] His widow, Elizabeth, applied for a pension in 1875 after Hinds died of tuberculosis.[66]

June 24, 1867

Was also engaged in the battle of Groveton or second Bull Run, August 29 1862, at which time, and late in the afternoon, I received a gunshot wound in my right arm between the shoulder and elbow shattering the bone and mangling the arm so badly as to necessitate amputation at [the] upper third.

In this condition I was held in possession of the Rebels for three days and then sent into our lines under flag of truce.

Was honorably discharged from the service November 12 1862. In September 1863, I enlisted in the Veteran Reserve Corps and was discharged from

64. Darius Hinds, Contest Entry, 2nd ser., no. 51, Bourne Papers; 1860 U.S. Census, Kent Co., MI, pop. sched., Ada, p. 176, dwelling 1475, family 1319, Darius Hinds, NARA RG 29, M653, roll 550.

65. *Register of Officers and Agents, Civil, Military, and Naval, . . . 1871,* 157.

66. Darius Hinds, Pension File, application 221859, certificate 180310, NARA RG 15,T288, roll 218.

that organization April 10 1865 by reason of circular order No. 63 from the War Department.[67]

While a member of the V.R.C. and from the time my arm was amputated, I experienced incessant pains in the remaining portion, to obviate which, it was thought best to cut open the stump and remove the cause. The operation was performed by a skillful surgeon, Dr. D. O. Farrand, and nearly cost me my life. It was necessary to cut the artery, and in taking it up they could not at first stop the flow of blood, and were compelled to burn it with a hot iron. For twelve hours they worked at my arm; during the greater part of the time, I was kept under the influence of chloroform. The flow of blood was finally stopped and the cause of the pain as they supposed removed.

But I now suffer from the same pains that I experienced previous to the operation, and I think it impossible to cure. At least I have no desire to attempt another operation.

JAMES TURNER BICKNELL

Second Lieutenant, Co. K, 22nd Massachusetts Volunteer Infantry
Second Lieutenant, Co. 36, 2nd Battallion Veteran Reserve Corps

Bicknell, a married bookbinder in his late forties, enlisted (apparently passing as a forty-three-year-old) on August 28, 1861, and was appointed sergeant.[68] He fought during the Peninsula Campaign and was wounded at Gaines's Mill. Appointed second lieutenant of the 22nd, he was transferred to the VRC and served at Harewood Hospital in Washington, D.C. After the war, he lived with his wife and four children in Roxbury, Massachusetts, and worked as a letter carrier and newsdealer.[69] In 1880, paralysis set in on his right side and spread to the rest of his body, rendering him speechless and unable to write; he died later that year.[70]

67. The official report on the VRC does not mention a Circular Order No. 63, but a general order in June 1865 stipulated that men who had transferred to the VRC could muster out with their former regiments. James Turner Bicknell (see below) mentions Special Order No. 317 (July 3, 1866) as the impetus for his mustering out. See *War of the Rebellion,* ser. 3, 5:559.

68. James T. Bicknell, Contest Entry, 2nd ser., no. 56, Bourne Papers (spelling and punctuation edited); Bicknell, *History and Genealogy of the Bicknell Family,* 228.

69. Bicknell, *History and Genealogy of the Bicknell Family,* 228; "A Stricken Soldier," *Boston Globe,* Feb. 21, 1880, 4.

70. "Stricken Soldier," 4; Bicknell, *History and Genealogy of the Bicknell Family,* 228.

June 20, 1867

Military and Hospital life of a Soldier are connected so much, that one does not exist without the other. Five years' service in the U. S. Army brings too many scenes which cannot be put on paper. When I was wounded, the ball struck the right elbow joint, passing down between the two bones in the lower arm, coming out on the inside halfway down, shattering them above and below the joint. I wanted to save my arm if possible. I made up my bundle of bones and nursed them with care. This was to be done in the hot month of July 1862 at the Libby Prison Richmond, VA, in a room with 300 wounded and dying men. I soon become too weak to take proper care of myself, allowing the flies full sway. In a short time my wound was alive with maggots and finally my body was covered with them. I one day actually took the vermin out of my eyes. This was almost madness to me in the condition I was in. After I was exchanged and taken to the Saterlee U.S.G.[71] Hospital, West Philadelphia, PA, I was too weak for an operation, and a delay was ordered to recuperate until Sept. 3rd 1862. Before the time expired I was on the decline. As soon as Surgeon Agnew knew my case, amputation was performed without more delay on the right arm at the middle upper third. I gained in strength some weeks. Then a decline again. Finally I was permitted to go home in the Steamer *Saxton* and arrived in Roxbury October 18th 1862, which was more than the Surgeons expected when I started. Their remark was: that I could not live to get home. I did however, in time, regain my health, and strength. In July 1863, paid them a visit at the Hospital in Phila. much to their surprise. They then told me what my condition was supposed by them at the time I left the Hospital for home. I thought this was true as I was questioned closely about myself. I have been in the service three years since as an Officer. Received a Parchment Commission signed by President Lincoln. And thought it was for life, but Mr. Grant did not like the Veteran Reserve Corps and after fighting Congress a long time on that line, he succeeded to disband the Corps.[72] Only four V. R. C. Regiments are in the Army, and they would not be there now had not Congress

71. United States General.

72. Grant, head of the regular army after the war ended, oversaw the disbanding of the VRC. Contemporary articles reported that most of the members of the VRC wished to be discharged, though some wanted to transfer to the regular army. One article claimed all but the officers wanted to muster out and that Grant supported the enlisted men in their desire to be released. In October

acted against the ungrateful G[rant]. I made application to be retained in service and no notice was taken of it. After 6 or 8 months I asked that my papers be returned to me and that was complied with quickly. I have no regrets that I have served my country five years in good faith, coming out with only one arm to help along in the path of duty in life. I look back on my military life with the satisfaction of doing nothing but a duty performed for one's own Country, which country I love better now than before the war. This war has cost life and money in large amounts. But the good that will grow out of it, in future time will in the end, pay the country *as a nation.* Notwithstanding [that] my application for continuance in the service was slighted by officials, I am quite comfortable and shall always do my duty to my Country. As I trust I have under fire in the army. I hope to have strength and health to perform all the allotted work in a manner that will please Him that doeth all things Well.

JOHN WESLEY NORTHROP JR.

Private, Co. F, 103rd Ohio Volunteer Infantry

Northrop, born in Ohio in 1843, sent his submission at the encouragement of his "friend and comrade" John Blanchard, another member of the Left-Armed Corps.[73] Lawrence A. Kreiser's study of the 103rd Ohio found that Northrop's comrades largely made successful transitions to civilian life.[74] Unfortunately, Northrop, an unmarried physician, entered a home for disabled soldiers in 1871 and died in 1872 from an inflammation of the brain.[75]

1865, congressmen sent a petition to the secretary of war protesting the discharge of twenty-four VRC regiments. Nevertheless, by November, almost all had been mustered out. See "Telegraphic News," *Louisville (KY) Courier-Journal,* Oct. 25, 1865, 1; "Veteran Reserve Corps," *Philadelphia Inquirer,* Sept. 21, 1865, 4; "The Proposed Discharge of the Veteran Reserve Corps," ibid., Oct. 6, 1865, 1; and "Veteran Reserve Corps," *Lawrence (KS) Tribune,* Nov. 30, 1865.

73. John W. Northrop, Contest Entry, 2nd ser., no. 65, Bourne Papers.

74. Kreiser, "Socioeconomic Study of Veterans of the 103rd Ohio Volunteer Infantry Regiment," 175.

75. Historical Register of National Homes for Disabled Volunteer Soldiers, 1866–1938, John Northrop, NARA RG 15, M1749, roll 31; Records of Headstones Provided for Deceased Union Civil War Veterans, ca. 1879–ca. 1903, NARA RG 92, M1845, John W. Northrop; "John Northrop, Jr.," *Dayton (OH) Daily Journal,* Sept. 7, 1872, 1.

June 25, 1867

Having lost the use of my Right Arm, and for several years have been struggling hard to acquire a passable hand I now take great pleasure in improving this opportunity of enrolling my name—if nothing more—among those who are my *comrades*—participating in so Benevolent an Enterprise.

Nearly six years since I enlisted in a company being gotten up in one of our western counties which was to march immediately for the front. 'Twas late in the fall of '61 and I was only eightteen at that time and ere I was "sworn in" my Dear Mother who was nearly "three score" remonstrated and the same resulted in my Father's interference and I was compelled to remain at home for a time—Only a short time elapsed and that mother was suddenly called into Eternity. A few months more and I was steaming away for a point 200 miles to this village—Oberlin—where on the 11th day of August 1862 I with two other Brothers was enlisted in the Company of F 103rd O.V.I. and immediately sworn into the U. S. Service for three years or during the war. We went at once to the front.

They were in Kentucky until September 1863, after which their regiment moved to Knoxville, Tennessee, and helped erect fortifications. Confederate troops under Lieutenant General James Longstreet besieged the city on November 17, 1863.

When the Siege commenced us three Brothers were ready "for the fight" while I "went in" for the Union and Humanity and was the only one of the "Trio" who was struck by the "Dreaded Minnie." On the 25th of November '63 while in the heat of the action on the Heights above the city I was struck by a Minnie Ball in the Right arm just below the Shoulder shattering the Shaft of the humerus for several inches almost to atoms—the Ball passing out directly under the arm and for some unaccountable reason did not enter my side. Was sent to the City Hospital at once and received immediate attention from a very Skillful Surgeon [G. B. Coggswell] who "Resected" the upper half of the middle third and the lower half of the upper third of the Right Humerus—Extracting four inches of the entire shaft of the Bone. I kept my couch for nearly eleven weeks while I was unable to travel for about four months. Was sent north April first '64 and remained in Hospital at Cleveland for three months when I was discharged with my arm yet in a sling and encased in a machine of no little worth to my arm which was gotten up by that Skillful Surgeon and excellent man, Dr. Weber of Cleveland. Suffice it to say that I was compelled to have my arm remain in a sling eighteen months and two years elapsed ere the wound closed although it was ever in a healthy condition. I now am in good *general* health however my nervous system is much impaired in consequence of that wound. I use no stimulants and do not know the taste of Ardent Spirits. Have no means of support save my own energies. Papers are now at Washington for increase of Pension. A Younger Sister is dependent on myself for her entire support also. While I write with my left hand and which never executed my name previous to my receiving the severe wound a Knoxville.

~~~

JOHN M. THOMPSON

Captain, Co. A, 49th Pennsylvania Volunteer Infantry
Brevet Lieutenant Colonel, U.S. Volunteers

Thompson, a carriage maker before the war, enlisted in September 1861 and fought in twenty battles.[76] In a congratulatory letter, Brigadier General John W. Geary lauded Thompson, the fellow Pennsylvanian he selected to win his premium: "I must also compliment you highly for the good use to which your left arm has been applied since the loss of its right companion, as well as for the gallant services you have rendered the government." In 1866, when Geary successfully ran for governor, Thompson was on his Union Republican ticket, nominated for prothonotary, or chief clerk; the party called on voters to "show their love for the defenders of the country by giving this maimed, disabled hero their undivided support."[77] In 1874, while serving as superintendent of the state arsenal, Thompson "caught a cold . . . which settled in his wounds and caused his death."[78] The state legislature observed a moment of silence in his honor; a state representative remembered Thompson as "a faithful and respected citizen, a public officer who honored the army to which he belonged and the republic to which he gave his blood to maintain."[79]

76. John M. Thompson, Contest Entry, 2nd ser., no. 63, Bourne Papers (punctuation corrected).
77. "The Ticket," *Juniata (PA) Sentinel*, May 23, 1866, 2.
78. "Death of Col. Jno. M. Thompson," *Harrisburg (PA) Telegraph*, Mar. 16, 1874, 3.
79. "Local Intelligence," *Juniata Sentinel and Republican* (Mifflintown, PA), Mar. 25, 1874, 3.
~~~

June 26, 1867

Promoted to sergeant major in January 1862, Thompson fought in the Peninsula and Maryland Campaigns. He was promoted to second lieutenant and then first lieutenant in October and November 1862, respectively. He commanded his company at both Fredericksburg and Gettysburg. After helping process drafted men in Pennsylvania, Thompson reported to his regiment in time for the Battle of the Wilderness and was wounded at Spotsylvania Court House in May 1864.

Early, on the morning of the 11th while sitting near a road behind some bushes (for we had to conceal ourselves), I was shot in the left arm, between the wrist and elbow joints, with a minie ball from a Sharpshooter's rifle. The ball followed the bone, and lodged above the elbow, causing a very severe, and painful wound. I went to the rear immediately and had the ball extracted and my wound dressed, and was sent the same day with others from corps Hospital to Washington. I was admitted to Seminary Hospital at Georgetown on the 13th at five o'clock p.m. I was very faint from pain, loss of blood, and sleep, for we travelled at night as well as day. My wound had not been dressed from leaving the Hospital in the field, until my arrival there, nearly three days. My arm and hand was very much swollen. At one time it was decided to amputate, but upon a careful examination it was found that the bone was not much injured, therefore my arm was saved. Alas: how much better for me had I lost it then, for by it I would have been kept from the field thereby avoiding the suffering of which I am about to speak. By a very wise arrangement of divine Providence we are prevented from knowing what is before us, which no doubt is for our good. I remained in the Seminary Hospital about three weeks, when my arm was so far recovered, that a leave of absence was granted me for thirty days to go to my home in Penn'a. . . .

After his furlough, Thompson rejoined his regiment but could not fight due to his sore arm. He served as provost marshal at Gettysburg before rejoining his regiment at Harpers Ferry. He was appointed captain in September 1864.

I was mustered for three years, but my term of service was destined to be of short duration as will be seen. Our Regiment was relieved in a few days, and ordered to join the corps then encamped near Charlestown, VA. On the 19th day of September the battle of Winchester[80] was fought under General Sheridan.... When the actions became general, the sixth corps took position on the left of the road leading from Harpers Ferry through Winchester. Our Brigade (Genl. Russell's)[81] was lying in column by battalion, awaiting orders to advance, when a shell from a Rebel gun in sight of our column exploded near my right side, scattering its fragments and loading[82] in a fearful manner. One of them broke my right arm, immediately above the elbow joint, which was amputated soon after, a few inches from the shoulder. A metal ball struck my right leg and lodged in the bone just below the knee, causing a very serious fracture, and nearly resulting in amputation, but I preferred death rather than lose both an arm and leg. Consequently the ball was extracted and care taken of the wound. It healed up finally and is now nearly as strong as ever. Another ball or fragment struck my right foot carrying away nearly the entire top of my boot and part of the little toe. Another passed through my right hand, breaking one and tearing another of my fingers, but as that hand was afterwards amputated, no account was taken of that wound. Another tore a ring and the flesh from the little finger of the left hand, carrying off one of the bands from my sword scabbard, which was in my hand at the time. Two other balls entered my groin (or near it) together carrying with them into the wound portions of my clothing. They lodged near the hip joint. I was carried immediately to the field Hospital about half a mile in the rear of the line of battle, where my arm was amputated and my wounds dressed. I remained there until the next morning when with the others I was removed to Winchester and put into the Taylor House[83] then to be used as a Hospital for our wounded, the Rebels having been driven from the town the day previous. It was on the 20th day of September I was taken to Winchester and for ten day[s] I remained unconscious, nor do I remember to this day anything that transpired during that time. I remained in the Hospital...

80. Also called Opequon Creek, this was the third major battle at Winchester.

81. Brigadier General David Allen Russell (1820–64).

82. Components of the shell, most likely balls.

83. A hotel.

until the tenth day of November when I was granted a leave of absence, and in company with my sister (who was with me) and servant, I started for home on my bed. It was a very dangerous trip for we had twenty two miles to travel in the ambulance from Winchester to Martinsburg. I was so far exhausted when reaching the latter place that we were compelled to remain from Friday until Monday. I reached home however on the fifteenth without accident or injury save a severe cold. The wound in my left hip caused me a great amount of suffering. The balls remained imbedded near the joint for a period of nearly eleven months, suppurating continuously, and producing the severest pain conceivable. Had it not been for morphine, I could not have endured it. Several efforts were made to extract them but without success. From lying on my back all the time, they worked their way downwards gradually until finally they made their appearance and were taken out nearly opposite the place they entered, by Dr. G. M. Graham. One was taken out whole, and the other in five pieces; how it was broken is a mystery, for the pieces fitted to each other making a perfect ball. They were taken out as discovered, at intervals of three and four weeks. All the balls taken from my body (and which are now in my possession) weigh just three ounces. From the effects of the wound last named my left hip joint is stiffened and the leg shortened nearly three inches, making me a permanent cripple. I was discharged on the 13th day of Jan. 1865 not quite four months after I was wounded by reason of being permanently unfit for service. As will be seen from the foregoing, I have been wounded in both legs, and both arms, the right being amputated. I have learned to write with my left hand entirely, since losing my right. I have seventeen scars on my body made by bullets and surgical instruments. My wounds are now all healed up sound, and I experience no inconvenience from them more than that of doing without my right arm, and the full use of my left hip, and I suppose there is no language fully adequate to describe the extent of that inconvenience, nor can anyone realize how great it is except those who by sad experience are called upon to bear it.

It has been said "they get pensions, they are not so bad off after all." True we do get pensions, and we thank our noble Government for that care over us; but how far short does it come of paying us for the loss we have sustained. To be compelled just in the prime of life (when teeming with anticipations of future prosperity and pleasure) to consent to be a permanent cripple for life, and to depend entirely upon others for assistance is a matter of no small moment. Then we lose more than the arm or leg; we lose in a great measure our place in society, which to many of us is a great sacrifice. Our loss in this respect may be, and I have no doubt is, more imaginary than real, but we cannot take the same part in social life we once could; consequently our enjoyments are less. But how many have given more than us in this great struggle, even their lives, and when I think of the fearful carnage of some of the battles in which we were engaged, I wonder at our escape from death. What we ask now, and desire most of all to see, is that the work that has cost each of us so much, and the nation at large such a vast amount of blood, of treasure, and of grief, be carried forward to an honorable and permanent consummation. I believe the day is not far distant when the surviving victims of the war against Treason and Rebellion will be held in higher esteem than at the present. We have given three years of the best of our time, and have been disabled for life; what more can we do. It remains now for those who are placed in high positions, of honor and of trust, to do their work well and securely. At the same time let us not forget the motto of our Government, "In God we Trust." He shielded us in the day of battle and He will not forsake those that trust in Him. Since I was discharged I have been commissioned to the rank of Major, and Lieut. Colonel by Brevet. In writing this narrative, I have endeavored to be as brief as possible; many incidents that might have been of interest, have necessarily been passed by without notice. If those whose business it is to compose, and write, had the facts, as we, by experience have them, a great History would soon be written.

5.

NEW AMERICANS

In the crucible of war, men became Americans by fighting for their adopted country. Foreign-born soldiers constituted one-quarter of Union troops, and at least thirty of them signed Bourne's hospital reminiscence books, including one Welshman, a Corsican, seven Englishmen, four Germans, three Canadians, four Irishmen, one Pole, one Norwegian, and six Frenchmen, one of whom wrote that he "perdu un bras pour une bonne cause" (lost an arm for a good cause).[1] Around 200,000 Germans enlisted in the Union army, constituting 10 percent of the total fighting force, while upward of 150,000 Irishmen joined the ranks.[2] While Irish soldiers commonly linked Irish independence to the Union cause, some German recruits hoped to bolster the kind of republic the German revolutions of 1848 and 1849 had failed to establish.[3] Though military service expedited assimilation for some, German troops faced nativist antagonism and were blamed for the Union defeat at Chancellorsville; historian Christian B. Keller argues that increased "ethnic consciousness" as opposed to Americanization resulted from this backlash.[4] Irish soldiers also faced discrimination but

1. McPherson, *Battle Cry of Freedom,* 606; Civil War Reminiscences by Soldiers and Sailors in Central Park Hospital, William Oland Bourne Papers.

2. Engel, "Yankee Dutchmen," 19–20; Bruce, *Harp and the Eagle,* 2.

3. Bruce, *Harp and the Eagle,* 1; Engel, "Yankee Dutchmen," 16.

4. Keller, *Chancellorsville and the Germans,* 4.

passionately demanded citizenship on the basis of their loyalty and service.[5] An act passed in July 1862 stipulated that honorably discharged veterans could petition for naturalization after one year of residency, expediting the process for those who had proved their dedication to the Constitution.[6] Black soldiers would have to wait until 1865 and the Fourteenth Amendment before their sacrifice was rewarded with citizenship.

Bourne was well aware of the multicultural and multilingual makeup of the Union army. In May 1867, he announced publication of *Der Soldaten-Freund,* a German-language version of his newspaper.[7] One potential reader, August Schmidt, submitted left-handed penmanship in English and German, transcribing an English account of the Battle of Malvern Hill (July 1, 1862) and a portion of Friedrich Schiller's *The Piccolomini* that describes the homecoming of weary soldiers.[8] Unsurprisingly, more than fifty contestants were foreign born; some enlisted shortly after arriving, having emigrated intending to do so, while others had spent a decade or more in the United States. Like Michael Fitz James, they decided to "take up arms in defence of [their] adopted country." Their narratives not only echo those of native-born veterans in their references to defeating treason, defending "our country," and perpetuating liberty but also provide insight into how recently arrived soldiers understood the significance of their service. Members of the Left-Armed Corps may have hailed from England, Germany, Ireland, France, and Scotland, but all expressed loyalty to their new homeland and bore visible marks of their dedication.

JOHN BRYSON

Private, Co. A, 30th New York Volunteer Infantry

Bryson, born in Scotland, enlisted on April 24, 1861, and was wounded at Second Bull Run.[9] Back home in Lansingburgh, New York, for a few years, he moved his family to Washing-

5. See Samito, *Becoming American under Fire,* 103–33.

6. Ibid., 108.

7. "The Soldier's Friend in German," *Soldier's Friend, and Grand Army of the Republic,* May 1867, 2.

8. August Schmidt, Contest Entry, 1st ser., no. 56, Bourne Papers.

9. John Bryson, Contest Entries, 1st ser., no. 18, and 2nd ser., no. 23, Bourne Papers (punctuation edited).

ton, D.C., to work as a government clerk. They eventually returned to New York. In 1901 and 1911, the *Brooklyn Daily Eagle* printed Bryson's letters to the editor, which praised the 14th Brooklyn Regiment in eloquent prose; an "ardent geologist," he also sent a letter regarding New York's Block Island.[10] Superintendent of multiple national cemeteries, Bryson also wrote a history of the 30th New York for a reunion of the regiment and was "always ready with both pen and tongue to enliven" gatherings.[11] When he died in 1919 at the age of eighty-five, survived by two children, Bryson was "one of the most prominent geologists of Long Island."[12] He requested that he be buried with his GAR pin and his "old flag."[13]

***First Entry:* August 28, 1865**

I have hesitated somewhat in sending this to you, feeling confident that there are others who have made greater proficiency with the left hand than I have; still, deeming myself entitled to some little credit, I have ventured to submit this to your notice.

I am a native of Scotland, and emigrated to this country at the age of eighteen. I was not long in learning to appreciate the blessings of your free Institutions, and for the perpetuity of which I was willing to risk my life. So when armed traitors arose with intent to destroy them, I was among the first to go forth to do battle, in defense of our country's cause. . . .

I have selected a few sketches of scenes thru which I passed during Gen. Pope's campaign in Virginia, commencing with a description of the field a few days after the battle of Cedar Mountain.

August 13th 1862. Being anxious to visit the battle ground I eluded the pickets and soon arrived near the foot of Cedar Mountain. Here everything bore evidence of the recent conflict. Fields of corn were trampled underfoot and torn up with artillery. Broken accoutrements were everywhere strewed around. Dead horses lay unburied all over the field. Here and there a little red

10. "To the Gallant Fourteenth," *Brooklyn Daily Eagle,* May 13, 1911, 15; "War Reminiscences," ibid., Feb. 25, 1901, 8; "Block Island's Formation," ibid., Sept. 5, 1905, 20.

11. 1900 U.S. Census, Suffolk Co., NY, pop. sched., Southampton, p. 6, dwelling 152, family 153, John Bryson, NARA RG 29, T623, roll 1166; Reed, *Original Iron Brigade,* x; "Old Hunters' Picnic," *Brooklyn Times Union,* Aug. 13, 1904, 7.

12. "Obituary," *Brooklyn Times Union,* June 19, 1919, 9; "Obituaries," *Brooklyn Standard Union,* June 17, 1919, 14.

13. "Wills Civil War Relics," *Brooklyn Daily Eagle,* July 12, 1919, 3.

mound showed where some soldier was sleeping his last sleep. A little further on between two woods—here is where the conflict has raged the fiercest. Here the 28th N.Y. Vols. charged under a murderous fire upon the rebel lines. Every tree and fence around were marked with bullet holes. Caps and jackets clotted with blood lay scattered all around.

The long line of newly covered trenches were sad monuments of the bravery of those who slept beneath. But quietly they rested there beneath the forest boughs. No alarm will wake them from their slumbers. The drums may beat again to action, but they will heed not their call, for their warfare is over.

Passing over to where the rebel lines had been formed a revolting sight met my view. Here the dead were only partly buried. Feet and hands protruded from their shallow graves. They had died to promote the aggrandizement of traitors and this was their reward. Not allowed enough of earth to cover their ghastly forms, but left exposed a prey to the hungry vultures.

I turned away full of sadness from the scene, with a silent but fervent prayer, that the cruel strife would cease in our land. I desired to visit no more battlefields.

In a few days after this our division advanced a few miles when we encamped along the base of the Mountain. In company with a friend I ascended to its summit. The day was clear and beautiful. The soft sunlight lay like a flood of gold in the plain beneath us. Far away beyond, we could faintly trace the windings of the Rapidan. The Blue Ridge in the distance lit up with the golden sunbeams looked grand and sublime, as it towered up against the sky. . . .

My friend and I lingered entranced upon the mountain top until the evening shadows began to gather around us. When we came down, and reached our camp we found it all in commotion. Orders had been received "to pack up." We struck tents, packed everything up, when we fell "into line." Stacked arms and was told "to lie down as quietly as possible." We could not divine what was up but a dark foreboding of evil settled down upon us. We feared that all was not well, so we lay down in sadness; but we did not have long to rest, for soon the word was quietly passed along the line to "Fall in."

Bryson's division marched toward Rappahannock Station, eventually crossing the river. Attacked by a rebel battery, they moved out of range and attempted to rest. Falling back, they met the enemy at Gainesville, encountering heavy shelling.

The shells were bursting right in front of us, tearing up the ground and covering us with dust. A young man belonging to my company, and who lay beside me, had half of his head carried way, killing him instantly. When the artillery had ceased, a heavy musketry fire commenced on our left. Gibbons' brigade composed of the brave Wisconsin and Indiana boys had engaged the enemy. Sometimes the firing would slacken a little as if both sides were losing heart, and then again a wild shout would rend the air, when the firing louder and more fierce than ever would burst from their thinned ranks. Thus the battle raged until after dusk, both sides seeming unwilling to give up the contest. At length the 30th was ordered from the "right" to support the "left." As we marched up the road, the scene was awful, tho' grand—the shouts of the combatants—the rattle of musketry, and to render it more terrific, a caisson was blown up lighting up the darkness with a lurid glare while the earth seemed to tremble beneath the shock.

On reaching Gibbons' line, the 30th went in cheering with all its might, while the enemy, I presume, thinking that reinforcements had arrived, withdrew from the field. Gibbons' brigade then fell back to the turnpike leaving our regiment to hold the line, and never will I forget that awful night. There we had to stand among the dead and dying, while the groans and shrieks of the wounded were heartrending to hear. We held the field until twelve o'clock that night when for some reason or other we were ordered to fall back to Manassas Junction which place we reached about daylight in the morning. Having had no rest all night and after marching and fighting all the day before, we felt weary and depressed in spirits; but after being refreshed with a cup of coffee, and Gen. Porter's[14] corps coming up we felt somewhat revived, so that when the order came for us to advance again, we obeyed it with alacrity.

We now came to the battle of Groveton. On the afternoon of the 29th of August, our forces came up with the enemy again driving him considerable ways. Our division was kept in reserve until nearly dark when we ordered to advance. [Maj.] Gen. [Irvin] McDowell rode up to us and said, "Boys the enemy is retreating, follow him up, and when you find him pitch in to him." Encouraged by these words, we advanced at brisk pace up the road; but we had not gone far when all at once, a rebel battery opened on [us] with grape and canister, sweeping the road in a fearful manner.

14. Major General Fitz John Porter (1822–1901), commander of V Corps, AOTP.

We were then ordered to file by the left flank into an open field where we tried to form in line of battle, but seemingly from all sides, the rebels poured into us a most deadly fire. The attack was so sudden and unexpected, that before we could form line we were thrown into confusion, and began to retreat back in considerable disorder, as it was getting so dark that we could hardly distinguish friend from foe. The rebels, elated with success, advanced, yelling like demons, pouring volley after volley into our broken ranks. It was a fearful night, the men were scattered here and there, not knowing in the darkness where to go and all was uncertainty as to who, and how many of our comrades had fallen in the fight.

Next morning we commenced picking up the fragments of our brigade. All forenoon they kept coming in, but alas there were many who would join us no more who lay cold and silent on the other side of the stream. And then again there were many who did come back after all the fighting was over—*skulkers* who had hid away and deserted their flag in the hour of danger.

Our brigade was so badly cut up that we did not expect to be put into the fight again that day but in the afternoon the "Old Iron Brigade"[15] had to go at it again. We crossed the same stream we did the night before, and advanced behind the skirmishers. Soon bang-bang went the sharpshooter's rifle, indicating that the enemy was "still there." Slowly and silently we advance[d] until we reach[ed] the edge of a wood facing the bank of the new railroad behind which the rebels were entrenched. As soon as they discovered us, they welcomed us with a withering volley, causing many of our number to bite the dust. Still we heeded it not but with a shout of defiance we charged up upon their lines, when we commenced firing, but as the rebels were concealed partly by the embankment of the railroad they did not of course suffer as much as we did, standing as we were on the brow of the hill, fully exposed to a galling fire, from both infantry, and Artillery.

Half of our number had already fallen. . . . I received two severe wounds, one in the foot, the other in the right hand, and though my wounds were bleeding profusely I managed to leave the field unaided, but I will not weary you with an account of my sufferings.

15. A storied brigade comprising "western" regiments from Wisconsin, Indiana, and Michigan, its soldiers wearing distinctive black slouch hats. It did not receive its nickname, however, until the Antietam Campaign.

In closing allow me to say, that although I have suffered much I murmured not amid it all, nor did I ever regret that I had followed that dear old flag amid its perilous course, during the late rebellion.

***Second Entry:* June 11, 1867**

. . . I was wounded in the left foot, and right hand, the latter so severely, that amputation was deemed necessary. I was conveyed from the field, and taken to Eckington Hospital, Washington D.C., where I remained, until I recovered from my wounds.

I was discharged from service November 7th 1862. Returning home to my family, with nothing but an "empty sleeve," I felt naturally anxious as to how I was going to provide for them, still I was not discouraged feeling confident that some way would open up, and I was not disappointed.

In the following Spring, I was elected tax collector, for the Town, and Village, of Lansingburgh, NY. Served one term, and was elected again, but resigned, to accept an appointment under the Government, at Washington, where I am now employed as clerk, in the Adjutant General's Office.

~~~

ALFRED D. WHITEHOUSE

Private, Co. D, 8th New York State Militia ("Washington Grays")

Whitehouse, who called himself Bourne's "left arm soldier friend," was born in London, England, in 1839, and became a U.S. citizen in 1861.[16] Prior to enlisting, he lived with his parents and worked as a sign painter in New York City.[17] After the war, he married and lived in Brooklyn, continuing to paint with his left hand; he even crafted an "elegant, substantial" sign for the office of *The Soldier's Friend.*[18] He was a trustee of the Fifteenth Street Baptist Church

16. Alfred D. Whitehouse, Contest Entries, 1st ser., no. 163, and 2nd ser., no. 73, Bourne Papers (punctuation edited); Index (Soundex) to Naturalization Petitions Filed in Federal, State, and Local Courts in New York City, 1792–1906, Alfred D. Whitehouse, NARA M1674, roll 281.

17. 1860 U.S. Census, New York Co., NY, pop. sched., New York City, p. 263 (stamped), dwelling 101, family 274, Alfred D. Whitehouse, NARA RG 29, M653, roll 806.

18. 1870 U.S. Census, Kings Co., NY, pop. sched., Brooklyn, p. 578A (stamped), dwelling 652, family 843, Alfred Whitehouse, NARA RG 29, M593, roll 951; "Left-Hand Painting," *Soldier's Friend*, Dec. 1865, 2.
~~~

Title page for Alfred D. Whitehouse's first entry.
Courtesy William Oland Bourne Papers, Manuscript Division, Library of Congress.

and was elected chaplain of his post of the GAR in 1909.[19] By 1910, he was a postal clerk and also worked as an appraiser for the New York customs service.[20] He died in 1919, survived by four children.[21] Whitehouse submitted his impressive penmanship to both contests; his first entry received a twenty-dollar prize for ornamental penmanship.[22]

First Entry: October 6, 1865

I left London for New York on April 14th, 1849, and have been in the United States ever since. I enlisted in Company D. Eighth Regt. Washington

19. "Pulpit and Pew," *Brooklyn Standard Union,* Nov. 4, 1899, 4; "Grand Army News," *Brooklyn Daily Eagle,* Dec. 5, 1909, 45.

20. 1910 U.S. Census, Kings Co., NY, pop. sched., Brooklyn, p. 15B, dwelling 180, family 327, Alfred D. Whitehouse, NARA RG 29, T624, roll 971; "Obituary," *Brooklyn Times Union,* Feb. 10, 1919, 3.

21. "Obituary," 3.

22. Exhibition of Left-Hand Penmanship, Bourne Papers.

Grays New York State Militia, February 1st 1859. I lost my right arm at the battle of Bull Run Manassas, Virginia, on Sunday July 21st, 1861. I wrote this with my left hand October 6th, 1865.

Friends, and Soldiers, Of Our glorious Republic,

I have had the honor of sharing with you the prosperity, and happiness, as well as the perils through which Our beloved country has so recently passed, the honor of having my name written among the first pensioners of this great Rebellion, the honor of being in the ranks of the Eighth Regt. as it marched with steady and well trained steps, down Broadway New York City on the 23rd day of April 1861, to the seat of war, amidst the cheering multitude whose eyes beheld many of us for the last time, for in the all wise providence of God, the time had arrived for Right, Justice, and Liberty to enter into fierce combat with Wrong, Unjust, and Oppressive principles of every satanic kind, that we might still rejoice with grateful hearts in the impartial Liberty that God by the hand of Our Forefathers gave us, that we might still retain Our beloved Land, as a receptacle for the down trodden and oppressed, but freedom loving people of all nations, and cursed be the man, whose lot has been to be the recipient of so benign a nation, to turn his back upon it, and become its foe, to return evil, for good, he is a ungrateful wretch, worthy only of the scorn, and contempt of all true men.

We embarked on board the steamship *Alabama,* and before dark the Old Metropolis had faded from view; then it is that the thoughts are turned homeward, when the ship is silently plowing the wide water, bearing us away from those we love, and naught is seen but the blue horizon, wondering if Providence shall permit us to see again our own dear native land or the land of our adoption, and meet with those dear friends whose tearful eyes watched our departure.—Who can tell. Duty to our country is to lead us where death and danger is, and upon many battlefields before we return. . . .

Whitehouse's regiment arrived in Annapolis on April 26 and was officially mustered into service May 24.

On the 26th of May 1861, we left Kaloroma Heights, crossed the Potomac River, over Long Bridge, and encamped on Arlington Heights, at which place we remained until everything was ready to give the rebels battle. Accordingly on the 16th of July 1861, Brig. Gen. McDowell, commanding on the west side of the Potomac, advanced towards Manassas with 50,000 men, arranged in five divisions. He was to drive the rebel Gen. Beauregard from Manassas, while Gen. Patterson pressed upon Johnston at Winchester to prevent a Junction of the rebel forces. On the 18th our first division reached Bull Run, and after a brisk skirmish with the enemy, fell back on Centreville. Bull Run is a small stream running North, and South, about four miles from Manassas Junction. The Enemy were strongly entrenched on the West side.

Early on the morning of the 21st of July 1861, a beautiful Sunday morning calm and serene, too sacred to be disturbed by the horrid din of battle, so a Christian would think as he contemplated the lovely day and the ominous quiet of nature. It was a day long to be remembered by those engaged in it, and by millions of liberty loving people. . . .

After hard fighting the Enemy were forced back one and a half miles, being driven beyond the Warrenton turnpike. But at this point the tide of battle turned. Gen. Patterson, believing his strength to be insufficient to cope with Johnston, had remained at Martinsburg. Johnston had therefore without opposition reached the scene of action, and was at 3 p.m. rapidly bringing up fresh troops from Winchester. . . .

Worn out with the labors of the day and faint for want of food for they had eaten nothing since 2 a.m., the federal troops gave way and fell back on their old positions at Arlington Heights. In this battle our loss was 83 Officers, and 1,409 men killed and wounded, besides a large number of prisoners and a large quantity of ammunition, provisions, etc. The acknowledged loss of the rebels in killed and wounded was 1,599.[23]

I was wounded about 3 p.m. in the right arm by a rifle ball near the shoulder and after remaining upon the battlefield about six days among my wounded and dying comrades, till my shattered arm was full of maggots, then I was put with many others on board of dirty cattle cars, without even straw to cover the manure on the floor of the cars where we lay. From three to five died in each car going from Manassas Junction to Richmond, VA, as prisoners. Such was rebel humanity towards wounded men. While I was in Richmond my right arm was amputated. On October 6th 1861, sixty-three

23. The official report of the Union assistant adjutant general matches Whitehouse's statistics. Confederate authorities reported 1,969 killed and wounded. See *War of the Rebellion,* ser. 1, 2:327, 570.

of us wounded, myself included, were sent by flag of truce to Ft. Monroe. On the 7th arrived at Ft. Monroe. On the 8th arrived at Baltimore, detained in general hospital for fourteen days, left Baltimore for New York. On the 21st arrived the same day at 7 p.m. On November 12th 1861, I was discharged from the service of the United States on account of the loss of my right arm. Now my friends, having no room to say any more, I close by saying I thank God who hath spared my life to see Victory and Peace, although at a terrible sacrifice, dawn upon our beloved land once more.

ROBERT A. BAIN

First Sergeant, Co. K, 24th Michigan Volunteer Infantry

Bain, born in Scotland in 1842, enlisted in the fall of 1862.[24] After sacrificing his right arm, as one biographer put it, "to appease the wrath of treason," Bain attended Oberlin College for two years and then worked in the Detroit Custom House until 1867, when he relocated to Nebraska "for the purpose of regaining his health, having never recovered from the shock of his wound."[25] He settled in Lincoln, married, and was elected county clerk in 1869; in 1871, he was elected treasurer.[26] Due to "failing health," Bain resigned in 1873; he died in 1882.[27] His effusive biographer summed him up with the following: "Politically, a life long republican, without a democratic relation. Religiously, a Methodist. In business, fair dealing, and as a citizen, true as the magnet."[28]

August 20, 1865

You stated that the literary part of the work might be of any choice, therefore I will give you a little history as people are far more fond of poorly written history than dry essays or orations.

24. R. A. Bain, Contest Entry, 1st ser., no. 55, Bourne Papers (punctuation edited); Edmunds, *Pen Sketches of Nebraskans,* 277.

25. Ibid.

26. Ibid., 278.

27. "Financial Sketches," *Nebraska State Journal* (Lincoln), May 30, 1882, 4; Robert A. Bain, Pension File, application 312613, certificate 222461, NARA RG 15, T288, roll 17.

28. Edmunds, *Pen Sketches of Nebraskans,* 278.

Many will wonder when they read my pages filed with the many specimens of left hand penmanship who I am. It might seem interesting to some few to know this, so I will proceed to give you a brief sketch.

When I was in the fourth year of my age, my father on account of embarrassment in business was compelled to leave the land of my birth (the city of Wick, Scotland) and come to America. He had heard much of the beauty of the prairies of Illinois and being fascinated by their described grandeur took up his departure for them, and settled in the central part of the County of Ogle. My father died soon after reaching here, leaving my mother to take charge of three children and attend to the duties of a large farm. . . .

At sixteen, Bain decided to leave the farm due to "family jars" with his mother's second husband.

On the seventh of August 1859, on one of those beautiful mornings which seems to clothe nature in its richest robes of grandeur and beauty, I packed up my few pieces of wearing apparel and started for the station (my mother being my only escort).

After having received a few words of Mother's kind advice—a parting kiss—a stroke of the locomotive's bell and a wave of the moistened handkerchief informed us that we had parted. At five o'clock p.m. I entered the city of Chicago, an object which never before did I look upon. This was a day of great interest to me—much did I see that only before I had formed boyish ideas of. There was a mother left to sigh and weep for with anxiety a young son who was just starting out into the world.

The crowded and noisy city, whose docks were crowded with vessels of all description. The blue sheet of water to the east of the city dotted here and there with white canvas floating from the masts of objects which have long excited my curiosity. This is a picture which can never be obliterated from my memory so long as I live.

At 7 p.m. we took the cars on the M.C.R.R.[29] and at 7 a.m. the next morning I found myself at my Uncle's a short distance from Detroit. . . . Uncle asked me one day how I should like to learn the dry goods trade; to this I did not

29. Michigan Central Railroad.

answer in the negative, as anything to occupy my time was acceptable. I had often had the idea enter my head, that I was intended for a dry goods man, and of course the proposition was a congenial one.

On the first of September, Uncle took me into Detroit and made application for me a situation in the "Scotch Store," the leading dry goods establishment of the place. I entered in a short time as junior apprentice and progressed nicely with the dry goods having worked my way up from ticket maker and marker to a department in the retail room. Three years had elapsed since I first entered the store and during that time I had underwent all the torture and persecution applicable to an apprentice's life (you who have served as such know full well what I mean by those words).

One afternoon while I was filling and preparing some hosiery for retail, I overheard a lady who was looking at some articles nearby telling of her son who had but a short time since joined the army as [a] volunteer to "fight rebels and put down rebellion," say the following, which fell upon my ears as if it had been shot from a 12 lb. *howitzer*, "If I had a son who would not respond to his country's call, when it needs his services as it now does, I would disown him." This was more than I could endure; it caused the red hot coals of patriotism which were partially covered with the ashes of fear and thought of leaving my mother in this world, to burst forth with unquenchable flames. I threw my box of hosiery aside and went straight to the nearest recruiting office, and there left my autograph on an enlistment paper for the 24th Regt. Mich. Infantry Vols.

Thirty days from that time my regiment reached Washington city, and at the close of that fatal Saturday on the 13th of Dec 1862, when the left wing of the army of the Potomac made their last and final charge on the enemy's impregnable stronghold at Fredericksburg, Va., a cannon shot from the masked battery which opened upon us from the left, cut off my right arm just below the elbow. Hoping you will pardon me for troubling you with so long a discourse I am

Most respectfully Your Obdt. Servt.

~ ~ ~

CONRAD DIPPEL

Private, Co. I, 37th Wisconsin Volunteer Infantry

Dippel, a competitor in both contests, was called away "from [his] daily pursuits of business and from the happy family circle of [his] wife and three children" in 1863.[30] Out of the twenty-nine men drafted in his neighborhood, he claimed, only he chose not to pay $300 for a substitute. Dippel was born in Saxony (now part of Germany) in 1831 and arrived in the United States in 1849, settling in Watertown, Wisconsin, in 1855 and working as a mason; he became a naturalized citizen in 1880.[31] As he narrates below, he worked as a schoolteacher after the war. He was still teaching in 1870 but a decade later had switched to farming, beekeeping, and (at least in 1880) census enumerating.[32] Surgeon for his local GAR post (meaning he was in charge of medical records), Dippel married twice and was widowed for a second time by 1900, when he worked as a notary public and was well known for his beekeeping.[33] In 1910, a local newspaper reported on his eightieth-birthday celebration, noting that Dippel was "in vigorous health and in the enjoyment of his faculties"; he had "many interesting incidents to relate of his experiences during that period which tried men's souls, and he was helping to make national history."[34] When Dippel died two years later, his obituary appeared on the front page of the *Watertown News*.[35]

***First Entry:* November 22, 1865**

Having lost my right arm in the battle before Petersburg, VA, on the 17th of June 1864 my physical powers are broke down to a great extent and I am obliged to take resort to the employment of my higher and better

30. Conrad Dippel, Contest Entries, 1st ser., no. 128, and 2nd ser., no. 29, Bourne Papers.

31. 1870 U.S. Census, Dodge Co., WI, pop. sched., Watertown, p. 556A (stamped), dwelling 68, family 68, Conrad Dippel, NARA RG 29, M593, roll 1711; 1910 U.S. Census, Dodge Co., WI, pop. sched., Watertown, p. 11A, dwelling 256, family 288, Conrad Dippel, ibid., T624, roll 1707; "Old Veteran Called," *Watertown (WI) News,* June 7, 1912, 1; *U.S. Naturalization Record Indexes, 1791–1992,* Conrad Dippel, NARA RG 85, M1285, roll 40.

32. 1870 U.S. Census, Dodge Co., WI, pop. sched., Watertown, p. 556A; 1880 U.S. Census, Dodge Co., WI., pop. sched., Watertown, p. 445A (stamped), dwelling 163, family 173, Conrad Dippel, NARA RG 29, T9, roll 1423. Dippel himself signed the 1880 Census page.

33. "Societies Elect Officers," *Watertown (WI) News,* Dec. 17, 1909, 8; 1900 U.S. Census, Dodge Co., WI, pop. sched., Watertown, p. 4, dwelling 83, family 93, Conrad Dippel, NARA RG 29, T623, roll 1785.

34. "Old Veteran Celebrates," *Watertown (WI) News,* Nov. 18, 1910, 4.

35. "Old Veteran Called," 1.

faculties and also to the talents of my left hand in former times so often disrespected and disregarded. The first attempts to write with it I made at Mount Pleasant Hospital, Washington, D.C., in the summer of 1864 when I sent letters to my family. I tried to improve ever since and lately encouraged by your offering of premiums and in view of some honorable position I practiced every leisure hour to fit my hand to a practical business style of penmanship.

I was a Private of Comp F, 37th Reg. Wis. Vols. and when I came to Virginia in May 1864 I found the most striking contrast between the quiet business and peaceful homes in Wisconsin and the noisy, warlike undertakings in [the] "Old Dominion." Drilling, guarding prisoners, building breastworks, marching and actual engagements soon followed one after another. While encamped at White House Landing, VA, in June 1864, thousands of our soldiers wounded in the battle in the Wilderness and in the engagements on the way to Cold-Harbor came in. Also the contrabands[36] from all the surrounding country and also the prisoners taken from the enemy in several large squads. A detachment of our regiment together with a New York regiment were detailed to guard a squad of 638 rebel prisoners among whom was a young sturdy woman dressed in our uniform. My post happened to be near the place where her tent was; she once came to the allowed inside line, four paces near the beat,[37] towards me and my next comrades on guard, and sat down to have a talk. Besides many other questions she was asked how she liked her present situation. In answer to this she expressed her wishes to be brought back by us to the lines of her friends and made the clever proposition to return her thanks by giving some of us a discharge and some others a furlough. We understood it and took it as an unpleasant joke. At night, while on guard, it rained and we had to stand the weather some distance off from our camp, whilst the prisoners were lying snuggly in tents, their tents and blankets mostly being captured, having the U.S. mark on them. . . .

36. Formerly enslaved people who have entered Union lines. In the summer of 1861, General Butler, commanding at Fort Monroe in Virginia, had labeled such persons legally "contraband of war" to prevent having to return them to their rebellious slaveowners under the Fugitive Slave Act (1850).

37. Area covered by a guard or sentinel. See Cable, *Famous Adventures and Prison Escapes of the Civil War*, 209.

Dippel's regiment marched to Cold Harbor, crossed the Chickahominy River toward Malvern Hill, and continued on to Petersburg.

What a long wearisome march it was, is hard to imagine by anyone who never went through such hardships. We had from the 10th until the 17th of June but very little rest by night and at daytime the sun shone so hot and scorching while we all were almost smothered by the dust, many falling out of the ranks tired out and sunstruck. On the 16th of June we marched over a fresh battle field, where a few hours before a division of U.S. colored troops had taken two batteries from the enemy;[38] the wounded men were lying in the adjoining houses and dead horses in our path. We kept going on slowly and late in the afternoon we took possession of the most outside entrenchments of Petersburg. We were lying in there with our breasts flat on the ground all night by a beautiful moonlight, the enemy firing furiously with his batteries and long lines of musketry and the balls whistling dreadful all around us. It seemed as if the Heavens had opened and poured down an incessant flash of lightning and a hail of bullets out of the clear sky of a bright moonshiny summernight. We expected an attack, had our rifles loaded, bayonets fixed, ready to receive the enemy, but the steady fire of our artillery closely brought it to a comparative stillstand [*sic*] about midnight; and early in the morning following several squads of rebel-prisoners were taken. The yells, threats, and curses I heard on this occasion I shall never forget; the prisoners were passed off on our left. The same day, the 17th of June, we were commanded to forward march. The next line of the enemy's breastworks in front of us being on a ridge of rising ground, little ways before the Norfolk & Petersburg R.R. We passed over a little brook, our battle-line was fixed, we went forward in a cornfield within shooting distance, were ordered to lay down, when immediately the balls of a terrible volley from the enemy passed a few inches over us. At the same time our batteries gave a steady fire from a hill behind us, the shell and shot passing us above our heads and making large breaches into the rebel works in which they piled their dead. We were commanded to fix bayonets, trail arms,[39] forward march and went forth as ordered. Running

38. In his second submission, Dippel added that the USCT division "encouraged us, cheered us, and refreshed us with some cool water."

39. A drill order involving keeping the rifle butt a few inches off the ground and angling the muzzle toward the front. See Holbrook, *Military Tactics,* 37–38.

up hill in this cornfield we received some awful, and deadly volleys. Here I was struck by a minieball in my right arm, was overcome with tiredness and fell, the balls whistling and the shells shrilling all around me. While lying on the ground during this unearthly noise I thanked the Lord for all the blessings I received; His ways are really wonderful and unsearchable forever. After some time and with much difficulty I rose, laid my dangling right arm upon my left across my breast and went toward the brook. . . . By a comrade I was led to the field-hospital and about sunset on the same day while under the influence of chloroform my right arm was amputated in the middle between elbow and shoulder. I recollect having had very pleasant feeling[s] during the time of operation, dreaming I was at play with quite a number of young girls and children. But when I awoke I found myself in a tent lying on the ground with my head leaning against the stump of a tree without my right arm, without coat, and without blanket amidst acres and acres full of wounded and dying men. A few paces off were some severely wounded rebels groaning loud, they being little discouraged by the Surgeons' reply that our men had to be attended first. On the third day after, a long ambulance train with wounded men went from the field hospital to City Point. By the attending Surgeon I was seated alongside the driver in one of the ambulances. On the way I saw again the rebel-prisoners who were captured in the morning of the 17th of June; now they were encamped along the roadside in an open field and guarded by U.S. colored troops in double file. This gave me really the greatest satisfaction and I forgot all about my suffering in reflecting how quick Providence turns the luck of man and does justice to everyone. But while so absorbed in thoughts about the past I was startled by many sudden cries of distress uttered by our wounded men especially those with newly amputated limbs, their pain being magnified by the wagons striking often in the road; it was a rough and hard road to travel.

When near City Point, our driver getting [a] little dry, left the ambulance and gave me the lines to lead the horses. They were dry too, like their driver, [and] became rather unruly and consequently it was very difficult for me to keep them steady with my only hand. All at once my fainting strength was aroused by the commanding cry, "take care of the horses," spoken by one of the men lying in the ambulance: a Sergeant of a Pennsylvania regiment with an amputated leg. O, what an amount of suffering a man can heap upon his fellow beings just by going to "take a drink."

By and by we received refreshments through the agents of the Christian Commission[40] which helped me along again for some time; although when I came to the steamboat-landing these utmost and over-powering exertions I had made reduced and exhausted my strength so that I was not able to walk without help. The pain was then not so much in the stump of my arm, but I found the most weakness in my legs and in my head. On board the steamboat en-route for Washington, D.C., I received again refreshments and clean clothes by the Agents of the Sanitary and Christian Commission what lessened my suffering greatly and for which I cannot be thankful enough. The next day I came to Mount Pleasant Hospital, Washington, D.C., in Tent 3, where by help of God and through good care of the Hospital Surgeon and with the best of attendance of the nurses I grew stronger every day.

I was discharged from the U.S. service on the 8th December 1864 and received my Pension Certificate, the number of which is 39,400. I had lived in and near Watertown, Wisconsin, for about ten years and had worked very hard at the mason and plastering business, but had not succeeded in collecting any earthly treasures. As soon as I came home I was entrusted with the care and tuition of a class of scholars in one of our schools and I am now engaged as a teacher for more than eleven months. Thus making use of the education I received at a Polytechnic Institution in my younger years. I give satisfaction to the public in general but received as far as now a pecuniary compensation rather small and often wish for a better situation under the government.

~~~

MICHAEL J. FITZ JAMES

Private, Co. D, 32nd New York Volunteer Infantry
Private, Co. H, 121st New York Volunteer Infantry

Fitz James was born in Ireland around 1846 and arrived in the United States in 1861; a muster roll for the 32nd New York lists him as twenty-eight but later census records indi-

40. Charitable organization founded by the New York YMCA that attended to the spiritual and physical needs of Union soldiers.
~~~

cate he was around sixteen when he enlisted (unless he later lied about his age).[41] After his first regiment's enlistment expired, he transferred to the 121st New York. He fought in nine battles, including Fredericksburg, Gettysburg, and Brandy Station. After the war, he worked at a carpet mill.[42] Married for forty-five years, he and his wife, Bridget, both died in 1917, survived by one son.[43]

December 18, 1865

My dear readers I take my pen in the left hand to inform you that I enlisted in Amsterdam, Montgomery Co., State of New York the 24th of August '62, to take up arms in defence of my adopted country. . . .

The battle of the Wilderness May 5th, where I received my honorable scar, which has left me disabled of the right hand. Genl. Upton[44] and Col. Olcott were the two first that came to my assistance and tied my arm carefully with their pockethandkerchiefs. I kept very calm; my first word was, it is all for a good cause: for freedom and Union. I only laughed, in order to give my companions good courage. There were two men detailed to carry me from the battle field to the Regimental Hospital. After my wound had been dressed by the Assistant Surgeon, I was conveyed in an ambulance to the Division Hospital near Germanna Ford, where Dr. [John O.] Slocum our Regimental Surgeon amputated my hand. I rested among the wounded that night. . . . This day we had the battle of the sixth: there was awful musketry and cannonading the whole day. All the wounded in our Division Hospital would have been taken prisoners, but for a Brigade of colored troops who made a gallant fight and repulsed a whole division of the enemy. In the night at 12 a.m. orders came to move the wounded; the worst cases were carried off in ambulances and army wagons, the rest had to walk the best

41. Michael J. Fitz James. Contest Entry, 1st ser., no. 144, Bourne Papers; 1910 U.S. Census, Montgomery Co., NY, pop. sched., Amsterdam, p. 8A, dwelling 65, family 134, Michael J. Fitz James, NARA RG 29, T624, roll 993.

42. 1880 U.S. Census, Montgomery Co., NY, pop. sched., Amsterdam, p. 44D, dwelling 350, family 451, Michael Fitz James, NARA RG 29, T9, roll 865.

43. New York State Death Index, 1917, certificate 50722, Michael J. Fitz James, New York Department of Health, Albany.

44. Brigadier General Emory Upton (1839–81). Upton was a colonel at the Wilderness but promoted to brigadier general after Spotsylvania.

way they could. We reached Chancellorsville at 6 a.m. The hospital tents were erected, and our wounds dressed. Oh! what an awful sight it was to see our brave men stretched that day under the scorching sun, some groaning, others laughing and thinking of the loved ones at home, whilst the rest were making their peace with the Almighty, perhaps never to see the light of the following day. No one knows what a soldier has to suffer but himself, or the honorable Ladies and Gentlemen of the Sanitary Commission who spared no pains in our assistance. The one half of us would not be alive this day but for this noble institution: their patriotic labor will never be forgotten by us wounded soldiers. At 6 o'clock p.m. we were escorted in ambulances and wagons and reached Fredericksburg at 3 a.m. Hospitals were made of all the churches and houses in the city. Some refused to let us in until our teamsters had forced in the doors. We remained here for three days. On the 11th a lady came to see us and gave us some writing paper and envelopes. I cannot tell her name. I heard she was a daughter of the Mayor of the city; if she was it was one of the first charitable turns I eve[r] had seen from a Southern lady. Next day we were sent to Bell[e] Plain Landing to take transportation for Washington. When we reached this city, the best of care was taken of us by the Sanitary Commission; everything in the line of eatables and clothing was prepared; it was very welcome for us hungry soldiers, some of us not having eaten any food since the day we were wounded. The minute we tasted of the delicious [illegible; possibly "brownies"] we got weak and could not eat [more] of them. When ready we were put into ambulances to be distributed among the hospitals by order of that benevolent Lady Miss Dix.[45] I was among the squad that was sent to the Finley Hospital.[46] After being a few days in this hospital I was taken very ill with a fever that lasted for three weeks. As soon as I got well I got a relapse of another with erysipelas[47] in my arm. I always had borne everything patiently, and got over all my trouble. By the month of October '64 my wound was healed. I took a notion to write a letter, the first one I ever did with my left hand, to see if I could get permission to join my regt. again. I received an answer in a few days; it read as follows:

45. Dorothea Dix (1802–87), superintendent of army nurses.

46. One of several hospitals in Washington, D.C.

47. A bacterial skin infection.

My Dear Fitz James

Yours of the 19 inst. is just received. You can perhaps imagine how glad I was to hear from you. Your courage and fortitude is well remembered by me and I wish that every soldier was actuated by motives as yours, and patriotic. Thomas McHerinan died in rebel prison. Gagin was killed near Petersburg June 22nd. Jacob Heintz died in Hospital at Washington June 2nd. W.H. Van Schanck was killed in the battle of 19 inst.[48]

Bekert, Lamphere, Goodspeed, Norris, and Milo Monger are back to the Co. Our loss the 19th was severe especially in Officers. Maj. Galpin was wounded again. Fret was killed. Burrell, Douw, and Johnson wounded.

Col. Scott commands the Brigade. Capt. Jackson and myself are the only Officers left. Write soon.

E.C. Weaver Adjt.

When I had seen there was no encouragement to join my regiment, I took my discharge in the month of January '65. I am happy to say from the date of my enlistment to the date of my discharge, no Officer ever reprimanded me for the least turn. I was always attentive to everything belonging to military discipline. The morals and unbounded patriotism of both men and Officers of the 121st N.Y. could not be excelled. The greater part of this Regt. was raised in Herkimer Co. NY. Their motto was "always unanimous."

~ ~ ~

THOMAS MOORE GIFFORD BROWNE

Private, Co. F, 48th New York Volunteer Infantry

Browne, born in Ireland in 1831, arrived in the United States prior to 1859, the year of his marriage; he enlisted in December 1861.[49] In November 1866, eleven months after sending his contest entry, Browne sent a letter to Bourne imploring him to speak to New York governor Reuben Fenton and ask for an appointment for Browne.[50] "I want to make a change in

48. The Battle of Cedar Creek, Virginia.

49. Thomas M. G. Browne, Contest Entry, 1st ser., no. 192, Bourne Papers (punctuation edited); Methodist Episcopal Church Records in New York City and Vicinity, Seventh Street Church Marriage and Other Records, 1836–1893, vol. 353-56, Thomas M. G. Browne, Manuscripts and Archives Division of the New York Public Library, New York City.

50. Thomas Moore Gifford Browne to William Oland Bourne, Nov. 10, 1866, William Oland Bourne Left-Handed Penmanship Papers, New-York Historical Society.

my habits, manners and customs, and particularly in my employment, for the better up to best," he wrote. Working as a watchman in 1870, by 1880, Browne was a store clerk, so Bourne seems to have failed to come through.[51] Browne died in 1905.[52]

January 1, 1866

I cannot give you all the dates referring to the different incidents connected with expeditions, and battles, in my military career, as I many times thought it was useless to attempt to take notes of what I have heard and seen, as death cast upon me, at times, his ghastly reflection. At Hilton Head, SC, I was engaged in throwing up fortifications and learning my drill. Occasionally, the regt. was ordered to Daufuskie Island, SC.[53] From that location we had a good view of Ft. Pulaski, GA,[54] then in possession of the rebels. A painter in language could not illustrate or describe the fatigue we had to endure on this island, also on Bird and Jones Islands,[55] in doing picket duty on land and river, throwing up breastworks and creating batteries on those swampy slimy islands, visited by daily inundations, hard fare, and hard beds and irregular rest. 'Twas enough to appall the bravest and stoutest recruit of that time, at 13 dollars a month.

After helping capture Fort Pulaski on April 12, 1862, the regiment targeted Folly and Morris Islands, successfully taking rebel batteries and in the process "losing brave and valuable men." The 48th New York then moved to Saint Augustine, Florida, to rest before returning to Hilton Head.

From then on we were removed to Jacksonville, Fla., marched over 50 miles into the interior of that state, fought a battle with our Secession

51. 1870 U.S. Census, New York Co., NY, pop. sched., New York City, p. 330A (stamped), dwelling 152, family 366, Thomas Browne, NARA RG 29, M593, roll 1013; 1880 U.S. Census, New York Co., NY, pop. sched., New York City, p. 463D, dwelling 352, family 319, Thomas M.G. Brown, ibid., T9, roll 889.

52. New York State Death Index, 1905, certificate 42541, Thomas M. G. Brown.

53. One of the Sea Islands, located near Hilton Head Island, South Carolina.

54. Masonry coastal fortification on Cockspur Island, near Savannah, Georgia.

55. Bird Island, Georgia, and Jones Island, South Carolina. Both are in the Savannah River near where it empties into the Atlantic.

enemies at *Olustee*, lost nearly one half of our braves, and a few officers. I shall not attempt to describe our sufferings, etc. in Florida.[56] At this battle, I received a wound on the upper [part] of the left foot, in the early part of the engagement. I remained on the field until the fight discontinued. . . . From Florida our route lay by way of Fortress Monroe found opposite Yorktown. From thence to Chester Heights, VA. We fought the rebels at Drewry's Bluff.[57] We were commanded by Butler of Massachusetts. From Drewry's Bluff we skirmished with our enemies on our onwards march to Petersburg, built fortifications and erected batteries, done picket duty in the face of death and behaved ourselves like patriot-soldiers, arrived in front of Petersburg, faced death indifferently. Went on the extreme outpost, picket duty, fatigue, and received the usual: rebel complimentary shells, mortar-bombs, musketry, etc. At daytime under the burning sun, we rested under our small short shelter tents. At sundown they were taken down, and we had the imperative privilege to lie under the canopy of heaven. On the evening of July 29th, 1864, the regt. was ordered to prepare to leave the trenches, we not knowing anything about our destination. We arrived early next morning July 30th in time to support and assist the charge on Cemetery Hill (a short time after Lieut. Genl. U. S. Grant's mine exploded) in front [of] Petersburg, VA, about 12 o'clock noon, in obedience to an order issued by Lieut. D'Arcy of my company. I formed in line, covering the afore-mentioned Lieut. on march to the rear. At that time I received a bullet from the enemy in my right arm, close to the shoulder, breaking the bone from which cause I lost my right arm by amputation at the shoulder socket. When wounded I was assisted to the rear by Private Jackson of Company B of the 48th and others. I was forwarded to the 9th Corps hospital, a temporary structure erected a short distance from the scene of strife. From the early part of August 1864 until the 5th day of November following date of my discharge, I was an inmate, and patient, in Campbell Hospital, situ-

56. Browne potentially alludes to racial atrocities following battles in Florida. After Olustee, Confederate soldiers murdered wounded Black soldiers and mistreated Black prisoners. See David J. Coles, "'Shooting Niggers Sir': Confederate Mistreatment of Union Black Soldiers at the Battle of Olustee," in *Black Flag over Dixie: Racial Atrocities and Reprisals in the Civil War*, ed. Gregory J. W. Urwin (Carbondale: Southern Illinois University Press, 2004), 65–88.

57. Second Battle of Drewry's Bluff, May 12–16, 1864.

ated at [the] foot of 7th St. Washington, D.C. I want my readers to understand that I cannot narrate every circumstance, date, etc. connected with my military career. 'Tis my desire to exhibit a specimen of my *left* hand penmanship to the able and disabled Soldiers of our glorious union. Also to the mothers, widows, wives, and orphans of our daring and gallant braves.

I was born in the townland of Drumralla in the residence of my much respected Grandfather, Captain John Moore of the Wattle Bridge Yeomanry,[58] on Wednesday the 20th day of April 1831. My father, James Gifford Browne, deceased, was a Primitive Wesleyan Methodist Preacher of the Irish Conference. He married Jane Moore, daughter to the afore-mentioned Capt. John Moore of the townland of Drumralla near Newtown Butler County of Fermanagh, Province of Ulster, Ireland, "my dear old country."

In conclusion, I wish to say to my readers, I never tried to write with my left hand, until I lost my right arm. Please excuse all grammatical errors. This is my 2nd attempt to write this letter. . . . I am very nervous indeed.

~ ~ ~

WILLIAM KIPLING

Private, Co. E, 3rd United States Artillery

Born in Surrey, England, Kipling arrived in New York in 1861 when he was thirty years old.[59] After his discharge, he petitioned for naturalization and became a citizen in 1864.[60] Information about his postwar life is unavailable, though it is possible he died of tuberculosis in 1869.[61]

January 1866

I trust that whoever reads this will pardon my presumption in sending in such a scrawl. I do not profess to be a scholar but will try and write a few lines.

58. A volunteer cavalry unit in Wattle Bridge, County Fermanagh, Ireland.

59. William Kipling, Contest Entry, 1st ser., no. 231, Bourne Papers; U.S. Army, Register of Enlistments, 1859–63, William Kipling, NARA RG 94, M233, roll 27.

60. Moak, *Military Petitions for Naturalization Filed in the Philadelphia [County] District Court,* 20.

61. Massachusetts Vital Records, 1840–1911, William Kipling, 1869, New England Historic Genealogical Society, Boston.

I beg to state I am an Englishman by birth though a citizen of America now. I came to America in April 1861 with the determination to join the army and fight for the Union. I landed in America the end of April 1861. Wm. Kipling enlisted as a private in NY on the 10th May 1861 to serve in the regular army for 5 years. Was put in Co. E, 3rd US Artillery, Sherman's Battery of Mexican fame.[62]

I joined my Company at Fort Corcoran in Virginia. While there I was instructed in artillery drill and I went on picket duty a few times but had no engagements with the rebels there. On General [Thomas W.] Sherman's expedition going to Hilton Head, SC, my battery was ordered to go with it. General Sherman, I heard, made the remark at the War Department that he would sooner have his favorite battery than two regiments of infantry. We sailed from Annapolis, MD, and arrived at Hilton Head, SC, about the 5th Nov. 1861. . . .

Kipling fought at Port Royal, James Island (June 10, 1862), and Fort Wagner.

On the 18 July 1863 about 4 p.m. while loading the cannon and in the act of drawing out the rammer I lost my right hand which was blown off by the premature discharge of the piece; however I am thankful I did not lose both—Dr. [Joseph L.] Mulford of the 48th N.Y.V. skillfully amputated my hand 1 inch above the wrist.

I was discharged in consequence on the 28th Aug. 1863 and received a good character, which I have maintained since as my references will prove. I landed a stranger in a strange land on purpose to fight for the Union and thank God I have found some good friends amongst the Americans which consoles me for the loss of my once dear right hand. If this should meet the eye of any kind person who can get me some permanent employment I shall feel thankful.

~~~

62. Major Thomas West Sherman was an officer in the 3rd U.S. Artillery during the Mexican-American War (1846–48). Eicher and Eicher, *Civil War High Commands,* 484.
~~~

JAMES MANGAN

Private, Co. D, 15th New Jersey Volunteer Infantry

Mangan was a married laborer with two children in Sussex County, New Jersey, prior to enlisting.[63] He was wounded fighting for the "Bloody Angle" at Spotsylvania Court House, his regiment losing 151 men in under thirty minutes while advancing on entrenched Confederates.[64] Two months after he submitted his penmanship specimen, Mangan was admitted to the New Jersey Home for Disabled Soldiers, where he died of asphyxia in 1869.[65]

June 4, 1867

In response to your call for a specimen of the left armed writing I have the honor to submit the following and if not the best it is as good as can be at present.

I lost the right arm: three years ago twelfth of last May. Was four months a prisoner and eight months in hospital after I got home. Has spent the last two years selling books. Has got to make my living at that or something else. Has not practiced writing only what I done to transact my business for I love reading more than writing and has to read a great deal to keep posted in the nature of the books I canvass for. And I do not believe I ever wrote my name with my left hand til I lost the right. I am now 39 years old. Was 34 when I enlisted.

So now for the narrative.

I emigrated from the north of Ireland to America in 1848 and after spending one year in the city of New York I moved out to Sussex Co. in New Jersey because I never liked a crowded city probably owing to my being raised in the country.

I took no part in politics til I could legally vote in 53. Then voted a Democrat ticket and kept on so to the split of 57 on the Kansas question.[66] Then I quit that

63. James Mangan, Contest Entry, 2nd ser., no. 17, Bourne Papers; 1860 U.S. Census, Sussex Co., NJ, pop. sched., Green, p. 690, dwelling 69, family 69, James Mangan, NARA RG 29, M653, roll 709.

64. Carmichael, "We Respect a *Good* Soldier," 203.

65. *Documents of the Ninety-Fifth Legislature of the State of New Jersey,* 1128.

66. Some northern Democrats broke with their party and aligned with Republicans over the question of Kansas's status as a free or slave state and the adoption of the Lecompton Constitution. See Kenneth M. Stampp, *America in 1857: A Nation on the Brink* (New York: Oxford University Press, 1992).

party for I thought the Kansas people were terribly abused through Pierce and Buchanan's administrations.

And in 60 I voted for the free state candidate.[67] I never once thought the south would undertake a war against the government, over which they had full control, and could hardly believe my eyes when I read the bombardment of Fort Sumter in the papers, but then I knew the Ball was opened and only one power knew where it would close. I believed it was the duty of every good citizen to support the government as it is the only one in existence that I know of based on the will of the people and people going to war for a privilege that they were in full enjoyment of was more than I could then understand but so it was. And so I decided to take part with the government and watch the course of events.

I read all the accounts of the war with intense interest and watched McClellan's going to Richmond and his repulse therefrom with extreme anxiety. And on the issuing of the president's proclamation for 300,000 men I enlisted in Co. D 15th N.J.V. on the 15th Aug. 1862. . . .

Mangan fought in nine battles and skirmishes, including Fredericksburg, Gettysburg, Rappahannock Station, Mine Run, and "The Wilderness and Spotsylvania from May 4th to 12th, 1864."

The reason I include the 4th to the 12th of May 64 in one battle is the 15th N.J. fought every day and skirmished or was on picket every night. And I was with it in every battle and skirmish from it entered the field til I fell at Spotsylvania on the 12th May 64, it being the last charge I was on. I will endeavor to give a faint description of it.

The night of the 11th it rained all night. We had rations served out to us in the rain and by daylight the next morning we got under way. Hancock had made his famous charge in the g[r]ay of the morning, capturing some guns and prisoners, but failed to hold the works his men had gained. He fell back with his prisoners, and the 1st div. of 6th Corps marched up to breast the storm. The 1st N.J. brigade in advance, the brigade was formed in two

67. A reference to Abraham Lincoln, whose name appeared on the ballot only in the nonslaveholding states in the 1860 election.

lines for the charge. . . . When we made the attempt the first line broke in confusion but the second stood firm until they reformed in our rear. . . . We then marched about 100 yards by a right flank and parallel to the enemy's works when the word halt front was given. Then charge double quick, but I thought nothing of that for we had been charging so much that I took it as a matter of course. But on we went til about 50 yards of the enemy's lines when we got a volley that killed or wounded half of the 15th, but the rest kept steadily on up to the breast works. I saw my captain (James Walker) mount the breast work and heard a rebel say, "Cap, are you going to take these works alone?"

Almost instantly I fell pierced with five bullets and [was] taken prisoner, for I fell into the enemy's works. My captain was killed instantly. I saw 64 of my regiment lay dead inside their lines. Our second line did not come to our support, for what reason I do not know. Whether their [enlistment] time was so near out that they would not or whether the charge was unauthorized from headquarters I never could learn. We did not carry the works and what of my regiment could get back done so and the rest was killed or taken prisoners. After that charge the regiment mustered about 50 men.

When night closed in the enemy fell back. In the meantime a Scotch man in the rebel army on hearing me talk supposed I was a Scotch man also, and got me on his back and carried me to the rear about 100 yards and put me into a log cabin. I was very weak and faint from loss of blood, but I lay on the floor and watched the battle from an opening in the logs. Pretty soon I saw a squad of the enemy running up a battery to fire on our men when suddenly there came a shot from our side and struck in a large oak tree just where they were going to post their guns. It scared them and they stopped a little. Directly another come and dismounted one of their guns. Then I laughed bad as I was. One of the rebels jumped up and said he, "you d[amn] Yank, you would laugh at that if you were dead, wouldn't you." "No," said I, "if I was dead I could laugh at nothing." Another rebel rebuked him for saying anything to a wounded man. I lay in the cabin all that night and the next day they carried me and others back with them to what they were pleased to call a field hospital which was nothing less or more than a pine woods without shelter of any kind but the trees and about three miles in rear of where we fought on the 12th. There about sundown on the 13th in a Virginia pine swamp I had my good right arm taken off and buried in the cold clay. The operation was performed by Drs. Minn[68] and Greene of the rebel Army. It was done without chloroform. I lay and watched them doing it. Dr. Greene said he never saw a man do the like in his life before. My other wounds were flesh wound[s] and soon got well but the arm had to be taken out in the shoulder joint and consequently took it about 3 months to heal up. I lay 11 days in the woods without any shelter when they put up tents at the old courthouse of Spotsylvania. But my prison life does [not] vary much from others similarly circumstanced. I got away from them in September with my life for which I have often since most fervently thanked God who alone could preserve it. That is the power I looked to for help and He never has failed me.

The question is often asked how a man feels when wounded in battle. For my part I did not feel the least fear. I thought I would be killed anyhow and I wanted to sell my life as dear as I could, but when I lay wounded I thought if God would spare me to see my youngest child I would like it very much.

God did spare me to see him for which I will ever be thankful.

~~~

THEODORE BRUNO GUENTHER

Private, Co. I, 41st New York Volunteer Infantry

Married a week after his discharge, Guenther and his wife settled in Missouri after the war; by 1870, they had five children, and Guenther was a saloon proprietor.[69] In 1877, working as a letter carrier, he gained notoriety for allegedly disappearing along with "two or three money packages"; the *St. Louis Globe-Democrat* reported that he had "been drinking very hard of late" and "disappeared under very suspicious circumstances."[70] After his "uniform was

68. *The Medical and Surgical History* identifies Dr. H. A. Minor of the Confederate army as Mangan's surgeon and notes that Mangan suffered a "copious hemorrhage." *Medical and Surgical History of the War of the Rebellion,* 2(2):625.

69. Theodore B. Guenther, Contest Entry, 2nd ser., no. 96, Bourne Papers; District of Columbia Compiled Marriage Index, 1830–1921, film 1303264, Theodore Bruno Guenther, accessed via FamilySearch, 2013; 1870 U.S. Census, Jackson Co., MO, pop. sched., Kansas City, p. 507B (stamped), dwelling 892, family 985, Theodore Guenther, NARA RG 29, M593, roll 782.

70. "Man and Money Missing," *St. Louis Globe-Democrat,* Nov. 25, 1877, 3.
~~~

found on the bank of the Missouri River," authorities "presumed that he committed suicide, as he left two letters threatening the act." Fortunately for his family, Guenther resurfaced in December telling a "pitiful story," having left Kansas City in fear; though he was unable to account for the missing packages, the *Globe-Democrat* reported, "the impression that he left here is that he is more fool than a knave."[71] The article added, "he is a one-armed veteran of the Union Army, and that helps in begetting sympathy." Having apparently lost his position as a letter carrier, Guenther worked in a mill by 1880; in the meantime, his family had added four children.[72] He died ten years later.[73]

June 25, 1867

I was born in the Kingdom of Hanover in the year 1839, entered the Army of that state, when about 18 years of age and served 5 years. During that service I availed myself of the advantages of military schooling and the means of education, which the European Military system generally provides for the education of the soldier. When in the year 1861 the great rebellion in this country broke out, and the existence of this government depended entirely upon the patriotism of its citizens, I at once concluded to immigrate, and shoulder the musket to fight for right, justice and liberty.

Having arrived in the City of New York on the 5th day of November 1861, I joined at once the 113th Regt. New York Vol. Infantry, which Regt. was just then organizing. I was just for a short time on recruiting service, when once several of my old European fellow soldiers, who had also immigrated to the country and joined the U.S. Army, paid me a visit and invited me to see them in their lodging at Helds Hotel. According to this invitation I in company with Corpl. Hesse went to Helds Hotel one evening and partook of about 2 or 3 glasses of wine with my friends, which must have been mixed with some narcotic drug, for a sudden drowsiness befell me and I became completely unconscious. When again I came to my senses, I and my companion, dressed in other uniform[s], found ourselves in a carriage, which conducted us to

71. "Crime at Quincy," *St. Louis Globe-Democrat,* Dec. 23, 1877, 5.

72. 1880 U.S. Census, Jackson Co., MO, pop. sched., Westport, p. 258B, dwelling 83, family 112, T. B. Guenther, NARA RG 29, T9, roll 694.

73. Grand Army of the Republic Post Reports, Wyandotte Post #456, 1888–90, Kansas Historical Society.

a depot, from whence we proceeded to Washington City. In the vicinity of this city, by Hunter's Chapel,[74] where the 41st regt. of New York Volunteers was stationed. To this regt. did those friends belong, who had the kindness to treat me and my companion so generously. We were at once put into the ranks of this regt., in spite of our protests and remonstrations. On the 10th of March 1862 we left Hunter's Chapel, to operate with the Army of the Potomac against Richmond, but at Warrenton Junction our division was attached to the Army of West Virginia. Near Winchester we joined General Rosenkranz [*sic*], thence we marched to Romney,[75] participated in the fight of Strasburg[76] under the command of General Fremont,[77] also in the race in the Shenandoah Valley and the Battle of Cross Keys.[78] Genrl. Fremont was then relieved and General Sigel took his command under whom I fought in the battles at Cedar Mountain, Rappahannock Station,[79] Silver Spring,[80] Waterloo Bridge,[81] and at last in the 2nd battle of Bull Run, where I lost my right hand by a cannonball on the 30th day of August 1862. I also was there taken prisoner by the rebels, was however paroled 3 days after I had been taken, and was compelled to walk to Alexandria on foot, even after I had reached our lines. Our surgeon who was in charge of the ambulance train refused to take me into one of the ambulances, although most of them were not occupied by any sick or wounded. From Alexandria I was sent to Georgetown D.C., where I remained 4 1/2 months, until my wounded arm was restored, although my hand had to be amputated. The operation was skillfully performed by Surgeon DeWitt of the College Hospital. Having but one hand, I of course was unfit for further service and received my discharge on the 15th day of January 1863.

~~~

74. Located in Arlington, Virginia.
75. A small town in what is now West Virginia.
76. A town in Virginia's Shenandoah Valley.
77. Major General John C. Frémont (1813–90).
78. Part of Jackson's Valley Campaign, this battle took place on June 8, 1862.
79. The First Battle of Rappahannock Station, August 22–25, 1862.
80. Possibly Sulphur Springs, north of Rappahannock Station near the river.
81. Another location on the Rappahannock where skirmishing occurred in August 1862.
~~~

FRANCIS XAVIA BURGER

Captain, Co. E, 4th Pennsylvania Reserves / 33rd Pennsylvania Volunteer Infantry

Burger, having arrived in New York in 1854, enlisted when he was thirty-eight.[82] He fought in seven battles, including Mechanicsville (June 26, 1862), Gaines's Mill, Second Bull Run, South Mountain, and Antietam. General Meade, who selected Burger's submission as the winner of his premium, wrote him a letter of recommendation, attesting to his "efficient services, and his good character"; Burger included a transcription of the letter, intended to help him obtain a position in the Invalid Corps, with his submission. He also included a poem entitled "Antietam" by his comrade Colonel George P. Webster, which includes these laudatory verses: "Firm at his post, and foremost in the fight, / Brave Burger stood, to battle for the right, / Oppression's Chain he wore beyond the sea, / And knew full well the worth of liberty." When he sent his penmanship specimen, he was employed as a copying clerk at the Depot of Army Clothing and Equipage; his supervisor, whose testimonial he also transcribed, wrote that Burger's record books were "models of neatness and beauty." By 1870, Burger was living with his wife and daughter in New York State, working at a lighthouse depot.[83] He died in 1873.[84]

[undated]

I was born at Buchau, in the Kingdom of Wurttemberg, Germany, on the 15th of August 1824. My father was a high Officer at the Court of the Prince Thurn & Taxis. After completing my studies at the Polytechnical School, at Munich, I was engaged as Civil Engineer and Architect, in laying out the railroad between the Fortress Ulm and Frederick's Haven.[85]

In the year 1848, when the War broke out between the German States and Denmark, I voluntarily offered my services and filled the position of Sergeant

82. Francis X. Burger, Contest Entry, 2nd ser., no. 101, Bourne Papers (punctuation edited).

83. 1870 U.S. Census, Richmond Co., NY, pop. sched., Castleton, p. 13A (stamped), dwelling 138, family 199, NARA RG 29, M593, roll 1086.

84. Queens, NY, Letters of Administration, vol. M–N, 1869–73, p. 10, Francis Xavia Burger, U.S. Wills and Probate Records, 1659–1999, New York County, District, and Probate Courts, New York City.

85. Locations in Baden-Württemberg, Germany. Frederick's Haven is the city of Friedrichshafen.

in the first Battery of Flying Artillery.[86] After a cessation of the troubles the Army was reduced and, prospective promotion being but slight, I left the service and sailed for the United States, and arrived at New York in August 1854.

I received my final papers and became a citizen of the United States in 1859. At the Commencement of the rebellion, in 1861, I was a Citizen of Lycoming County, Pa., and organized a Company of intelligent men, was elected its Captain, and my command was known as Comp'y E. of the 4th Regiment of Pennsylvania Reserves. . . .

At the battle of Charles City Cross Roads,[87] June 30th, 1862, I was severely wounded by a Musket ball passing through my left Arm; but kind nursing enabled me to become sufficiently convalescent to join my Regiment on the 1st of the following August.

At the bloody battle of Antietam, on the 17th day of September 1862, my right arm was shattered by a shell from the enemy and was amputated the same day at Boonsboro, Maryland. Notwithstanding this heavy misfortune I found myself able to report to my Regiment again for duty on the 4th of December 1862, but little over two months after the loss of my right arm, and, on the recommendation of Genl. Meade, was ordered on recruiting service January 8th 1863.

In the month of November 1863, I made application to be transferred to the Invalid Corps. I was appointed 1st Lieut. and summoned to appear on the 12th of January 1864, before the Board of Examiners at Washington. For this purpose I received leave of absence at the headquarters of the recruiting service, Harrisburg, and left for Washington. I had in charge 26 recruits and deserters, destined for Baltimore: On January 12th I found myself in the last car of the R.R. train, with my squad, when at 4 o'clock p.m., 34 miles from Baltimore, our car was run into by an express train. Two of the men in my

86. Burger refers to the first of two wars (1848-50 and 1864) over Schleswig-Holstein, a region in what is now northern Germany. A "flying artillery" involved mounted soldiers as opposed to foot soldiers accompanying horse-drawn artillery. "Schleswig-Holstein Question," *Encyclopedia Britannica,* Dec. 16, 2016, https://www.britannica.com/event/Schleswig-Holstein-question.

87. Also known as the Battle of Frayser's Farm, part of the Seven Days' Battles.

charge were killed—one so badly hurt as to require amputation of one of his legs, and several others more or less injured. I was injured myself, and when I recovered from the contusions, I returned baffled and disappointed in my application for a transfer, to my recruiting Station, where I served until my regiment was mustered out of Service, June 17th 1864.

This ended my Military Career. Since July 1866, I have been employed at the Depot of Army Clothing and Equipage New York, where I am at present engaged. I never used my left hand in writing until after the loss of my right arm; and I may say, that until within the last year, or more particularly, within the past six months, my progress or proficiency as a left-hand writer, was not marked.

6.

THE POETS

Poetry was one of the primary ways in which Americans, both northern and southern, responded to the Civil War.[1] Professionals and amateurs submitted lyrics and odes about the war to newspapers, memorializing and commemorating the fallen and documenting the stakes and effects of the conflict. Though the contests' instructions asked entrants to submit personal accounts of military service, a number of veterans sent in verse. Some demonstrated their penmanship skills by copying popular poems (a practice that was common at the time, as evidenced by mid-nineteenth-century commonplace and scrapbooks), but others, including the veterans below, submitted original verse concerning their time as soldiers and their experience of amputation and life after it. The poems are of varying literary quality but represent wounded men's attempts to narrate and understand their experiences and feelings with a form instantly recognizable to their readers. Thomas Perrine employed the extremely common ballad stanza (alternating four-syllable and three-syllable lines), while Charles A. Edmonds stuck to tetrameter (Bourne did the same in his "Ho! Brothers on the Battlefield!").[2] Others apostrophized their missing limbs, poetically turning to

1. For poetry during the Civil War, see Barrett, *To Fight Aloud Is Very Brave,* 6–13.

2. William Oland Bourne, "Ho! Brothers on the Battlefield!," *Soldier's Friend,* Jan. 1865, 2.

their absent arms while simultaneously confronting ever-present stumps and pain.[3] Both humor and pathos pervade the poems as contestants reflect on the physical, social, emotional, and political ramifications of their wounds. Newspapers and periodicals were full of paeans to empty sleeves that spoke for silent and suffering soldiers, calling for pity instead of recognition for individual experiences of loss and adjustment.[4] In contrast, the contestants primarily focus on their mangled right or newly abled left arms. In doing so, they add their unique voices, perspectives, and bodies to the literary record of the war.

BURRITT STILES

Private, Co. A, 14th Connecticut Volunteers

Burritt Stiles.
Courtesy William Oland Bourne Papers, Manuscript Division, Library of Congress.

3. For my discussion of this phenomenon, see Johnson, *Scars We Carve,* 110–15.
4. For "empty sleeve," see ibid., 95–103; and Nelson, *Ruin Nation,* 179–200.

Born in Southbury, Connecticut, in 1838, at nineteen years old, Stiles traveled as far west as the Rocky Mountains before working for the Mississippi Central Railroad.[5] In giving Bourne a "sketch of how [he] was unfortunate and lost [his right arm] while a soldier in Uncle Sam's army," Stiles explained his circuitous route to enlistment. He arrived in New Orleans on April 21, 1861, just over a week after the bombardment of Fort Sumter. "All *should have been content* with the laws of the Great Republic," Stiles wrote, "but instead a rebelious people were the *oposite*." Unable to return to his "northern home," he sailed to Cuba, "ship[p]ed as sailor on a vessel" bound for San Salvador, and, "being satisfied with [his] sailor life," joined the crew of a brigantine headed to Europe. Returning to the U.S. in April 1862, he "found employment" before being drafted in August 1863. He fought at Bristoe Station and Morton's Ford before being wounded during the Wilderness. "I was no coward," Stiles averred, "but I must confess that I availed myself of the first good chance of getting to the rear where the field hospitals were located and where that dear Right Arm was soon taken from me *forever*." At the end of 1864, he was transferred from a Connecticut hospital to Central Park Hospital "for the purpose of getting an artificial arm." While there, he signed Bourne's autograph book and wrote the poem below.[6] Two years later, Stiles competed in the second penmanship contest and sent Bourne multiple photographs of himself, one featuring his artificial arm holding a violin bow; Bourne potentially referred to Stiles when he mentioned witnessing a "young man, furnished with an artificial limb . . . quietly seated with some of his comrades, discoursing to them skillfully from the strings of a violin."[7] He married in 1865 while employed as a laborer; by 1870, he was a farmer.[8] Stiles died in Florida in 1912 at the age of seventy-three.[9]

May 5, 1865

I am incompetent and unworthy to add my little mite
For I've seen but little fighting but that little was for rights
That all loyal sons of freedom is willing to sustain
And march to the field of battle until peace greater is again

5. Burritt Stiles, Contest Entry, 2nd ser., no. 70, William Oland Bourne Papers.

6. Civil War Reminiscences by Soldiers and Sailors in Central Park Hospital, Bourne Papers.

7. "Writing with Artificial Hands," *Soldier's Friend,* Sept. 1865, 2.

8. Massachusetts Vital Records, 1840–1911, Burritt Stiles, 1865, New England Historic Genealogical Society, Boston; 1870 U.S. Census, Franklin Co., MA, pop. sched., Wendell, p. 417B (stamped), dwelling 84, family 81, Burritt Stiles, NARA RG 29, M593, roll 615.

9. Burritt Stiles, Pension File, application 987127, certificate 747074, NARA RG 15, T288, roll 454.

In Connecticut I was drafted in New Haven Co.
And felt myself quite honored and would not refuse to go
It was on the 8th of Aug. eighteen hundred and 63
That I joined the Union army when the drums beat reveille
I was in camp on grape vine point[10] for weeks some two or three
Before they sent me to help fight the rebel Gen. Lee
The regt was the 14th Connecticut Volunteers
Colonel Ellis was commander and Hays[11] was our brigadier
The Co. they assigned me to of it one word I'll say
And before preceding further will name it Co. A
John C. Broatch was chosen captain A strictly military man
We all soon learned to love him and march at his command
We marched from near Culpeper towards the rising of the sun
When we met the rebel forces and they numbered two to one
It was at Bristo[e] Station[12] where we met and had the fight
And all was glad to get away by leaving in the night
The month it was October the year 1863
But the date is quite forgotten by much better men than me
It was but a short detention and our wounded were but few
And we marched on through Virginia to the Union proving true
Now we'll stop at Stony Mountain where we rested many nights
And where we were drilled daily to fit as for the fight
It was the six of Feb. on that eventful day
We crossed the river at Martin's Ford[13] to drive the rebs away
I must be brief and this I'll state in the month of May
We met the rebs by thousands and fought both night and day
The year was 1864 the dates from six to nine
That we faced our enemy's strong hold in the Wilderness sublime
We will go to Spottsylvania where the conflict was severe
Where we charged the 12 of May or that time very near

10. Grapevine Point in New Haven, also called "Conscript Camp." Peck, *Recruit before Petersburg*, 5.

11. Brigadier General Alexander Hays (1819–64).

12. Battle of Bristoe Station, Virginia, October 14, 1863.

13. Morton's Ford.

We won the fight took many guns and prisoners by the score
I never shall forget that day two arms I had no more
I [illegible] was in Washington there had the best of care
And many were the friends I found among the ladies fair
One year since then has not rolled round
And new friends daily I have found.

~ ~ ~

HENRY C. ALLEN

Private, Co. E, 1st Massachusetts Volunteer Cavalry

Henry C. Allen.
Courtesy William Oland Bourne Papers, Manuscript Division, Library of Congress.

Allen submitted entries to both contests; his efforts for the first contest won him a twenty-dollar prize for literary merit.[14] Born in Massachusetts in 1842, he was a resident of Conway and a laborer when he enlisted in 1861.[15] After the war, he and his family relocated to the Midwest. Working as a traveling salesman, Allen married in 1867; the couple lived with his parents in Beloit, Wisconsin.[16] He also compiled war records as a clerk for Wisconsin's adjutant general.[17] A widower, Allen relocated to Missouri, remarried in 1894, and died in 1911.[18]

14. Henry C. Allen, Contest Entries, 1st ser., no. 15, and 2nd ser., no. 99, Bourne Papers; Exhibition of Left-Hand Penmanship, ibid.

15. Consolidated Lists of Civil War Draft Registration Records, NARA RG 110, Henry C. Allen.

16. 1880 U.S. Census, Rock Co., WI, pop. sched., Beloit, p. 24A (stamped), dwelling 114, family 127, Henry C. Allen, NARA RG 29, T9, roll 1444.

17. Cunningham, *Blue Book of the State Wisconsin.*

18. 1910 U.S. Census, Cedar Co., MO, pop. sched., El Dorado Springs, p. 23A, dwelling 620, family 620, Henry C. Allen, NARA RG 29, T624, roll 768; "Henry Allen Passes Away," *Beloit (WI) Daily News,* Sept. 14, 1911, 1.

First Entry: **August 21, 1865**

If I had attended the writing schools that some have since losing their arms, I should think I stood an even chance for the prize. I have had no practice in penmanship, except the carrying on of a limited correspondence with some of my friends, and therefore do not expect to win even the lowest prize. Should the committee consider my penmanship worthy even of a commendation in words, my expectations will be fully realized; and I shall consider myself well recompensed for the hour spent in penning my manuscript.

I am no literary genius, and cannot write any manuscript worthy a place in the columns of the *Soldier's Friend.* I can, however, comply with your request and in my own plain way give you the outlines of my military experience in the "slaveholders' rebellion," or the war for Union, Justice, and Liberty. . . .

Allen served as an orderly for Major General David B. Birney (1825–64) in the spring and summer of 1863, "pass[ing] through the battles of Chancellorsville, Gettysburg, and Manassas Gap." He rejoined his regiment in September and was wounded soon after.

People often ask me, if I am not sorry that I ever entered the army. I answer them truly when I tell them *no.* I often think that were such a thing possible as the restoration of my arm, I would not have it restored. I consider it an honor and am proud of it when I think that I gave my right arm to save the "old flag," for which so many have given their lives. I said, when I left my quiet home for the strife and turmoil of war, that I wanted to bring a mark home with me to show that I had been where danger came near me. I have that mark, and so conspicuous, that all can see it and I am proud of it; no man can say that Allen was a coward and hid from danger. I have written recommendations from my officers: but better than those, I have an honorable scar that speaks plainer than words of deeds gone by.

Some young men that have lost an arm or a leg in the war seem to think that they cannot gain an honest living, but are dependent upon the charity of others. I think my living would be poor enough did I depend upon others for it. While regarding a one legged soldier that was begging through the cars for a livelihood a few days since, I thought if he came to me for alms

I should say to him I will only give to those that try to earn something themselves. I did not make the remarks that came into my mind, but I let him pass by without giving him anything. Now that young man could very easily learn the shoemaker's trade and earn a good support therefrom for he had every appearance of enjoying perfect health. I made up my mind that he was an indolent fellow before he went to war. There is no young man who has lost an arm or a leg, if his health be good and he is in all other respects uninjured, but can earn a good support with the limbs left him, if he will only select some pursuit in life and apply himself closely to it. I am dependent upon the strength of my left hand and the few brains I have in my head for my living and just so long as I am blessed with good health I shall earn it and a good one too. The world owes no man a living except he does something to earn it. I never expect others to help me unless I try to help myself.

To the Union Soldiers

Comrades! now the war is over
Is there nothing we can do
To defend our country's honor
From a blind relentless foe?

"Yes there is!" is quickly answered.
By every Union Soldier brave
We can vote and use our influence
Our nations honor still to save.

At the *White House* or in Congress
Traitorous acts, must be put down.
Proud rebellions cannot flourish
With Union Patriots all around.

We have suffered cold and hunger.
We have marched o'er hill and plain:
We have fought in many battle.
Won and lost and won again.

Many noble ones have fallen.
Many wounded yet remain,
Tell me comrades true and loyal,
Have our sufferings been in vain?

Must this union yet be severed
And "*our flag*" be rent in twain?
Must the "Freedman" still be bonded
In *wicked, hellish* chains?

Comrades, gather round the standard
Sound your voices through the land:
Beat the drum, and blow the bugle
Firm, undaunted, Take your stand.

Let them try in vain to ruin
That which we have fought to save
"Our Country" yet shall thrive, and flourish.
The states united, the "Union" saved.

Show the rebel hordes and traitors
Who now menace:—that we stand
"Freedom's Banner" floating o'er us
Still to keep our own free land.

These lines were suggested by the vetoing of the Freedman's Bureau Bill by President Johnson[19] and are sent as an extra contribution to the long list of left hand specimens, or rather [as] Specimens of left hand penmanship.

***Second Entry:* June 29, 1867**

Early in the year of 1861, the little village of Conway, situate[d] among the hills of Franklin County, Massachusetts, was startled into a fever of excite-

19. Allen wrote the poem on February 24, 1866, shortly after Andrew Johnson vetoed a bill that would have extended and expanded the Freedmen's Bureau.

ment by the announcement, that Fort Sumter had fallen, and that the Stars and Stripes had been fired upon, and desecrated by Southern Traitors. This was enough to arouse all the Puritan blood of the inhabitants of that New England village: drums were beaten; torchlight processions formed; alarm meetings were called; and men, both old and young were marching and drilling "in preparation for war."

Urged on by the excitement, I joined with the crowd in marching through the streets, making all the noise possible; thinking at the time, that the traitors would be conquered immediately, and that by adding to the confusion everywhere prevalent, I was aiding an insulted Nation in subduing its enemies.

A few weeks after the first excitement had passed away, we received the startling intelligence that Massachusetts men had been fired upon by rioters and traitors while passing peaceably through the streets of Baltimore.[20] New England blood was now thoroughly aroused and "up to the boiling pitch": nothing but "war" was talked about and nothing but "war" was thought about. . . . Such desires were aroused within me and I urged my Father to give me his consent, and in September 1861, he gave me a written permission to enlist in the 1st Massachusetts Cavalry. . . .

By September 1863, Allen's regiment was near Culpeper, Virginia.

On the morning of the 14th after partaking of our early "coffee," we resumed our "line of march"; but we saw nothing of the rebels, till we came within range of their heavy guns, on the heights across the Rapidan, where the army of the rebel Genl. Lee, were entrenched. While reconnoitering their position, we were opened upon by a masked battery, close to the river's edge; the first discharge killed two men, and made me a member of "the left armed corps." With the assistance of a "dismounted man," I bound up the remnant of what was once my right arm, and turned my horse's head rearward immediately thereafter. A horseback, of one mile or more, and an ambulance ride of three or four miles brought me to the "old church" where the amputation was so skillfully performed by Dr. Hazelton, Brigade

20. During the Baltimore Riot on April 19, 1861, secessionists attacked regiments reporting for duty. Four soldiers from Massachusetts were killed. See Brown, *Baltimore and the Nineteenth of April, 1861,* 42–59.

Surgeon.[21] From this place, I went via ambulance and freight car accommodations to Washington, where I was placed in Lincoln General Hospital.

There, under the skillful surgical treatment of Dr. W. F. Peck (now resident in Davenport, Iowa), and the tender ministrations of "Sister Ellen," my wound healed very rapidly, and in just five weeks after the amputation, it was perfectly healed, and to all appearances as sound as it is at this present time.

On the 8th of November I received my discharge, and the day following I started for my home in Massachusetts, where anxious friends gladly hailed my arrival, even in so dilapidated a condition. Once safe at home, my military experiences ended. My left hand has written them out on these few pages, not, that I think my career an exemplary one, but to show to all who may peruse these "specimens of left hand penmanship," that there is truth in the maxim, "where there is a will, there is a way." When deprived of the right hand, the left hand can be taught to do the work formerly done by both, and every member of "the left armed corps" can learn to excel in penmanship, if we but exert ourselves in that direction.

Practice, makes perfect, is said to be true.
Tis equally applicable to one hand, or two.
So honorable members of "the left armed corps,"
If, "practice makes perfect," then practice the more.
To excel, in your penmanship, and such prizes win.
As will gladden your hearts, and bring you the "tin."

~~~

THOMAS A. PERRINE

Second Sergeant, Co. G, 140th Pennsylvania Volunteer Infantry

One month shy of twenty-years-old and enrolled in college, Perrine enlisted in August 1862 as one of what he called, paraphrasing a popular poem and song, "'six hundred thousand more' who so melodiously informed Father Abraham that they were coming."[22] He was

21. Allen's surgeon was William B. Hezless of the 3rd Pennsylvania Cavalry. *Medical and Surgical History of the War of the Rebellion,* 2(2):700.

22. Thomas A. Perrine, Contest Entry, 1st ser., no. 50, Bourne Papers.
~~~

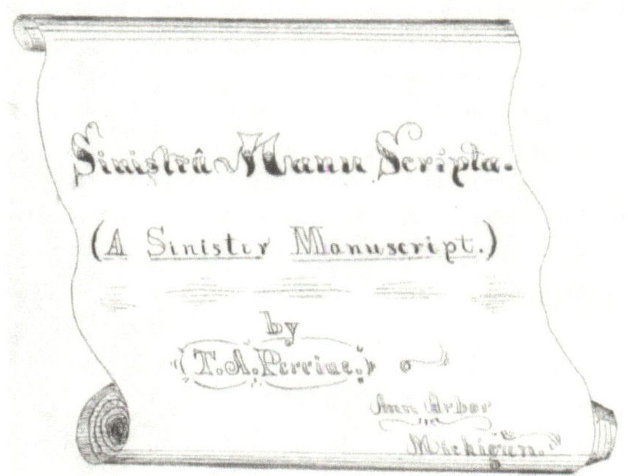
Sinistrâ Manu Scripta.
(A Sinister Manuscript.)
by
T.A. Perrine.
Ann Arbor
Michigan.

Title page of Thomas A. Perrine's entry.
Courtesy William Oland Bourne Papers, Manuscript Division, Library of Congress.

wounded at Chancellorsville, his first and only battle. After his discharge, Perrine returned to college and graduated in 1865.[23] He sent his entry, which won a twenty-dollar premium, from Ann Arbor, Michigan, where he was attending law school. In an explanatory note accompanying the affidavit attesting to his injury, Perrine allowed that his "little escapade does not profess to be wholly true"; indeed, he struck out the portion of the affidavit that read "the contents thereof are true to the best of his knowledge and belief." Perrine was an attorney, a judge, and a newspaper editor in Minnesota before moving to Colorado in hopes of benefiting his health.[24] Despite the concerns about his romantic potential he expresses in his "Sinister Manuscript," Perrine married in 1878; was living with his wife, Inez, and two step-daughters in Colorado by 1880; and welcomed a son in 1886; the census lists his profession as "dairying."[25] He died in 1890 at the age of forty-eight as a result of his wounds. The local GAR post, of which Perrine was junior vice commander, mourned him as "an active and generous comrade."[26]

September 25, 1865

Sinistra Manu Scripta
A Sinister Manuscript
"Arma Virumque Cano"[27]

23. "Mortuary Record," *Canonsburg (PA) Weekly Notes,* Sept. 13, 1890, 1.

24. "Mr. T. A. Perrine Moving to Colorado and Ending Connection to Monticello Times," *Princeton (MN) Union,* Dec. 18, 1878, 1.

25. 1880 U.S. Census, Douglas Co., CO, pop. sched., p. 358A (stamped), dwelling 3, family 3, Thomas A. Perrine, NARA RG 29, T9, roll 90.

26. "Mortuary Record," 1; "Mustered Out," *National Tribune* (Washington, DC), Aug. 21, 1890, 4.

27. The first line of Virgil's *Aeneid,* which translates to "I sing of arms and of a man."

'Twas in the year of Sixty three,
And on the third of May,
A rebel shell brought harm to me
And took an arm away.

This game of "give and take," I thought,
Might fun for rebels be,
But surely, what was sport to them
Was death a'most to me.

Hard by a road, within a wood,
We lay flat on the ground:
('Tis said that only cowards strike
A foe when he is down.)

With six and eight and ten pound shell
So carelessly they shot,
You would have swore they'd hit you on
The head as soon as not.

A shrapnel burst above our heads
And filled us with alarms;
A fragment struck my Humerus vein,
And so I grounded arms.

They placed me on a litter then
Without the least ado.
(This portion of my tale, observe,
Is literally true.)

They bore me to a hospital
And gave me chloroform;
I slept—and when I woke again
Was minus a right arm.

From hospital to hospital
They carried me about,
And though they watered well the stump,
They couldn't make it sprout.

And though an arm this empty sleeve
Again shall never fill,
Not bootless was the surgeon's skill
Which made the wound to heal.

Sure May-day never, never brought
Such griefs to anyone,
For, Reader dear, the tale of woe
Alas! is not yet done.

That May-day made a maid a jilt!
(Miss May Dey was her name.)
May day like that come ne'er again
So fraught with grief and shame.

To accept my hand she had agreed,
"Her love would ne'er grow cold":
But when I lost my hand, she said,
The bargain didn't hold.

I offered her my other hand
Uninjured by the fight;
'Twas all that I had left, I said,—
She said, 'twould not be right.

"Gaze on these features, Dear," I cried,
"They're fair as you will see."
"Without two hands," she made reply,
"You cannot handsome be."

O woful day! that took away
My arm and sweetheart too:—
An empty sleeve, an empty heart—
'Twould make a Darkey blue.

"These negroes all," Judge Taney said,[28]
"A white man's rights do lack":
The rebels left not right to me—
I might as well be black.

One consolation, still, I have:
When wars again shall be,
And Congressmen shall cry, "Two Arms!"
They can't say that to me.

And when again to Canada
True patriots shall flee,
The provost marshal with his draft
Can't come it over me.

Alternate ending:[29]

And when true patriots shall fly
To Canada again,
The draft-enrolling-officer
Shall take my name in vain.

~~~

28. Chief Justice Roger B. Taney presided over the Dred Scott decision in 1857.

29. Perrine sent two copies of his poem.
~~~

CHARLES A. EDMONDS

First Lieutenant, Battery A, 1st Michigan Volunteer Light Artillery
Captain, Co. H, 17th Michigan Volunteer Infantry

Born in New York in 1830 and a carpenter prior to enlisting, Edmonds was wounded while leading a charge at South Mountain.[30] After working as the register of deeds for Branch County, Michigan, he ran successfully for state commissioner of lands as a Republican.[31] In 1872, the Michigan Senate tried him for impeachment, citing "corrupt conduct in office, crimes and misdemeanors," including embezzling, drunkenness, adulterous activities (specifically, frequenting brothels), and publishing an obscene newspaper about a political opponent; the trial lasted six weeks and cost the state $19,151.28.[32] A reporter described Edmonds's appearance in court, noting that the "stump of his right arm suggests patriotic service and stirs a feeling of sympathy for the soldier, but his face is not so frank and open as one would choose to behold in looking upon a great and noble specimen of a man."[33] Though Edmonds was acquitted, his tenure as commissioner remained infamous and set the precedent for impeaching state officials. In 1943, the *Detroit Free Press* unearthed the scandal, reporting that Edmonds ran afoul of the "Old Guard"; after the trial, he "lost his reputation" and returned home.[34] He worked as a carpenter afterward and died in 1907.[35] Prior to his downfall, Edmonds sent a poem to Bourne's first contest. Two months later, he sent a "revised" and "corrected copy" of his work, telling Bourne, "I think it would be a good plan to destroy my first specimen." Both poems, excerpted below, tell the story of the conflict and end with political commentary on the issue of Reconstruction and suffrage for Black men; Edmond's views on the latter are less progressive in the edited version, perhaps reflecting the shifting politics of the time.

30. Charles A. Edmonds, Contest Entry, 1st ser., no. 51, Bourne Papers; "State Officers Elect," *Rock Island (IL) Argus,* Nov. 15, 1870, 1.

31. Collin, *Twentieth Century History and Biographical Record of Branch County,* 298.

32. "The Impeachment Trial," *Detroit Free Press,* Apr. 13, 1872, 5; "The Edmonds Investigation," ibid., Mar. 28, 1872, 1; "An Expensive Impeachment Trial," ibid., Jan. 16, 1873, 2.

33. "The Impeachment Trial," 5.

34. "Impeachment Trial Was Noisy," *Detroit Free Press,* Feb. 28, 1943, 53.

35. Michigan Death Records, 1907, Charles A. Edmonds, Division for Vital Records and Health Statistics, Michigan Department of Community Health, Lansing.

September 25, 1865

The Great Rebellion

The poem begins in 1860 and describes the defense and eventual fall of Fort Sumter.

Volunteers of hardy Freemen
Then came forth, to meet the Rebels;
Then came men of all professions;
Farmers, Merchants, Lawyers, Doctors,
Dressed themselves in blue, as soldiers. . . .

Soon they came where hostile armies
Had assembled for the conflict:
Then began the awful struggle—
On one side the Rebels fighting:
On the other, Union Soldiers,
Who were trying to protect them;
Even guarding their old Hog-pens,
And their orchards, and their henroosts,
and their cornfields, and their "niggers,"
Who were helping their old Masters.

But, this kind of peaceful Tactics
Soon played out with Uncle Samuel,
When three times five hundred thousand
Men had been called in to battle,
Then he thought of little "Sambo"[36]—
Sambo, helping Rebel Masters
Hoe the corn and dig the trenches,
That his soldiers might not labor,
And, of course, could fight the harder.
And he thought to make a Freeman—

36. A stereotypical name for an African American man.

Then resolved to make a Soldier—
Soldier, true, to do the fighting,
And to save so many White Men
By the use of little "Sambo."
Now, Jeff Davis and McClellan
Didn't like the way 'twas going
Didn't like the Confiscation
Of the little "Nigger Sambo":
So they got a big Convention[37]
In the City of Chicago,
Where they talked about a "Failure"
Of the war, to conquer Rebels,
And they got old Vallandigham[38]
Then to make them a "Peace Platform";
And they thought to make McClellan
Captain of the Union Forces:
That they might give peace to Rebels:
But, they found themselves mistaken—
Greatly, grandly, all mistaken!

General Grant and General Sherman,
With their white and colored Soldiers,
One a pushing up to Richmond;
One a driving down through Georgia—
Got the Rebels—Lee and Johnston,
And their Captain—Old Jeff Davis,
And the host of Rebel Soldiers,
In the bushes, on the Mountains.
There the Volunteers, and "Sambo"
Had surrounded all the Rebels;
And they forced them to surrender. . . .

37. 1864 Democratic National Convention, which nominated General McClellan for president of the United States.

38. Clement Vallandigham (1820–71), Ohio politician and antiwar Democrat.

Thus the End of the Rebellion;
Now, the question "What of Sambo?"
Echoed to us from our Statesmen:
Some are Saying "Let us make him
Equal to the Whites in voting."

Some Say, "No, our country never
Was intended for the Nigger";
Still they clamor for the Rebels.
And they say they are Entitled
To their rights within the Union,
For it is the "Constitution."
I have been a Union Soldier,
Fighting, side by side with Sambo;
We have fought the "Rebs" together;
I, for country, he, for freedom:
Fighting to maintain the Union—
Rebels fighting to destroy it.

Now, the Rebels, they are conquered,
And, the time of "Reconstruction"
has arrived, when we must settle
What the status of the Rebel;
What the status of poor Sambo.
I'm in favor, now of giving
Hemp to all the leading Rebels,
Freedom and the right of voting,
To the true "American Citizens of African
descent," who have so nobly dared, so freely
bled; to aid the Union cause, and to secure their
blessings of liberty to themselves and to
their posterity Forever.

December 25, 1865

The Great Rebellion—Its Beginning and End—1860–1865

In this edited version, Edmonds begins by describing the Democratic National Convention and the national election of 1860, the secession crisis, and the fall of Fort Sumter.

So, out comes the Proclamation
To the Rebels, in the army,
If they still kept up their fighting
They would surely lose the "nigger"—
Rebels heeded not the warning.
But they still kept up their fighting.
Now the Hundred days are over.
Shackles fall from off the Bondman!
Suddenly the skies are brightened.
And our army greatly strengthened
By Two Hundred Thousand soldiers.
Who, before, had helped the Rebels. . . .

Now the things that must be settled
Are what kind of Reconstruction
Must the Congress of the Nation
Give, to get the states in motion?—
And the question "What of Sambo?"
Echoes to us from our Statesmen. . . .

Is the great Rebellion ended?
If it is, the conquered party
Must accept such propositions,
As the Rulers of the Nation,
Now and then, see fit to give them.

I'm in favor, now of giving
Freedom and the right of voting,
In the south, to all the Loyal
Who can read the Constitution
And can write as good as I can!![39]
I'm in favor, too, of keeping
Leading Rebels on probation
Till we're sure they are converted
From the error of their ways.
If they have committed Treason,
I would give them "nary" pardon,
But I'd teach them to be faithful
To the Laws and Constitution....

~~~

JOHN BLANCHARD

Private, Co. B, 1st Ohio Volunteer Light Artillery

Blanchard, a resident of Penfield, Ohio, enlisted in August 1862 when he was twenty and living on his father's farm; he was discharged on May 14, 1863, after being wounded at Stones River and briefly taken prisoner.[40] He attended business college, married, taught school, and was a member of his local GAR post.[41] In 1873, he ran for the office of county recorder on the Republican ticket and served for three three-year terms; afterward, he was secretary and treasurer for a coal company.[42] He put his penmanship to good use in 1890, enumerating survivors of the war and their widows for the census.[43] Blanchard and his wife had four children; he died suddenly in 1912 at the age of sixty-nine.[44]

39. Such a literacy requirement would prevent many formerly enslaved men from voting.

40. John Blanchard, Contest Entries, 1st ser., no. 75, and 2nd ser., no. 57, Bourne Papers.

41. Galbreath, *History of Ohio*, 69; *Proceedings of the Thirty-Fifth Annual Encampment of the Department of Ohio, Grand Army of the Republic*, 202.

42. Galbreath, *History of Ohio*, 69; "Republican State Ticket," *Elyria (OH) Independent*, Sept. 24, 1873, 5; "Candidate for Recorder," *Wellington (OH) Enterprise*, May 20, 1891, 4.

43. 1890 U.S. Census, Lorain Co., OH, vet. sched., Elyria, p. 1, dwelling 1, family 1, John Blanchard, Special Schedules Enumerating Union Veterans and Widows of Union Veterans of the Civil War, NARA RG 15, M123.

44. Galbreath, *History of Ohio*, 69.
~~~

First Entry: **September 29, 1865**

Amputated

With a dim and dizzy brain
As after idle revel with its glare of painted pomp
Its wildering dream of light and wine and love
That flits away at morning thus I wake
From what?—to what?

The air is faint
With a strange odor sweet and sick
That hangs about my bed. I just remember
How the heart beats sounded in my ear.
Thicker and faster till I seemed to float
On pinions from my shoulders newly grown.
A dancing above in the buoyant space
Soaring away, I knew not, cared not whither
Until, Icarus like, I rose too high and fell
As something struck my pinions off.
Who speaks? Who said, "He wakes."

Ah, now I know
"Quick, Surgeon, with your work. What, is it off?"
"Ay, even so, there lies your arm."

I groaned tis true, done
But not with pain for what the knife had done
So skillfully and well. I groaned good bye.
It was the hand that long ago my mother held
And mated with its fellow for the evening prayer
Beside her knee, and that since then
Has clasped hers, parting by the farm house door
That laid right proudly in her lap the
Scholar's prize, hard won but fairly.

'Tis the hand
That held sweet, dying Minnie's till her arm was cold
And linked to Death and then was not ashamed
To dash away a brother's tear.

It flung the horse
Quite mad from peril back.
That autumn time when Madeline Dubray
Thanked God and me and then grew faint.
That idle arm off yonder held her then
Without rebuke. Ah, Madeline, I bring you back
The honors which you bid me win for you.
Pray God you do not turn away when one poor hand
With halting awkward gestures seek your own.
And watching eyes appeal for promised love.
Have pity, Madeline, for that I lose today.
Oh give me back the heart lost long ago.
Good bye right arm! Your work is done
Forever. What remains before your comrade comes
To join you in the quiet church yard.
Only one all-seeing knows. Pray God the left
May never shame the right. Good-bye, good-bye.

Second Entry

I am not much of a scribe, but I felt it to be my duty to contribute my mite toward this great and noble work. I know not what the feelings of others may be with regard to this subject, but I feel first as though there were others that felt for us in our misfortunes, and that these inducements were held out to stir us if possible to still greater exertion. There are many places of honor and profit we might fill and be useful to our fellow men if we are only qualified to do so. This should be our first aim. Now, for a brief history of my experience as a soldier for my country. . . .

On the morn of the 26th of December [1862] we left our camp for the bloody field of Stone[s] River. I was No. 1 man on rammer; on the afternoon of the 26th we were fighting the Rebs near La Vergne.[45] I was loading the gun or ramming the cartridge home when it went off prematurely blowing my right hand off above the wrist joint. This of course put an end to all my fun. My hand was amputated about 8 o'clock in the evening. On New Year's I was taken prisoner by Wheeler's cavalry[46] whilst lying in the hospital at La Vergne but was immediately paroled. This ends my experience with the exception of six months of hospital life.

~~~

ROBERT D. CHAMPION

Private, Co. C, 157th Regiment New York Volunteer Infantry

Born in 1838, Champion enlisted in August 1862 and mustered into service on September 19, leaving behind his farm, his wife, and two sons, "one four, the other one."[47] His regiment fought at Gettysburg and Chancellorsville before taking a steamer to South Carolina; he was wounded at Honey Hill. By 1870, Champion and his wife lived on a farm in Lincklaen, New York, and had four children.[48] He died and was buried there in 1883.[49]

June 22, 1867

Champion's regiment fought two engagements on John's Island, South Carolina, and then traveled to Florida.

45. A town located about midway between Nashville and Murfreesboro.

46. Brigadier General Joseph Wheeler (1836–1906), the Army of Tennessee's cavalry commander.

47. R. D. Champion, Contest Entry, 2nd ser., no. 48, Bourne Papers (punctuation edited).

48. 1870 U.S. Census, Chenango Co., NY, pop. sched., Lincklaen, p. 183B (stamped), dwelling 145, family 157, Robert D. Champion, NARA RG 29, M593, roll 916.

49. Robert D. Champion, Pension File, application 307162, certificate 217166, NARA RG 15, T288, roll 78.
~~~

[T]he ninth day of December 1864 I was wounded in the right arm and left leg and sent to the Hospittle at Beaufort whare I [had] my right arm amputated the twenty seventh day of December, 64. Gangreen when I became convalescent in a short time. The nineteenth day of February 65 I was sent to Grant's General Hospittle, Willets Point, NY, whare I stayed until the ninth day of May and was discharged. Went up to the city and got my pay and started for home the twelfth day. This endes my service for my bleeding country but long shall I remember the day that made me a cripple for life. I arived home and found my family well and waiting my return, may our country never kneed the service we have rendered again, may the star spangled banner ever wave over the free, and may the name of our brave officers ever be held in long and loving remembrance and ever may the right triumph is the best wish of a wounded soldier and your humble servant, R. D. Champion.

Union Patriotic Song

Come all good union patriots
Come listen to my song
Concerning this rebellion
Thoug I'll not detain you long

I'll speak of trater Davis
And his secesheon crew
Of how they ronged our dear old flag
The red white and blue

Twas down in Charleston harbour
This rebellion first began
By firing on fort Sumpter
And majour Anderson[50]

They fired on our Stars and Stripes
From moultry[51] on the shore

50. Major Robert Anderson (1805–71) was the commander of Fort Sumter.

51. Fort Moultrie, on Sullivan's Island northeast of Fort Sumter.

Then they murderd Massachusets troops
In the streets of Baltimore[52]

They robbed our mints arsnells[53]
Our fourts and ships likewise
Then we shut their port from Georgia trade
Which took them by surprise

Then Butler and old Faragut[54]
In spite of all their scheme
Sailed a round and took fort Jackson
And they captured neworleans

Then it was our Cheaf Comander
McClellon was his name
Went down to take old Richmon
Upon the river James

But he could not stand the pesher[55]
As every one does know
So he jumped on board of a Iron Clad
And to City Point did go

Then the rebels flushed with sucsess
Soon started north a gain
They drove old Pope throug Centervill
And captured quite a train

But they got repulsed at Anteatum
Which grieved their General so
That he ordered them to face a bout
And back to Dicksey[56] go

52. See note 20 above.

53. Arsenals.

54. Rear Admiral David Farragut (1801–70).

55. Pressure.

56. Dixie.

Then from the Mississippi
The glad tidings we did hear
That Grant had taken donelson[57]
With the veteron volunteers

That Iland Ten[58] and Shilow
Had both become our own
That Rosencrens[59] had whipped the rebs
Down on the river Stone

Then Burnside and Jo Hooker
Although good fighting men
Both got repulsed at Fredricks burg
By General Lee and then

The Rebs struck up the vally[60]
All early in the Lead
Got whiped like smoke at Getesburg
By patriotic Mead[e].

Next of the noble Sheridan
My object is to sing
That victories in the vallies
Has made the Mountains ring

Next is the news that U.S. Grant
Has taken Chief Command
That he whiped Lee's boasted Cavelry
Down on the Rappadan

57. Fort Donelson, overlooking the Cumberland River, just south of the Tennessee-Kentucky border.

58. Battle of Island Number 10, a Confederate stronghold in the Mississippi River along the Tennessee border, February 28–April 8, 1862.

59. Rosecrans.

60. Virginia's Shenandoah Valley.

Then he moved up to the River Bank
And threw a crost his right
The Rebels met him on the Bank
And fought a stuburn fight

But soon we got Reenforced
And forced them to givway
We drove them through the Wilderness
And thus we gained the day

At Spoteselvania Court House
They made another stand
But as soon as Burnsides Nigs[61] came up
The Rebs again got tand

Grant flanked them then upon the left
Which caused their Chief to see
That the only way to save him self
Is to pack up traps and flee

They Started of[f] for Richmon
As fast as they could go
With General Grant to spur his pace
Twas not to[o] auffle[62] slow

He halted on the Rappadan
Whare he thought to make a stand
But Holdfast[63] flanked on the left
So he fell back again

61. Champion refers to a division of USCT that were part of Burnside's XI Corps, attached to the AOTP during the Overland Campaign.

62. Awful.

63. Apparently a nickname for Grant, who told Thomas at Chattanooga to "hold fast." "Career of General Grant," *Wilmington (NC) Herald,* Apr. 28, 1865, 3.

They fell into their trenchments
In something like a rout
When the yankees took their Bayonetts
And forked the Johnies out.

He soon drew up near Richmon
And placed his men about
Then planted all his mighty Guns
Two keep the Yankees out

Then hurr[i]ed to the white House
Their President to see
And tell him how the yankee boys
Has whipped his Cavelry

How are you to Lee said Jeff
Who met him on the way
What makes you look so sad my boy
What brought you here to day

Oh Jeff you cursed simple Head
Hav you not hurd of late
That the yanks at las[t] has found a man
All hell cant make retreat

He met us in the Wilderness
He told his men to move
Then our pet lambs before them
Right through the Woods they drove

Then they put on their bayonetts
And made us turn our Backs
Why I rather whip a dozzen Popes
Or forty little Mcs[64]

64. "Little Mac" was a nickname for McClellan.

I tell you Jeff old Grant a Hoss
The Devil cannot flog
And General Sherman to[o] you know
Has proved a pluckey dog

And thares that Beastly Buttler
Is bound our town to Shell
So I think Secesh is a bout played out
And kinder gone to Hell

Well General Lee I must confess
Our case looks mighty hard
For just the other day old Buttler
Whiped our Beauragard

And if he brings his Guns to bear
Upon this stinking town
I think the best thing we can do
Is to lay our muskets down.

For Brag[g] you know has lost his grip
And kinder seems to me
That if Abraham gets holt of us
Heel make us climb a tree

If I was out of Richmon now
Secesh might go to Hell
For it kinder seems to me old boy
That hemp begins to smell.

PHINEAS P. WHITEHOUSE

Corporal, Co. C, 6th New Hampshire Volunteer Infantry

In October 1865, Whitehouse sent Bourne a "few stray attempts at versification" produced "in camp and hospital," including "On Picket." He sent "My Crippled Arm" with his second submission. For Whitehouse's biography, see chapter 3.

"On Picket"

This was written in the winter of 1863 some time after the battle of Fredericksburg when the Army of the Potomac was under command of Gen. Burnside. The Sixth New Hampshire regiment was on picket duty nearly opposite the city several days.

On the bank of the Rappahannock,
With my rifle by my side,
I stand at my long post watching
The river's swift flowing tide.

'Tis the silent hour of midnight
And scarce a sound I hear,
Save of the gliding waters
Or a brother picket near.

Overhead dark clouds are hovering,
Obscuring the moon's cheering light,
Save when, now and then, through an opening
She peeps with a smile on the night.

Before me, just over the river,
Rising dark from the waters below,
Stands the ruined and desolate city,
Once the glory and pride of the foe.

No signs of life 'mid the darkness,
Save here and there a stray gleam
From the fires of the rebel pickets,
Along the bank of the stream.

My thoughts half unconsciously wander,
Far away over mountain and dell
To the snow clad hills of New England,
And the scenes I love so well.

I forget 'tis the hour of midnight,
And fancy it evening there,
When the farmers sit by their firesides,
Just relieved from toil and care.

'Mong the hills, all quiet and peaceful,
By the stooping willow tree,
Just beyond old towering Powow,[65]
My own happy home I see.

There the cheerful fire is glowing,
And familiar objects appear;
The old clock ticks in the corner,
The voices of loved ones I hear.

And there, by the cheerful fireside,
I am sitting once again,
Surrounded by blessings as precious
As were ever bestowed upon men.

—But hark! there's a sound of footsteps
And I must "Halt! Who goes there?"
"Relief!" is the welcome answer.
And I to my quarters repair.
Falmouth, Virginia Jan 31st 1863

65. Powow Hill in Salisbury, Massachusetts. Whitehouse explains in a note that "the poet Whittier's residence is at its foot, and scenery in the vicinity has been many times graphically pictured in the charming productions of the distinguished Quaker."

Second Entry: **August 1866**

"My Crippled Arm"

'Twas hardy once, and strong for manly labor,
And grew not weary at the sound of toil;
Could shoulder musket or could turn the sabre,
Could wield the pen or till New England soil.

A faithful servant, it was ever by me,
A friend in need to keep the wolf away;
However sharply Fortune seemed to try me,
That strong right arm would always win the day.

But Fortune frowned. A rebel bullet's madness
Shattered that arm on Spottsylvania's field,
And many hours of pain and days of sadness
In gloom succeeded, ere the fracture healed.

A trusty, helping friend to me no longer,
A weak and feeble patient it has grown,
And, day by day, I watch to find it stronger,
But watch in vain—for there's a missing bone.

I look upon the tender, child-like fingers,
The crooked wrist which tells when storm is nigh,
The shapeless arm where still the dull pain lingers,
Where the rough scar still wakens many a sigh,—

I look at this, the feeble thing before me—
The piteous wreck of what was once an arm—
And can you wonder if a cloud comes o'er me?
If smiles are vain, and kind words cease to charm?

The cloud does come, at times, but does not tarry;
It passes over, and again 'tis fair;

Ungrateful I, to murmur, or to carry
A heavy burden which I need not bear.

What matters it one arm its task has ended?
'Tis well, it may be, why should I repine?
For Life's stern conflicts I am still defended,
While, true and faithful, one stout arm is mine.

With that, and Heaven to aid me, let me labor
With cheerful heart, whate'er my lot may be;
And though may rust the rifle and the sabre,
May that lone arm a final victory see.

FRANCIS J. IRWIN

Sergeant, Co. K, 140th New York Volunteer Infantry

Irwin enlisted in August 1862, one month shy of his eighteenth birthday.[66] During his two years as a soldier, he fought in the Battles of Fredericksburg, Chancellorsville, Gettysburg, Second Rappahannock Station, Spotsylvania, Cold Harbor, and Petersburg, among others. He lost his right arm "above the elbow" at Weldon Railroad. His poem on the power of the pen was inspired by his time learning to write with his left hand at Eastman's Commercial College and dedicated to his penmanship instructor; his studies there secured him employment as a bookkeeper. Irwin lived in Rochester with his wife and two daughters, working as a city messenger, or clerk, after being elected to the post in 1876.[67] A member of the GAR, he died in 1898 at the age of fifty-three, survived by two daughters and remembered as "a good companion and a fearless soldier."[68]

66. Francis J. Irwin, Contest Entry, 1st ser., no. 104, Bourne Papers.

67. 1880 U.S. Census, Monroe Co., NY, pop. sched., Rochester, p. 203B (stamped), dwelling 131, family 141, Frank J. Irwin, NARA RG 29, T9, roll 864; "In Common Council, April 3d, 1876," *Rochester (NY) Democrat and Chronicle,* Apr. 6, 1876, 3.

68. "Francis J. Irwin," *Rochester (NY) Democrat and Chronicle,* Jan. 27, 1898, 11; "Excellent War Record," ibid., Jan. 28, 1898, 8.

September 26, 1865

How great is the power for good or evil,
How mighty the scepter he wields over men.
Who knows how [to] speak with the mind of the absent,
The potent, the true, the victorious pen!

He scorneth the limits of time and of distance,
His reign may extend over the land and the sea,
To the pinions of thought there can be no resistance,
Though the body be fettered the mind may be free.

The friend whom he loves may receive his fond greeting
Though long dreary miles may their pathways divide.
And earth-care forbid them the pleasure of meeting,
The pen speaks—and lo! they are now side by side.

His words may go forth to the lofty and lowly;
His messages soothe the keen pangs of distress—
Oh! who would not prize a possession so holy?
Nor seek with the boon the whole nation to bless?

The pen on its point hangs the praise or dishonor
Of those who have sought for the laurels of fame:
The forms of the past, from the sepulcher rising,
Demand of the living a place for their name.

The hero whose sword reaped a pathway to glory;
The martyr who died for the truth and the right;
The noble immortals of song and of story,
Whose names greet the world with a thrill of delight;

All these would have perished; and forthcoming ages
Would lose the sweet influence, their life labor shed,
Did the pen have no record on history's pages;
To embalm, in remembrance, the glorious dead.

The time has gone by when men deemed it merit
To jot down their thought in illegible scrawl;
A mark of great talents to write so obscurely
That none could decipher their meaning at all!

Tis an age of progression; and darkness and error
No longer asserting tyrannical sway,
Are shrinking abashed in confusion and terror;
Neath the clear sunny light of a beautiful day.

The clown must give place to the man of refinement.
For bothers, henceforth, there will be no demand;
To genius, and culture, and skill we are looking
For the growth and success of our time-honored land.

And penmanship too, shall assert her dominion,
Bad writing be counted a mark of disgrace.
The scribbler who seeketh a good situation,
Shall weary himself in search of a place.

CURLEY L. VANBRIMMER

Private, Co. I, 3rd Regiment Ohio Volunteer Infantry

Vanbrimmer was born in Indiana in 1841 and was farming when he enlisted in 1861.[69] Wounded at Perryville, he lived in Ohio after the war with his wife and two sons, working as a house painter.[70] Vanbrimmer died in 1899.[71]

69. Curley Vanbrimmer, Contest Entry, 1st ser., no. 111, Bourne Papers (punctuation edited).

70. 1880 U.S. Census, Morrow Co., OH, pop. sched., Cardington, p. 401B (stamped), dwelling 164, family 168, Lavon Vanbrimer, NARA RG 29, T9, roll 1053.

71. "Cardington Notes," *Marion (OH) Star*, Apr. 14, 1899, 4.

October 5, 1865

Dear Sir I saw your advertisement in the daly for the best left hand riters but I am won of the poorest but I will do the best I can for you an that will be poo[r] a nuf. In fact I have but little time to rite I wouldent of ritten a lott but the old woman my mother insisted on me to try my hand.

Well it was the 19 of April 1861 Early in the morning that my patriotic blood began to boil. At last she boils clear over. Beaing not myself started for Cardington[72] the nearest recruiting office bound to inlist soon. Reached the office and in less than an ower I was changed that from a sitizen to a soldier. Not beaing asigned to any company or regiment we lay at Cardington some two weaks from thar to Columbus lay thar thre weaks. Twas thar and at Camp Den[n]ison that soldiern was but fun. After laying at camp Denison som time we then started to the frount in Western Virginia. We roved about thre months in that gods forsken country then was transferd to Kentucky. Was thar whar we had plenty of hard marches untill we at last wound our way to Huntsville Alabama whar we had a pleasant camp onley disturbed now an then by the bushwhackers. From thar we took that great retreat march back to Louisville made but a short stay but marched on to Perrysville whar I met the fatal blow which left me ne more fit for field duty which was ca[u]sed by the fragment of a shell passing through the elbow taring the right arme from me. This was don near Sunset an was near twellv befor I got any asistenc. The day after the battel was gloomy a nuf but al this is for som good. Prehaps had better be me than any won else.

He is gon our noble soldier boy
He fell amid the battels roar,
And we are left alas to grieve
For one that shall return no more,
Mid hope and fear we left our homes
Yet hoping that we might return,
But oh he met the fatal blow
Whitch left but won to return
But we ar not alone in this
For many brave men has fallen

72. A village in Morrow County, Ohio.

Who cheerfully left ther childhood homes
Obedient to ther countrys call
And went to meet the Southern fo
With hearts So noble and So brave
Regardless both of weal or woe
And now they lie in Soldiers graves
Now near whear we resid
His lonley place we oft do visit
He is No more disturbed by battels din
Awaiting the last great trumpet Sound
God grant that we prepard may be
To meet our loved ones in the Skies
From Sin and Sorrow to be free
And tears no more Shall dim our eys

Riten on the death of a brother who sacrifised his life fore his Countrys Caus, we wer both in the Same Company an faithful did I watch over him untill his death.

You must excuse this poor Scribling.

~~~

JAMES OTIS LADD

Private, Co. I, 15th Massachusetts Volunteer Infantry
Captain, Co. K, 35th Infantry United States Colored Troops/1st North Carolina Colored Infantry

A Massachusetts native, Ladd was eighteen and a farmer when he enlisted.[73] After losing his arm, he was appointed second lieutenant of the 1st North Carolina Colored Troops and led the regiment in South Carolina and Florida; he was promoted to first lieutenant in March 1864. Captured a few weeks later, Ladd spent seven months as a prisoner, was paroled in December 1864, and rejoined his command in South Carolina. He was appointed captain of his regiment in 1866 by order of the secretary of war.[74] He penned his entry in South Carolina and married

73. James O. Ladd, Contest Entry, 1st ser., no. 218, Bourne Papers (punctuation edited).

74. Compiled Military Service Records of Volunteer Union Soldiers Who Served with the United States Colored Troops, James O. Ladd, NARA RG 94, M1992, roll 94.
~~~

a local woman, remaining in the state for the rest of his life and raising four children.[75] He worked as a clerk for the Freedmen's Bureau and later the state treasury, served for over two years as postmaster (before being replaced by a Democrat), collected internal revenue, was a member of GAR Anderson Post No. 7, and became a circuit-court commissioner in 1876.[76] Ladd died in 1931 at the age of eighty-seven.[77]

December 20, 1865

I know of nothing that seems more beautiful than my imagination has pictured those motives to be, which gave birth to the appointment of a "Committee of Awards" for the best specimen of left hand writing by soldiers who have lost their right arms in the service during the late civil war from the cruel enactments of which our Country has so recently recovered. My feelings of admiration at such a manifestation of remembrance are unbounded, for I behold therein such appreciation of our soldiers' laborious hardships, sufferings and dangers as none but thankful hearts can evince that seek to place such incentive before the unfortunate "war worn Veterans" as shall, though maimed for life, inspire them with courage for the future, as well as to show them that their deeds are remembered by an ever grateful People, and I can well imagine many a grateful expression from the hundreds of hearts whose life's blood flowed freely, as the right arm that so faithfully had served them was severed, never to serve them more. . . .

On the 18th of October 1861, I placed my name on the rolls of our Volunteer force from Windsor, Mass. The following few weeks were spent in drilling and preparing for the duties connected with a soldier's life. I afterwards joined the 15th Mass. Volunteers and on the 8th of December 1861 was assigned to the ranks of Co. "I" of that command. With it I passed through nearly all the battles of the ever memorable Peninsula Campaign of 1862 from Yorktown to Fair Oaks and Seven Pines, and on that dread seven days retreat that struck terror to all hearts. . . .

75. South Carolina Death Records, 1821–1965, Dorchester Co., vol. 16, Priscilla Catherine Ladd, South Carolina Department of Archives and History, Columbia.

76. 1870 U.S. Census, Richland Co., SC, pop. sched., Columbia, p. 93B (stamped), dwelling 525, family 615, James O. Ladd, NARA RG 29, M593, roll 1507; Ladd, *Ladd Family,* 221–23.

77. South Carolina Death Records, Dorchester Co., vol. 14, James Otis Ladd.

Ladd's regiment covered retreating troops after Second Bull Run and then pursued "the rebel army through Maryland."

South Mountain will never cease to tell its silent tales of horror as they yet can be distinctly traced in the rocky recesses of her almost perpendicular heights, and the succeeding battle of Antietam will ever find its place of long remembrance of deeds of valor, suffering and death in the hearts that compose many a family circle from the East to the unbounded West of our Republic. To my participation of its strongly contested and bloody fields can be traced the data of that misfortune that enables me to pen these lines, for during the struggle of the 17th of September, when the contest raged in its fiercest terror I received a wound that dropped my right arm helpless at my side and from the cause of which I had to suffer the amputation thereof at the upper third on September 19th 1862.

My misfortune soon had initiated me to the Hospital life of the Soldier of which I was before quite ignorant. I remained in General Hospital on the battle field until the date of my discharge on [the] 13th of January 1863. I will here insert a few lines of verse as composed by me during the tedious hours of hospital life.

1
"Antietam! Antietam!" Tis the cry of the Nation.
Oh! Where are our loved ones that went to thy shore.
Those that fought o'er thy bosom in battle, Antietam!
And with bright glistening bayonets thy waters charged o'er.

2
Far back on thy shores they fought with the Traitor
The Contest raged fierce, with the dismal cannons' boom,
Midst the shrieks of the dying, as in life's blood they weltered,
And the closing of ranks when the fallen made room.

3
From morn until eve raged the muskets' fierce clatter,
The leaden message sped its way on its errand of death,
While the flash gave new lurid, as the fire of the crater,
Neath dense volumes of smoke many breathed their last breath.

4
Midst the clashing of Arms did brave Mansfield's steel glitter,
He with thousands, wounds mortal received in the strife.
We would not recall them from the arms of their Maker,
For their Country *they yielded* the sweetness of Life.

5
The heart of the Nation is full to o'erflowing
This wound ne'er will heal while this wide world we roam.
Let us hope that our *Loved Ones* with *Jesus* are pleading,
To the *God* of our Country on *His Heavenly Throne*.

Perhaps I have overdone myself in the exertion and hasty composition of these lines. I however do submit willingly to whatever fate may be in store for them, knowing that thousands like myself will have done the same ere this late hour. I however do not regret the loss of my right arm, for I would not barter the experience its loss has forced upon me and with it shall ever be happy to subscribe myself as the

Ever Obedient Servant of My Country
James O. Ladd

CHARLES A. QUINCY NORTON

Private, Co. K, 1st Maine Volunteer Cavalry
Private, Co. K, 7th New Hampshire Volunteer Infantry

Born in Bangor, Maine, in 1841, Norton began his military career with the 1st Maine Cavalry and was severely wounded in 1862; a bullet lodged in his left shoulder plagued him until it was removed twenty years later.[78] Though Norton claimed he lost his arm at Fort Fisher on

78. Charles A. Norton, Contest Entry, 1st ser., no. 250, Bourne Papers; 1870 U.S. Census, Penobscot Co., ME, pop. sched., Patten, p. 394A (stamped), dwelling 108, family 114, Charles A. Norton, NARA RG 29, M593, roll 555; *Medical and Surgical History of the War of the Rebellion,* 2(3):748.

January 15, 1865, an official regimental history reports that he "shot himself through the hand and wrist" while onboard a transport steamer on the twelfth; nevertheless, a description of his case in *The Medical and Surgical History of the War of the Rebellion* confirms Fort Fisher as the site of his injury.[79] Having married in 1864, Norton lived with his wife and children in Maine and Massachusetts after the war and worked as a physician.[80] In 1890, the Senate granted him a higher pension, noting he suffered from heart disease, partial blindness, and "nervous prostration"; his condition, the committee concluded, was a result of "three subsequent amputations and four other separate and distinct surgical operations," which rendered him incapable of practicing medicine or dressing himself.[81] By 1900, he lived with his sister in Hartford, Connecticut; both he and his wife, now living in different states, claimed to be widowed, though she filed for his pension when he actually died at the age of seventy-four in 1915.[82] Newspapers referred to Norton as "Captain"; one recounted how he "proved that the courage which lost him an arm in the siege of Fort Fisher in the sixties, had not oozed out with the years" when the "one-armed veteran" led the charge against a swindling steamboat crew.[83] The article reported he was "prominent in the Grand Army" and "a good public speaker" with "abundant pluck."[84] Norton was also an expert on antique lamps, a "correspondent of several historical and archaeological societies," and a "pioneer in Christian Science healing."[85]

79. *Medical and Surgical History of the War of the Rebellion,* 2(3):748; Little, *Seventh Regiment New Hampshire Volunteers,* 506. The author offers no explanation for the discrepancy, noting only that Norton's hand was amputated as a result.

80. Maine Marriage Records, 1713–1922, Charles A. Norton, Maine State Archives, roll 81; 1870 U.S. Census, Penobscot Co., ME, pop. sched., Patten, p. 384A; 1880 U.S. Census, Essex Co., MA, pop. sched., Salisbury, p. 364A (stamped), dwelling 7, family 9, Chas. A. Norton, NARA RG 29, T9, roll 528.

81. *Reports of Committees of the Senate of the United States for the First Session of the Fifty-First Congress,* Report 483.

82. 1900 U.S. Census, Hartford Co., CT., pop. sched., Hartford, p. 15, dwelling 107, family 272, Charles A. Norton, NARA RG 29, T623, roll 137; 1910 U.S. Census, Cumberland Co., ME, pop. sched., Portland, p. 2B, dwelling 26, family 30, Lizzie D. Norton, ibid., T624, roll 540; Charles A. Q. Norton, Pension File, application 1041995, certificate 72399, NARA RG 15, T288, roll 351; "Death Roll of Veterans Grows," *Hartford (CT) Courant,* May 20, 1915, 5.

83. "Capt. Norton's Pluck," *Hartford (CT) Courant,* Oct. 9, 1899, 1.

84. Ibid., 2.

85. Norton, "Lights and Lamps of Early New England," 501–13; "Captain C. A. Q. Norton Dead," *Boston Globe,* Feb. 3, 1915, 11.

January 18, 1866

The Author of the lines that you will receive with this letter, has been a Soldier in the Union Army from the commencement of the war. . . . I do not write for the Premium because I know that I cannot get any but I should like a Book to see what the left armed men can do. . . .

Long Bridge crosses the Potomac from Washington to the VA side. Over this Bridge have gone the long lines of proud Soldiers hastening to their Country's defense. Back across this Bridge have come the heavy loaded ambulances, filled with sick and wounded Soldiers. In fact this Bridge has been the great vein, through which has rushed the grandest Army the world ever saw.

Long Bridge

Many are the feet that pressed that Bridge, never to press it again.
Many noble souls that went over that Bridge, now are numbered with the slain.
Many brave men crossed that Bridge, determined their Country to save.
Many brave men were soon laid low, low, in a Soldier's grave,
Over the Bridge.

Acrost that Bridge went the Country's hope, strong with vigor and might.
Acrost that Bridge went the thronging hosts, hastening on to the fight.
Acrost that Bridge went many light hearts, fresh from their native town.
Acrost that Bridge many have gan who laid their bodies down,
Over the Bridge.

Over that Bridge many have gan, gan to the Prison's cell.
Over that Bridge many have gan, who bid their home a last farewell.
Over that Bridge many have passed into the foul dungeon's door.
Over that Bridge, O how many went, went to come back no more,
Over the Bridge.

Some have come back over that Bridge, wounded, mangled and torn.
Some have gan back to their homes, all sick and battle worn,
Some have marched back over that Bridge, proud of the victory won,
Some have been brought back over that Bridge, with an arm forever gan,
Over the Bridge.

Those that never returned, who went over with the thronging band,
Those have passed to a happier home, in the far off better land.
Those that found a Soldier's grave, when their marches and battles were o'er,
Those have all been mustered in on the bright and shining shore,
Over the Bridge.

Through another Bridge we all must pass, when done with this world of strife,
Through that Bridge we all must pass, that leads to the River of Life.
Through this Bridge which is the Tomb we all must pass to the other shore.
Through this Bridge, we all must go to sing God's praises evermore,
Over the Bridge.

Lines on the Death of My Mess Mate

Rest, hero rest, the Battle's done.
The fight is ended, and the victory won.
The Potomac washes along the shore,
With a sadder sound, than e'er before,
The stars shine bright o'er your lone low grave,
Your name lives on, with the good and Brave.
Rest, here rest, Heaven's own at last,
Life's tempests o'er, and its dangers passed.
You fell for the land you dearly love,
You'll reap your rewards, in the home above,
Rest, hero rest, from the Battle's alarms,
You fled for repose in your Savior's arms.

DANIEL J. SHERMAN

Private, Co. I, 17th New York Volunteer Infantry
Unassigned Veteran Reserve Corps

Sherman was twenty-one, married, and a farmer when he enlisted.[86] The poem that accompanies his narrative of service is brief but poignant. Unfortunately, his life was also brief; Sherman died of tuberculosis in 1869 at the age of twenty-seven.[87]

April 25, 1867

I enlisted the 12th of Sep. 1861 in Ontario, Wayne Co., N.Y. in company I the 17th New York regiment and served two years and I lost my right arm on the 30th day of August 1862 in the second Bull Run fight and was discharged in December 1862 and after my arm got well I enlisted in [the] invalid corps. I served 7 months a guarding the hospittle in Elmyra[88] and was discharged on May the 21, 1863. I was a privet in both inlistments. I was in two battles . . . and after I was wounded I lay on the battle field two days and then was taken prisoner by the Johnnys and was with them one weak and then was porowled and was sent to Washington and my arm was amputated in Clifton hospittle.

Give me work that I can dowe
I am disabled but I am not disheartend
I lost my right hand fighting at my cuntrys call
And it is my left hand that now has to dow my all

~~~

86. Daniel J. Sherman, Contest Entry, 2nd ser., no. 10, Bourne Papers; New York Town Clerks' Registers of Men Who Served in the Civil War, ca. 1861–1865, Daniel J. Sherman, New York State Archives, Collection 13774, box 67, roll 36.

87. 1869 New York State Census, mortality sched., Monroe Co., line 24, Daniel J. Sherman, New York State Library, roll M6.

88. Elmira, New York, originally site of a training camp for Union recruits, it hosted a prison for captured Confederates later in the war.
~~~

ALFRED D. WHITEHOUSE

Private, Co. D, 8th New York State Militia ("Washington Grays")

For Whitehouse's biography and a description of his military service, see chapter 5.

***Second Entry:* June 17, 1867**

The right arm's gone,
the nation yet remaines,
Tho many perished, yet we are saved,
The right, will triumph over wrong,
Tho it leave us but, one left arm strong,

The Pen is mightier than the sword, And can be wield from right, to left,
with great ef[f]ect.

"Give us Work, that we can do!
And dont be afraid of what we cant do,
Because one arm, is not two,
So deny us the right.

"Give us work that we can do—
For God hath decreed and blessed be he
That all men from labor should not be free'd,
Till death shall call us hence.

"Give us work that we can do
For Soldiers in War, Citizens in peace,
Our cause it was Just, and God hath us Blessed,
So why these blessings retain."

7.

POLITICS, PHILOSOPHY, AND PATRIOTISM

As possible subjects for original sketches, contest instructions suggested topics including "Essays on the War, its Purposes, its Results; the Vindication of Democracy, the Ideas of the War; Republicanism Magnified by the Struggle; [and] the American Future."[1] The veterans below, and other contestants like them, reflected on the significance of their individual service as well as the larger political and societal repercussions of the internecine struggle. For many, it was the duty of those who survived the war to protect the memory of those who did not and to fulfill the promise of their service and sacrifice by securing equality for the freedmen and by caring for their fallen comrades' loved ones. While some praised the courage and dedication of the "volunteer soldiery," others focused on the implications of Union victory for the country's future and the way in which the federal government should deal with former Confederates. Almost to a man, the veterans believed in and expressed the United States' great promise and its exceptional qualities. Born in England, Joseph Wiley Gelray wrote of the differences between volunteer soldiers in the United States and

1. "Left-Hand Writing," *Soldier's Friend,* Oct. 1865, 2.

career soldiers in European armies; the American soldier "is no machine, but a living breathing *thinking* patriot." A number of left-armed veterans waxed philosophical and political, proving that they were indeed "thinking patriots."

Even as the nation moved toward reconciliation, the failure of Reconstruction, and the betrayal of the freedmen, members of the Left-Armed Corps remained focused on their part in ending slavery and crushing rebellion. Yankee soldiers' sentiments on the peculiar institution have long been debated, but there is no doubt that fighting—often alongside Black men—to preserve the Union and defeat treason convinced many of the necessity of emancipation and citizenship for African Americans.[2] Though their opinions may have changed in later years, it is clear that many members of the Left-Armed Corps remained engaged in politics and proudly wore their GAR pins, mementoes of an organization that (for the most part) welcomed Black veterans and remained committed to the memory of abolishing slavery—though not, perhaps, to the ongoing struggle for equality.[3] In the early twentieth century, members of the Left-Armed Corps were living reminders of a war against what Ezra Dayton Hilts called the "infamous system of slavery." Alonzo L. Mabbett, whose entry is included in chapter 3, delivered the main address at a celebration of Washington's Birthday in 1911, referring to the fight against "human slavery" led by Lincoln, "the patron saint of every veteran of the Civil War."[4] His words, and those of his comrades, live on, a reminder of where our country has been and where it still has to go. Speaking from the past to our present moment, Rufus L. Robinson (whose first submission appears below) wrote:

> If we would command the respect of other nations and secure the blessings of Omnipotence, we must be consistent, and our laws must be tempered with justice. It is not sufficient that we have free Institutions, free Speech and freedom of the press, we must have freedom at the

2. Historian Bell Irvin Wiley claims that less than one-tenth of Union soldiers cared about emancipation. See *Life of Billy Yank,* 40. For refutations of this, see McPherson, *For Cause and Comrades,* 117–18; and Chandra Manning, *What This Cruel War Was Over: Soldiers, Slavery, and the Civil War* (New York: Vintage Civil War Library, 2007).

3. Gannon, *The Won Cause,* 146.

4. "School Classes Transfer Flags," *Rochester (NY) Democrat and Chronicle,* Feb. 23, 1911, 12.

> Ballot Box. We cannot be true to the principles of republicanism while we say to the Colored Man, You have no rights at the ballot-box that we are bound to respect, for we have said to him, Take the musket, and gain your freedom. Not till Universal suffrage becomes a law will our country stand forth in all her greatness and grandeur United, Disenthralled, and Redeemed.[5]

Like the men included in this chapter, Robinson remembered the past while looking to the future.

~~~

EZRA DAYTON HILTS

Corporal, Battery D, 1st New York Volunteer Light Artillery

For Hilts's biography and reminiscence of the Siege of Yorktown, see chapter 2.

November 12, 1865
Results of the War

The results of the war through which we have just passed have been sad enough, and although it has cost rivers of blood, and immense treasure and the sacrifice of half a million of brave men, yet as a whole it has resulted in the highest blessing to us as a Nation.

We are one people more than ever before. The wicked spirit which sought to sever the bonds of our Union and overthrow the government, served only to cement our Union more strongly, and to strengthen the whole framework of our government. The infamous system of slavery, which breeds rebels and assassins, has been torn up by the roots in our land as the greatest evil in Christian civilization, and the proud spirit of a slaveholding oligarchy has, we hope, vanished from among us. The strength and grandeur of our government has been proved to the world, and stands out in gratifying prominence to shield us from the insolence of our foes

5. Rufus L. Robinson, Contest Entry, 2nd ser., no. 80, William Oland Bourne Papers.
~~~

and to afford a beacon and hope to the oppressed of other lands. The war has also taught the South a severe lesson. Let the people of the South turn from the "error of their way" and swear allegiance to the government and we will extend to them "the right hand of fellowship"[6] and welcome them back beneath the folds of the old Flag. But I would not pardon rebels, especially the leaders, until they should first kneel in the dust of humiliation and show by their deeds that they sincerely repent. I fear our President[7] is too lenient. Justice should be done to the perpetrators and leaders of the wicked rebellion. The tens of thousands of our brothers who were starved in Andersonvill[e] and the other prison pens in the South cry from the ground for justice. Our work is not yet finished. We must build schoolhouses and educate the masses in the principles of eternal truth and liberty, and this will form a basis of our government as firm as the everlasting hills. We must elect loyal men to fill places of trust: our public men—our rulers—must be men who will work for the good of the whole country, and the interests of the people instead of working to gratify their own selfish ambition. They must possess wisdom, honesty and decision. Then will the Nation continue to prosper and be exalted for truly "righteousness exhalteth a nation but sin is a reproach to any people."[8]

THOMAS T. SANBORN

Sergeant, Co. A, 15th Vermont Volunteer Infantry
Sergeant, Co. I, 17th Vermont Volunteer Infantry

Sanborn, who enlisted for nine months in 1862 with the 15th Vermont Volunteers and then reenlisted with the 17th, lost his arm at the Battle of Poplar Grove Church (south of Petersburg) on September 30, 1864.[9] Born in 1823, he married in 1847 and was a tailor making

6. Galatians 2:9.
7. Andrew Johnson.
8. Proverbs 14:34.
9. Thomas T. Sanborn, Contest Entry, 1st ser., no. 102, Bourne Papers.

"neat, tasty, and fashionable garments" when he enlisted.[10] After the war, he was a deputy collector of customs.[11] Sanborn married twice, had two children, and died in 1889 at the age of sixty-five.[12]

September 29, 1865
Plain Dealings With the South

We may safely assume that the people of the South understand one thing, and that is that they have been beaten. They may acknowledge it or they may not; their young men, and some of them old enough to know better, may report about being merely "over-powered," and trying the struggle over again at the first opportunity; but we may rely upon it that a people who have fought as the Southerners have for the last four years, know perfectly well when they are whipped, and to what an extent they are at the mercy of the conqueror. But there is another thing which may not be so well understood at the South, and that is the precise sum of the requirements to be made on each seceded State as an evidence of due repentance and a condition of readmission to Congress and the Union. We are apt to think that any Southern man truly submissive to the Government ought to understand all this. But why should he necessarily? He finds the whole foundation of the social and industrial systems [with] which he is habitueded [*sic*] suddenly knocked from under his feet, and he is required to [illegible] another with which he is totally unfamiliar to fit into the general framework of the Government. Allowing that he has the best of intentions, he may err here as to what and how much his State is called upon to do. His conscience may not be a suffi-

10. 1860 U.S. Census, Orange Co., VT, pop. sched., Strafford, p. 391 (stamped), dwelling 1767, family 1888, Thomas T. Sanborn, NARA RG 29, M653, roll 1323; "Marriages," *Vermont Watchman and State Journal* (Montpelier), June 17, 1847, 3; "New Tailoring Establishment," *Vermont Family Gazette* (Bradford), Nov. 10, 1847, 4.

11. *Register of Officers and Agents, Civil, Military, and Naval, . . . 1871,* 147.

12. "Personal," *Burlington (VT) Free Press,* Apr. 19, 1889, 8; Thomas T. Sanborn, Pension File, application 393935, certificate 340047, NARA RG 15, T288, roll 411; 1870 U.S. Census, Chittenden Co., VT, pop. sched., Burlington, p. 302B (stamped), dwelling 157, family 157, Thomas T. Sanborn, NARA RG 29, M593, roll 1617.

cient guide, for he may have been sincere in his whole devotion to slavery. His intelligence may be inadequate, for he may have never really comprehended the free institutions of the North. . . .

Now it becomes the people of the North to see to it that no mistakes are hereafter made by the South in her efforts at reconstruction for want of that light of a definite understanding which it is in our power to supply. President Johnson led the way in this duty when he had his plain talk with the South Carolina delegation.[13] It ought to be made clear at the South that twenty millions of loyal freemen are backing up the President, not only in the policy which he has thought best to adopt for the time being, but [also] in the grand aims toward which that policy is an experiment. In other words, slavery being annihilated by the fiat of the sword, the South is to be brought into full and complete harmony with the free institutions of the land. To this end it is not enough merely to acknowledge emancipation and repudiate secession. In passing from the narrow gauge of slavery to [the] broad gauge of freedom, something more is necessary than to throw away the old axles and get longer [ones]—the whole dimensions and proportions of [the railroad] car and engine are to be remodeled.

So in Southern society, all the relations betwixt man and man, all political claims and rights are henceforth to be based on impartial principles and not on the false distinction of color or class. How far in this direction must the seceded States go as an earnest of their fitness for the Union? That is for the public opinion of the North, uttered through the press, her orators, and her conventions to say explicitly and to say promptly. This is the formative period of the South and the will of the North should be made known to her dispassionately, but plainly and emphatically, so that there will be no excuse for any Southern State if she shall pursue the wrong course, have her delegates to Congress sent back to her, and shall find herself remitted to a military guardianship of indefinite duration.

~~~

13. Sanborn's confidence in Johnson was misplaced, as the president's policies would eventually betray the freedmen. See Eric Foner, *Reconstruction: America's Unfinished Revolution, 1863–1877* (New York: HarperCollins, 1988).
~~~

JOSEPH WILEY GELRAY

Colonel, 59th Massachusetts Volunteers

Gelray was born in Manchester, England, in 1837 and emigrated in 1844.[14] A printer in Lowell, Massachusetts, he enlisted in the 2nd Massachusetts Infantry in May 1861.[15] He was appointed corporal and then transferred to another company, having been promoted to sergeant in December.[16] Wounded in the right shoulder and right thigh at Antietam, he was made second lieutenant in December 1862 and first lieutenant on July 23, 1863.[17] Gelray was wounded at Gettysburg in the right arm "so near the former wound as to require amputation."[18] Nevertheless, the officer continued to rise up the ranks, commissioned captain of the 57th Massachusetts on July 25, 1864, and major of the 4th Massachusetts Heavy Artillery later that year. Finally, Gelray was "brevetted major and lieutenant-colonel for gallant and meritorious service."[19] Following the war, he became a captain in the regular army and served in a number of states and territories, including Kentucky, Utah, and Montana; an obituary reported that he retired in 1870 due to "disability resulting from wounds received in line of duty."[20] Yet in 1871, he was still on the books as a captain in the army, and the 1880 Census identifies his occupation as colonel.[21] Living in Boston, he remained involved in the GAR and presided over reunions.[22] Gelray died from apoplexy in 1900 at the age of sixty-three and is buried in Arlington National Cemetery.[23] Word of his death appeared in newspapers across the country; one obituary, titled "Gave Country His Right Arm," noted that the colonel never

14. Joseph W. Gelray, Contest Entry, 1st ser., no. 108, Bourne Papers; Quint, *Record of the Second Massachusetts Infantry*, 503–4.

15. Quint, *Record of the Second Massachusetts Infantry*, 503; "Captain Joseph W. Gelray," *New York Tribune*, Mar. 13, 1900, 7.

16. Quint, *Record of the Second Massachusetts Infantry*, 504.

17. Ibid.; "Captain Joseph W. Gelray," 7.

18. Quint, *Record of the Second Massachusetts Infantry*, 504.

19. "Captain Joseph W. Gelray," 7.

20. "Members of the Staff," *Boston Globe*, Sept. 1, 1880, 1.

21. *Register of Officers and Agents, Civil, Military, and Naval, . . . 1871*, 249; 1880 U.S. Census, Suffolk Co., MA, pop. sched., Boston, p. 36C (stamped), dwelling 17, family 17, Joseph W. Gelray, NARA RG 29, T9, roll 558.

22. "Col. Gelray's Funeral," *Boston Globe*, Mar. 13, 1900, 7; "Old Soldiers Gather," ibid., Sept. 17, 1894, 1.

23. "Captain Joseph W. Gelray," 7.

married and had "traveled extensively" prior to his death in hopes of "recovering his health."[24] His entry below won twenty dollars for literary merit.[25]

September 30, 1865

The permanency of our country and her institutions depend upon the patriotism and valor of her sons.

While the above might be said with some degree of truth of every country on the earth, it is eminently true when applied to America only. Men born under Monarchical rule may be thoroughly patriotic and courageous, but their very patriotism and valor may lead them to take up arms against the constituted authorities of their own country and make war upon her institutions. They feel and know that they are, as it were, the property of their Sovereign, and consequently their individuality is, in a measure, destroyed. They have little to say in the affairs of their government, and they naturally feel themselves non-responsible for its errors or mistakes. It is, then, evident, that, however just their patriotism may be, it can be of no power or use in maintaining the government, which is supposed to protect and foster the interests of its subjects. In case of war or invasion, their countries have large standing armies to place in the field either for offense or defense, and so thoroughly are these armies disciplined, that the great majority of the men composing them, entirely lose their individuality, and become part of "one stupendous whole"[26] which is guided and controlled like a vast machine by its officers who are its only thinking men. These armies are educated and drilled to fight; it is their legitimate occupation, and, when war ensues, they enter the contest without a thought of the justice of the cause and fight as well against, as for, the interests of their country and of mankind. In these countries the farmer, the mechanic, the merchant, and the student pursue uninterrupted their several avocations during a war, no matter how long or desolating it may be. They are not called upon to sacri-

24. "Gave Country His Right Arm," *Lyndonville (VT) Journal,* Mar. 14, 1900, 2.

25. "Left-Hand Penmanship by Disabled Soldiers—Report of the Committee," *Philadelphia Evening Telegraph,* Mar. 8, 1866, 6.

26. From Alexander Pope, *An Essay on Man: Epistle I* (1734), sec. 9, line 9.

fice much to either patriotism or courage. Nothing of all the horrors of war touches them. They suffer no inconveniences, except perhaps, they may pay an increased tax.

How different is the case in our country where so few make war their trade! At the first sound of war's stern alarms, patriotism demands that we not only loosen our purse strings, but that all of us no matter what our business may be shall leave it and join the ranks of our citizen soldiery. Fathers, mothers, wives and little ones must be for the time forgotten, each man armed with that which the European soldier deems of no account—patriotism—must bare his bosom to his and his country's foes, and the valor which is born of knowledge gives him the victory. He is no machine, but a living breathing *thinking* patriot. Thus far the patriotism of the people of this country has been equal to any emergency; but should we not use every means in our power to foster and encourage the growth of that which has been the saving of our national life? We should commence this work by rewarding its possessors, who after passing through the late war—many of them returning to us wanting a limb, or otherwise disabled, and now dependent upon the country they have saved for their daily bread. A simple sense of justice, which every generous human must feel, would demand that this should be supplied, and that they be tenderly cared for. Our duty to posterity demands it! The sight of a poor soldier with one arm, and one leg lost in his country's service standing on the corner of a street in *Boston* with two little children shivering by his side begging for pennies to buy bread, is not a spectacle calculated to inspire our youth with patriotism or convince them of the honor which attends those who nobly do battle for the Republic, and who by shedding their life-blood upheld her rights and preserved her honor.

Thousands of dollars are spent annually by the different states and [the] United States government in perfecting the militia system. If one half the money thus applied was expended in making these scarred heroes comfortable, it would do more to increase the military spirit of the country than millions of dollars spent in any other way. The unjust treatment of the soldiers of the revolution forms one of the darkest pages in American history. Let us take warning in time! Do not let us suffer these men to grow[?] out of our memories. Let us convince them that the sacrifice is appreciated. Let them have no cause to say, as they *have said*, that instead of losing their arm or a leg, they wished they had lost their lives, since they were suffered to beg, or starve, in the midst of a people whose houses and whose fields they had guarded and protected.

JOHN STEWART

Sergeant, Co. C, 3rd New Jersey Volunteer Infantry

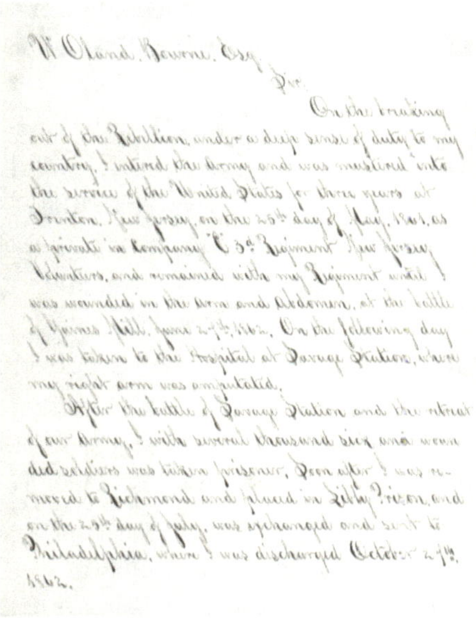
W. Oland Bourne, Esq.

Sir:

On the breaking out of the Rebellion, under a deep sense of duty to my country, I entered the Army and was mustered into the service of the United States for three years at Trenton, New Jersey, on the 25th day of May, 1861, as a private in Company "C" 3d Regiment New Jersey Volunteers, and remained with my Regiment until I was wounded in the Arm and Abdomen, at the battle of Gaines Mill, June 27th, 1862. On the following day I was taken to the Hospital at Savage Station, where my right arm was amputated.

After the battle of Savage Station and the retreat of our Army, I with several thousand sick and wounded soldiers was taken prisoner. Soon after I was removed to Richmond and placed in Libby Prison, and on the 25th day of July, was exchanged and sent to Philadelphia, where I was discharged October 27th, 1862.

A sample of John Stewart's penmanship.
Courtesy William Oland Bourne Papers, Manuscript Division, Library of Congress.

Born in Scotland in 1837, Stewart emigrated in 1842 and enlisted in May 1861 "under a deep sense of duty to [his] country"; he lost his arm at Gaines's Mill and spent a month in Libby Prison.[27] Married in 1860, he and his wife settled in Philadelphia after the war and had four children who survived to adulthood; Stewart worked as an accountant and bookkeeper.[28] In 1910, he was widowed and worked as a watchman at the U.S. customs house; he had previously worked as a bookkeeper there.[29] Stewart died one year later.[30] He won a twenty-dollar second-class-penmanship prize for this entry.[31]

27. John Stewart, Contest Entry, 1st ser., no. 93, Bourne Papers (punctuation edited); 1910 U.S. Census, Philadelphia Co., PA, pop. sched., Philadelphia, p. 1A, dwelling 8, family 5, John Stewart, NARA RG 29, T624, roll 1410.

28. 1880 U.S. Census, Philadelphia Co., PA, pop. sched., Philadelphia, p. 274A (stamped), dwelling 35, family 39, John Stewart, NARA RG 29, T9, roll 1189; 1900 U.S. Census, Philadelphia Co., PA, pop. sched., Philadelphia, p. 14, dwelling 281, family 307, John Stewart, ibid., T623, roll 1472.

29. 1910 U.S. Census, Philadelphia Co., PA, pop. sched., Philadelphia, p. 1A.

30. "Died," *Philadelphia Inquirer*, Sept. 12, 1911, 7.

31. Exhibition of Left-Hand Penmanship, Bourne Papers.

September 30, 1865

I purpose according to terms of your circular published in "The Soldiers Friend," to offer a few thoughts to my fellow Soldiers, amongst whom feelings fraternal ought to exist.

Fellow Soldiers:

Previous to the Rebellion the major part of us had thought that in the United States, the age of Bullets had been suspended by the age of Ballots; but the inauguration of a causeless and bloody Rebellion by the Slaveholders of the South undeceived us, and revealed to us our utter ignorance of the civilization begotten of Slavery.

The Masses of the Free States were ignorant of the fact that the relations of Capital and Labor in the South induced that condition of mind that lead[s] to the settlement of difficulties rather by brute force, than as with us of the North by the dispassionate sway of reason and reflection.

The fiendish attack on our Flag when the "Star of the West,"[32] freighted with provisions for a starving Garrison, sought entrance to Charleston Harbor; the traitorous attack on Fort Sumter headed by one doubly accursed as having no personal grievance to redress and no cause of complaint against the Government that gave him his military education without charge;[33] aroused the latent patriotism of the North and we flew to arms for the life of a Nation, to secure to ourselves and to our children the continuance of Constitutional Government; and thank God the Nation has been saved, Liberty has awakened to a brighter and more extended existence and the Soldiers of the Union feel that not in vain have they braved the cannon's mouth, nor the deadly breach; nor in vain have they suffered the pangs of consuming hunger, the slow torture of the parched lips, or the weary fatigue of the march. We have crushed to annihilation the most formidable Rebellion the world ever witnessed—against open foes in front and secret traitors in our rear, we have fought and conquered. True, hundreds of thousands of our brave comrades in arms sleep their last sleep in honor and loneliness upon many a battle field, whilst others called to greater sufferings have succumbed under the more

32. Steamship tasked with resupplying the U.S. troops at Fort Sumter.

33. P. G. T. Beauregard, commanding Confederate forces at Charleston, was an alumnus of West Point.

cruel treatment received in Rebel Prisons, perpetuating to eternal infamy alike the cause which they fought against, and [the] men who promoted it. Thousands of us who have survived the shock of battle are maimed for life and bear on our bodies honorable scars earned in battling for Justice and Liberty. Every hamlet, town and city of the Union witness[es] the shattered constitutions and mutilated forms of those who counted not their lives dear unto them so that Liberty should be Triumphant.

Fellow Soldiers! My mind reverts to these scenes and endeavoring in vain to aggregate the sacrifice and impelled by its magnitude I ask—Why this amount of suffering? What has the Nation been guilty of that required the shedding of so much blood? The answer comes with the interrogation. God's truth, holy and immutable, declares—Nations (as individuals) that sin must suffer. Having secured the salvation of the Government at such a terrible sacrifice to ourselves may we not, fellow Soldiers, justly lay claim to be heard in the Nation's Councils, and shall we not as a recognition of our sufferings insist with one heart and one mind that in the reconstruction of the States there shall not be tolerated one principle at variance with the natural rights of any human being. Then shall be removed all cause for future disruption as the end of injustice will insure the end of war.

Whether good or evil predominates as the result of this war for Liberty and the Union, is a question that perplexes many. With me there is not a doubt. The evil is present and palpable as all evil necessarily is. The good, though watered with many tears, is permanent and abiding: and slow of growth as the oak which braves the storms of a thousand years.

Hitherto we have been looked upon as a nation of money worshippers unwilling to make one sacrifice to defend a principle in our all absorbing love for money and its power; but, in the good that this war has developed, I see millions of men rushing to arms when the principle of self-government is menaced. I see Slavery, accursed of God and man, swept from the land as with a beesom[34] of destruction. I see the wealth of the nation poured out to alleviate the pain of the dying Soldier, to enhance his comfort on the march, to add to his pleasure on his return. I see the Womanhood of the nation laid in death from excessive sympathy and labor for the man who left his home and kindred

34. Besom, or broom. The phrase "besom of destruction" is from Isaiah 14:23.

to secure a Continent to Liberty: to posterity; a Government the wisest and the best man ever framed.

As a nation we are more powerful than ever, and challenge the respect of those who recently despised us. We, fellow Soldiers of the Union, sharers of the glory of aiding to develop to the nations of the earth the benevolence and disinterestedness enshrined in the American character; and we cannot but contemplate for our common country a career more brilliant and prosperous than ever.

The Aristocracies of the Old World saw in the conservation of Slavery on this continent immunity for themselves in their power over the masses and hence their common sympathy for the Rebellion; and were it only for the prestige of Serfdom broken by the war, who will venture to estimate the good to all nations that will arise from it.

The Nation educated to a higher humanity, to a more exalted appreciation of justice, to a greater reverence for the principle of Freedom; it is a matter of proud consciousness to us fellow Soldiers that with our lives in our hands we have aided to secure these inestimable blessings to our beloved country.

It has been the painful experience of many of us on our return to our homes to find a sentiment prevailing among many "that with our return there would be an increase of crime consequent on the demoralization incident to camp life."

Soldiers, we know the source of such fears. I have found that they are uniformly entertained by men whose loyalty is doubtful. I have never met a truly loyal man nor read a truly loyal journal who have given expression to such sentiments, persons alone who have had no sympathy with the objects of the war, but whose sympathies were with the enemies of their country, and whose conduct in our rear caused the fall of many a hero. Soldiers, this sentiment of distrust comes not from our friends but from our enemies.

That crime may have increased with the return of the Army may be true, but who are the criminals; not as a rule the returned Veteran but a set of craven, cowardly time servers who have been preying on the Government and its defenders since the war began.

In conclusion, fellow Soldiers, may what we have suffered for our country increase our love for her and may we always be found the defenders of our Government and never consent to trust with any man the administration of State or National affairs who in the trying times of our Country has been of doubtful Loyalty.

HENRY L. KRAHL

Private, Co. H, 13th United States Infantry

Krahl enlisted in 1862 and was wounded at Arkansas Post (January 10–11, 1863), his second battle.[35] A farmer prior to enlisting, he worked as a clerk after losing his arm and was swindled by a confidence man who employed him in 1867. Asking the veteran to collect money for his real-estate agency, the swindler required a security deposit of $200; Krahl could only afford to loan the man $150 and received a total of $21 in wages despite being promised $15 a week.[36] After the conman was arrested, the *Chicago Tribune* reported that Krahl was "a young man, of gentlemanly address, who has lost an arm in the service of his country, and one whom none but a scamp of the first water would have the meanness to cheat."[37] Married in 1868, Krahl worked in insurance and real estate and as a purchasing agent, a pension agent, and a notary public.[38] When he ran for city clerk in 1884 before withdrawing from the contest, a Chicago paper reported that his "'armless sleeve' tells of a sacrifice, which none but a cripple can estimate. . . . Though he has lost his right arm he writes rapidly with his left, and is an excellent accountant."[39] Krahl died in Aurora, Illinois, in 1908, a "prominent businessman."[40]

October 27, 1865

I, without lamentation, bear a deep and lasting memento of the war for the Union in the loss of my right arm. . . .

But thank God, our Country is saved; though it has been with sacrifice of the lives of many thousands and the maiming of many thousands more. And now since war's dread alarms are over, and victory complete has perched upon our National Banner, and the armies are being disbanded; issues of great and paramount importance are rising before us. Among these is that of restricted and universal suffrage.

35. Henry L. Krahl, Contest Entry, 1st ser., no. 120, Bourne Papers.

36. "An Old Swindler Caught," *Chicago Tribune*, Jan. 5, 1867, 4.

37. Ibid.

38. 1900 U.S. Census, Kane Co., IL, pop. sched., Aurora, p. 9, dwelling 177, family 206, Henry L. Krahl, NARA RG 29, T623, roll 312; 1880 U.S. Census, Kane Co., IL, pop. sched., Aurora, p. 141C (stamped), dwelling 432, family 449, Henry Krahl, ibid., T9, roll 218; *Daily News Aurora City Directory*, 216; *Every Office Favorite*.

39. "Aurora Bulletin," *Chicago Inter Ocean*, Jan. 26, 1884, 16; "Aurora Bulletin," ibid., Feb. 2, 1884, 15.

40. "H. L. Krahl Dies," *Davenport (IA) Daily Times*, Nov. 4, 1908, 2.

This question is to be regarded as more vital to the future of our country than any which has arisen since the settlement of the great question of Union or *no* Union by the stern decision of the battle-field.

And since by the valor of the national arms, and the wise statesmanship of the martyred and lamented President, under the blessing, sanction, and guidance of an over-ruling Providence this great struggle has resulted in the freedom of the slave, can we remand him back to servitude, or can we bestow upon him the priceless boon of Freedom, and at the same time withhold the rights belonging thereto?

I think all history will show, and our knowledge of human nature will teach us, that it would be a most hazardous experiment to clothe a large part of the citizens of a State with freedom and yet deny to them the *rights and franchise of citizens.*

Are we to suppose that 4,000,000 of men made free by the results of a gigantic war, in which they themselves have borne no small part, will be satisfied with anything short of entire citizenship with all its consequent rights?

May we not reasonably expect that mob violence and petty rebellions will constantly disturb the peace and harmony of the country in case they be with-held?

Is not the alternative of citizens or savages held out to us in this question?

And again, where is the justice of accepting the strong arm and the steady valor of the Negro at a time when his help was sorely needed, then denying to him the hard earned fruits of his fidelity and courage when his services in the field are no more required? Of his valor and might in battle, Fort Wagner, Fort Pillow,[41] Milliken's Bend, and many other well-fought battles will forever testify.

Can this government clothe with its military insignia a soldier to struggle for its freedom and preservation, and at the same time deny that soldier the privileges of a free government?

Such presumption would forever blast the fair fame of our glorious and blood-bought, beloved and redeemed Republic: for the dignity of a nation, as

41. Battle in Tennessee along the Mississippi River on April 12, 1864, at which Confederate troops murdered surrendering Black soldiers.

well as its stability, rests upon its integrity, and in the justice shown to even the humblest citizens. What better security can we have for the peace, loyalty and prosperity of the south than this just measure of universal suffrage? Let the ballot of the loyal black man balance that of the disloyal white.

~ ~ ~

WILLIAM MILLER DECAMP

Private, Co. B, 1st Iowa Volunteer Infantry
First Lieutenant, Co. G, 22nd Iowa Volunteer Infantry
First Lieutenant, Co. 161, 2nd Battalion Veteran Reserve Corps

DeCamp, born in New York City in 1818, was an Iowa farmer when he enlisted in response to Lincoln's first call for volunteers and was mustered into service in May 1861.[42] He fought in Missouri at Wilson's Creek (August 10, 1861), suffering a "severe flesh wound." DeCamp spent three months in the hospital, a prisoner for two-thirds of that time. After reenlisting in August 1862, he was appointed second lieutenant in January 1863. DeCamp was involved in Grant's campaign against Vicksburg and fought at Port Gibson (May 30, 1862), where he was "severely wounded in [the] right shoulder and arm, which resulted in the contraction and partial paralysis of [his] right hand, which is now almost entirely useless." He was promoted to first lieutenant in May 1863.[43] Put in command of a battalion of VRC at a hospital in New Orleans, DeCamp rejoined his regiment in the Shenandoah Valley and "was present at the surprise battle of Cedar Creek, Virginia" (October 19, 1864). In November 1864, he was summoned by an examining board in Washington, D.C., "for decision in regard to [his] fitness for commission in V.R.C." He could not appear due to "army diarrhea," an illness that lasted nine months. DeCamp was honorably discharged in April 1865. His initial affidavit noted that he could write with his toes, but he later requested that Bourne remove that "somewhat inelegant" information, believing it "not calculated to appear or sound well 'historically.'" From the late 1870s onward, he spent significant time in National Homes for Disabled Volunteer Soldiers, including branches in Dayton, Ohio; Milwaukee, Wisconsin; and Hampton,

42. Wm. M. DeCamp, Contest Entry, 1st ser., no. 147, Bourne Papers (punctuation edited); 1856 Iowa State Census, Johnson Co., pop. sched., Scott, State Historical Society of Iowa Library and Research Center, p. 630.

43. Pryce, *Vanishing Footprints*, 47.

Virginia.[44] In 1904, DeCamp attempted suicide while a patient in Dayton; when he died there in 1905 from a cerebral hemorrhage, the register identified him as a widowed schoolteacher.[45] In 1872, the *Chicago Tribune* called him a "zealous liberal"; the essay DeCamp submitted, which won twenty dollars for literary merit, fits the label.[46]

December 15, 1865

With no hope of deserving any of the premiums offered to left-handed writers, I esteem it an honor to comply with your polite invitation, and therefore send a specimen. I will endeavor very briefly to give my ideas of the causes, and objects of our late civil war; state in what the crowning excellence of a representative government consists; remark upon the relative merits of white and black men; and conclude with a few items of personal history.

The *Cause* of the war may be stated in one word, *Selfishness*! or that tyrannical, monarchial, domineering, and aggrandizing spirit, which is unavoidably created in the slave owner; which curtails all freedom of speech or the press, and can only thrive satisfactorily under a despotic form of Government.

Call to mind the insults, indignities, destruction of life or business, and general spirit of intolerance practiced toward *all* (born North or South) who would *dare*, in a slave community (and even before whites only) to express the opinion that Slavery was an evil, and should be abolished.

Oh *Abolition*! that awful word, at once a bane and bugbear to all Rebels and rebel sympathisers. Demagogues have ever been disposed to saddle on parties the individual acts and sayings of single persons supposed to belong to said parties, when it is well known by all *thinking* men, that a party is only responsible for the official acts of said party; hence the hue and cry of "Abolitionism" (in its offensive sense) against the old Republican party was thoroughly unjust. With the same propriety might the present sham Democ-

44. Historical Register of National Homes for Disabled Volunteer Soldiers, 1866–1938, William M. DeCamp, NARA RG 15, M1749, rolls 35, 158, 230.

45. Ibid.; "After Style of Old Romans," *Dayton (OH) Daily News,* Jan. 3, 1904, 11.

46. "Political," *Chicago Tribune,* Sept. 3, 1872, 4; Exhibition of Left-Hand Penmanship, Bourne Papers.

racy be charged of being composed of all Foreigners, or all Roman Catholics, because containing more of these classes, than the opposite party: or a church might be called a Gamblers Church, because one or more gamblers might have contributed to its erection.

Much has been said about the relative merits of the *White and Black Man.* The blacks are charged with laziness and improvidence. It is a Physiological and Phrenological fact, that exercise gives power, either of mind or body. Take away from a human being the legal power to possess and accumulate property, the privilege of education, and the control of one's own children, and what motives are left as incentives to action? Comparatively none!

The Blacks have been in this condition for many generations. Would not many of the Whites have similar characters, under similar restrictions, which deny them all those mental incentives and activities, so *necessary* to mental development. The *most inferior Whites* are loudest in their denunciation of Blacks, and insist, that the colored race cannot by any possibility equal them, under any circumstances. Such will frequently ask a more liberal minded opponent this question: "Do you consider a 'Nigger' as good as you are?" To such I have replied in this manner: "That will depend upon circumstances; it is possible for a Negro to be even *better* than I am." If he can do a harder day's work, or can carry a heavier burthen a longer distance, with less fatigue than I can, he is *Physically* better.

If he can write a letter better, or make a better speech, he is *Intellectually* better.

If he tells the truth more often, more fully abstains from Profanity or Obscenity in thought and deed; and can be tempted with a larger amount of money, without theft or embezzlement, he is *Morally* better. If the Negro exhibits more fidelity as a friend, and treats his family more kindly, he is *Socially* better.

If he abstains from the use of Tobacco and Alcohol, his *Example* is better. Nothing I believe remains, but the consideration of Beauty. It then becomes a matter of taste, whether the color of yellow, or black, is more desirable than white, and which has the most symmetrically arranged features. It is well known that there are some extremely vile and heartless *white* men in the World, who will remorselessly lie, cheat, steal, murder, be guilty of seduction, or commit a rape whenever opportunity offers. Will any sane man, pretend to say, that said white man is superior to an honest and well behaved black man? In what respect superior? The idea is absurd! In short, the unkind feeling against the black man is a selfish, ignorant, and vulgar prejudice, the offspring of a narrow, contracted, and ungenerous mind.

Admitting the alleged inferiority of the Negro race, it should prompt us to charity, magnanimity, and kindness, rather than to proscription and persecution.

The advocate of *Political* equality for the black man is taunted with an equal desire for his *Social* equality, desire for promiscuous marriages, etc. etc. As well accuse the advocate of kindness toward horses of a desire to marry said horses. There is a wide difference between Political equality, and Social equality, and he who cannot distinguish the difference, certainly lacks education, or sense, or both. There is many a *white* man whom we would defend in his political rights, and at the same time we would be very reluctant to make him a social companion, or invite him to our houses and families.

Although the intermarriage of Whites and Blacks is not in accordance with my taste, and I esteem it my privilege to discourage the same, by the mild agencies of remonstrance and argument, yet strictly speaking, if a white man chooses to marry a black woman, or the reverse, it is simply none of my business: *nor is it any other man's business*; so long as they behave peaceably, quietly, in violation of no law, and do not intrude themselves upon the sanctities of other people's houses and residences. It were as well to dictate to our neighbors, what color of dress they shall wear, as what color of skin they shall marry. . . .

Taking the teachings of Christ, or of Common Sense Justice as our guide, the Black man should be judged as all other classes of men are judged, namely, upon their merits, without regard to color.

Legal interference prohibiting the intermarriage of different races can only be justified, upon a presumption *amply sustained*, that the offspring of such marriages, are of necessity, abnormal or degenerate, insane, fools, or in some sense inferior in mind or body to both of the parents, hence the Bible injunction against the intermarriage of Cousins. . . .

I will state this fact, which is entirely beyond refutation. The weight of medical testimony is decidedly in favor of crossing or mixing temperaments or races, with the object or intention, of improving the offspring. . . . This reasoning is supposed to account for the superiority of many Americans over any class of Europeans. Said Americans are the offspring of different classes of European emigrants.

Whether this rule will warrant the intermarriage of Whites and Blacks, we are not prepared to say. Before legislative interference is invoked to prohibit said intermarriages, the soundest and most reliable medical testimony should be consulted, and this testimony should exert a controlling influence.

Unprohibited! A "Government of Law" says, "Hands off," said intermarriages are none of your business! . . .

Believing that Slavery has received its death blow in our beloved Country, it now only remains that the Freedman be endowed with all his Natural Rights: Life, Liberty, and the pursuit of Happiness (including the right of Suffrage), as justly set forth in the Declaration of Independence.

A wise restriction for all voters, White or Black, Native or Foreign, would be to require an ability to *read*, which alone would tend greatly to advance Universal Education.

~ ~ ~

MICHAEL J. FITZ JAMES

Private, Co. D, 32nd New York Volunteer Infantry
Private, Co. H, 121st New York Volunteer Infantry

For Fitz James's biography and narrative of his service, see chapter 5.

December 18, 1865

Two years ago when our country was in danger the talk of a great many was that our Northern forces would never subdue the South. But with hearts of flint and Yankee steel we showed these Copper Heads what we could do. No one ever heard a soldier speaking in this manner unless a coward or a runagate;[47] there are plenty of these all over the North and always talking bad of one of the best governments in the known world. We have had four years' war in this country fighting for freedom and Union. How often were our armies repulsed during that time! Several times to my own knowledge, when we had to shoulder our muskets and march over the same ground both day and night, in heat, rain and cold, to fight the same battles over and over

47. Deserter.

again. We fought with perseverance, trusting in God's mercy, until we put an end to this bloody rebellion. We have our beloved country in a way that it stands in a higher and firmer scale than it ever was before, not only in our own eyes but in the eyes of foreign nations. We have shown them what we "Yanks" can do.

Now, the war is all over; we have abolished slavery and subdued the proud aristocracy of the South. There is a certain party, if they see one of our poor disabled soldiers looking for employment, the first word that is said to him, "you had no right to go and fight for Nigars [*sic*]." This is the way our brave men are scrutinized with disgust and horror by this party. Every man of us knows that we have fought for freedom and Union to maintain our republic which is one of the best forms of government in the world. They who do not abide the laws of such a government as this, are not worthy to be called citizens. My fellow soldiers and citizens, we ought to feel proud to see the spirit of independence prevailing among us this day. If we did not gain our independence, how would we be. We would be treated and knocked around worse than the dogs of the street. We ought ever to be thankful to God who gave us faith and courage to fight the glorious battles of our Country. We must not indulge hatred against our fellow creatures for being black although they differ in dialects, custom and manners in this world. It must be remembered that we will not in the next. When all and every one of us will appear body and soul before the Heavenly tribunal to be judged according to our works, with no distinction of person whatsoever, the Negro will be as good in the sight of God as the white man if he be obedient to His Commandments; therefore it is our duty to love one another in this world that God may love us hereafter in Heaven. With those contemptible men, we have nothing to say or do, but to pray to God for their forgiveness that he may cast away all evil from their hearts. We soldiers know the cause that we hazarded our lives and spilt our blood for. The cause our beloved President was assassinated for. We should maintain and never desist from this cause as long as we live. I hope and trust that God will give us grace to persevere in this to the end.

~~~
~~~

WILLIAM HANNIBAL THOMAS

Sergeant, Co. I, 5th United States Colored Infantry

Born in Ohio in 1843, Thomas served in the same regiment as Robert A. Pinn (see chapter 1).[48] Prior to the war, he was the first African American student admitted to Otterbein University in Westerville, Ohio; met with verbal and physical hostility on campus, he left before the end of the first term.[49] Prior to the advent of the USCT, Thomas served as a noncombatant starting in 1861; perhaps not surprisingly, he begins his account with his 1863 enlistment.[50] After the war, Thomas entered a seminary and requested Bourne's help in obtaining theological texts; he hoped to secure a position teaching freedmen, explaining, "I don't expect to secure a position as clerk being proscribed on account of my color." Bourne printed his request and readers responded by sending more than fifty volumes; in thanks, Thomas wrote that the "tokens of kindness" showed that "there are at least some hearts who are grateful to our country's soldiers, and who . . . will not forget those who added their mites in support of the Union—some giving a scar, others an arm, and many others a leg, while hundreds and thousands gave their life's blood, pouring it out upon the altar of Liberty for universal freedom."[51] In later years as a preacher, legislator, and journalist, Thomas worked for the uplift of Black people.[52] In 1901, however, the biracial Thomas published *The American Negro: What He Was, What He Is, and What He May Become,* an extremely racist treatise. John David Smith's biography of Thomas's fascinating life bears the title *Black Judas* and argues that the "excruciating physical pain" that resulted from amputation had combined with other "physical and psychical traumas" to foster "Thomas' pessimism and the venomous anti-Negro racial ideology he espoused."[53]

December 30, 1865

It is a question which suggests itself to the mind, but which prudence forbids to ask, when conversing with the brave soldiers, Did you enlist from

48. William H. Thomas, Contest Entry, 1st ser., no. 193, Bourne Papers.
49. Smith, *Black Judas,* 17–18.
50. Ibid., 22–23.
51. "A Wounded Soldier," *Soldier's Friend,* Feb. 1866, 2.
52. Smith, *Black Judas,* xxiv.
53. Ibid., xiv.

patriotic, or mercenary motives? In my own case I will not say, but relate the incidents, and leave an impartial public to decide.

I enlisted at camp Delaware, Ohio, Sept. 28, 1863, in the fifth Regiment U.S. Col'd Infantry, in company I, in which I served as Sergeant until my discharge.

At that time no bounty was paid to colored soldiers, and $7.00 per month was paid to such as would accept. It was under these circumstances that I, with many other young men, entered the service, and for a year we received no pay. . . .

Thomas was wounded and lost his right arm at Wilmington, North Carolina.

I was removed north to Hospital, where I remained [until] July 25, '65, when I was discharged from the service.

Here my narration ends; but I will add, that the *government*, seeing the injustice did me in regard to pay, paid me the same as other soldiers from January 1st, 64.

In conclusion, we ask no favors in our behalf, but we do ask, if such devotion is not a test of Loyalty? And since the evidence is so conclusive, and we have shared alike in the dangers and vicissitudes of the war, ought we not to partake of all the immunities pertaining to the rights of citizens, even, as our Anglo Saxon Brothers? What say you?

We ask this in the name of the noble braves, who, first at Milliken's Bend, by untiring zeal and fidelity to the union, succeeding in repelling a vast horde of would-be conquerors; and again at Port Hudson, where by their deeds of valor, they showed to the world their fearlessness of death in the cause of liberty and justice. And again at Fort Wagner, and Olustee, and time warns us to desist. When Petersburg, New Market Heights, Fort Gilmer, and Honey Hill, Nashville, Wilmington, and Fort Fisher,[54] with their wounded and dying

54. Thomas lists battles in which Black soldiers fought valiantly and made significant contributions. New Market Heights and Fort Gilmer were both sites of fighting during the Battle of Chaffin's Farm. Black troops helped secure victory at Nashville, in December 1864, and capture Wilmington in February 1865.

heroes present themselves to our mental visions, asking that justice may be meted out to those living defenders of American Liberty.

~~~

MARTIN DOUGLASS HAMILTON

First Sergeant, Co. G, 17th Indiana Volunteer Infantry

For Hamilton's biography and a narrative of his service, see chapter 2.

January 23, 1868

I write not with the expectation of gaining the premium offered to the best penman, for I know that is entirely out of the question for many reasons. But as I am one of the one-armed corps I of course am somewhat interested in this work and think it no harm in exposing my ignorance by becoming one of the contributors. As my notice is so very short and having no time to think of this matter I of course am excusable by everybody for going it rough shod. So hear goes never to[o] late to do good. I will not dwell long so do not get impatient my readers. . . .

Hamilton was mustered into service June 1861.

[D]uring the knight of July the 25/61 hea[r]d the bugle sound the alarm. That sound I never will forget. The long roll was beat and all the peculiar noises thatt all the Soldiers had to become acquainted with. Anyway "fall in" was the cry so hear we went over ditches fences and whatever might hapen Now our line was formed and with throbbing harts we awaited them. As we thought now the order was fire now the guns that long had been loaded was in that forest exploded and I asure you that Rebs would not [have] been safe even 30 feet up the trees and I asure you thare was not many braves but what quivered in his boots and I am in hopes every Buter-nut[55] may have my

55. "Butternut" was slang for a Confederate soldier, referring to the color of their uniforms dyed at home with butternut squashes.
~~~

feelings on that knight eaven if it is down whare they are shore to go. Hear I would lik to give you my opinion of the thing but as I must hasten as my time is limated I will just say when I think of my condition and then whar a part of my soul layes I cannot help but think that I would like [to] have the powr in my one left-hand to smash them with evry Rebe[l] and cast the seed from off the face of the earth. But my one armed fellows I can say I hope thare is a beter time coming and I am Boldly for striking for higher wages and give us enough to board us at $2.50 per wk. any how if nothing for clothing and whoe has any beter right than we criples do who helped defend this property of the north I say let us strik[e] for higher wages than $8 a month.[56] I am shore that had I not had a good home to have come to I might [have] starved to death before this time. I cannot get in any kind of imploy now what is to be done. I am now ready for a situation if anybody has any thing that I can doe. But on I must go and get don my scribbling.

PHILIP KEPPEL FAULK

Private, Co. F, 11th Pennsylvania Volunteer Infantry
Second Lieutenant, Co. C, 54th Pennsylvania Volunteer Militia
Second Corporal, Co. F, 11th Pennsylvania Volunteer Infantry

For Faulk's biography and his description of his last battle, see chapter 3. What follows is his second entry, undated.

A Word with Comrades

The scenes of carnage—the fiery storm of war—the red deluge of blood, and the terrible mimicry of hell that for four long years enshrouded our land in a pall black as Egyptian night have all passed away. The war drum no longer calls to arms, and no serried hosts now marshal for the fray, but instead the light of Heaven shines serenely down upon a peaceful people, and flagrant flowers blossom undisturbed upon the graves of the heroic dead. The unsullied flag of the free—prouder than the eagles of ancient Rome—floats in triumph from the frozen pines of the North to the flaunting Palmettos of the

56. By wages, Hamilton means the pension payment for disabled veterans.

South. Stained with precious blood, and blackened with battle smoke it still waves in full glory, and will live long as the star of freedom lights up in effulgent splendor the newborn Western World. An ocean of blood and millions of Treasure it has cost to vindicate the honor or that emblem of a free nationality, and to preserve unbroken the bonds of union sealed by that sacred compact—the immortal Declaration of Independence.

The foul blot—human slavery—early introduced into the Thirteen Colonies, which threatened to exist for all time, a curse to all, and a deadly insult to the very principles of human progress, and the religious and political rights we vauntingly boasted of, is by the bloody arbitrament of the sword, erased forever from our escutcheon. As a free, proud nationality we now stand forth to the world, no longer the target for ridicule and derision, but as the home of the free—the refuge of the oppressed, and the hope of unborn millions. The star of the West, whose radiance flashes into the uttermost parts of the earth.

From the wreck and havoc of war, good has risen Phoenix-like, and already blots out the crimson stains upon the fair face of Nature, but it cannot dry the tear of anguish or suppress one emotion of heart-bursting grief. It cannot restore the lost husband to his widowed wife, the once lithe and active son to the bereaved mother, or the fallen father to the weeping and helpless orphan. While momentous results for good, viewed in a moral and political light, owe their origin to the war, and exert a deep and lasting influence upon the future of our country, we cannot forget that suffering, sorrow, and the most poignant agony are felt in many a lonely and desolate hearth.

Who can estimate the grief, weigh the tears, or measure the bitterness of heart that weigh down and oppress thousands upon thousands all over our war scourged land. Broken hearts, ruined hopes, and blasted prospects are intimately associated or connected with every life that has been sacrificed, and with every honorable scar received upon the field of deadly strife. In every valley and upon every hill, in the dark mountains, and upon the broad prairies, a voice of weeping cries aloud into the ears of the God of Battles. It is the cry of lament[at]ion—"Rachel mourning" for her first-born.[57] It is the bitter memory of the stain that will never die, long as the page of history blazons the gory chapter.

57. A reference to Matthew 2:18, itself referencing Jeremiah 31:15.

As comrades, who marched side by side with the fallen, who witnessed the death blow, and listened to their last dying messages, in the desperate hour of conflict, when the air was hot with flames sulphurous as Dante's hell, do we not owe a duty to those who are left to mourn, that no effort or sympathy or charity on our part, can lessen? Should we not remember in our prosperity that orphans and widows have been deprived of their strong stay and are homeless, friendless and penniless? Perhaps a father fell by your side, you closed his eyes in death while his thoughts clung fondly to his distant home and family. The widow's only son was with you in the loathsome prison hell at Andersonville and breathed out his life there. Perchance you pillowed his dying, languishing head, when the gaunt destroyer conquered him. Can you remember his last faintly breathed message to his poor old mother far away in her Northern home? Did you not witness that death scene in the cheerless hospital? That husband passing into the dark valley, slowly, and with gasping [illegible] effort, whispering a farewell to a waiting, anxious wife? Have we not all witnessed such scenes, and can we soon forget them? Will we stand by and behold the heartless, selfish world pass the soldier's widow or the soldier's orphan, with its cold unfeeling eyes? No! We cannot and must not do it. *"We cannot forget the soldier"*—our comrade, nor can we forget those who sleep beside his grave.

We leave all that to the *clerical hypocrite,* who has garnered unenviable notoriety in that particular. Let us extend that sympathy that is practical—not theoretical pity. We can care for the needy, help the maimed, and comfort the widow and fatherless. By doing so, God, the Father of all, will bless us. "Charity hideth a multitude of sins,"[58] and "it is more blessed to give than to receive"[59] says the Word of God. We can realize the truth of these word of inspiration by protecting and cherishing the Republic's mourners.

It is the source of much gratification to know that the surviving soldiers, aided by many citizens of the State of Pennsylvania, have, in a noble spirit of benevolence and philanthropy, made ample and efficient provision for the orphans of the soldiers of that State, who fell during the Rebellion. May Heaven bless and prosper all who assisted in the laudable enterprise, and may the "Children of the State" do honor to the memory of her Sainted patriots.

58. 1 Peter 4:8.

59. Acts 20:35.

One word more. Does not your heart, comrade, sometimes swell with exultation and pride when you reflect or realize that you stood by the Stars and Stripes in the dark and terrible hour of battle—that you beheld its stained and shattered shreds float high and far in the smoking front, until every traitorous assailant yielded before its invincible power. Are you not conscious that you were not mingling in the strife at the behests of a despot, or for the purpose of conquest—not waging war for plunder at the nod of an adventurer, but standing up nobly, voluntarily in defense of your country's free Government? You realized that you were no hireling or mercenary. Fortified by these reflections and conscious of duty fearlessly discharged, no misfortune, no calamity or adversity however overwhelming, can rob you of that light within and self gratulation, which not even all the world can burn down or destroy. All your veteran scars are enduring, priceless mementoes of glory won in the deadly breach at the cannon's mouth, and in the heat of the fierce charge. They tell of unfading laurels plucked from the jaws of death, and speak of deeds of noble daring performed, where none but the true and brave could venture. They proclaim your patriotism in language more eloquent than human tongue. They picture the price of liberty and union, and are richer ornaments than the purest gold—more valuable than the treasures and gems from Golconda's mine.[60]

Though we realize all this, we must not be content with the record of the past, but ever stand up fearlessly for the right. We must assist the distressed, and aid and encourage our brethren who strike for the principles of liberty and justice, whenever it is consistent to do so, remembering also, that life is a continual warfare—temporal as well as spiritual. And while upholding the vital principles of religious and political liberty, let us also wage perpetual war against the emissaries of Satan who strike at our character, our reputations, and our immortal souls. We have conquered a mortal foe—let us also strive persistently to vanquish the unceasing and insidious assaults of the Powers of Darkness. Put on the whole armor of God, and fight valiantly under the blood-stained Banner of King Emanuel, and ultimately the great Prince of Peace will wash away forever our blood and tears.

60. A diamond mine in India.

8.

LIFE AS ONE-ARMED MEN

All of the contest entries are testaments to recovery, adjustment, and rehabilitation. The veterans in this chapter, however, spent considerable time describing their post-amputation lives and thus provide insight into varied experiences, struggles, and mindsets. Bourne believed that the left arm was a fitting substitute for the right—perseverance would enable a nearly seamless transference of duties from right to left. The prosthetics industry, already in operation but invigorated during the war as thousands of men lost limbs, marketed a similar rhetoric: men with artificial arms and/or legs could reenter civilian life and provide for themselves and their families. Prior to legislation in 1862 entitling Union amputees to "government" arms or legs, newly limbless men had to purchase their own; later, manufacturers were assigned to hospitals and fit eligible soldiers with prosthetics.[1] In 1865, men signing Bourne's hospital

1. On the Civil War–era prosthetics industry, see Hasegawa, *Mending Broken Soldiers.*

reminiscence book had come to Central Park Hospital to receive theirs. A few contestants complained about uncomfortable artificial limbs, while others emphasized their continued ability to engage in manual labor or secure gainful employment; most never mentioned prosthetics, though Burritt Stiles sent Bourne photographs proudly featuring both his stump and his artificial arm. In his examination of the prosthetics industry during the conflict, historian Guy R. Hasegawa notes that artificial limbs enabled amputees, in part, to cover their injuries in order to avoid public scrutiny.[2] By participating in a contest that underscored their reconfigured bodies and presented the products thereof to the public, the Left-Armed Corps chose to bare their wounds and tell their stories.

Some contestants addressed heart-felt exhortations to their fellow left-armed veterans, reaching out to men they believed would understand and relate to their experiences. Others bid farewell to their missing right arms or mourned their diminished limbs. Returning home, the veterans had to determine how to support themselves and their families while simultaneously recovering from the physical and emotional trauma of their wounds. Bourne proposed occupations that required legible penmanship as possible solutions, and a number of contestants wrote while attending commercial colleges, institutions that, among other business-related subjects, provided penmanship instruction. Many were still learning to shape legible letters with their left hands when they submitted their specimens; the process of recovery, therefore, was not complete. Ira Broshears describes how losing a limb "unmans the energy," indicating what historian Sarah Handley-Cousins terms the "gendered crisis" of a wounded body; disability was tied to dependency and unmanliness, and left-armed veterans aspired to present a new form of manhood—one that did not depend on bodily wholeness but instead on proven loyalty and perseverance.[3] As they asserted their ability to continue farm work or lamented their lack of job opportunities, the contestants navigated expectations of self-reliance and bodily labor in the face of potential reliance on pensions or charity. Broshears links "labor-greatness" to American identity and refers twice to the "conflict of life," while Jonathan McKinstry Allison greets his comrades as they enter the "great 'drama' of life." Both were determined to thrive as (to quote Allison) "living monuments of the late cruel and bloody Rebellion" and

2. Ibid., 21.

3. Handley-Cousins, *Bodies in Blue*, 12.

as examples of American resilience. Regardless of their situation, the men included below and others like them recognized their membership in a brotherhood of one-armed soldiers.

IRA BROSHEARS

Sergeant, Co. B, 27th Indiana Volunteers

Broshears, an Indiana native and farmer, enlisted in 1861 and lost his right arm at Chancellorsville.[4] In 1867, he was appointed assistant clerk to the Indiana House of Representatives.[5] By 1880, he and his family lived in Iowa, where Broshears was a postmaster.[6] After 1890, he lived with his family in the Washington, D.C., area, where he served as a government clerk and a minister.[7] Despite lamenting he was "hastening probably to an early grave," Broshears lived to be ninety-one.[8] His entry won a twenty-dollar prize for literary merit.[9]

September 27, 1865
That Lost Right Arm

That right arm was my daily companion and helper in the years of innocent childhood. How readily it learned the Yankee art of whittling, with a boy's first prize the universal "Barlow."[10] With what a vague anxiety that hand fumbled in the first pocket for something not there—for what boy never lost his first jack-knife? That mishap however did not paralyze its energies—it grew apace with the days and years—it was an apt scholar and learned the use of many things beside a pocket knife. Often it assisted the truant in climbing the fruit trees that surrounded the paternal mansion.

How many depredations it committed upon the premises of the neighbors the left hand must not tell, for "the partaker is as bad as the thief."[11] Nor need

4. Ira Broshears, Contest Entry, 1st ser., no. 64, William Oland Bourne Papers.

5. "State Items," *Evansville (IN) Daily Journal,* Jan. 12, 1867, 4.

6. 1880 U.S. Census, O'Brien Co., IA, pop. sched., Sanborn, p. 272 (stamped), dwelling 2, family 2, Ira Broshears, NARA RG 29, T9, roll 358.

7. *Washington, D.C., City Directory, 1890;* 1900 U.S. Census, DC, pop. sched., Washington City, p. 20, dwelling 388, family 448, Ira Broshears, NARA RG 29, T623, roll 160.

8. Death Certificate, July 5, 1924, file 16034, Reverend Ira Broshears, Virginia Department of Health.

9. Exhibition of Left-Hand Penmanship, Bourne Papers.

10. A popular folding pocket knife, usually single-bladed.

11. Adage similar to Proverbs 29:24.

be told the mishaps that befell it in rambles after berries and nuts—suffice it to say, good dame Nature soon effaced each sorrow and healed every little wound made by burr or briar.

Then came school days—Yes, in that old log school house, encompassed as it was by giant oaks, beneath whose boughs the Indian learned to use the bow and arrow—where too they made his grave, when the chase and battle of life were ended.

In that primitive temple of knowledge that hand made many an effort to learn the art chirographical,[12] and for its awkwardness and ink blots sometimes received the master's ferule.[13]

But recess long waited for would come at last with its games of bat and ball and a hundred et ceteras. What cunning and strength were brought into play by that same right arm and hand, the old playground might tell, if voice and memory were only given it. But it is a field now, and of those who played there and studied also, some now sleep in the sunny south, while others mingle in the great life-conflict of today.

That hand too swung the scythe, guided the plow and curbed the steed in the noble art of agriculture—wiped the sweat from the brow of manly toil, and deposited in the ballot box the vote of an American freeman, liberty's richest legacy and the highest of all earthly honors.

Fort Sumter was fired upon—the nation flew to arms—fathers, brothers, husbands, sons, all rushed to the field, eager to meet the traitor foe. What pen shall portray the heart-grief of the loved ones left behind—ah! those weary days and nights of waiting and no tidings save—"the army is moving."

Over that bloody field, those ghastly forms, that gory stump of an arm, let us draw a veil—Its work is done—no more may the foeman fear the steel it bore, or the bullet which it flashed on a death-errand. That right hand served its owner and his country well, and now it sleeps in death, under some cedar, pine, or palm. Its virtue and untimely loss is briefly here recorded, by the inheritor of its labors, the lone

Left Hand

12. Handwriting.

13. Ruler used to discipline schoolchildren.

March 19, 1866

Yours of the 14th inst. enclosing check for $20 came duly to hand. Very unexpectedly indeed came the announcement in the March number of the *Friend*—and least of all for literary merit. To the position of authorship I have never aspired—my education is not sufficiently varied and extensive, nor have I enjoyed so much of life's comforts as allowed leisure for the mental cultivation and intellectual training necessary to excellence in this direction. My boyhood was spent upon a farm—my education was mainly acquired in log-schoolhouses or at the fireside and is the result of my own exertions. Since my majority I have carved my own way in life and now at the age of 32 I am a cripple with a broken constitution hastening probably to an early grave. My wife and little ones look confidingly to me for a support and having but little property I have provided for them by life insurance.

Save those loving ones I have no ties that hold me earthward. Disabled physically and a daily sufferer I look only for a resting place in that land which knows no pain or death or sin.

No one can imagine except by actual trial, how spirit-crushing, soul-saddening and heart-burning, is that sense of helplessness that is felt by a crippled man who has devoted his life to active pursuits. It curbs the ambition, dampens the ardor and unmans the energy, thrusting him down soul and body to a treadmill existence in the great conflict of life.

Hence words of cheer coming from any source are hailed as harbingers of good, as an evidence that we still live in the affections and esteem of those for whom we fought and bled. Our surroundings are often lone and dreary on account of the neglect and cold-heartedness of our fellow beings, who have wealth and influence.

Well I need not repine. I am enjoying more than I deserve and doubtless more than many of my brave comrades. Go on in your noble enterprise and may success abundantly attend you. . . . A few weeks ago I surveyed the farm once owned by Lincoln's father where the "Rail Splitter" was mainly brought up—and where he learned to read and write. I loved my country better than ever before as I saw and felt that we have no *born-greatness* but much of *labor-greatness*, which alone can make the man of nobility. . . .

~~~
~~~

JONATHAN MCKINSTRY ALLISON

Corporal, Co. I, 111th Illinois Volunteer Infantry

Allison enlisted in August 1862 and was elected corporal.[14] His regiment traveled to and through Kentucky, Tennessee, and Alabama before joining Sherman's command for the Atlanta Campaign. He lost his right arm during his first battle after a Minié ball "struck [his] right arm half way between the shoulder and elbow," necessitating amputation. Despite the "bright future" he hoped for in his narrative, Allison died in 1867 while attending Illinois Soldiers' College.[15] He sent two submissions, both to the first competition. The second addressed his fellow "one armed" soldiers.

September 23, 1865

I have the honor of transmitting to you a sample of my left hand penmanship: having acquired this art to this perfection since I lost my right arm. . . .

I am now going to school at the Monmouth College to try and qualify myself for some useful position in future life. I don't know if I will succeed or not, for I am a poor boy and all I have to school me is the savings of a three years' campaign and what bounty I received with the small pension I will receive.

Boarding, food, and all necessary are so high, it is almost discouraging.[16] But "Nil desperandum"[17] has been my motto in the past and shall be in the future. With it and the sympathy of a good, true, and loyal people I hope to succeed and accomplish something in the bright future just dawning before me.

I would like to write more and on some other subject but my time will not permit me. I also get very tired and nervous. Hoping this scribbled page may meet your hearty approval and consideration. I offer this as my contribution to a cause worthier of a better specimen of penmanship. . . .

14. Jonathan M. Allison, Contest Entry, 1st ser., no. 67, Bourne Papers.

15. *Catalogue and Circular of the Illinois Soldiers' College*, 7.

16. Though Allison attended Monmouth College when he submitted his entry, the institution he would later attend, the Illinois Soldiers' College, listed expenses for students as $15 to $26 dollars, the equivalent of $250 to $450 today. *Catalogue and Circular of the Illinois Soldiers' College*, 22.

17. Latin for "never despair."

December 26, 1865

I was in but one battle, that of Resaca, Georgia, May 14th 1864, where I lost my *Right Arm*. Since that time I have learned to write to this perfection. It was rather awkward for me to write because I was naturally right handed. But I can pick up a pen now and go to writing with some little science. I believe I can by practice become equally as good with my left hand as I was with my right hand before I was wounded. . . .

TO THE "ONE ARMED" SOLDIERS OF THE "U. S. A."

Wounded Comrades: We are the living monuments of the late cruel and bloody Rebellion. We now retire from fields of blood and carnage, to prepare to act another part in the great "drama" of life. The question now presents itself to us. "What will we do now to make a livelihood?"

Why, one says you can keep "Saloon" as good as anybody. Almost invariably this is the first suggestion made an armless soldier by his comrades. And by the repeated quotation of this and similar suggestions induces many to go at it to get a livelihood. And they will quote several good reasons as they may think to induce you to comply with their plan for your support. As one who has lost my right arm in the cause of the Union I would consider it the height of impudence to [be] accosted thus, and the suggestion unbecoming a Union solider. I do not think the lives of so many brave soldiers were spared on fields of strife and death, to degrade themselves in as low, mean, base calling as a "Saloonkeeper."

No. Soldiers you can fill higher and better positions in life than that, or any one similar to it. If we act as becomes soldiers or good citizens. Your misfortune and sacrifice in behalf of your country has not rendered you incapable of filling important positions in life. Your friends and country hold you doubly dear, and you have the sympathy and best wishes of all good loyal people for your success and welfare in the future. You can see already the patriotic effort on now to fit and prepare the disabled soldiers of our country for lucrative positions in [the] honorable business of life.

Before many years we will see "One Armed" Preachers, Lawyers, Lecturers, Literary writers, Teachers, Statesmen, and in a great many civil offices through the country. Those very officers will arise out of our number, and are we going to drift down the tide of time and not row our frail barques to the side of honor and distinction? Where we may write our names in characters of living light to [be] handed down to succeeding generations in grateful remembrance as among those who lived for their country, and the freedom of mankind. Always set your aim high and never fall below it. But beware lest vaulting ambition overleaps itself. Always avoid extremes.

Qualify yourselves for honorable positions in life: and you will be successful in your undertakings either in public or private life.

Perhaps the One-legged Soldiers may think I have forgotten them but I do not desire to detract from their honor or praise due to them, one single letter no—not one. I will let some Bass-wood-toed[18] writer advocate their cause.

The few brief remarks I have advanced in this page I hope may be beneficial to some.

~~~

RUFUS LEWIS ROBINSON

Private, Co. D, 121st New York Volunteer Infantry

Robinson was a thirty-four-year-old married farmer when he enlisted in 1862.[19] He fought in nine battles, including first and second Fredericksburg and Gettysburg, and lost his arm "by a minie ball through the wrist" at Fort Fisher. When he submitted his entry, he had "been practicing but three weeks" and was sure it would not measure up to submissions from those who had "lost their arms soon after the war commenced, and some who were always left-handed, and doubtless some [who] have been learning at Commercial Colleges." Nevertheless, he received honorable mention.[20] Robinson married twice, had five children, and worked as a merchant, dying in 1916.[21]

18. Basswood, also known as linden, is a type of tree. Allison refers to veterans with wooden prosthetic legs or feet.

19. Rufus L. Robinson, Contest Entry, 1st ser., no. 71, Bourne Papers (punctuation edited); New York Town Clerks' Registers of Men Who Served in the Civil War, ca. 1861–1865, Rufus L. Robinson, New York State Archives, Collection 13774, box 27, roll 15; New York Civil War Muster Roll Abstracts, 1861–1900, Rufus L. Robinson, ibid., Collection 13775-83, box 504, roll 160.

20. Exhibition of Left-Hand Penmanship, Bourne Papers.

21. 1875 New York State Census, Herkimer Co., pop. sched., Frankfort Village, p. 21, dwelling 76, family 234, Rufus L. Robinson, New York State Library; 1880 U.S. Census, Herkimer Co., NY, pop. sched., Frankfort, p. 51B (stamped), dwelling 60, family 66, Rufus L. Robinson, NARA RG 29, T9, roll 837; Rufus L. Robinson Pension File, application 1083116, certificate 846478, NARA RG 15, T288, roll 400.
~~~

September 30, 1865
To The Disabled Soldiers of the Union

Through the blessings of Divine Providence, we have been permitted to return to our homes. The dark clouds of war which for four years enveloped our nation, have passed away, and peace, the inestimable prize for which we so long contended, has come again. The terrible battle field. The long and tedious march. The exposure to the pelting storm, and piercing cold, and many other trials, incident to a soldier's life, will never be forgotten while life and reason last.

But though we cannot forget the many unpleasant scenes through which we have passed, let us not dwell mournfully on them, but look manfully forward to the future, with the same unfaltering trust in the God of the universe, that enabled us to stand firm and unyielding, on so many closely contested battle fields, and which inspired us with hope, when our cause looked darkest.

Although our career as soldiers is ended, there are yet many trials for us to pass through in the future. Before we left our homes to fight our country's battles, we felt that with our strong arms, and vigorous constitutions, aided by God's blessing, we were abundantly able to provide for the wants of ourselves, and those who were dependent on us, by following such pursuits as best suited our inclinations. Now, through the fortunes of war, we must labor under different circumstances. Instead of selecting our employment, we must adapt ourselves to such pursuits as are available, however distasteful to our feelings. But let us bear in mind that any honest employment is commendable.

Doubtless we shall meet with many rebuffs, and insults, not only from that class who sympathized with treason, but also from the empty-headed, *heartless*, and *soulless* votaries of fashion. But thank God, there is another class, who are living to some purpose. Whose deeds are daily recorded in Heaven. They will not fail to appreciate, and encourage, honest industry; neither will they permit the defenders of our common country's dearest rights to come to want, should they be incapable of self-support.

With the exception of such as are totally disabled, we should all desire some employment. If not necessary for our support, it is essential to our happiness, and well-being, and we should all make a wise improvement of time, and what talents we possess, if we would secure to ourselves the greatest amount of happiness, both in this life and in that which is to come.

Doubtless there are many in the catalogue of disabled soldiers who possess talents of a high order, which, from the force of circumstances, have never been brought into action, and which might, if rightly understood and improved, be made not only the stepping stone to ease and affluence, but might win for their possessors a high position upon the ladders of fame.

Our experience has taught us that we little knew what could be achieved by us physically, until we entered the field as soldiers, and the same rule applies to us mentally. It is a true saying that much of our success in life depends on knowing ourselves; therefore we should strive to fully understand our abilities before laying our plans for future action. The broad fields of science and knowledge are accessible to all alike. No other government can boast of such institutions as ours, and no people are more munificent in awarding to all their proper merit, and we may rest assured that in whatever enterprise we may embark, if we devote to it all our energies, and rightly understand our abilities, our efforts will be crowned with success. Nor should we forget our duties as citizens. Proud as is the record which the American Soldier bears, embellished as it is with innumerable acts of heroism and self-sacrifice, let not its bright pages be tarnished by any unbecoming act of ours. Let not the disgusting and pernicious examples of many of our officers in the field be imitated by us. Let us be true to ourselves, our fellow men, and our country. Then will a grateful posterity venerate our memory and generations unborn will imitate our virtues.

~~~

HENRY W. PALMER

Private, Co. H, 31st Maine Volunteer Infantry

Palmer was eighteen when he enlisted in 1864.[22] The affidavit verifying his identity and amputation also included the testimony of three selectmen of Corinth, Maine, who attested to Palmer's high moral character, writing that "the said Henry W. comes back to us, though

22. Henry W. Palmer, Contest Entry, 1st ser., no. 73, Bourne Papers; *Alphabetical Index of Maine Volunteers,* 1019.
~~~

injured in body, yet possessing those moral excellences which he has at all time[s] exhibited in life." From 1867 to 1878, Palmer lived in the Northwestern Branch of the National Home for Disabled Volunteer Soldiers in Milwaukee.[23] In 1880, he was back in Maine and living with his parents, managing his father's farm along with his brother.[24] Twenty years later, he remained a bachelor, lodging with a Boston family and working as a bookkeeper.[25] Palmer seems to have married before his death; a woman identifying herself as his widow applied for a pension in 1925.[26]

September 1865

I immediately left home for Camp Coburn, Augusta (Maine) at which place our said Company remained some twelve days, during which time I was detailed for the purpose of writing—I then possessed two hands, and my right hand (now lost) was as ready at all times to wield the pen in Camp as pull the trigger on battle field—

Lost right arm! thou wert a member of a perfect body, given to Country in her day of trial, and while Virginia's soil is enriched by thy decay, the remnant of that Soldier-body is reserved for such further duties as Country may demand—

From Camp Coburn we were conveyed by rail to Alexandria (Va.) and made a rapid march toward the battle grounds for which we were destined—Before reaching the Enemy, I found that my three comrades, who enlisted at the same time, and were my townsmen, had given out by the way-side.[27] Early on the morning of the twelfth of May, we were before the enemy and joined in the great battle of Spotsylvania Court House—Of that battle, let the Historian speak—It was my first Soldier effort, and after discharging my musket a few times, I was as calm and collected as one could possibly be, who was

23. Historical Register of National Homes for Disabled Volunteer Soldiers, 1866–1938, Henry W. Palmer, NARA RG 15, M1749, roll 160.

24. 1880 U.S. Census, Penobscot Co., ME, pop. sched., Corinth, p. 485C (stamped), dwelling 254, family 266, Henry W. Palmer, NARA RG 29, ser. T9, roll 485; *History of Penobscot County, Maine,* 315.

25. 1900 U.S. Census, Suffolk Co., MA, pop. sched., Boston, p. 2, dwelling 12, family 12, Henry W. Palmer, NARA RG 29, T623, roll 681.

26. Henry W. Palmer, Pension File, application 1239948, certificate 972435, NARA RG 15, T288, roll 360.

27. Apparently, they had deserted.

anxious for the result of his doings—Personal fear gave place to confidence of success—My gun strangely won my confidence, and I regarded it much as a child regards the protection of a father—failed never in the discharge of duty, and was fired with love of Country—It spoke in audible tones not easily misunderstood, and sent its leaden yet forcible messages to Rebels, declaring that the "Union must be preserved"—At this instant, while raising my gun to my shoulder, a strange sensation seized my right arm, and my gun fell to the ground—stooping to recover it, my right arm for the first time failed in duty—became way-ward and unmanageable—unmindful alike of entreaty or rebuke—my left arm sought immediate promotion, and at once assumed the office of right arm—but alas! it was no veteran at the trigger pulling—and with gun at the wrong shoulder, the eye refused to see the *sight*—Thus foiled, the Military Court Martial I caused to be held upon the conduct of my right arm, was brief, and disclosed the fact that a minie ball penetrated the center of the bone, pulverizing it to a powder.

While the battle yet raged, and hope grew strong, and confidence gained ground, I was compelled to leave the field sorrowing that in my first battle I was compelled to lay down my arms—In an hour, after amputation I was again in open air—among the limbs amputated, I sought my own right arm, and did chide myself that for a moment, I should have censured, upon battle field in thought, that arm ever faithful—that right arm, which inscribed two months before, my name upon the Soldiers' Roll.

Strange sensations are those of him standing beside the grave of a member of his own body—strange communings between the quick and the dead—My right arm, as if conscious of approaching dissolution, seemingly bequeathed unto the left arm, all the properties of which it died seized and possessed—The seal of this last Will and Testament was the blood seal of amputation—Patriotism, Love of Country, and Equal Rights were the subscribing witnesses to the Instrument—The body from which the arm was severed was the Executor—in Heaven's Court the Will was proved, allowed and recorded—The left arm thus became the Devisee of all and singular the right arm possessed or could devise—And timidly today attempts to imitate the handwriting of its Testator, but strangely fails for want of practice, and trembles through fear of failure—But a few months of careful attention will accomplish the purpose so eagerly sought.

The day after my arm was amputated I walked fifteen miles to the hospital, but the effort was too much and even now I feel the effect of that over-exertion—but seeing hundreds of my wounded associates unable to walk I determined to be in no one's way, and thank heaven my Locomotive powers went unharmed—I laid my own track—got up steam, and made for the Hospital as best I could, and without stopping to "wood and water" failed not for steam, tho' I had none to spare, even to *whistle* as I approached.

Weeks elapsed before I reached Christian Street Hospital, Philadelphia—at the various Hospitals on my way, I generally received good attention, but my journey was tedious and I found my bodily health fast leaving me; and on my arrival the Typhoid fever had set in, and I was sick indeed—When I contemplated my situation—away from my home—mutilated—sick among the sick and dying, despondency knocked at the door of my heart and entered unbidden—I reflected upon the bad condition of our Country—Rebels, South in open rebellion—in the North in secret conclave, plotting ruin;—Many Union men, sighing over a bleeding Country, and were daily bleeding that Country by robbing her Treasury—; then it was that I could have subscribed to the belief of man's total depravity.

My fever increased, and I was scarce conscious of what was passing—at intervals I slept—It was my first sleep for a long time—in my dreams, home—Country—Mother, were before me—I felt the warm pressure of a soft hand upon my aching brow—and a sweet voice said, "my Soldier boy"—I knew I was called, and started into wakefulness—Bending over me stood a Samaritan woman, in whose eyes shone woman's goodness of heart who inquired what she could do to alleviate my sufferings—I then felt that human nature was not totally depraved, and that the Ladies of Philadelphia were teaching the world that there is *yet* upon earth *Christianity and Patriotism*—The names of Mrs. Eliza B. Hill—Miss Austin—Dorr and many others will be held in grateful remembrance while memory remains, for to them, and a kind and skillful Physician (Dr. Barr) I owe my life.

I am again at home—an artificial Lincoln arm[28] is doing what it can to

28. A popular artificial limb patented and manufactured by Marvin Lincoln and advertised and distributed by Benjamin Franklin Palmer's American Artificial Limb Company. Lincoln formerly worked for Palmer, who was known for the "Palmer leg." See Hasegawa, *Mending Broken Soldiers*, 37.

supply the place of my right arm—it is somewhat awkward, and tho' it is the mate of the remaining arm, yet it seems to be destitute of a "fellow feeling"—I chide it not!—God forbid that my Country should ever want my services again on field of battle—yet if desired *there* or *elsewhere*, I am in readiness—all that I now am—*all that I can make myself*, is at command of Country now and ever.

December 6, 1865[29]

Herewith please receive my photograph, which I hope may find a place among the likenesses of those who, in defending our Country from Treason's grasp received those outwards marks which tell of devotion to that Country—I love the faithful Soldier as I love my kindred in the flesh, and the wounded Soldier I claim as a brother to whom I would gladly extend the right hand of fellowship, was not that right hand now enriching a Southern soil, in which I trust the sown seeds of loyalty will generate and send forth an abundant harvest.

Could my feelings find suitable embodiment in expression I would speak to the thousands of mutilated Soldiers who are receiving, not only help from our Government, but the kind regard of benevolent and distinguished individuals, *and urge* that we deserve the notice and the aid bestowed upon us—Shall we be indolent because we are maimed? Has our Country, for which we fought, no further need of our body members unharmed, and a stirring brain strong in growing manhood? Our Country demands the wakeful, watchful, far seeing eye—the prudent tongue—the sober exemplary life—Patriotism—Sobriety—Zeal.

Possessing these (tho' minus the right arm) we shall be around for life's battles and do good service for the Country we love—The spared hand from the battle field may gather the smooth stones from life's running brook, which may be hurled at the Foreign Goliath, or with nerved left arm and accuracy of aim, sink deeply into the forehead of traitors found upon our own homestead.

~~~

29. Bourne published this letter in *The Soldier's Friend* in January 1866.
~~~

FRANK H. EVANS

Corporal, Co. A, 3rd New Hampshire Volunteer Infantry

Evans, born in Vermont to Methodist minister and New Thought proponent Reverend Warren F. Evans, was working as an operator for the U.S. Military Telegraph Service in Virginia when he submitted his penmanship specimen.[30] In a letter to Bourne accompanying his submission, Evans explained: "I served in the army two years and three months as a private soldier. During the time I was with my regiment, we saw but little active service, being stationed most of the time along the coast of South Carolina." His regiment participated in "only three regular engagements," but he was seriously wounded at Fort Wagner when a shell "tore [his] right hand from the arm and inflicted severe wounds in both legs." Evans married in 1870; he and his wife lived in Washington, D.C., where he worked as a clerk for the War Department and was a member of GAR Lincoln Post No. 3.[31] He remained in that position until his death in 1911 at the age of seventy.[32]

November 28, 1865
The Empty Coat Sleeve

In passing through the streets of any of our cities, how many men we meet with an empty coat sleeve hanging by their sides! A large share of those sleeves were made empty by the war—most of these men losing their arms while defending the Stars and Stripes and the noble government they represent.

There is a strange history connected with each of those empty sleeves—a history of hardships such as the soldier only knows—of long marches, now through the rain and cold, and now beneath a burning sun—of fearful conflicts amid roaring shells and hissing bullets, rattling of musketry and thunder of cannon. Shouts and yells of excited men and groans of the dying and wounded—in which those arms that no longer hang by their sides

30. Frank Evans, Contest Entry, 1st ser., no. 133, Bourne Papers. For New Thought and "mental healing," see John F. Teahan, "Warren Felt Evans and Mental Healing: Romantic Idealism and Practical Mysticism in Nineteenth-Century America," *Church History* 48, no. 1 (Mar. 1979): 63–80.

31. 1910 U.S. Census, DC, pop. sched., Washington City, p. 7B, dwelling 133, family 173, Frank H. Evans, NARA RG 29, T624, roll 152; "Funeral Services for Veteran of Civil War," *Washington Times*, Sept. 26, 1911, 9.

32. "Funeral Services for Veteran of Civil War," 9.

doubtless have struck many effective blows for the liberty and honor of our nation, and caused many a traitor to bite the dust as a punishment for his treason.

There is also a secret history connected with the empty coat sleeve which none can understand who have not had the misfortune to lose an arm. The bitter disappointments and ruined hopes connected with the empty coat sleeve cannot be written, but which every soldier who has lost an arm well understands.

But those arms were not lost in vain. The Union still remains firmer than ever, the Stars and Stripes proudly float in the faces of the humbled traitors who would have destroyed the best government on which the sun ever shone; the rebel armies have been beaten and dispersed; the plotters and leaders of the rebellion are in our hands; and the death of thousands of our comrades whose bones lie bleaching in southern sands is avenged.

It is sad to lose an arm, yet it is gratifying to know it was not lost in vain and that the cause for which the sacrifice was made was an honorable one—a cause that no man will ever be ashamed of having helped to sustain.

Well may the union soldiers be proud of their empty coat-sleeves. To have lost an arm in the service of one's country is a life-long honor, increasing with advancing years, and all may, who will, live in the memory and esteem of good and true men and the *empty coat-sleeve* be a badge of honor to the maimed soldier who must wear it in his march to the Celestial land.

PHINEAS P. WHITEHOUSE

Corporal, Co. C, 6th New Hampshire Volunteer Infantry

In a letter to Bourne acknowledging his receipt of a twenty-five-dollar premium, Whitehouse discussed his postwar situation: "I have been quite pleasantly situated this winter now past. My school closed two or three weeks since, having continued nearly four months. I am having a little leisure now, and do not know hardly what I shall be called to do next. There was some prospect of my securing some government employment, but that will be somewhat doubtful, as such business is requiring a fewer number of hands each succeeding day." Whitehouse wrote the following letter and essay for *The Soldier's Friend*. For his biography, see chapter 3; for his poetry, see chapter 6.

April 27, 1865
"A Letter to the Left-Armed Corps"

Mr. Bourne: With your permission, I wish to say a few words to the soldier readers of your *Soldier's Friend,* who have been so unfortunate as to lose a *right arm* in the service. To none is this a greater misfortune than to those who consider the exercise of the pen useful and instructive as an employment, and peculiarly interesting as a pastime and amusement. Many of those who have occupied many long hours in camp and hospital in writing to loved ones at home, are now deprived of this delightful exercise by the loss of the very hand which used to pen the thoughts and words so eagerly awaited for at the old homestead. What an unmeasured happiness would it be to such, if, while they are waiting for the aching stump to heal, or the artificial limb to be provided, they could occupy the long period of wearisome leisure in their old cherished employment!

With a view to induce you to become more independent of your lost or withered right arm, I now address you, *left-handed* soldiers. There is only one way for you to arrive at this independence of which I speak. *Learn immediately to write with your left hand.* Many of you have an idea that this can never be done to any degree of perfection; but in this you are mistaken. You have no idea how readily you can make your left hand do the same things formerly done by your right, if you are really *in earnest,* and take hold of the pen *with a determination to succeed.* I have seen as fair and round a handwriting executed with the left hand, as any I should care to imitate; and most of the few soldiers of my acquaintance, who have practiced left-hand penmanship since the loss of an arm, can write *as rapidly,* also, as the majority of those who use the right hand in writing.

For the encouragement of those who may be induced to "break in" the left hand, I will say a word in regard to my own experience. I lost the use of my right arm a little less than a year ago, and began practicing with my left hand in a few days afterwards. In less than a month I could write a letter of four pages without weariness, but, of course, necessarily slower than formerly with the right. In the course of three months it was no more of a task for me to write a letter with the left hand than I considered it with the other before I was wounded. Since the rebel Minié found its way into my arm I have written not less than *two hundred* letters with the left hand, besides other scribbling.

I can now write very nearly as rapidly, if not quite as well, as when I had two good hands.

Bourne's editorial comment follows:

We most cheerfully publish the above letter to the left-armed corps, as it is so much in accordance with our own observations and the thoughts we have endeavored to impress upon various audiences of soldiers we have had the honor to address. There are men who cannot read or write, and others who have lost their right hand, who spend more hours and days of time in card-playing and other diversion, than would make them proficient as readers and penmen. We do not expect all men to write like copperplate engraving, but they can attain a fair degree of skill, and can make themselves better fitted for earning money, where brains will take the place of hands. What say you, friends? Will you try it?

December 5, 1865

"A Few Words to Our Returning Soldiers"

Soldier brothers! The war is over—the Rebellion is virtually at an end. The object for which we have so long been fighting is at last accomplished, and we are now returning to our homes. Some have already taken their old places in the family circle, others are on their homeward journey, and many more are soon to follow in the same track. We come from the army of the Potomac, whose journeys from Washington to Richmond, though lone and wearisome, was so successfully performed; from the army of Sheridan, whose brilliant campaign in the Valley[33] will long live in the memories of the surviving participants; from the army of Sherman, whose grand march from Atlanta to Savannah, Charleston, and Richmond,[34] will compare favorably with the deeds of the great Napoleon; and from the armies of the West, who can point to many bloody fields in Kentucky, Tennessee, Missouri, Alabama,

33. Sheridan's 1864 campaign in the Shenandoah Valley.

34. Sherman's forces were still in North Carolina at war's end. Perhaps Whitehouse meant Raleigh instead of Richmond.

Mississippi, and Louisiana, where they have fought and conquered, during the last four years of Rebellion. . . .

From these scenes of hardship, privation and peril, of war and courage, we are now returning, to re-occupy in our Northern homes the places made vacant one, two, three or four years ago, when we responded to the call of our country. Our fathers, mothers, sisters, wives, children—all dear to us by the ties of nature—will give us a hearty welcome, a happy greeting, as we return to them with the cheering story that our work is done. Some of us return with broken constitutions, with feeble limbs and weary steps, from long confinement in the hated dens of Libby, Andersonville and Salisbury;[35] many bear marks of wounds received at Vicksburg, at Lookout Mountain, at Gettysburg, or in the last campaign, at the terrible battles of the Wilderness, Spottsylvania, Petersburg, or Richmond. Some came back with disfigured faces, some with deformed bodies and crooked limbs, some with missing foot or vacant sleeve. Others, comprising a large number, return from the fields of victory in all their wonted health and vigor. All are received with gladness, many with tears of joy. The father listens with pride to the long story of his son's experiences; the mother blesses God, with tear-wet eyes, that He has brought back her boy in safety; the loving wife presses to her bosom her returning husband, with a sigh of gratitude that the war is over, and the laughing little sister strives in vain to express her joy that brother has come at last.

Thousands have already experienced these happy greetings, and thousands more yet see them in the perspective, which will soon be changed to a vision of reality. A little while and all these touching scenes of reunion will be over, and we shall mingle with our friends in civil life, as in days gone by. Gradually shall we fall back into the old channels in which we once moved and the individual duties and responsibilities of life will again press upon us. Then will our friends and the world know what we have lost or gained by our participation in the war for preservation of the Union. How to meet these duties and responsibilities manfully, is now a question which claims our individual attention. Returning soldiers, will you listen to a few suggestions, bearing on this subject, from one of your own number?

A few words first, to the young man who returns from the front, in the

35. Confederate prison camps in Virginia, Georgia, and North Carolina, respectively.

same health and vigor of four years ago. . . . After months, or years perhaps, of roaming in the "Sunny Southland," after a long period of toils and marches and battles, many weary days of hunger and thirst and sickness, and many perilous nights on picket and bivouac, you have returned strong and hardy to the scenes of home and friends. Everybody thanks you for what you have done, all honor you for the self-sacrificing spirit you have exhibited, *but remember that your patriotic services in the past will not of themselves provide for your future welfare or elevate your position in society for days to come.* It is for you, by your own conduct, to prove to those around you, that he who is a good soldier on the battlefield, can make a worthy citizen at home in the quiet pursuits of civil life. . . .

And now a few words to the unfortunate class of returning veterans, who came back from the scenes of strife crippled or permanently disabled. Among that number is he who pens you this friendly line. Some of you are already at home, others are waiting in hospitals for artificial limbs, and will soon follow. In a little while we shall all say "good-by" to the service, and go where we can make out our own "passes" and "furloughs," and be our own men again. The kind services of the Christian and Sanitary Commissions will soon cease to affect us, and the many benevolent ladies connected with our hospitals, who have so faithfully attended to our wants, will soon be out of our reach. In view of these significant facts, it is important that we be able to answer to ourselves the question, What are we to do at home? It is certain that many of us cannot resume the occupations we followed before the war. Among us are farmers and shoemakers, who return with the strong right hand missing, or a sleeve altogether empty, and carpenters with fractured shoulders and footless legs. The greater portion of these are men whose daily labor in their respective lines of business has been their only means of support at home. Many, too, are young men who have apparently a long life before them. What, my crippled friends, are your plans and purposes for the future? Are you to sit down at the street corners—as you have seen some of our number in the metropolis—and depend upon the charities of the people for a support? Are you to entertain the idea that, because you have suffered so much in your country's service, the world owes you a living and you have a right to sit idle and demand it? No; I am sure you will not do this, while there remains in you a spark of that patriotism that prompted you to seize the musket, or a semblance of that manhood you exhibited on the field of battle! You will rather seek at once for permanent, honorable employment; of which, if you are steady, trustworthy and persevering, you will find an abundance throughout our land. There are many branches of business, in which a man with an artificial leg, or with only one arm, can be advantageously employed; and we have the assurance from many prominent business men throughout the country that these situations will be given to crippled soldiers. As clerks in mercantile establishments, in post offices and in custom houses, or as express messengers, telegraph operators, and employees in other departments of light, easy business there will be opportunities for you to obtain desirable lucrative situations. But many a discharged soldier is ready with the objection: "I am not qualified to fill such responsible positions, and it is too late to prepare myself for such duties now." No, my friend, it is *not* too late, even though you have passed the season of youth and early manhood—not too late for you to fit yourself for an honorable employment. There are commercial colleges in every state, where all who wish can at small expense become acquainted with everything in the line of penmanship or the transaction of business that is requisite for the practical duties of such a calling. Select that occupation for which you think yourself best adapted, and be not content till you are fully prepared to enter upon its duties. And you, my left-armed brothers, be not discouraged because your right hand lies buried far away beneath the green sod in Virginia. You have one good arm left you—with patient and persevering effort make the best of that, and there is nothing to prevent you from becoming useful, respected and honored citizens of our regenerated Republic.

~~~

STEPHEN D. WILBUR

Private, Co. E, 109th New York Volunteer Infantry

A student when he sent his submission in 1865, Wilbur was still attending school in 1870 and living with his parents; he employed his penmanship skills when filling out census forms that year.[36] After finishing school, Wilbur became a teacher and continued to work in public educa-

36. Stephen D. Wilbur, Contest Entry, 1st ser., no. 185, Bourne Papers; 1870 U.S. Census, Broome Co., NY, pop. sched., Binghamton, p. 19A (stamped), dwelling 1, family 1, Stephen D. Wilbur, NARA RG 29, M593, roll 906.
~~~

tion until he retired, serving for a time as school superintendent and ending his career as a truant officer.[37] His obituary notes that, "though handicapped by the loss of an arm, he always rode a bicycle from school to school in discharging his duties."[38] He and his wife adopted a daughter, and he was a member of GAR Bartlett Post No. 108.[39] Wilbur died in 1920 at the age of seventy-eight after falling from a tree while picking cherries.[40]

December 29, 1865

The War which has been carried on for the last four years in the United States by an Aristocratic and Rebellious People trying to overthrow the best Government the Sun ever shone upon, has draped our land with Mourning from the Executive Mansion down to the humble Cot and Logcabbin. The dark Spectre War which has haunted our land so long has at last passed away and with it Slavery has passed out of existence in our land, yet we can see in every Hamlet or Village and in almost every household the ravages it has made upon our fellow beings. It would be hard to find a family who have not been called to mourn for some Relative or dear friend who fell on the battle field beneath a Southern Sun. Others have been taken from the field amid the dreadful carnage and shower of death bleeding and mangled, suffered amputation and after many hours and days suffering in a Hospital have returned home to their friends, but not as they went away. No! the empty sleeve or leg to plainly show that they are Crippled for life.

When the war broke out in '61, I was 19 years old and lived with my father on a farm, would [have] joined the Army when the first call for Volunteers was made had it not been for the objections raised to it by our family, so I stayed at home until August '62 when I became of the age when young men consider themselves their own master. I then on the 9th day of that month at Binghamton, Broome Co., NY, enlisted for three years in a new regiment. . . .

37. "Stephen D. Wilbur Dies Following Fall from Tree," *Binghamton (NY) Press and Sun-Bulletin,* July 7, 1920, 3.

38. Ibid.

39. 1910 U.S. Census, Broome Co., NY, pop. sched., Binghamton, p. 4B, dwelling 86, family 94, Stephen D. Wilbur, NARA RG 29, T624, roll 925; "Stephen D. Wilbur," *Binghamton (NY) Press and Sun-Bulletin,* July 10, 1920, 5.

40. "Stephen D. Wilbur Dies Following Fall from Tree," 3.

We were mustered into the United States Service Aug. 27th '62 and left for the seat of war the 29th but by our Colonel being what we styled a Political Officer or some other reason unknown to us we were put into the Department of Washington and did not go into the field until April '64. . . .

Wilbur fought in the Wilderness before falling sick at Fredericksburg. He rejoined his regiment at Petersburg.

I was struck with a fragment of Shell in the right forearm causing Amputation and was sent to Washington so I did not have the pleasure of marching into the Rebel Capitol with my comrades. I arrived at Washington April 5th, was sent to Harewood Hospital, was there three Months before I was able to come home, and it was some time after that before I could get around much. I did not used to be left handed so I have had to learn to write in a very short time. When a boy I did not have a very good chance to go to School so my Education is rather limited, but I am going to School now and working hard for an Education that by it I may find a livelihood.

~~~

JOHN ARMSTRONG ROBISON

Corporal, Co. F, 96th Illinois Volunteer Infantry

Robison was born in Illinois in 1837 and worked as a farmer both before and after the war.[41] Married in 1859, he and his wife had seven children.[42] In later years, he worked as an insurance agent and was a member and commander of GAR Hawk Post No. 406. Robison died in 1910 at the age of seventy-two.[43]

41. John A. Robison, Contest Entry, 1st ser., no. 266, Bourne Papers; 1870 U.S. Census, Carroll Co., IL, pop. sched., Washington, p. 251A (stamped), dwelling 33, family 33, John A. Robison, NARA RG 29, M593, roll 191.

42. Illinois Marriage Index, 1860–1920, John A. Robison, accessed via Ancestry.com, 2015; 1880 U.S. Census, Carroll Co., IL, pop. sched., Savanna, p. 578A (stamped), dwelling 206, family 208, John A. Robison, NARA RG 29, T9, roll 178.

43. 1900 U.S. Census, Carroll Co., IL, pop. sched., Savanna, p. 2, dwelling 36, family 37, John A. Robison, NARA RG 29, T623, roll 239; John A. Robison Pension File, application 944057, certificate 708942, NARA RG 15, T288, roll 401; *Proceedings of the Forty-First Annual Encampment of the Department of Illinois G.A.R.*, 53.
~~~

January 25, 1866

I do not make this effort as a competition for the premiums which you very kindly offer but simply because I think you are engaged in a worthy undertaking. I never claimed to be a good penman even when I had a right arm; and now that I must write with my left hand exclusively I find it more tedious and difficult. . . .

Robison was elected corporal of his regiment at its formation, serving on the color guard (on the left of the flag) and as company commissary.

I was wounded on Sunday Sept. 20th 1863 at the battle of Chickamauga by a rebel ball which passed through my right arm and forearm while in the act of returning the rammer, as I was loading my piece. Our regiment was very closely engaged by a superior force of rebel infantry which was supported by artillery. Our men were being mown down, as it were, when our regiment began to fall back, firing as fast as we could while we were doing so. It was at this time that I received my first and only wound. I suppose the man that deprived me of my right arm was within 65 paces of me at the time he fired. . . .

Robison walked thirty-eight miles in two days and then took a train to Nashville.

I was taken to Hospital No. 16. I remained there two days before my arm received much attention. It was then eight days since I had received the wound. Upon examination it was found that mortification had taken place. In less than half an hour my arm was amputated within about 1 1/2 inches of my shoulder joint. I remained in hospital about three months, and was not mustered out of the service until the 16th of March 1864. I am 28 years old a farmer by occupation and have remained on and carried on my farming ever since I received my discharge. By practice my left arm has become quite strong. I chop my own firewood, harness and drive my own team, and do all the general labor on my farm. All of which I do much more efficiently than I can write. I used my pen in my right hand altogether before I was wounded.

BARNABAS "BARNEY" DORR PALMER

First Sergeant, Co. C, 9th Kansas Volunteer Cavalry
Captain, Co. K, 5th United States Volunteer Infantry

Barnabas D. Palmer, far left, and fellow officers of the 5th U.S. Volunteer Infantry. Courtesy Wilson's Creek National Battlefield.

Palmer submitted to both contests and won the Grant Premium for his second entry; three local papers reported on his success and printed the general's congratulatory letter.[44] An 1879 biography claimed he walked from Colorado, where he was mining for gold in 1861, back to Kansas in order to enlist; Palmer wrote that he rode a horse.[45] He served as a captain in the 5th U.S. Volunteer Infantry on the frontier following the war but returned to civilian life in 1866 due to declining health. Back home, he "was obliged to depend upon his left hand for clerical work by which to secure a living, and became very expert in penmanship."[46] He was elected district-court clerk in Douglas County in 1866 and was reelected seven times.[47] Palmer married in 1867, had two children, and was in his late thirties when he died after months of "delicate health"; an obituary in a Lawrence newspaper reported that his "disease assumed the form of quick consumption."[48] A memorial resolution passed by the county bar sang his praises and noted his sacrifice: "as a soldier for the preservation of our nationality . . . he lost his right arm and bore most honorable scars, a constant reminder to us of his patriotism, of his bravery and zeal."[49] Obituaries published in three different Lawrence papers and an 1879

44. B. D. Palmer, Contest Entries, 1st ser., no. 134, and 2nd ser., no. 28, Bourne Papers; "A High Compliment," *Daily Kansas Tribune* (Lawrence), Jan. 3, 1868, 3; "Prize Received," ibid., July 17, 1868, 3; "Prize Received," *Wyandotte Commercial Gazette* (Kansas City, KS), July 25, 1868, 2.

45. *United States Biographical Dictionary, Kansas,* 106.

46. Ibid.

47. Ibid., 107.

48. Ibid.; "Death of Capt. Barney Palmer," *Spirit of Kansas* (Lawrence), Oct. 20, 1880, 5.

49. "Memorial Resolutions," *Lawrence (KS) Daily Journal,* Oct. 21, 1880, 4.

biography all highlighted the Grant Premium, quoting the former president's brief note. The biographer declared, "it will doubtless be handed down from generation to generation as a souvenir of the great war and become one of the family heirlooms."[50]

***First Entry:* January 28, 1863**

I was born in Andover, State of Mass., in 1844 where I lived until the spring of 1856 when my father and family migrated to Kansas and located at Lawrence. Although but a boy I participated in the Troubles of 56, 57 and 58 under Old John Brown a part of the time.[51] In 1861 I entered the U.S.A[rmy]. under Jim Lane of Kansas.[52] I participated in seventeen different battles during my enlistment. The last one which was on the 2nd day of July 1863 was where I lost my arm besides receiving five other shots in my person. . . .

After I sufficiently recovered from my wounds to be moved I was taken to Lawrence which was in Nov. 1863. As soon as I regained my health enough to sit up I commenced practicing writing. At first I thought it impossible to even learn but I persevered and you see the results of my labor.

The sacking and burning of Lawrence reduced me to poverty and I feared at one time that I should either have to live off of the charity of my friends (of which I had not a few) or go to the poor house. But I did not have to resort to either and don't think I ever shall.

In 1865, Palmer joined the 5th U.S. Volunteer Infantry and served in Colorado and New Mexico.

50. "Death of Capt. Barney D. Palmer," *Western Home Journal* (Lawrence, KS), Oct. 21, 1880, 3; *United States Biographical Dictionary, Kansas,* 106; "Death of Capt. Barney D. Palmer," *Kansas Daily Tribune* (Lawrence), Oct. 19, 1880, 4; *Lawrence (KS) Daily Journal,* Oct. 19, 1880, 4.

51. Palmer refers to "Bleeding Kansas," a series of conflicts between antislavery and proslavery settlers in Kansas. John Brown (1800–1859) and accomplices killed five proslavery settlers as retaliation for the burning of Lawrence in May 1856. See Thomas Goodrich, *War to the Knife: Bleeding Kansas, 1854–1861* (Mechanicsburg, PA: Stackpole Books, 1998).

52. Brigadier General James Henry Lane (1814–66) also served as one of the original U.S. senators for Kansas from 1861 to 1866. Prior to the war, he was a Free-Soil proponent and militant leader during Bleeding Kansas as well as president of the antislavery Topeka Constitution convention. See Ian Michael Spurgeon, *Man of Douglas, Man of Lincoln: The Political Odyssey of James Henry Lane* (Columbia: University of Missouri Press, 2008).

I have not been in this territory but a short time and the greater part of that I have been bound up in snow. Doubtless some think it a romantic thing to wander six hundred miles from civilization to see the Rocky Mountains and procure if possible some of the rich dust that so many crave but get less of than they expect. If I could get a living in the states, early spring or as soon as the grass begins to show its green tips in the valleys of the La Platte[53] would find me wending my way toward America and civilization.

***Second Entry:* June 12, 1867**

My arm was amputated on the 12th day of July, 1863.—Shortly after the amputation of my arm I received the sad news of the Lawrence Massacre, Aug. 21st, 1863, and the names of my father and brother were among the victims of that black hearted villain Quantrell.[54] They wounded my father, tied his hands, threw him into his store and burned him alive, because he had a large number of government arms, repairing them; my brother was two years my senior, was a printer by profession, and was working at his trade at the time he was murdered;[55] he entered the army in 1861, was wounded severely at the battle of Bull Run, got an honorable discharge and retired home. I came to Lawrence the following October, was taken sick again and did not leave my room for several months in consequence of a poor amputation by an intoxicated surgeon.

On the 13th day of January 1864 I made my first letters with my left hand; it was very hard at first, but a few months' practice enabled me to earn a living as clerk in a hotel. . . .

~~~

53. The Platte River, which waters a broad area in Nebraska.

54. William Quantrill (1837–65), a Confederate guerilla leader from Missouri. He and his Raiders attacked civilians in Lawrence on August 21, 1863, killing over 150 people and burning several buildings in what became known as the Sack of Lawrence. See Thomas Goodrich, *Bloody Dawn: The Story of the Lawrence Massacre* (Kent: Kent State University Press, 1991).

55. In his first submission, Palmer explains that his brother was an editor of a Lawrence newspaper.
~~~

WILLIAM AUGUSTUS MACNULTY

Sergeant, Co. A, 10th New York Volunteer Infantry
Second Lieutenant, Co. I, 16th Veteran Reserve Corps
Brevet Captain, U.S. Volunteers

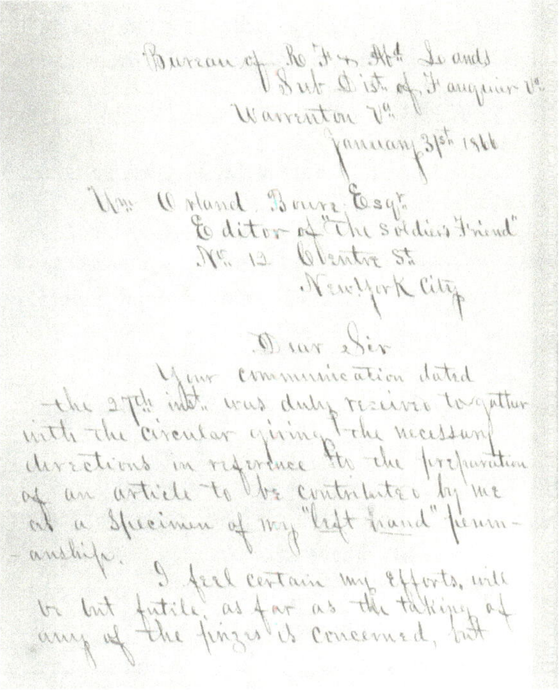
Bureau of Re F. & Ab'd Lands
Sub Dist. of Fauquier Va.
Warrenton Va.
January 31st 1866

Wm. Oland Bourne Esqr.
Editor of "The Soldiers Friend"
No. 12 Centre St.
New York City

Dear Sir

Your communication dated the 27th inst. was duly received together with the circular giving the necessary directions in reference to the preparation of an article to be contributed by me as a specimen of my "left hand" penmanship.

I feel certain my efforts will be but futile, as far as the taking of any of the prizes is concerned, but

A sample of William A. MacNulty's penmanship.
Courtesy William Oland Bourne Papers, Manuscript Division, Library of Congress.

Born in Maine in 1836, MacNulty was working in New York City when he enlisted.[56] He married in 1865 and remained in Virginia after finishing his work for the Freedmen's Bureau.[57] He served as postmaster for Culpeper and as chairman of the Republican county committee.[58] In 1872, he was a candidate for the postmastership of the U.S. Senate and was employed by the Washington, D.C., Post Office until he retired.[59] A member of GAR Kearney Post No. 11, he had two daughters and two sons.[60] MacNulty was a widower when he died in 1920 at the age of eighty-four.[61]

56. W. Augustus MacNulty, 1st ser., no. 238, Bourne Papers; "Capt. W. A. MacNulty Dies," *Washington Evening Star,* Apr. 7, 1920, 7.

57. "Capt. W. A. MacNulty Dies," 7.

58. 1870 U.S. Census, Culpeper Co., VA, pop. sched., 2nd District, p. 688A (stamped), dwelling 992, family 982, W. A. MacNulty, NARA RG 29, M593, roll 1641; "Grand Rally of the Republicans of Culpeper," *Alexandria (VA) Daily State Journal,* Sept. 13, 1863, 1.

59. "The Washington *Chronicle* Says," *Alexandria (VA) Daily State Journal,* Nov. 18, 1872, 2.

60. "Capt. W. A. MacNulty Dies," 7.

61. Ibid.

Letter to award committee: January 20, 1866

I am aware of my inability to compare with any degree my penmanship with that of others of my brother soldiers who like me have been deprived of their "good right arm" but feel certain that we can all feel that we have reasons to be very grateful to our heavenly father that it is as well with us as it is today. To sacrifice an arm especially the right, is indeed a great sacrifice, but when one's country is in danger no sacrifice is too great to be made for its defense and security from foes, foreign and domestic. . . .

Contest Entry: January 31, 1866

I feel certain my efforts will be but futile, as far as the taking of any of the prizes is concerned, but at the same time feel proud to know I am permitted to contribute my mite toward so laudable an enterprise as is proposed in publication of a book devoted to the productions and narratives of the "one armed" soldiers of our country. I feel proud to know I am included in the list of those who were willing to sacrifice their lives if necessary for the perpetuation of civil and religious liberty. . . .

I entered the service of our common country as a private in Co A 10th Regt N.Y.V. the 21st day of April with the full determination of performing my whole duty to God and my native land. I served through the Virginia Campaign under McClellan, also the Maryland Campaign and remained with the Regt. until the 13th of December 1862 on which date at the battle of Fredericksburg, VA, I parted with my "good right [arm]" from the shoulder socket and after enduring a long and painful confinement of six months in "Harewood Hospital" Washington, D.C., I once more set my face homeward. I was mustered out of service May 6th 1863 on account of expiration of term of service (two years).

I subsequently received my present position as second lieutenant U.S. VRC from our dear departed President Abraham Lincoln dated May 9th 1864 for which I shall ever feel grateful as it is a proof of the appreciation of my government for my humble services in a just and holy cause.

I am at present on duty in the "Freedmen's Bureau" as Assistant Superintendent of the sub-district of Fauquier, VA, and am trying in my humble sphere to do all in my power for the amelioration of the condition of the poor yet patient negro and am bound, God being my helper, to see that their rights and privileges as "Freemen" are not infringed upon by those who would wish to still oppress them.

~~~

HENRY KARSNITZ

Private, Co. B, 93rd Pennsylvania Volunteer Infantry

Karsnitz, a tailor's apprentice, enlisted in 1861 for three years and reenlisted in 1863; he fought at Williamsburg, the Seven Days' Battles, both battles of Fredericksburg, Gettysburg, the Wilderness, Spotsylvania, Cedar Mountain, and Second Rappahannock Station and was wounded at Fort Fisher in March 1865.[62] Karsnitz was married when he died of typhoid fever in 1869 at the age of twenty-five.[63]

May 10, 1867

I had much pain and got amputated about 3 hours after the fight at our Division Hospital Headquarters. . . . I did not like to loose my right arm I would have sooner lost my left arm I received an Artificial arm last winter and I can not use it, it dose not work the way it was informed I received it from Blanck & Son No. 1635 Market Street Philadelphia I was to pay $80 which the Gov. was to pay $50 but I pay $30 Cash before I received it and in case the arm works well I will then send the Ballence ($50) and so I cant use the arm I did sent him few lines states all about it and that they should send me my money then I would send arm back as I received it and no answer yet.

~~~

62. Henry Karsnitz, Contest Entry, 2nd ser., no. 9, Bourne Papers.

63. 1870 U.S. Census, mortality sched., Berks Co., PA, p. 1, line 18, Henry Karsnitz, NARA RG 29, M1838, roll 5.

HARRISON OTIS THOMAS

Private, Co. L, 3rd Regiment Massachusetts Volunteer Militia
("New Bedford City Guards")
Corporal, Co. D, 18th Regiment Massachusetts Volunteers

Harrison O. Thomas.
From Nason, *History and Complete Roster of the Massachusetts Regiments (1910).*

"Harry" Thomas was twenty-one and a grocery clerk when he enlisted as one of the "Minutemen of 1861."[64] After his three months' service was up, he reenlisted and participated in the Peninsula and Maryland Campaigns, then was wounded at Fredericksburg. Afterward, Thomas volunteered extensively in a field hospital, earning the nickname "Citizen Thomas."[65] He married in 1868 and was a "dealer in fancy goods," including embossed stationery that he made with "machine and dies . . . imported from Paris."[66] Starting in 1893, he worked as a vault custodian at a trust company.[67] Thomas was the first member of his local GAR post, serving as post historian and publishing a book of autobiographical sketches of local veterans. He also contributed an essay on the "Spirit of '61" when he was "71 years young," recalling "those stirring days of 50 years ago" when he and other Massachusetts men met on Boston Common three days after the bombardment of Fort Sumter and joined up.[68] When Thomas died in 1916 at the age of seventy-six, the *Boston Globe* reported that he "was one of the best-known citizens of the city."[69]

64. Harry O. Thomas, Contest Entries, 1st ser., no. 78, and 2nd ser., no. 58, Bourne Papers.

65. Nason, *History and Complete Roster of the Massachusetts Regiments,* 34–35.

66. Massachusetts Marriage Records, 1840–1915, Harrison Otis Thomas, New England Historic Genealogical Society.

67. "Fought in War without Pay," *Boston Globe,* July 28, 1916, 5.

68. Ibid.; "Are There Striking Contrasts between the Spirit of '61 and the Spirit of Today?," *Boston Globe,* Apr. 16, 1911, 46.

69. "Fought in War without Pay," 5.

Second Entry: **June 15, 1867**

My motive in writing as a member of the "left arm corps" will be the same at this time as before, mainly to add to your collection of specimens, thinking it to be the duty of every one, if for no other purpose than to encourage you, one whose whole heart seems to be for the interest of those who have been in the army. . . .

I was wounded in battle at Fredericksburg, VA, Dec. 13th, 1862. A minie ball entered on the inside of my right fore-arm, half way between the elbow and the wrist, passing through, at the same time shattering the radius bone so badly that it could not be set, therefore the arm was opened, and an excetion performed taking three inches of the bone. The operation was performed with honor, by the surgeons of the 50th New York Engineer Corps, but by neglect of the surgeon at the hospital in Washington, the hand was wrongly shaped, or placed, so that now, the hand is turned palm outward, and as the thumb and index finger are paralyzed, I lose the power of penmanship.

I was discharged from the service in March 1863. Up to the time of my being wounded, I never was absent from duty a day on account of sickness, furlough or pass, in the meantime never drank of spirituous liquors nor coffee.

In March 1864, my regiment came home on Veteran furlough; when they returned to the army, I accompanied them as a citizen and former comrade, and for nearly fourteen months labored with the sick and wounded of the 1st Division 5th Corps Field Hospital, for many weeks of which time I only had to eat such as I could get by returning to and sleeping with my former comrades, though many times my return was late at night, and then to lay with them under fire of the enemy. Such was the case all through the Wilderness to Cold Harbor; by this the surgeons noticed my labor and rewarded it by giving me food.

Through the Sanitary and Christian commissions, and by constant labor, I was enabled, I trust, to do much good, and to alleviate much suffering. I was personally with over four hundred death scenes. When the army was marching, I usually marched in the ranks of my former comrades.

In the field and in time of action my labors were confined to the worst cases; many times after my acquaintance with the Surgeons, they gave to me special charge of cases which needed special care and attention. I will not try to describe my free labor, only write as I have, to open a way to say that none know of it as do the Surgeons, nurses and chaplains of the 1st Division, 5th Corps Field Hospital, especially Surgeon in Chief ([W. R.] Dewitt) and Surgeon in Charge (Thomas), and should they or any of the surgeons see this, I hope they will accept my thanks for their kindness and assistance in all my labors; had they not encouraged me, I could not have labored as I did.

I have no proof to show for labor, and I take this opportunity to invite any soldier who has received care from me, or any surgeon, or chaplain, or nurse, who knows of my labor, to address me with some letter or testimony of the facts, especially Surgeon Dewitt and Surgeon Thomas.

I desire the above only to assist me in gaining permission to do the *same* again, should opportunity *ever* in my life afford, from such I never wish to be exempt, though from the ranks I am sorry to be.

Can I but gain such testimony and writings as will gain for me permission to do the same again, as Free Nurse in the field, should there ever be another war, I shall be well paid for all my labor.

After Lee's surrender I joined the Sanitary Commission and was put in charge at Petersburg, where I served until the 28th of June 1865 and then returned arriving at my home about 18 hours after my Old Comrades arrived in Boston, though I had known nothing of them after my marching with them from Petersburg to Richmond.

~~~

WILLIAM MCLEOD

Private, Co. G, 104th New York Volunteer Infantry

Born to Scottish immigrants (his father was a member of the 93rd Highlanders Regiment) in Ontario, Canada, in 1841, McLeod came to New York in 1852.[70] He worked on his family's farm and was learning blacksmithing when the war commenced; he assumed his father, given his military experience, would not want him to enlist, but found out he was mistaken and enlisted in October.[71] A biographical sketch in a history of New York's Livingston County

70. William McLeod, Contest Entries, 1st ser., no. 105, and 2nd ser., no. 100, Bourne Papers; Doty, *History of Livingston County New York,* 33; 1920 U.S. Census, Monroe Co., NY, pop. sched., Rochester, p. 6B, dwelling 112, family 113, William McLeod, NARA RG 29, T625, roll 1124.

71. Doty, *History of Livingston County New York,* 34.
~~~

William McLeod.
Courtesy William Oland Bourne Papers Manuscript Division, Library of Congress.

describes McLeod's post-amputation journey to Washington in more detail than the narrative below: "Being taken prisoner after he was wounded he had nothing to eat, save what he had in his haversack. . . . This was six army crackers and coffee and sugar for six cups"; McLeod gave half of his rations to other prisoners and painstakingly made his way to Washington, "so weak he dared not sit down."[72] McLeod "has no political ambitions," the sketch continues, "save a desire to better the conditions of society, so that he may feel that he did not give his good right arm in vain." In 1880, he lived with his parents in Livonia, New York, and remained upstate for the rest of his life; he does not appear to have married.[73] According to an obituary, McLeod "maintained an observatory in his barn . . . and became famed locally for his ability to read the signs of the heavens."[74] A member of GAR Gilbert Post No. 382, he died in 1924 at the age of eighty-three.[75] His first submission received honorable mention.[76]

Second Entry: **June 29, 1867**

I have not been in any business where I have had writing to do. I have made this sketch as brief as I could and have it plain . . . I appreciate the efforts you are making to have the soldiers become *men*. I am not getting rich, but thanks to a liberal government, I have been under no necessity of accepting charity, though I have had it tendered. . . .

The 9th of August [1862] found us at Cedar Mountain, a reserve to Gen. Banks while he fought that battle. We were called up [with] only time enough to support battery a spell. Next we were on the Rappahannock, and at second

72. Ibid., 34–35.

73. 1880 U.S. Census, Livingston Co., NY, pop. sched., Livonia, p. 179D (stamped), dwelling 138, family 142, William McLeod, NARA RG 29, T9, roll 859.

74. "Death of William McLeod," *Livonia (NY) Gazette,* Apr. 18, 1924, 1.

75. *Abstract of General Orders and Proceedings of the Fortieth Annual Encampment, Department of New York, G.A.R.,* 115; "William McLeod," *Rochester (NY) Democrat and Chronicle,* Apr. 17, 1924, 26.

76. Exhibition of Left-Hand Penmanship, Bourne Papers.

Bull Run we were brought in in earnest. I had been on the skirmish line considerable during the day, and was thinking I was going to get out all safe, when along came a bullet, passing through my right arm. It was on Saturday, August 30th, and on Monday it was taken off near the shoulder. It was taken off near the field, and on Wednesday morning I started for Washington, where I arrived Sept. 6th. I walked the whole way except six miles. I was assigned to the Epiphany Hospital. Discharged Nov. 12, '62. . . .

Shortly after returning from the army I was one day talking with a friend, when he made the remark, that of those young men who returned from the army minus arms and legs, the majority would be better off than [as] though they had come back as they went away. It sounded strange to me, but the more I thought of it, the more I thought he was right.

In the first place, a number of them were farmers, and losing a leg incapacitated them for following that pursuit, and they had to turn their attention to something else. All we have to do now is to go into the cities and villages, and step into the harness and other shops, to see them earning as good livings as they could at farming, and much easier. They are of my acquaintance now, who are carrying on business on their new accounts, who, in all probability would not be doing as well if they had their bodies sound.

Nor is this the best, any more than it is the worst. A good many of the maimed ones went into the army as I did, under age, and when they had been to school but little. Coming back unfit for farmers and mechanics, many of them went at improving their minds, and are today teachers, and men qualified to conduct almost any business. The mental discipline they have received; the expanded and liberal views they now hold of life and its surroundings; but above all, the self-knowledge they have acquired, will in a great measure compensate, if not entirely repay them for the parts of their bodies they left on the different fields of strife. And I have in my mind now, "boys of blue" who are in positions of trust and honor, who today, but for the change which rendered it imperative upon them to cultivate their minds, would be working with their muscles to the almost complete neglect of those parts of their organizations which should receive their first considerations. And who will say now, that their enlarged intellects, and the influence they exert on society are not ample reparations for the inconvenience they suffer from the loss of an arm or a leg. This may sound like poor reasoning to those who find trouble adapting themselves to circumstances, who find it hard work to write with their left hands, etc., but let them think it over carefully and see if they will not have to come to the same conclusion that I did. I think they will. I think I speak knowingly as I left an arm on Virginia's soil. I can do a great many things with one hand. I may someday tell you what I can do, and how I do it.

APPENDIX A

List of Contestants

Contestant names, birth and death dates, residence at time of submission, regiment and company, service dates (enlistment–discharge),[1] wounding location and date, amputation date (if available; if n/a, identification of surgery or disability, if specified), contest (first or second) and entry number (* indicates entry is missing from the William Oland Bourne Papers and/or not part of digitized collection).

—	amputation date same as wounding date
Art.	Artillery
amp.	amputation
Batt.	Battery
Bvt.	Brevet
Cav.	Cavalry
exc.	excision
Ind.	Independent
POW	prisoner of war
Vols.	Volunteers

1. Official enlistment and discharge dates sometimes differ from veterans' statements; in such cases, I have used the dates provided by the veterans.

Name (Dates)	Residence	Regiment, Company (rank if above private)
Akers, George W. (1840–74)	Enfield, IL	40th IL, C
Allen, Henry C. (1842–1911)	Conway, MA	1st MA Cav., E
Allison, Jonathan McKinstry (1837–67)	Monmouth, IL	Cpl., 111th IL, I
Amsden, Mark Alonzo (1815–82)	Willoughby Lake, VT	10th VT, K
Anthony, James H. (1837–1915)	Pittsfield, MA	125th NY, K
Arnold, Edmund C. (1839–96)	Washington, DC; Uxbridge, MA	15th MA, H
Atchison, Henry K. (1820–93)	New Geneva, PA	85th PA, G
Bail, Lewis (1839–70)	Chester, PA	26th PA, K
Bailey, Turner Smith (1841–1913)	Iowa City, IA	3rd IA, A
Bain, Robert A. (1842–82)	Marshall, MI	1st Sgt., 24th MI, K
Barber, Richard M. (1847–1930)	Albany, NY	16th NY Heavy Art.; 148th NY, B; 2nd Lt., 2nd Battalion VRC, 4; Bvt. Capt., NY Vols.
Barger, Frederick C. (1842–1923)	Westfield, NY	1st Lt., 49th NY, G
Barker, Frederic L. (1843–94)	New York, NY	Sgt., 3rd MI, K; Capt., 5th MI, H
Barlow, Alfred (1844–97)	Detroit, MI	14th MI, C
Barnum/Bainum, D. W. (?–?)	Warrenville, OH	2nd Lt., 7th OH, D
Barr, Samuel L. (1839–70)	Bellefonte, PA	Lt., 148th PA, B; 2nd Lt., 18th VRC, A
Bates, Dorus E. (1843–80)	Pittsfield, IL	Bugler, 2nd IL Cav., K; Bvt. Capt., 13th U.S.
Baumgardner, Morgan (1840–1918)	Mechanicsville, IA	1st Sgt., 9th IA, B
Baumhager, Herman (1842–before 1911)	Shakopee, MN	5th MN, E
Beaver, Anthony J. (1832–99)	James Creek, PA	Sgt. 53rd PA, C; , 2nd Battalion VRC, 39
Beck, Grandison D. (1845–99)	Beck Creek, IL	35th IL, B
Beerbower, Samuel T. (1842–1902)	Marion, OH	Sgt., 64th OH, B
Bergin, William S. (1849–77)	Columbus, OH	121st OH, A

Service	Wounding location and date	Amputation date	Contest and entry
10/5/61–4/13/63	Shiloh, 4/6/62	4/19/62	1:114
9/17/61–11/8/63	near the Rapidan, 9/14/63	—	1:15; 2:99
8/11/62–6/7/65	Resaca, 5/14/64	—	1:67
7/28/62–9/9/65	Cold Harbor, 6/1/64	n/a; paralysis	1:113
8/15/62–7/6/65	Southside Road, VA, 4/2/65	—, exc.	1:42*
7/12/61–4/7/62	Ball's Bluff, VA, 10/21/61	10/22/61	1:148
9/20/61–11/22/64	Petersburg, 9/1/64	—	1:80
5/5/61–?	Spotsylvania, 5/15/64		1:112
5/22/61–10/5/63	Jackson, MS, 7/12/63	7/24/63	1:85
8/4/62–2/11/63	Fredericksburg, 12/13/62	—	1:55
1/2/64–7/21/65	Petersburg, 6/15/64	—	2:59
8/8/61–5/11/64	Fredericksburg, 12/13/62	—; 2nd amp. at home	1:81
5/9/61–7/5/65	Wilderness, 5/6/64	n/a; shot through shoulder and lung	1:150
10/18/61–6/22/65	Jonesboro, GA, 9/1/64	9/2/64	2:112
Not on roster	Lookout Mountain, 11/24/63		1:45*
8/15/62–6/30/66	Bristoe Station, VA, 10/15/63	—	2:92
7/30/61–1/25/65	Vicksburg, 5/19/63		1:7
8/12/61–11/30/63	Vicksburg, 5/22/63	10/2/63	2:39
4/2/62–10/10/62	Clear Creek, MS, 6/14/62	n/a; paralysis	1:53; 2:38
9/16/61–8/21/65	Bristoe Station, VA, 10/14/63	10/15/63	1:162
7/3/61–9/27/64	Pickett's Mill, GA, 5/27/64	5/28/64; 3 amps. in following 3 months	2:109
10/23/61–3/24/63	Missionary Ridge, TN, 11/25/63	n/a; hand and arm paralyzed	1:107
3/1/64–10/25/64	Allatoona Mountain, GA, 6/2/64	6/19/64	1:109

Name (Dates)	Residence	Regiment, Company (rank if above private)
Bicknell, James Turner (1813–80)	Roxbury, MA	2nd Lt., 22nd MA, K; 2nd Battalion VRC, 36
Bishop, Roswell Peter (1843–1920)	Oneonta, NY	43rd NY, C
Bissell, Edward B. (1847–1928)	Wardsboro, VT	9th VT, K
Blanchard, John (1842–1912)	Penfield, OH	1st OH Light Art., B
Blanchard, Thomas W. (1845–1906)	New Ipswich, NH	Cpl., 13th NH, G
Blood, Alvin (1836–82)	Stevens Point, WI	32nd WI, E
Blood, Samuel L. (1846–1925)	Manchester, NH	11th MA, K
Blotner, John (1834–1900)	Versailles, OH	40th OH, E
Bohn, Albert Julius (1843–84)	Milwaukee, WI	36th WI, I
Bolen, John (?–?)	Athol Depot, MA	20th CT, A
Boos, Louis J. (1840–83)	Philadelphia, PA	Sgt., 6th PA Cav., B
Bostaph, William Marion (1845–1935)	Gallatin, MO	Cpl., 103rd PA, F
Bottom, William H. (1842–85)	Norwich, CT	Sgt., 11th CT, H
Bowker, Hubert "Hugh" Demarest (1842–1927)	Fitchville, OH	1st Lt., 8th OH, D; Sgt., 2nd Battalion VRC, 111; 1st Lt. 122nd USCT, B (postwar)
Bowron, Lyman E. (1841–1922)	Champlain, NY	Sgt., 98th NY, D
Bresnahan, John (1839–1918)	Washington, DC	27th IN, A
Brewster, Caleb (1844–1927)	Waverly, NY	69th NY, K
Broadfoot, James (1837–1903)	Kirkwood, NY	137th NY, F
Brooks, Edwin A. (1844–93)	New Haven, CT	10th CT, K
Broshears, Ira (1833–1924)	Rockport, IN	Sgt., 27th IN, B
Brougher, Ira Day (1843–1920)	Siddonsburg, PA	130th PA, F
Brown, George A. (1841–93)	Boston, MA	11th CT, D
Brown, John Lee (1838–1906)	Danville, IN	Cpl., 70th IN, A
Browne, Thomas Moore Gifford (1831–1905)	New York, NY	48th NY, F

Service	Wounding location and date	Amputation date	Contest and entry
8/28/61–7/30/66	Gaines's Mill, 6/27/62	8/3/62	2:56
8/6/61–12/10/62	Yorktown, 4/28/62	—	1:224
12/8/63–7/25/65	Fair Oaks, 10/27/64	—	1:261; 2:84
8/8/62–5/14/63	Stones River, 12/26/62	—	1:75; 2:57
8/12/62–5/31/65	Chaffin's Farm (Petersburg), 9/29/64	—	1:186
8/12/62–7/17/65	Beaufort, SC, 2/3/65	—	1:269
3/18/64–7/25/65	Wilderness, 5/5/64	5/6/64	1:251
9/20/61–2/13/64	Chickamauga, 9/20/63	9/23/63	1:239
2/27/64–2/11/65	Cold Harbor, 6/3/64	7/18/64	1:258
8/24/63–6/19/65	Peach Tree Creek, GA, 7/22/64		1:151
11/19/61–11/29/64	Todd's Tavern, VA, 5/7/64	5/13/64	1:10; 2:19
10/30/61–?	Fair Oaks, 5/31/62	n/a; hand paralyzed	1:66
12/2/61–7/15/65	Petersburg, 8/5/64	n/a; shoulder wound	1:9
4/17/61–1/16/65	Martinsburg, VA, 3/23/62	n/a; shot in right breast	1:90
10/16/61–1/12/65	Fort Harrison, VA, 9/29/64		1:166*
8/19/61–3/8/64	Chancellorsville, 5/3/63	5/9/63	2:64
3/29/64–3/2/65	Spotsylvania, 5/12/64	n/a; hand disabled	2:32
8/13/62–12/30/63	Gettysburg, 7/2/63	7/3/63	1:201
9/1/61–5/9/63	Seabrook Island, SC, 3/28/63	n/a	1:39
8/10/61–6/17/63	Chancellorsville, 5/3/63	—	1:64
8/8/62–12/25/62	Antietam, 9/17/62	9/18/62	2:113*
12/1/61–11/10/62	New Bern, NC, 3/14/62	—	1:65
7/21/62–3/3/65	Resaca, 5/15/64	5/17/64	2:66
12/11/61–11/21/64	Cemetery Hill, Petersburg, 7/30/64	—	1:192

Name (Dates)	Residence	Regiment, Company (rank if above private)
Brundage, Edgar Alonzo (1834–88)	Otsego, MI	11th MI Cav., F
Bryce, John (1821–1910?)	New York, NY	1st NY, H
Bryson, John (1834–1919)	Washington, DC	30th NY, A
Bucknam, George C. (1834–1915)	Charlestown, MA	3rd Ind. Batt., MA Light Art.
Burger, Francis Xavie (1824–73)	New York, NY	Capt., 4th PA Reserves (33rd PA), E
Burnett, Stephen J. (1832–94)	Warrensburg, MO	2nd Lt., 27th MO, D; Capt., 33rd MO, A
Burns, James R. (1838–1917)	New York, NY	Cpl., 74th NY, E; 2nd Battalion VRC, 4
Burroughs, Marvin (1846–1918)	Seneca Falls, NY	148th NY, A
Burt, Abellino S. (1835–1907)	Oxford, MA	12th MA, C
Bush, George W. (1839–90)	New York, NY	Sgt., 90th NY, G
Byers, Joseph King (1839–78)	Fryburg, PA; Sacketts Harbor, NY	1st Lt., 121st PA, F; 2nd Battalion VRC, 2; 1st Lt. and Quartermaster, 15th VRC, F
Byram, Charles E. (1843–1915)	Abingdon, IL	7th IL Cav., D
Call, George (1840–1917)	Keeseville, NY	6th NY Cav., D
Cameron, Alexander (1830–1908)	Detroit, MI	2nd Lt., 16th MI, G; 1st Lt., 2nd Battalion VRC, 63, 25, 173
Cargon, Silas (1838–1922)	Castleton-on-Hudson, NY	5th NY, B; 146 NY, G (US Navy, 1859–62)
Carpenter, Samuel A. (1846–1928)	Strongsville, OH	124th OH, A
Cavanaugh, Theodore J. (1819–95)	New York, NY	Sgt., 139th NY, E
Chaffee, Henry H. (1840–1912)	Rochester, VT	1st Sgt., 4th VT, E
Champion, Robert D. (1838–83)	Union Valley, NY	157th NY, C
Charmoille, Claude (1828–99)	Glenmore, NY	146th NY, B
Chase, John F. (1843–1914)	Augusta, ME	3rd ME, B; 5th ME Light Art.
Chatfield, Alonzo Bradley, Jr. (1842–1920)	Lisle Station, IL	33rd IL, B

Service	Wounding location and date	Amputation date	Contest and entry
10/15/63–3/20/65	Piketown, KY, 10/7/64	11/27/64	1:184
5/8/61–11/4/62	?	9/6/62	1:199
4/24/61–11/7/62	2nd Bull Run, 8/30/62	9/1/62	1:18; 2:23
8/12/62–9/16/64	Laurel Hill (Spotsylvania), 5/8/64	—	2:47
6/12/61–6/17/64	Antietam, 9/17/62	—	2:101
7/4/61–8/10/65	Helena, AR, 7/4/63	—	2:54
4/27/61–6/1/63	Williamsburg, 5/5/62	6/5/62	1:54; 2:67*
7/28/62–8/26/64	Cold Harbor, 6/3/64	6/27/64; undated 2nd amp.	1:167; 2:7
7/14/63–6/25/64	Wilderness, 5/5/64	5/6/64	1:63
12/21/61–8/31/63	Port Hudson, 6/14/63	—	2:72
8/16/62–4/23/67	Fredericksburg, 12/13/62	12/14/63	1:30; 2:44
12/30/63–6/22/65	Nashville, 12/15/64	—	2:46
9/10/61–6/15/65	Deep Bottom, VA, 7/28/64	—	1:187
8/4/61–6/30/66	Gettysburg, 7/2/63	—	1:103
8/21/62–1/20/65	Wilderness, 5/5/64	5/6/64; 2nd while POW	1:205
2/15/64–8/29/64	Dallas, GA, 5/27/64	5/28/64	1:248
8/21/62–10/5/64	Cold Harbor, 6/2/64	—	1:169
8/31/61–6/27/65	Cedar Creek, VA, 10/19/64	—	1:156
8/9/62–5/9/65	Honey Hill, SC, 12/9/64	12/27/64	2:48
9/6/62–4/26/65	Petersburg, 6/18/64	—	1:139
4/23/61–11/25/63	Gettysburg, 7/2/63	7/5/63	1:223
8/20/61–9/26/63	Big Black River, MS, 5/17/63	—	1:252

Name (Dates)	Residence	Regiment, Company (rank if above private)
Churchell, Amos (1842–1922)	Danby, IL	Cpl., 8th IL Cav., M; 1st Lt., 141st IL, H
Claffey, William (1843–1911)	Mattapan, MA	1st MA, D
Clobridge, Selden C. (1846–1918)	Saratoga, NY; New York, NY; Albany, NY	1st Lt., 115th NY, G
Cloyd, Samuel J. (1833–1925)	Washington, DC	2nd Lt., 12th PA Reserves (41st PA), I
Coleman, Charles T. (1840–1915)	Canton, IL	Cpl., 75th NY, B
Combs, James Rockwell (1843–1901)	Morris, IL	127th IL, D
Compton, William (1846–1911)	Gilboa, OH	25th OH, G
Conant, James H. (1828–1914)	Chester, IL	80th IL, A
Connor, William M. (1840–71)	Mount Clemens, MI	Cpl., 6th MI, C
Cook, Benjamin C. (1839–1906)	Mottville, NY; Newark, NJ	Sgt. 5th MI, H; 2nd Lt., 2nd Battalion VRC, 50; 24th VRC, D; Bvt. Capt. (1866)
Cook, Benjamin F. (1845–80)	Oregon, MO; Carondelet, MO	4th MO Cav., B
Cook, Willard L. (1823–1916)	Belleville, NY	Cpl., 94th NY, B
Courtney, William R. (1845–1907)	Philadelphia, PA	Sgt. Maj., 118th PA, G
Crosby, Josiah Quincy (1832–1908)	Stoneham, MA; Washington, DC	Sgt., 13th MA, G
Cruver, John H. (1842–1908)	Gilmer, IL	96th IL, B
Cullen, Richard J. (1841–1913)	Andover, MA	1st Sgt., 9th NH, F
Cunliffe, James G. (1844–?)	New York, NY	51st NY, E
Currier, Lewis D. (1845–1916)	Enfield, NH	Cpl., 11th NH, H
Cutler, Frederick R. (1843–73)	Chester, PA	72nd PA, K; 55, 2nd Batt. VRC
Dake, Frederick E. (c.1840–c.1880)	Washington, DC	Sgt., 139th PA, F
Dale, George W. (1845–1913)	Elmira, NY	4th PA Cav., K; 16th VRC, A

Service	Wounding location and date	Amputation date	Contest and entry
8/30/61–9/28/63; 6/16/64–10/10/64	Beverly Ford, VA, 6/9/63	6/10/63, exc. of elbow	1:3
10/26/61–11/22/62	2nd Bull Run, 8/29/62	9/13/62	1:27
7/18/62–7/28/65	Fort Gilmer (Petersburg), 9/29/64	–	1:189; 2:75
3/17/64–1/7/63	Antietam, 9/17/62	–	1:170; 2:85
9/16/61–9/3/63	Port Hudson, 6/14/63	6/15/63, exc.; 8/7/63, amp.	1:49
8/13/62–6/3/65	Atlanta, 7/28/64	–	1:259
10/5/64–5/16/65	Boyd's Point, SC, 2/7/65	–	1:236
7/28/62–6/7/65	near Kennesaw Mountain, GA, 7/4/64	10/1/64	1:40; 2:55
7/1/61–12/22/63	Port Hudson, 5/27/63	–	1:12
8/6/61–1/1/68	Gettysburg, 7/2/63	–, exc.; 7/19/63, amp.	1:154; 2:6
3/1/62–3/1/65	Big Blue River, MO, 10/23/64	–; 2nd at home	1:110; 2:81
11/6/61–9/13/62	2nd Bull Run, 8/30/62	–	1:60
8/9/62–6/8/65	Poplar Springs (Petersburg), 9/30/64	–	1:219
4/19/61–8/1/64	Spotsylvania, 5/8/64	5/9/64	1:222; 2:95
8/9/62–9/4/65	Chickamauga, 9/20/63	–, exc.; 3/5/65, 2nd exc.	1:96
6/28/62–6/5/65	Spotsylvania, 5/12/64	7/14/64; 5/1/65	1:230; 2:20
3/26/64–7/8/65	Poplar Grove Church (Petersburg), 9/30/64	10/1/64	1:157*
8/13/62–5/13/65	Poplar Grove Church (Petersburg), 9/30/64		1:245
8/10/61–3/15/63	Antietam, 9/17/62	10/19/62	1:241
9/1/62–7/13/63	Fredericksburg, 5/3/63	5/4/63	1:126
10/18/61–10/18/64	Elmira, NY (riot), 1/25/65	–	1:196; 2:30

Name (Dates)	Residence	Regiment, Company (rank if above private)
Davis, John W. (1840–1921)	Burlington, IL	Sgt., 36th IL Cav. (15th IL Cav.), B
Davis, William Watts Hart (1820–1910)	Doylestown, PA	Capt., 25th PA, I; Col., 104th PA; Bvt. Brig. Gen.
DeCamp, William Miller (1818–1905)	Iowa City, IA	1st IA, B; 1st Lt., 22nd IA, G; 2nd Battalion VRC, 161
Denison, Andrew Woods (1831–77)	Baltimore, MD	Col., 8th MD; Bvt. Maj. Gen.
Denney, William (1846–92)	Philadelphia, PA	29th PA, D
Dibble, Alvin H. (1845–?)	Nunda, NY; Washington, DC	33rd NY, F; 49th NY, A
Dickinson, Robert James (1836–1916)	Toulon, IL	127th IL, B
Dillon, George L. (1837–91)	Georgetown, IL	125th IL, D
Dippel, Conrad (1831–1912)	Watertown, WI	37th WI, I
Dodge, Charles W. (1843–80)	Washington, DC	Cpl., 13th NH, B; 1st Lt., 22nd USCT, B; 2nd Lt., 24th Regt. VRC, E
Dougal, William Henry (1845–1924)	Naugatuck, CT	6th CT, E
Dunton, Albert A. (1827–73)	Philadelphia, PA	Cpl., 27th PA, I
Durrah, Franklin H. (1844–1904)	Philadelphia, PA	31st PA (82nd PA), F
Eastham, Edmund (1840–84)	West Candor, NY	3rd NY Art., Batt. I
Eaton, Charles H. (1834–1903)	Lafayette, IN	1st Sgt., 79th IN, E
Eaton, Ulysses S. (1842–1931)	Cambridge City, IN	19th Batt. IN Light Art.
Edmonds, Charles A. (1830–1907)	Quincy, MI	1st Lt., 1st MI Light Art., Batt. A; Capt., 17th MI, H
Edwards, Edward Ames (1840–1927)	St. Paul, MN	15th IN, K
Egolf, Joseph (1830–93)	Troy, NY	1st Lt., 2nd NY, F; Capt., 125th NY
Elliott, James F. (1840–1909)	Greencastle, IN	8th IN, I
Evans, Frank H. (1841–1911)	Claremont, NH	Cpl., 3rd NH, A
Farley, George Rockwell (1840–1908)	Prospect, NY	Sgt., 117th NY, F
Farrington, Henry W. (1839–1920)	Cambridge, VT	4th VT, I

Service	Wounding location and date	Amputation date	Contest and entry
8/18/61–4/18/63	Murfreesboro, 12/31/62	1/12/63, exc.	1:76
4/28/61–9/30/64	John's Island, SC, 7/6/64	–	1:268
5/14/61–4/26/65	Port Gibson, MS, 5/1/63	n/a; partial paralysis	1:147; 2:14
9/12/62–5/31/65	Spotsylvania, 5/8/64	5/14/64	2:98
7/8/61–1/21/65	Resaca, 5/18/64	5/19/64	1:127
10/24/62–11/13/63	Fredericksburg, 5/3/63	5/4/63, exc.; 7/22/63, amp.	1:227
8/15/62–9/24/63	Vicksburg, 5/22/63	7/29/63	1:25
8/10/62–1/27/65	near Dallas, GA, 6/2/64	6/21/64	1:254
11/20/63–12/8/64	Norfolk and Petersburg RR, 6/17/64	–	1:128
8/15/62–11/10/68	Petersburg, 6/15/64	–	1:47
8/26/61–11/16/63	Fort Wagner, 7/18/63	8/7/63	1:98
10/2/62–9/19/63	Gettysburg, 7/1/63	8/1/63	1:177
8/24/61–12/12/62	Fair Oaks, 5/31/62	6/1/62	1:95
8/30/62–6/8/64	New Bern, NC, 2/2/64	–	1:202
8/7/62–2/3/65	Jonesboro, GA, 9/2/64	9/3/64	1:52
8/3/62–4/18/65	Resaca, 5/15/64	–	1:262
5/28/61–1/31/63	South Mountain, 9/14/62	–	1:51
6/14/61–3/20/63	Stones River, 12/31/62	n/a; lost two fingers	1:178
4/20/61–12/31/64	Ream's Station, VA, 8/25/64	8/26/64	1:207
8/18/61–11/30/64	Vicksburg, 5/22/63	5/27/63	2:36
8/19/61–11/9/63	Morris Island, SC, 7/10/63	–	1:133
7/23/62–12/30/64	Fort Gilmer (Petersburg), 9/29/64		1:86
7/17/63–2/5/65	Wilderness, 5/5/64	5/6/64	2:68

Name (Dates)	Residence	Regiment, Company (rank if above private)
Faulk, Philip Keppel (1840–1900)	Yankton, Dak. Terr.	11th PA, F; 2nd Lt., 54th PA Militia, C; 2nd Cpl., 11th PA, F
Fay, John S. (1840–1914)	Marlborough, MA	Sgt., 13th MA, F
Fenton, Philo Servetus (1841–1907)	Decatur, IL	Cpl., 116th IL, C
Fertig, Thaddeus (1837–1910)	Milroy, PA	45th PA, C
Finley, John F. (1842–1914)	Charlestown, MA	3rd MA Batt. Light Art., C
Fisher, Caleb B. (1844–1931)	Aurora, IL	Sgt., 143rd PA, A
Fitz James Michael J. (1846?–1917)	New York, NY	32nd NY, D; 121st NY, H
Foster, John Frye (1826–87)	Gloucester, MA	35th MA, F
French, Alfred (1843–1935)	East Rockport, OH	1st OH Light Art., Batt. B
Fries, Andrew J. (1836–81)	Joliet, IL	Cpl., 100th IL, E
Frizzell, William (1844–69)	Chicago, IL	Cpl., 2nd NY, H
Fuller, Elbert (1835–1915)	White Plains, NY	Cpl., 6th NY Heavy Art., B
Gates, David C. (1841–81)	Portsmouth, OH	1st OH, G
Gelray, Joseph Wiley (1837–1900)	Lowell, MA	Capt., 2nd MA, D; 57th MA, B; Maj., 4th MA Heavy Art.; Col., 59th MA
Gilbert, Smith S. (1837–1911)	Washington, DC	Lt., 11th CT, K
Gilman, John E. (1844–1921)	Boston, MA	12th MA, E
Granger, Harmon F. (1841–1925)	Prairie Ronde, MI	19th MI, F
Gray, Lorenzo J. (1840–1903)	Portland, WI	20th WI, B
Griffith, Thomas P. (1843–1925)	Johnsonville, IL	48th IL, I
Guenther, Theodore Bruno (1839–90)	St. Louis, MO	41st NY, I
Hall, Mosley Edwin (1841–1924)	Vergennes, VT	Sgt., 5th U.S. Art., Batt. G
Hamilton, Martin Douglass (1843–1926)	Clear Spring, IN	1st Sgt., 17th IN, G
Hamilton, Samuel H. (1839–1932)	Black Hawk, PA	10th PA Reserves (39th PA), F
Hanese, Jacob (1845–78)	Saline, MI	16th MI, E
Hardy, Amos E. (1843–1922)	Hampden, ME	18th ME (1st ME Heavy Art.), F

Service	Wounding location and date	Amputation date	Contest and entry
4/61?–7/61?; 11/9/61–1/3/63; 6/30/63–8/17/63; 2/29/64–11/3/64	Wilderness, 5/6/64	—	1:142; 2:91
6/29/61–9/9/63	Fredericksburg, 4/30/63	—; arm and leg	2:93
8/13/62–6/7/65	Dallas, GA, 6/3/64	—	1:100
2/23/64–6/23/65	Cold Harbor, 6/3/64	6/4/64	1:35
9/9/61–9/16/64	Weldon Railroad, 8/18/64	—; 9/1/64	1:225
8/6/62–12/16/64	Petersburg, 6/18/64	—	2:111
8/24/62–2/28/65	Wilderness, 5/5/64	—	1:144
8/11/62–3/15/63	Fredericksburg, 12/13/62	—	1:242
8/12/62–2/11/63	Stones River, 12/31/62	1/10/63	1:43*
8/12/62–4/18/64	Chickamauga, 9/19/63	10/31/63	1:256; 2:103
4/24/61–3/26/63	Chancellorsville, 5/3/63	—	1:79
8/18/62–10/22/64	Cold Harbor, 6/2/64	—	1:215
4/16/61–7/29/61	Vienna, VA, 6/17/61	7/3/61	1:20
5/11/61–6/17/65	Gettysburg, 7/3/63	—	1:108
10/10/61–10/17/64	Firing salute, New Bern, 1/1/66		2:108
8/4/62–10/28/63	Gettysburg, 7/2/63	—	2:11*
8/6/62–5/11/65	Peach Tree Creek, GA, 7/20/64	—	1:255
8/19/62–2/9/63	Prairie Grove, AR, 12/7/62	12/11/62	1:117
11/3/61–11/20/62	Shiloh, 4/7/62	—	1:44*
12/13/61–1/15/63	2nd Bull Run, 8/30/62	9/6/62	2:96
4/21/62–3/16/65	Red River Campaign, AR, 4/5/64	n/a; shoulder wound paralyzed right hand	1:69
6/12/61–8/29/65	skirmish near Selma, AL, 4/1/65	4/28/65	1:243
5/61–4/27/63	Fredericksburg, 12/13/62	—	1:84
12/16/62–9/13/65	Petersburg, 7/30/64	8/22/64	1:216; 2:?
7/19/62–8/30/65	Southside Railroad (Petersburg), 10/2/64	—	1:149

Name (Dates)	Residence	Regiment, Company (rank if above private)
Harrington, Charles W. (1831–98)	Dayton, OH	Sgt., 15th U.S. Infantry, F
Harrison, Albert J. (1835–89)	Cadiz, OH	2nd Lt., 126th OH, H; Asst. Adj. Gen. 3rd Brig. AOTP
Haskell, Samuel Frank (1839–1922)	Augusta, ME	Sgt., 17th ME, C
Hayes, Edward (1829–99)	Burghill, OH	Lt. Col., 29th OH
Hayward, Allen B. (1839–1922)	Marlboro Depot, NH	Sgt., 2nd NH, A
Hilts, Ezra Dayton (1839–1908)	Stone Mills, NY	Cpl., 1st NY Light Art., Batt. D
Hindman, John S. (1840–1921)	Clover Hill, PA	140th PA, E
Hinds, Darius (1834–75)	Washington, DC	3rd MI, A; 2nd Battalion VRC, 137
Hogg, Benjamin Franklin (1841–96)	New York, NY	Cpl., 104th NY, C
Holder, James (1844–1914)	Harlem Springs, OH	80th OH, D
Hooper, William H. (1835–1905)	Manchester-by-the-Sea, MA	12th MA, K
Horne, Charles Edwin (1839–1902)	Stoneham, MA	1st Lt., 13th MA, I
Horton, Lewis A. (1842–1916)	Newburyport, MA	USN steamer *Rhode Island*
Hosier, Sidney M. (1843–1902)	Blockville, NY	112th NY, D
Hosler, White Norman (1843–1901)	Fishing Creek, PA	143rd PA, I
Hubbard, Ozro N. (1843–71)	Washington, DC	16th NY, I
Hudson, William S., Jr. (1841–77)	Paterson, NJ	9th NY, C; Capt., 49th NY
Hunter, James Henry (1842–71)	Brooklyn, NY	Color Cpl., 12th NY, B
Huntington, John F. (1824–89)	Penfield, NY	1st Lt., 140th NY, K
Hurin/Huron, Eli (1836–1921)	Washington, DC	53rd IN, A
Hutchinson, William B. (1839–1937)	Ogdensburg, NY	Cpl., 142nd NY, G
Irish, Abel J. (1842–1901)	Moira, NY	106th NY, H
Irwin, Francis J. (1844–98)	Rochester, NY	Sgt., 140th NY, K

Service	Wounding location and date	Amputation date	Contest and entry
10/18/61–10/28/64	Utoy Creek, GA, 8/7/64	n/a; hand and arm disabled	1:2
8/15/62–12/20/64	Wilderness, 5/6/64	5/7/64	2:42
8/18/62–12/15/64	Petersburg, 6/16/64	—	1:61*
8/26/61–11/4/64	Dug Gap, GA, 5/8/64	—, exc.	1:220
5/22/61–6/21/64	Cold Harbor, 6/3/64	6/21/64	1:74
8/29/61–9/26/62	Williamsburg, 5/5/62	—	1:14; 2:50
8/13/62–4/20/65	near Spotsylvania, 6/19/64	—	2:24
5/13/61–4/10/65	2nd Bull Run, 8/29/62	8/30/62	2:51
10/9/61–11/25/63	Gettysburg, 7/1/63	7/2/63	1:137
8/27/62–8/21/63	Jackson, MS, 5/14/63	—	1:36; 2:5
6/26/61–4/6/64	Gettysburg, 7/3/63	7/4/63	1:28
7/16/61–9/9/64	Spotsylvania, 5/8/64		1:179
5/20/61–2/18/64	premature discharge, Cap-Haïtien, Haiti	Lost both arms	2:1
8/2/62–7/8/65	Chaffin's Farm (Petersburg), 9/29/64	—	2:53
8/9/64–7/20/65	Laurel Hill (Spotsylvania), 5/10/64	—	1:146
4/16/61–7/7/63	Fredericksburg, 5/3/63	5/4/63	1:97; 2:102
5/4/61–3/9/65	Spotsylvania, 5/18/64	—	1:38
11/11/61–9/6/62	Gaines's Mill, 6/27/62	7/7/62; 4/30/63	1:70; 2:15
8/30/62–1/12/65	Weldon Railroad, 8/19/64	n/a; partial paralysis	1:92
2/14/62–11/14/62	Hatchie River, MS, 10/4/62	10/9/62	1:145; 2:35
9/6/62–12/23/64	Drury's Bluff, VA, 5/20/64	n/a; shot through wrist	1:72
8/8/62–6/6/65	Spotsylvania, 5/12/64	5/17/64	1:235
8/22/62–4/3/65	Weldon Railroad, 8/19/64	8/20/64	1:104

Name (Dates)	Residence	Regiment, Company (rank if above private)
Jackson, Charles (1845–1926)	Willimantic, CT	8th CT, D; 3rd VRC, ?
Jennings, Edward M. (1842–1922)	Portageville, NY	130th NY, A
Johnson, George H. (1836–1906)	Blairsville, PA	2nd Sgt., 56th PA, B
Johnson, William M. (1844–98)	Vernon, OH	6th OH Cav., D
Johnston, John (1836–85)	Muhlenberg, KY	Sgt., 11th Kentucky, B
Jones, William J. (1839–1919)	Madison, WI	Bvt. Capt., 16th WI, C
Karsnitz, Henry (1844–69)	Myerstown, PA	93rd PA, B
Keller, Martin Van Buren (1840–1921)	Lititz, PA	1st PA Reserves (30th PA), B
Kent, Evarts B. (1843–1924)	Ripton, VT	6th VT, A; 2nd Battalion VRC, 171
Kenyon, Charles E. (1842–1914)	Newark Valley, NY	63rd NY, F
King, William C. (1826–72)	Hartford, KY	Sgt., 12th KY Cav., D
Kipling, William (1831–69?)	Brooklyn, NY	3rd U.S. Art., E
Kleckner, Jacob H. (1838–1910)	Ickesburg, PA	53rd PA, I
Kline, Lewis E. (1843–1905)	St. Louis, MO	33rd MO, C
Kneeland, James H. (1837–91)	Worcester, MA	Cpl., 15th MA, D; 2nd Battalion VRC, 99
Koster, John Smith (1841–1921)	Bond's Village, MA	Sgt., 21st MA, H
Krahl, Henry L. (1841-1908)	Grand View, IA; Geneva, IL	13th U.S. Infantry, H
Lacy, Joel L. (1840–1913)	Wilmington, DE	2nd DE, C
Ladd, James Otis (1843–1931)	Windsor, MA; Summerville, SC	15th MA, I; Capt., 35th USCT/1st NC Colored Inf., K
Lamley, David (1840–1921)	Blissfield, MI	18th MI, B
Lantz, Jacob Alexander (1841–93)	Akron, OH	19th OH, G; Cpl., 67th OH, C
LaRue, George S. (1836–1903)	Cincinnati, OH	Cpl., 6th OH, I
Lee, James E. (1840–98)	Paterson, NJ	3rd CT, C; 2nd Sgt., 6th NY Heavy Art., G

Service	Wounding location and date	Amputation date	Contest and entry
9/23/61–10/12/65	Antietam, 9/17/62	9/18/62	1:221
7/28/62–5/28/63	deserted farm, Suffolk, VA, 1/30/63	–	1:101
10/25/61–7/20/63	Fredericksburg, 4/30/63	5/1/63	2:21
2/24/64–7/8/65	Danville Railroad, VA, 9/30/64	10/1/64	1:226
9/28/61–12/16/64	near Atlanta, 8/6/64	–	2:26
12/28/61–11/1/62	Corinth, 10/3/62	10/4/62	1:132
9/30/61–6/24/65	Fort Fisher, 3/25/65	–	2:9
7/10/61–2/13/63	White Oak Swamp, VA, 6/30/62	7/28/62, fragments extracted; 9/1/62, exc.	1:213
2/6/64–2/24/65	Wilderness, 5/6/64	5/16/64, exc.	1:88*
3/29/64–10/24/64	Cold Harbor, 6/3/64	–	2:12
8/22/62–10/6/64	Knoxville, 11/18/63	–	1:68
5/10/61–8/28/63	Fort Wagner, 7/18/63		1:231
9/19/61–12/14/63	Gettysburg, 7/2/63	–	2:82
8/11/62–12/11/65	Old River Lake, AR, 6/6/64	–, exc.	1:41; 2:25
7/12/61–12/11/62; 5/29/63–6/1/66	Antietam, 9/17/62	–	2:90
8/5/61–8/30/64	Cold Harbor, 6/2/64	6/3/64	1:124
1/17/62–4/6/63	Arkansas Post, 1/11/63	–	1:120; 2:37
5/21/61–6/19/64	Cold Harbor, 6/5/64	–	2:18
10/18/61–1/13/63; 5/29/63–6/1/66	Antietam, 9/17/62	9/19/62	1:218
8/6/62–4/8/65	near Decatur, AL, 6/24/64	7/16/64	2:45
4/27/61–6/30/62	1st Kernstown, VA, 3/23/62	4/28/62	1:152
4/18/61–1/19/64	Chickamauga, 9/19/63	9/20/63	2:77
5/14/61–9/3/63	accidental rifle discharge, 8/2/63	8/4/63	1:57

Name (Dates)	Residence	Regiment, Company (rank if above private)
Lippincott, Isaac E. (1838–1920)	Gloucester County, NJ	Cpl., 95th PA, B
Littleton, John E. (1841–1909)	Philadelphia, PA	2nd Lt., 28th PA Veteran Vols., C
Livermore, William Byron (1837–1916)	Centre Lisle, NY	89th NY, F
Lombard, David C. (1840–92)	West Bath, ME	19th ME, K
Long, George Howard (1842–1908)	Boston, MA	1st Lt., 29th MA, H; 29th MA, E
Lott, Alexander H. (1846–1932)	McCutchenville, OH	123rd OH, D
Lowell, Delmer R. (1844–1912)	Middlefield, NY	121st NY, G
Lower, William H. (1841–79)	Trenton, IL	90th PA, H
Ludford, John A., Jr. (1847–88)	Bridgeport, CT	2nd CT Heavy Art., K
Mabbett, Alonzo L. (1835–1917)	Rochester, NY	Capt., 24th CT, I
MacNulty, William Augustus (1836–1920)	Warrenton, VA	Sgt., 10th NY, A; 2nd Lt., 16th VRC, I; Bvt. Capt., U.S. Vols.
Mangan, James (1828–69)	Gratitude, NJ	15th NJ, D
Mann, James (1838–78?)	Alma, Canada	5th NY Cav., I
Martratt, Matthew H. (1840–81)	Waterford, NY	169th NY, C
Masius, Leopold (1836–97)	New York, NY	Cpl., 66th NY, A
McEwan, William G. (1837–1925)	Philadelphia, PA	3rd Asst. Engineer, USS *Hartford*
McGeehan, Thomas A. (1839–84)	South Bergen, NJ; Albany, NY	11th NY, D; 47th NY, A; Sgt., 155th NY, D
McKean, Joshua L. (1822–89)	Coloma, MI	Cpl., 12th MI, B
McKinny, George J. (1843–68)	Reading, PA	Cpl., 128th PA, B
McLeod, William (1841–1924)	Hemlock Lake, NY	104th NY, G
McMillan, John M. (1812–93)	Gaines Station, MI	7th MI, H
Metcalf, Chesley L. (1844–1924)	Upper Stillwater, ME	1st ME Heavy Art., I
Miles, Richard (1839–1902)	Harrisburg, PA	4th PA, H; Cpl., 148th PA, H

Service	Wounding location and date	Amputation date	Contest and entry
8/26/61–3/18/65	Charlestown, VA, 8/21/64	–, exc.; 9/8/64	2:41
7/3/61–2/1/65	Pine Knob, TN, 6/16/64	right finger amputated at home	1:155
10/22/61–10/19/62	Antietam, 9/17/62	9/18/62	1:59
8/2/62–10/28/63	Gettysburg, 7/2/63	7/3/63	1:212
11/5/61–10/11/64	Cold Harbor, 6/1/64	6/3/64, exc.	1:16
1/29/64–7/25/65	Petersburg, 3/30/65	3/31/65	1:131
9/2/64–6/19/65	Sailor's Creek, VA, 4/6/65	4/7/65	1:228
12/31/61–10/12/63	Gettysburg, 7/1/63	7/2/63	1:175
8/16/62–2/25/65	Cold Harbor, 6/1/64	6/3/64	1:11
9/8/62–9/30/63	Port Hudson, 6/17/63	–; 7/8/63	1:176
4/21/61–5/6/63	Fredericksburg, 12/13/62	–	1:238
8/15/62–5/17/65	Spotsylvania, 5/12/64	5/13/64	2:17
1/7/64–6/65?	Wilderness, 5/5/64	5/15/64	1:138
8/25/62–7/27/65	Cold Harbor, 6/1/64	6/2/64	1:116
10/10/61–12/22/64	Ream's Station, VA, 8/25/64	8/26/64	1:191
12/24/63–c.1890?	Mobile Bay, 8/8/64		1:122*
4/20/61–7/4/65	Cold Harbor, 6/3/64	6/10/64	1:135; 2:33
9/6/61–9/28/63	Shiloh, 4/6/62	4/7/62	1:87
8/5/62–11/29/62	Antietam, 9/17/62	–	2:104
10/15/61–11/12/62	2nd Bull Run, 8/30/62	9/1/62	1:105; 2:100
2/5/64–9/8/64	Petersburg, 1864		1:143
7/27/62–3/22/65	Petersburg, 6/18/64	–	2:71
4/19/61–7/13/63	Chancellorsville, 5/5/63	–	1:13

Name (Dates)	Residence	Regiment, Company (rank if above private)
Moenninger, Charles V. (1829–94)	Floraville, IL	Cpl., 9th IL, D
Moffit, Andrew J. (1836–1926)	Ripley Landing, WV	Sgt., 3rd WV Cav., H
Moore, Wallace Mordecai (1841–1932)	East Charleston, PA	13th PA Reserves (1st PA Rifles), E; Cpl., 190th PA, E
Moore, William Fithian (1836–1908)	Bridgeton, NJ	Cpl., 12th NJ, K
Mulhall, William (1839–1914)	Washington, DC	4th U.S. Art., Batt. K
Mull, David O. (1844–90)	Columbus, OH	Sgt., 113th OH, H; 2nd Battalion VRC, 124
Myers, Henry W. (1841–78)	St. Louis, MO	30th IL, H
Newling, James E. (1845–1922)	Troy, NY	83rd NY, D; 97th NY, D; 2nd Battalion VRC, 75
Noble, [William Henry] Harrison (1832–1907)	North Norway, ME	Musician, 10th ME, G; Cpl., 29th ME, G
North, Edgar (1840–1915)	Watertown, NY	Cpl., 35th NY, G
Northrop, John Wesley, Jr. (1843–72)	Oberlin, OH	103rd OH, F
Northwood, John A. (1838–1922)	Flushing, MI	16th MI, C
Norton, Charles A. Quincy (1841–1915)	Bangor, ME	1st ME Cav., K; 7th NH, K
Norton, Francis M. (1842–1921)	Pine Grove, NY	76th NY, C
O'Connell, John (1841–1910)	Washington, DC	11th VT/1st VT Heavy Art., K; 14th VRC, H
Otis, Frank George (1842–78)	Colchester, CT; Kensington, CT	2nd Lt., 10th CT, G
Palmer, Barnabas Dorr (1844–80)	Lawrence, KS	1st Sgt., 9th KS Cav., C; Capt., 5th U.S. Vols., K
Palmer, Henry W. (1845–after 1910)	Corinth, ME	31st ME, H
Parker, Alvah J. (1838–1915)	Leominster, MA	2nd MA, G
Parmelee, Henry Spencer (1844–1902)	New Haven, CT	Sgt., 1st CT Cav., B
Patterson, Joseph M. (1830–1906)	Piqua, OH	Sgt., 110th OH, A
Pendergrast, Jesse S. (1835–97)	North Truro, MA	Cpl., 24th MA, F

Service	Wounding location and date	Amputation date	Contest and entry
8/10/61–9/27/62	Shiloh, 4/6/62	4/11/62	2:40
8/18/62–1/14/64	White Sulphur Springs, WV, 8/27/63	—	1:181
4/22/61–12/1/64	Weldon Railroad, 8/19/64	—	2:114
8/6/62–5/30/65	Wilderness, 5/12/64	n/a; disabled arm and hand	2:83
4/1/61–4/1/64	Chancellorsville, 5/3/63	—	1:119
8/22/62–12/27/64	Kennesaw Mountain, GA, 6/27/64	—	1:249
9/15/61–2/1/62	Belmont, MO, 11/7/61	11/14/61	1:83
12/28/63–6/5/65	Spotsylvania, 5/9/64	n/a	1:204
10/4/61–9/7/65	Cedar Creek, VA, 10/19/64	—	1:229
4/28/61–10/3/62	2nd Bull Run, 8/30/62	9/6/62	1:174
8/11/62–7/30/64	Knoxville, 11/25/63	—, exc.	2:65
8/9/61–8/18/62	Gaines's Mill, 6/27/62	6/28/62	1:8
6/26/62–4/28/65	Fort Fisher, 1/15/65	—	1:250
7/27/63–9/13/64	Wilderness, 5/5/64	—	1:197
7/14/62–12/23/64	Cold Harbor, 6/1/64	n/a	1:129
9/18/61–7/4/65	Fort Gregg (Petersburg), 4/2/65		1:62; 2:107
8/13/61–4/18/64; 4/19/65–7/3/66	near Fort Scott, KS, 7/2/63	7/12/63	1:134; 2:28
3/31/64–12/2/64	Spotsylvania, 5/12/64	—	1:73
5/21/61–10/21/62	Cedar Mountain, 8/9/62	8/11/62	1:182
9/8/62–6/20/65	Harper's Farms, VA, 4/6/65	—	1:94
8/20/62–3/14/65	Wilderness, 5/6/64	5/7/64	2:76
11/18/61–11/19/64	near Bermuda Hundred, VA, 6/17/64	—; also lost two fingers and thumb of left hand	1:118

Name (Dates)	Residence	Regiment, Company (rank if above private)
Perrine, Thomas A. (1842–90)	Monroe, OH	2nd Sgt., 140th PA, G
Perry, Frederick L. (1843–1909)	Springfield, MA	Cpl., 36th MA, E
Phair/Fair, Edwin [alias Thomas E. Elliott] (1845–96)	Brooklyn, NY	64th NY, A
Phillips, Josiah (1845–1900)	Haverstraw, NY	95th NY, F
Pickle, John (1844–1929)	Elderton, PA	Cpl., 63rd PA, G
Pinn, Robert A. (1843–1911)	Massillon, OH	1st Sgt., 5th U.S. Colored Inf., I
Platt, Frederick M. (1841–71)	Port Chester, NY	Cpl., 10th CT, G
Post, Charles R. (1842–1922)	Fort Hamilton, NY	173rd NY, F
Presley, Charles R. (1842–95)	New York, NY	Gunboat *Emma Duncan*
Putnam, Sylvanus B. (1835–95)	Manchester, NH	10th NH, D
Randolph, Alfred T. (1842–1919)	Shiloh, NJ	Cpl., 10th NJ, D
Raymond, John H. (1837–1901)	Augusta, ME	Sgt., 3rd ME, A
Reed, William W. (1816–85)	Cascade, WI	36th WI, E
Reynolds, John W. (1834–98)	Sycamore, OH	15th OH, G; Sgt., 49th OH, G
Richardson, William H. (1844–?)	Port Chester, NY	69th NY State Militia (182nd NY), F
Robins, William Bradley (1836–1912)	Sand Lake, NY	5th NY Heavy Art., H
Robinson, Rufus Lewis (1827–1916)	Frankfort, NY	121st NY, D
Robison, John Armstrong (1837–1910)	Savanna, IL	Cpl., 96th IL, F
Rockwood, Heman S. (1844–1915)	Parishville, NY	106th NY, E
Rockwood, Simeon Augustus (1838–73)	Boston, MA	Cpl., 25th MA, F
Roe, Alexander (1842–1920)	Randolph, OH	Cpl., 1st OH Light Art., A
Roripaugh, Buell (1844–73)	Cincinnatus, NY	157th NY, C
Ross, Frank (1844–1928)	Orneville, ME	Cpl., 14th ME, E
Roth, Lewis H. (1839–1916)	Slatington, PA	12th PA Reserves (41st PA), E

Service	Wounding location and date	Amputation date	Contest and entry
8/21/62–8/7/63	Chancellorsville, 5/3/63	—	1:50
7/17/62–11/14/62	Petersburg, 8/11/64	8/12/64	1:165; 2:78
9/14/64–11/25/65	Farmville (High Bridge), VA, 4/7/65	—	1:188
4/2/64–11/14/64	Wilderness, 5/5/64	n/a; shot through wrist	1:234
8/6/61–9/1/64	Wilderness, 5/5/64	5/12/64	2:49
9/5/63–9/20/65	Richmond, 9/29/64	n/a	1:29
8/31/61–8/27/63	Kinston, NC, 12/14/62	—	1:32
9/5/62–6/23/64	Cane River Crossing, LA, 4/23/64	—	1:89; 2:110
3/16/63–10/63	Green Bottom Bar, TN, 4/24/63	—	2:4
8/11/62–6/27/65	Cold Harbor, 6/3/64	—	2:43
10/9/61–4/6/65	near Winchester, 8/17/64	—	1:194
4/23/61–6/28/64	Chancellorsville, 5/2/63	n/a	1:21
2/20/64–1/6/65	Petersburg, 6/18/64		1:158*
4/19/61–5/29/65	Nashville, 12/16/64	—	1:240; 2:31
9/24/62–7/8/65	Cold Harbor, 6/3/64	—	1:77; 2:79
3/3/62–3/9/65	near Halltown, VA, 8/26/64	8/29/64	2:106
8/11/62–5/29/65	near Fort Fisher, 4/2/65	—	1:71; 2:80
8/15/62–3/16/64	Chickamauga, 9/20/63	9/28/63	1:266
8/8/62–2/18/65	3rd Winchester, 9/19/64	—	1:265
9/23/61–10/20/64	Arrowfield Church (Petersburg), 5/9/64	5/15/64	1:246
8/27/61–10/25/64	Resaca, 5/15/64	n/a; hand disabled	1:46*
8/11/62–4/13/64	Gettysburg, 7/1/63	7/2/63	1:82; 2:94
12/28/61–5/26/65	3rd Winchester, 9/19/64	—	1:253
5/30/61–12/15/62	South Mountain, 9/14/62	10/2/62	1:171; 2:89

Name (Dates)	Residence	Regiment, Company (rank if above private)
Rothwell, Robert J. (1818–c.1870?)	Blue Creek, OH	70th OH, C
Russ, George F. (1840–1927)	Dayton, OH	Sgt., 110th OH, B
Russell, Alexander M. (1844–80)	Janesville, WI	12th Batt., WI Light Art.
Sanborn, Thomas T. (1823–89)	South Strafford, VT	Sgt., 15th VT, A; 17th VT, I
Sanderson, Frederick L. (1840–86)	Petersham, MA	53rd MA, F
Sands, William Penn (1844–1901)	Columbus, OH	Sgt., 5th OH, C; Priv., 2nd Battalion VRC, 111
Savage, Joseph (1835–1912)	Harlem, NY	Sgt. Maj., 64th NY
Schmidt, August (1832–1905)	Grand Rapids, MI	Sgt., 3rd MI, C
Seague, Richard Watson (1837–1907)	White Pigeon, MI	1st Lt. and Quartermaster, 4th MI
Shaw, Junius B. (1839–1917)	Mansfield, OH	65th OH, D
Shaw, Walter B. (1838–192[illegible])	Vassalboro, ME; Washington, DC	Cpl., 19th ME, B
Sheldon, Henry H. (1843–1921)	Richmond, IL	45th IL, F
Shepard, Silas M. (1840–98)	Charleston, IL	1st Lt., 123rd IL, A
Sherman, Daniel J. (1842–69)	Williamson, NY	17th NY, I; VRC (unassigned)
Shurtleff, Albert T. (1837–1902)	Washington, DC	1st RI, D
Smith, Anselm J. (1844–1913)	Buffalo, NY	Sgt., 164th NY, D
Smith, James H. (1836–?)	Harlem, NY	4th NY Ind. Batt.; 5th PA Cav., H
Smith, John Milton (1831–1902)	Brooklyn, NY	26th NJ, C; 10th NJ, E
Smith, Joseph F. (1844–1931)	Moline, IL	37th IL, H
Smith, Matthias N. (1843–1914)	Point Pleasant, PA; New York, NY	1st PA Reserves (30th PA), G
Snider, Leonard A. (1841–78)	Lima, OH; Hogg Creek, OH	33rd OH, K
Soule, Martin Bradford (1838–1927)	Waterville, ME	Sgt., 16th ME, E
Spaulding, Edward Asa (1846–1927)	Churchville, NY	8th NY Heavy Art., K

Service	Wounding location and date	Amputation date	Contest and entry
11/29/61–8/23/62	Shiloh, 4/7/62	–	1:264*
8/9/62–7/21/65	Petersburg, 4/2/65	–	2:16
8/29/62–3/30/65	Savannah, 12/15/64	–	1:206
8/29/62–8/24/65	Poplar Grove Church (Petersburg), 9/30/64	10/1/64	1:102
9/15/62–6/28/63	Port Hudson, 6/14/63	–	1:244
4/20/61–6/3/62	Winchester, 3/23/62	3/27/62, exc.	1:6
10/30/61–1/19/64	Gettysburg, 7/2/63	–	1:232
5/13/61–10/12/62	2nd Bull Run, 8/29/62	–	1:56
6/3/61–12/31/63	Gettysburg, 7/2/63	n/a; shot through right lung	1:4
10/12/61–4/16/64	Chickamauga, 9/20/63	9/23/63	1:106
7/16/63–3/24/65	Spotsylvania, 5/12/64	–	1:180
12/3/61–12/7/63	Vicksburg, 6/25/63		1:99
9/6/62–8/8/63	Perryville, KY 10/8/62	n/a	1:34
9/12/61–5/21/63	2nd Bull Run, 8/30/62	9/5/62	2:10
4/17/61–10/30/61	1st Bull Run, 7/21/61	7/24/61	2:61
8/20/62–9/23/65	Spotsylvania, 5/18/64	–	1:190
8/29/62–6/17/65	Darbytown Road, VA, 10/7/64	–	1:233
9/1/62–5/15/65	Cedar Creek, VA, 10/19/64	10/24/64	1:130; 2:2
8/18/61–7/16/62	Pea Ridge, AR, 3/7/62	3/14/62	1:48
7/12/61–10/14/62	Charles City Crossroads, VA, 6/30/62	7/2/62	1:270
10/13/61–1/7/64	Chickamauga, 9/19/63	9/20/63	1:263; 2:62
8/14/62–6/4/64	Gettysburg, 7/1/63	10/29/63, exc.	1:159
1/5/64–10/3/64	Cold Harbor 6/3/64	6/4/64	1:257

Name (Dates)	Residence	Regiment, Company (rank if above private)
Stage, Joseph Fayette (1839–1916)	New York, NY	9th NY, A
Steen, Benjamin Strong (1840–1915	Brooklyn, NY	Cpl., 14th NY State Militia, C
Stephens, Robert Elder (1842–1916)	Newport, IN	Cpl., 71st IN (6th IN Cav.), K
Stewart, John (1837–1911)	Philadelphia, PA	Sgt., 3rd NJ, C
Stiles, Burritt (1838–1912)	Meriden, CT	14th CT, A
Stiles, Richard (1822–1908)	Benton, PA	199th PA, B
Stilwell, Daniel Duane (1837–1910)	Dansville, NY	Sgt., 13th NY, B
Stone, Augustus (1840–96)	Worcester, MA	25th MA, A; 2nd Lt., 4th MA Heavy Art., D
Stoutenburg, Hiram E. (1842–1910)	Delhi, NY	Sgt., 101st NY, G; 37th NY, A; 40th NY, E
Strayer, Adam F. (1846–1932)	Apple Grove, PA	21st PA Cav., C; 188th PA, B
Sutherland, Robert J. (1836–70)	Washington, DC	19th PA, F; 2nd Lt., 109th PA, B; 2nd Battalion VRC, 71; 24th VRC, G
Sutherland, Seth (1836–68)	Ironton, OH	1st Sgt., 18th OH, E; 3rd Sgt., 5th OH Light Art.
Taylor, George W. (1839–1926)	Washington, DC	1st Sgt., 9th NJ, H
Thomas, George W. (1845–1901)	Nantucket, MA	24th MA Veteran Vol., D
Thomas, Harrison Otis (1840–1916)	North Bridgewater, MA	3rd MA, L; Cpl., 18th MA, D
Thomas, William Hannibal (1843–1935)	Allegheny City, PA	Sgt., 5th U.S. Colored Inf., I
Thompson, John M. (1838–74)	Perrysville, PA	Capt., 49th PA, A
Till, William A. (1843–97)	Sandusky, OH	23rd OH, A; 2nd Battalion VRC, 111
Tolman, Minott (1823–1901)	West Camden, ME	1st ME Heavy Art., G
Touris/Tours/Turse, John M. (1840–1907)	Mianus, CT	Cpl., 70th NY, I
Tracy, Arunah (1845–79)	Carmel, ME	18th ME, F; Cpl., 1st ME Heavy Art., F
Trevor, Baxter (1843–1921)	Cleveland, OH	55th OH, D
Tucker, William J. (1840–77)	Dayton, OH	4th KY, E; 2nd Battalion VRC, 42

Service	Wounding location and date	Amputation date	Contest and entry
4/23/61–5/20/63	Camden, NC, 4/19/62	4/21/62	1:198
4/18/61–12/16/62	2nd Bull Run, 8/29/62	3/23/64	1:203
8/18/62–5/27/65	railroad accident near Dalton, GA, 11/4/64	c. 11/25/64	1:23
5/25/61–10/27/62	Gaines's Mill, 6/27/62	6/28/62	1:93
8/8/63–6/16/65	Wilderness, 5/12/64	—	2:70
2/22/65–6/19/65	Fort Gregg (Petersburg), 4/2/65	—	1:183
4/14/61–12/22/62	2nd Bull Run, 8/30/62	9/17/62	1:214
10/1/61–6/17/65	Arrowfield Church (Petersburg), 5/9/64	—	1:125
11/14/61–12/28/64	Petersburg, 9/10/64	9/11/64	1:140; 2:87
7/8/63–5/29/65	Chaffin's Farm (Petersburg), 9/29/64	9/30/64	2:13
5/18/61–6/30/66	Chancellorsville, 5/3/63	—	2:88
4/22/61–11/1/62	Shiloh, 4/6/62	—	1:1
10/3/61–8/23/64	Cold Harbor, 6/3/64	—	1:19
11/19/61–5/30/65	Deep Bottom, VA, 8/16/64	8/27/64	2:27
4/16/61–3/28/63	Fredericksburg, 12/13/62	—, exc.	1:78; 2:58
9/23/63–7/25/65	Wilmington, NC, 2/20/65	—	1:193
9/3/61–1/13/65	3rd Winchester, 9/19/64	—	2:63
5/18/61–12/11/62	Antietam, 9/17/62	10/24/62	1:17
12/28/63–6/14/65	Petersburg, 6/18/64	8/2/64	2:74
4/24/61–7/1/64	Spotsylvania, 5/12/64	—	1:173*
8/12/62–12/16/64	Petersburg, 6/18/64	6/19/64	1:161
10/7/64–6/14/65	near Goldsboro, NC, 3/19/65	—	1:211
8/27/61–11/7/64	railroad collision, Shohola, PA, 7/15/64	7/16/64	1:5

Name (Dates)	Residence	Regiment, Company (rank if above private)
Tuerk, Julius G. (1831–86)	Davenport, IA	4th U.S. Art., Batt. B; 1st Lt., 3rd NJ Batt.; 1st Lt. and Quartermaster, 114th USCT, A
Turner, John (1842–1918)	Bloomville, OH	Sgt., 49th OH, G
Turrell/Terrill, Jared D. (1841–1916)	Plymouth, MI; Washington, DC	1st MI Cav., H
Tuttle, Alfred B. (1843–1908)	Manlius, NY	23rd NY, H; 15th NY Cav., F
Tyler, George E. (1837–1905)	Painesville, OH	Sgt., 23rd OH, I
Vallereux, Frank G. (Francois Gustavers) (1842–1922)	Mount Sterling, IL	1st IL Light Art., Batt. C
Van Schaack, Peter G. (1834–1902)	Coxsackie, NY	120th NY, D
Vanbrimmer, Curley L. (1841–99)	Westfield, OH	3rd OH, I
Vignos, Augustus (1838–1926)	Louisville, OH	Musician, 19th OH, I; Maj., 107th OH
Vroman, Norman (1841–1929)	Flint, MI	Cpl., 60th NY, C
Wagner, Abram (1845–1906)	Vernon, IN	12th IN, A
Wait, George Addison (1840–73)	Fort Edward, NY; New York, NY	1st Lt., 122nd NY, K; 10th NY, F
Walbridge, Ora D. (1842–1917)	Marseilles, IL	104th IL, D
Walters, Thomas (1842–1910)	Bridgeport, CT	48th NY, G, E
Warner, George S. (1846–1911)	Zanesville, OH	13th OH Cav., F
Warren, Will, Jr. (1842–1937)	Evansville, IN	24th IN, F
Wasson, Andrew James (1843–1910)	Mariaville, NY	134th NY, H
Watson, William D. (1837–82)	Philadelphia, PA	71st PA, C; 2nd Lt., 71st PA, E
Weaver, Caius A. (1844–1925)	De Ruyter, NY	122nd NY, B
Weidner, William A. (1844–87)	College Corner, OH	Cpl., 37th IN, B
Weitershausen, Charles R. (1841–99)	Allegheny City, PA	9th PA Reserves (38th PA), B; Bvt. Maj. and Asst. Quartermaster, U.S. Vols.; Bvt. Maj. 44th U.S. Infantry
Whims, Jasper (1840–99)	Hookstown, PA	140th PA, H

Service	Wounding location and date	Amputation date	Contest and entry
3/1/52–5/5/67	Fort Haskell (Petersburg), 3/25/65	–	2:3
8/18/61–10/28/64	Dallas, GA, 5/27/64	5/28/64	1:172; 2:22
8/13/61–12/5/65	2nd Bull Run, 8/29/62	10/1/62	1:200
10/23/61–6/20/65	Appomattox Court House, 4/8/65	–	1:247
5/22/61–11/7/62	South Mountain, 9/14/62	–	1:58
9/8/61–9/13/64	Ruffin's Station, GA, 7/4/64	–	1:33
8/6/62–12/9/63	Gettysburg, 7/2/63	n/a; forearm wound	2:60
4/19/61–3/28/63	Perryville, KY, 10/8/62	–	1:111
4/27/61–9/30/64	Gettysburg, 7/1/63	7/3/63	1:195
8/27/61–2/13/65	Kennesaw Mountain, GA, 6/15/64	6/16/64	1:31
6/1/62–3/24/63	Richmond, KY, 8/30/62	n/a; 5 wounds in arm and hand	1:22
8/11/62–5/20/65	Spotsylvania, 5/11/64	5/13/64	1:123; 2:69
8/7/62–5/5/64	Heartsville, TN, 12/7/62	n/a; forearm wound	1:24
8/21/61–6/24/65	Petersburg, 7/30/64	–	1:209
3/3/64–7/27/65	High Bridge, VA, 4/7/65	–	1:260
3/4/62–10/23/62	Champion Hill, MS, 5/16/62	–	1:208
8/14/62–5/9/64	Gettysburg, 7/1/63	7/2/63	1:237
4/15/61–7/2/64	Cold Harbor, 6/3/64	–, exc.; 7/23/64; 10/12/65	1:210; 2:108
8/11/62–6/19/65	Fort Stevens, DC, 7/9/64	7/12/64	2:86
8/23/61–11/29/64	Atlanta, 7/21/64	7/29/64	2:97
4/18/61–9/28/62	Charles City Crossroads, VA, 6/30/62	c. 8/6/62, exc.	1:168
8/11/62–12/16/64	Spotsylvania, 5/12/64	–	1:37

Name (Dates)	Residence	Regiment, Company (rank if above private)
Whipple, John Frank (1842–1923)	Ipswich, MA	1st MI Cav.; 1st MA Heavy Art., L
White, George Quincy (1839–97)	Richmond, VA; Chicago, IL	Capt., 1st IL Light Art., Batt. B; Bvt. Maj. and Asst. Quartermaster, U.S. Vols.; Bvt. Maj. 44th U.S. Infantry
Whitehouse, Alfred D. (1839–1919)	New York, NY	8th NY State Militia, D
Whitehouse, Phineas P. (1842–1910)	South Hampton, NH	Cpl., 6th NH, C
Whitford, John Updike (1838–1920)	Wakefield, RI	USS *Rhode Island;* 1st RI Light Art., Batt. A
Wilbur, Stephen D. (1841–1920)	Hawleyton, NY	109th NY, E
Williams, Alva John (1842–96)	Sandy Hill, NY	22nd NY, B
Wise, Elisha R. (1838–1924)	Pittsburgh, PA	7th PA, A; 1st Sgt., 11th PA, F; 2nd Battalion VRC, 109
Wood, Julius V. (1839–1930)	Chesterville, OH	96th OH, C
Woods, James (1838?–?)	St. Louis, MO	7th MO, C
Wooster, Uri Tracy (1842–1902)	Windsor, NY	89th NY, G
Works, Frank P. (1835–1908)	East Brookfield, MA	24th MA, I

Service	Wounding location and date	Amputation date	Contest and entry
11/61–7/3/65	firing salute to surrender, Worcester, MA, 4/10/65	—	2:52
6/19/61–12/15/70	Belmont, MO, 11/7/61	—	1:141
2/1/59–11/12/61	1st Bull Run, 7/21/61	9/21/61	1:163; 2:73
8/25/62–8/15/65	Spotsylvania, 5/18/64	—, exc.	1:136; 2:8
7/22/62–8/20/63; 2/16/64–9/26/64	Cold Harbor, 6/3/64	6/4/64	1:91
8/9/62–6/23/65	Fort Hill (Petersburg), 4/2/65	—	1:185
4/23/61–11/18/62	South Mountain, 9/14/62	—	1:217
4/20/61–9/5/64	Gettysburg, 7/1/63	7/3/63	1:267; 2:34
8/8/62–1/16/64	Grand Coteau, LA, 11/3/63	—	1:115
6/1/61–9/9/63	Vicksburg, 5/22/63	—	1:153
10/19/61–10/31/64	Petersburg, 10/21/64	—, exc.	1:26
2/27/64–8/5/65	Richmond, 7/16/64	n/a; hand disabled	1:164

APPENDIX B

List of Battles

ANTIETAM (September 17, 1862). Culmination of the Antietam Campaign. McClellan's and Lee's armies met near Sharpsburg, Maryland, and battled west of Antietam Creek. Principal fighting shifted from the north to the south through the day, occurring in a cornfield and surrounding woods to the north, a sunken road that became known as "Bloody Lane" in the center, and to the south a bridge that Burnside's IX Corps encountered difficulties in taking and the hills beyond it, where A. P. Hill's late-arriving division pushed Burnside's troops back and ended the battle. McClellan chose not to attack on the eighteenth, and Lee retreated back to Virginia the following day. Militarily inconclusive and, with over 22,000 casualties, one of the bloodiest battles in American history. But Lee's retreat offered Lincoln the occasion to issue his preliminary Emancipation Proclamation. Also known as Sharpsburg.

BRANDY STATION (June 9, 1863). Largest cavalry battle of the war, fought in Virginia by Union cavalry of the Army of the Potomac (AOTP) and Stuart's Confederate cavalry of the Army of Northern Virginia (AONV). Inconclusive.

BULL RUN, first battle of (July 21, 1861). First major battle of the war. McDowell's forces met Beauregard's troops, defending the railroad junction at Manassas, Virginia, south of Bull Run creek. Joe Johnston and Jackson reinforced Beauregard by rail from the Shenandoah Valley, leading to Confederate victory and Union retreat. Also known as First Manassas.

BULL RUN, second battle of (August 28–30, 1862). Jackson attacked a column of Pope's Army of Virginia near Warrenton Turnpike on the twenty-eighth (often called the Battle of Groveton), and Pope counterattacked on the twenty-ninth. Longstreet destroyed the Union left on the thirtieth, leading to Confederate victory. Heavy casualties on both sides. Also known as Second Manassas.

CEDAR MOUNTAIN (August 9, 1862). Jackson attacked Banks's II Corps, Army of Virginia, outside Culpeper, Virginia. A. P. Hill reinforced Jackson, forcing Banks to retreat.

CHANCELLORSVILLE (April 30–May 5, 1863). Lee's AONV, outnumbered two to one, confronted Hooker's AOTP south of the Rapidan River in Spotsylvania County, Virginia. Lee divided his forces multiple times to launch aggressive attacks, eventually forcing Hooker to withdraw. Jackson, key to Confederate victory, was mortally wounded by friendly fire. Arguably Lee's greatest victory, it inspired his subsequent Gettysburg Campaign.

CHICKAHOMINY RIVER. *See Gaines's Mill.*

CHICKAMAUGA (September 18–20, 1863). Engagement in Georgia between Rosecrans's Army of the Cumberland (AOTC) and Bragg's Army of Tennessee. AONV forces under Longstreet arrived on the nineteenth, helping force a Union retreat to Chattanooga.

COLD HARBOR (May 31–June 12, 1864). Toward the end of the Overland Campaign, forces under Lee and Grant met near crossroads leading to Richmond. Grant eventually shifted his army south of the James River to attack Petersburg, outflanking Lee and attempting to take Richmond from the south.

CORINTH, siege of (April 29–May 30, 1862). After Shiloh, Beauregard retreated to Corinth, Mississippi, a strategic railroad town. Halleck began advancing on April 29 and started the siege in early May. His army weakened by disease and dirty water, Beauregard eventually withdrew.

FAIR OAKS (May 31–June 1, 1862). Inconclusive battle between forces under McClellan and Joe Johnston during Peninsula Campaign. Also known as Seven Pines.

FORT FISHER, second battle of (January 13–15, 1865). Naval forces under Porter and troops under Terry jointly attacked and captured the North Carolina fort, the last Confederate stronghold.

FORT WAGNER (July 10–September 7, 1863). Gillmore attempted to take the fort on Morris Island in Charleston Harbor multiple times. On July 18, the 54th Massachusetts of the USCT led an attack. This assault failed, but continued heavy bombardment eventually forced Confederate troops to abandon the position.

FREDERICKSBURG, first battle of (December 11–13, 1862). Burnside's AOTP crossed the Rappahannock here and faced Lee's well-placed and prepared AONV. Disastrous frontal assaults on the Confederates' elevated and fortified positions on the thirteenth led to more than 12,000 Union casualties. Burnside retreated back across the river.

FREDERICKSBURG, second battle of (May 3, 1863). While Hooker faced Lee at Chancellorsville, Early's Confederates remained in positions behind Fredericksburg and faced Union troops under Sedgwick. Early's troops retreated toward Chancellorsville and clashed with Sedgwick's at Salem Church.

GAINES'S MILL (June 27, 1862). One of the Seven Days' Battles, fought by Porter's V Corps, AOTP, and Lee's AONV near the Chickahominy River east of Richmond. Despite heavy casualties on both sides, Porter withdrew.

GETTYSBURG (July 1–3, 1863). One of the most significant battles of the war and a major turning point in the East and the war as a whole. Lee's AONV, advancing into Pennsylvania, met Meade's AOTP at the small crossroads town. Union forces included I Corps under Reynolds/Doubleday, II Corps under Gibbon, VI Corps under Sedgwick, and XI Corps under Howard; Confederate forces included Longstreet's First Corps, A. P. Hill's Third Corps, and Stuart's cavalry. Over 50,000 casualties made it the bloodiest battle of the war. Decisive Union victory forced Lee to retreat back to Virginia.

GROVETON (August 28, 1862). *See Bull Run, second battle of.*

HONEY HILL (November 30, 1864). Failed Union attempt to cut the railroad in South Carolina leading to Savannah, Georgia.

LOOKOUT MOUNTAIN (November 24, 1863). Grant ordered Hooker to capture the mountain, occupied by Confederate troops, southwest of the besieged AOTC within Chattanooga, Tennessee. The assault was successful, and Bragg removed his troops.

MILLIKEN'S BEND (June 7, 1863). Confederates attacked a supply depot on the Mississippi River in Louisiana supporting Grant's Vicksburg operations. The Union line held, but the USCT regiments defending it suffered heavy losses while proving that Black men could indeed fight.

MINE RUN (November 27–December 2, 1863). Meade's final attempt of 1863 against Lee's AONV, camped along the Rapidan River after Gettysburg. Inconclusive.

MORTON'S FORD (February 6–7, 1864). Part of Butler's plan to liberate Union prisoners held in Richmond. Stalemate, followed by withdrawal of Union troops.

OLUSTEE (February 20, 1864). Engagement in northern Florida. USCT troops, including the 54th Massachusetts, held off an attack on the withdrawing Union line. Confederate troops murdered wounded Black soldiers. The Union defeat ended attempts to take northern Florida.

PERRYVILLE (October 8, 1862). Battle in Kentucky between Buell's Army of the Ohio and Bragg's Army of Mississippi. Although a tactical Confederate victory, Bragg withdrew back into Tennessee, ending his Kentucky Campaign.

PETERSBURG, assault on (June 15–18, 1864). As part of his Overland Campaign, Grant moved on Petersburg, an important railroad junction south of Richmond, Virginia. Butler's Army of the James and Meade's AOTP converged on Petersburg and faced Confederate troops under Beauregard. Lee sent reinforcements that helped them retain control of the city, necessitating a siege.

PETERSBURG, siege of (June 15, 1864–April 2, 1865). Following the Union assault on Petersburg, both sides entrenched while Grant attempted to cut off Lee's supplies. A few weeks later, Burnside's troops detonated a mine underneath a portion of the Confederate works, leading to Battle of the Crater on July 30. His supplies severely diminished over the ensuing months, Lee evacuated Petersburg and Richmond after Grant's attack on April 2 cut the final rail line leading into the cities.

PITTSBURG LANDING. *See* Shiloh.

PORT HUDSON, siege of (May 22–July 9, 1863). While Grant attacked Vicksburg, Banks's Army of the Gulf targeted Port Hudson on the Mississippi River in Louisiana, surrounding it on May 22. Union troops attacked unsuccessfully on May 27, then began the siege. Following Vicksburg's capitulation, the Confederate garrison's commander surrendered, ensuring Union forces complete access to the Mississippi.

PORT ROYAL (November 7, 1861). Early Union victory securing this South Carolina port for blockade operations.

RAPPAHANNOCK STATION, second battle of (November 7, 1863). AOTP attacked AONV, encamped along the Rappahannock River. Union troops under Sedgwick routed Early's forces, and Lee's army retreated.

RESACA (May 14–15, 1864). Battle following Joe Johnston's withdrawal from Rocky Face Ridge during Sherman's Atlanta Campaign. Sherman's troops forced Johnston to retreat farther into Georgia.

ROCKY FACE RIDGE (May 7–13, 1864). Sherman attacked Joe Johnston's stronghold near the 500-foot ridge to open the Atlanta Campaign but was unable to force the Confederates' withdrawal.

SEVEN DAYS' BATTLES (June 25–July 1, 1862). Nearing Richmond during the Peninsula Campaign, McClellan spread his AOTP across the Chickahominy River. Lee attacked, using forces under Jackson, Longstreet, and A. P. Hill. The Confederates forced McClellan to retreat down the Peninsula, bringing the campaign to a close. Engagements included Mechanicsville (June 26), Savage's Station (June 29), White Oak Swamp (June 30), and Malvern Hill (July 1).

SHILOH (April 6–7, 1862). Battle in southwestern Tennessee between Grant's Army of the Tennessee, supported by Buell's Army of the Ohio, and the Confederate Army of the Mississippi under Albert Sidney Johnston and Beauregard. Johnston launched an attack on Grant's forces, camped near a log-cabin church called Shiloh. Buell's arrival on April 7 and the resulting Union counteroffensive forced the Confederates to withdraw, exposing northern Mississippi and jeopardizing Confederate control of key railroad connections there. With over 23,000 casualties, the battle was the bloodiest fought on American soil before Gettysburg. Also known as Pittsburg Landing.

SOUTH MOUNTAIN (September 14, 1862). After intercepting Lee's orders for the Antietam Campaign, McClellan moved on the AONV through gaps in South Mountain, Maryland. Fighting occurred at three gaps. The Confederates withdrew, but Lee's army was able to consolidate in time for Antietam.

SPOTSYLVANIA COURT HOUSE (May 8–21, 1864). Following the Wilderness, Grant sent the AOTP south, attempting to place it between Lee and Richmond as he continued his Overland Campaign. Stuart and Anderson quickly moved their Confederate forces to block the Union advance, and both sides began entrenching on May 9. After intense fighting and heavy casualties on both sides, Grant shifted the AOTP toward the North Anna River, attempting to flank Lee and get between the AONV and Richmond. The standard nineteenth-century spelling was "Spottsylvania."

STONES RIVER (December 31, 1862–January 2, 1863). Troops under Rosecrans and Bragg fought in Middle Tennessee near Murfreesboro. Bragg withdrew toward Chattanooga. Also known as Murfreesboro.

VICKSBURG, siege of (May 18–July 4, 1863). Vicksburg, Mississippi, was one of two remaining Confederate strongholds on the Mississippi River in 1863. Grant moved toward it starting in January 1863 and reached the city's outskirts on May 18. He initiated a siege after unsuccessful infantry assaults. Pemberton surrendered on July 4. After the surrender of Port Hudson, the Union controlled the Mississippi.

WELDON RAILROAD (August 18–21, 1864). Part of Grant's Petersburg Campaign. Union troops captured part of the railroad line linking Petersburg to Wilmington, North Carolina, cutting a line of supply for Lee's AONV.

WILDERNESS (May 5–7, 1864). First battle of the Overland Campaign. AOTP under Grant and Meade crossed the Rapidan River and attempted to move beyond the thickly wooded Wilderness west of Chancellorsville to get between the AONV and Richmond. Forces under Warren, Sedgwick, Hancock, and Burnside faced Confederate troops under Ewell and A. P. Hill. Longstreet arrived on May 6. Fighting was fierce, with heavy casualties on each side, but inconclusive. Grant then shifted his army southeast toward Spotsylvania Court House.

WILLIAMSBURG (May 5, 1862). A Peninsula Campaign engagement between McClellan's AOTP and Longstreet's division of Joe Johnston's army, following the Confederate withdrawal from Yorktown. Inconclusive.

WINCHESTER, third battle of (September 19, 1864). Sheridan's Army of the Shenandoah defeated Early's attacking Army of the Valley during the 1864 Valley Campaign. Also known as Opequon Creek.

YORKTOWN, siege of (April 5–May 4, 1862). First major action of the Peninsula Campaign.

Sources: *War of the Rebellion; Medical and Surgical History of the War of the Rebellion; Civil War Battlefield Guide;* American Battlefield Trust (battlefields.org); Jones, *Historical Dictionary of the Civil War.*

EMANCIPATION PROCLAMATION.

Whereas, On the Twenty-Second day of September, in the year of our Lord one thousand eight hundred and sixty-two, a Proclamation was issued by the President of the United States, containing, among other things the following, to wit:

"That on the first day of January, in the year of our Lord one thousand eight hundred and sixty-three, all persons held as slaves within any State or designated part of a State, the people whereof shall then be in rebellion against the United States, shall be then, thenceforth, and **FOREVER FREE**, and the **EXECUTIVE GOVERNMENT OF THE UNITED STATES**, including the military and naval authorities thereof, **WILL RECOGNIZE AND MAINTAIN THE FREEDOM** of such persons, and will do no act or acts to repress such persons, or any of them, in any efforts they may make for their actual freedom."

"That the Executive.

John H. Raymond's transcription of the Emancipation Proclamation. Courtesy William Oland Bourne Papers, Manuscript Division, Library of Congress.

BIBLIOGRAPHY

Unpublished Sources

1856 Iowa State Census. State Historical Society of Iowa Library and Research Center. Accessed via Ancestry.com, 2007.

1860, 1870, 1880, 1890, 1900, 1910, and 1920 U.S. Census. Records of the Bureau of the Census, RG 29, NARA. Microfilm.

1869 New York State Census. New York State Library, Albany. Microfilm.

1875 New York State Census. New York State Library, Albany. Microfilm.

1890 U.S. Census, Special Schedules Enumerating Union Veterans and Widows of Union Veterans of the Civil War. Records of the Department of Veterans Affairs, RG 15, NARA. Microfilm.

California Death Index, 1905–39. California Department of Health and Welfare, Sacramento. Microfilm.

Church Records, 1767–1970. The Episcopal Diocese of New York, New York City.

Civil War Soldiers: "Disabled but Not Disheartened." By the People Campaign, Library of Congress, Washington, DC. crowd.loc.gov/campaigns/civil-war-soldiers-disabled-but-not-disheartened.

Civil War Veteran Pension Files. Records of the Department of Veterans Affairs, RG 15, NARA. Microfilm.

Compiled Military Service Records of Volunteer Union Soldiers Who Served with the United States Colored Troops. Records of the Adjutant General's Office, 1780s–1917, RG 94, NARA. Microfilm.

Consolidated Lists of Civil War Draft Registration Records. Records of the Provost Marshal General's Bureau, RG 110, NARA.

District of Columbia Compiled Marriage Index, 1830–1921. Accessed via FamilySearch, 2013. https://www.familysearch.org/en/.

Grand Army of the Republic Post Reports, 1880–1940. Kansas Historical Society, Topeka.

Historical Register of National Homes for Disabled Volunteer Soldiers, 1866–1938. Records of the Department of Veterans Affairs, RG 15, NARA. Microfilm.

Illinois Marriage Index, 1860–1920. Accessed via Ancestry.com, 2015.

Index (Soundex) to Naturalization Petitions Filed in Federal, State, and Local Courts in New York City, 1792–1906. RG 85, NARA. Microfilm.

Indiana Death Certificates. Vital Records, State Archives, Indiana Archives and Records Administration, Indianapolis. Microfilm.

Iowa Department of Health. Marriage Records, 1880–1922. State Historical Society of Iowa, Des Moines, Iowa. Microfilm.

Iowa Grand Army of the Republic Membership Records, 1861–1949. RG 048, State Historical Department, Des Moines. Accessed via FamilySearch, 2020. https://www.familysearch.org/en/.

Maine Marriage Records, 1713–1922. Maine State Archives, Augusta.

Massachusetts Marriage Records, 1840–1915. New England Historic Genealogical Society, Boston.

Massachusetts Vital Records, 1840–1911. New England Historic Genealogical Society, Boston.

Methodist Episcopal Church Records in New York City and Vicinity. Manuscripts and Archives Division of the New York Public Library, New York City.

Michigan Death Records, 1907. Division for Vital Records and Health Statistics, Michigan Department of Community Health, Lansing.

New Hampshire Marriage Records Index, 1659–1947. New Hampshire Bureau of Vital Records, Concord.

New York Civil War Muster Roll Abstracts, 1861–1900. Collection 13775-83. New York State Archives, Albany. Microfilm.

New York Grand Army of the Republic Records, Post Descriptive Books. Sub-Series 11, Series B1706. New York State Archives, Albany.

New York State Death Index. New York Department of Health, Albany.

New York State Marriage Index. New York State Department of Health, Albany.

New York Town Clerks' Registers of Men Who Served in the Civil War, ca. 1861–1865. New York State Archives, Albany. Microfilm.

Ohio Department of Health. Death Records, 1908–1932. Ohio Historical Society, Columbus.

Pennsylvania Grand Army of the Republic Membership Records, 1865–1936. Accessed via FamilySearch, 2016. https://www.familysearch.org/en/.

Pennsylvania Veterans Burial Cards, 1777–2012. Bureau of Archives and History, Pennsylvania Historical and Museum Commission, Harrisburg.

Queens, NY, Letters of Administration. U.S. Wills and Probate Records, 1659–1999, New York County, District, and Probate Courts, New York City.

Record of Appointment of Postmasters, 1832–1971. Records of the Post Office Department, RG 28, NARA. Microfilm.

Records of Headstones Provided for Deceased Union Civil War Veterans, ca. 1879–1903. NARA, RG 92. Microfilm.

South Carolina Death Records, 1821–1965. South Carolina Department of Archives and History, Columbia.

U.S. Army, Register of Enlistments, 1798–1914. RG 94, NARA. Microfilm.

U.S. Naturalization Record Indexes, 1791–1992. Records of the Immigration and Naturalization Service, RG 85, NARA. Microfilm.
Virginia Department of Health, Richmond.
William Oland Bourne Left-Handed Penmanship Papers. New-York Historical Society, New York City.
William Oland Bourne Papers. Manuscript Division, Library of Congress, Washington, DC.

Newspapers and Periodicals

Akron (OH) Beacon Journal
Akron (OH) Daily Democrat
Alton Weekly (IL) Telegraph
Altoona (PA) Tribune
Appleton (WI) Post
Arcanum (OH) Times
Baltimore Daily Commercial
Baltimore Sun
Belmont Chronicle (Saint Clairsville, OH)
Beloit (WI) Daily News
Binghamton (NY) Press and Sun-Bulletin
Black Hills Weekly Journal (Rapid City, SD)
Bloomington (IL) Pantagraph
Boston Globe
Boston Post
Bridgeport (CT) Times and Evening Farmer
Brooklyn Daily Eagle
Brooklyn Evening Star
Brooklyn Standard Union
Brooklyn Times Union
Brooklyn Union
Brooklyn Weekly Eagle
Brookville (PA) Republican
Buffalo (NY) Advocate
Buffalo (NY) Commercial
Buffalo (NY) Courier
Buffalo (NY) Morning Express and Illustrated Buffalo Express
Buffalo (NY) Times
Burlington (VT) Free Press
Caldwell (KS) News
Canonsburg (PA) Weekly Notes

Carroll Free Press (Carrollton, OH)
Cedar Rapids (IA) Gazette
Chattanooga Sunday Times
Chicago Inter Ocean
Chicago Tribune
Chillicothe (OH) Gazette
Columbus (IN) Republican
Corvallis (OR) Gazette Times
Daily Kansas Tribune (Lawrence)
Daily Ohio Statesman (Columbus)
Daily State Journal (Alexandria, VA)
Dakota Farmers' Leader (Canton, SD)
Davenport (IA) Daily Times
Davenport (IA) Morning Democrat
Dayton (OH) Daily Journal
Dayton (OH) Daily News
Detroit Free Press
Elyria (OH) Independent
Evansville (IN) Daily Journal
Fall River (MA) Daily Evening News
Fitchburg (MA) Sentinel
Great Bend (KS) Tribune
Green-Mountain Freeman (Montpelier, VT)
Harper (KS) Advocate
Harper's Weekly (New York City)
Harrisburg (PA) Telegraph
Hartford (CT) Courant
Howard Union (Glasgow, MO)
Huntsville (AL) Weekly Democrat
Ilion (NY) Citizen
Indianapolis News
Indianapolis Star
Janesville (WI) Daily Gazette
Journal of the American Medical Association (Chicago)
Juniata (PA) Sentinel
Juniata Sentinel and Republican (Mifflintown, PA)
Kansas Daily Tribune (Lawrence)
Lake Geneva (WI) Herald
Lancaster (OH) Gazette
Lancaster (PA) Intelligencer
Lancaster (PA) Intelligencer Journal

Lancaster (PA) New Era
Lawrence (KS) Daily Journal
Lawrence (KS) Tribune
Lima (OH) Times-Democrat
Livonia (NY) Gazette
Los Angeles Evening Express
Los Angeles Times
Louisville (KY) Courier-Journal
Louisville (KY) Daily Courier
Ludington (MI) Daily News
Lyndonville (VT) Journal
Marion (OH) Star
Mason City (IA) Globe-Gazette
Methodist Quarterly Review (New York City)
Mineral Point (WI) Weekly Tribune
Moline (IL) Dispatch
Monmouth Inquirer (Freehold, NJ)
Montgomery (AL) Advertiser
Montpelier (VT) Daily Journal
N.J. Standard (Middletown-Point)
National Era (Washington, DC)
National Republican (Washington, DC)
Nebraska State Journal (Lincoln)
New Haven (CT) Morning Journal-Courier
New York Daily Herald
New York Sun
New York Times
New-York Tribune
North Carolina Times (New Bern)
Ogdensburg (NY) Journal
Perry County Democrat (Bloomfield, PA)
Philadelphia Evening Telegraph
Philadelphia Inquirer
Philadelphia Times
Piqua (OH) Democrat
Pittsburgh Post-Gazette
Portsmouth (OH) Daily Times
Princeton (MN) Union
Racine (WI) Journal Times
Richmond (IN) Palladium-Item
Rochester (NY) Democrat and Chronicle

Rock Island (IL) Argus
Sacramento Bee
Saint Paul (MN) Globe
St. Joseph (MI) Herald
St. Louis Post-Dispatch
St. Louis Globe-Democrat
St. Louis Republic
San Diego Evening Tribune
Scranton (PA) Times-Tribune
Soldier's Friend (New York City)
Soldier's Friend, and Grand Army of the Republic (New York City)
South Bergenite (Rutherford, NJ)
Spirit of Kansas (Lawrence)
Streator (IL) Times
Summit County Beacon (Akron, OH)
Sunday School (London, UK)
Vermont Chronicle (Bellows Falls)
Vermont Family Gazette (Bradford)
Vermont Watchman and State Journal (Montpelier)
Washington Evening Star
Washington Post
Washington Times
Watertown (WI) News
Weir (KS) Weekly Tribune
Wellington (OH) Enterprise
Wellsboro (PA) Gazette
Western Home Journal (Lawrence, KS)
Western Kansas World (WaKeeney)
Wilmington (NC) Herald
Woodstock (IL) Sentinel
Wyandotte Commercial Gazette (Kansas City, KS)
Yonkers (NY) Statesman
Zanesville (OH) Times Recorder

Published Sources

Abstract of General Orders and Proceedings of the Fortieth Annual Encampment, Department of New York, G.A.R. Albany: Brandow Print, 1906.

Alphabetical Index of Maine Volunteers. Augusta, ME: Stevens & Sayward, 1867.

American Battlefield Trust. https://www.battlefields.org/.

Annual Report of Indiana University, including the Catalogue for the Academical Year, MDCCCLXVI–VII. Indianapolis: Alexander H. Conner, 1867.

Annual Report of the Adjutant General of the State of New York for the Year [1894–1904]: Registers. Vols. 1–43. Albany: James B. Lyon, 1894–1906.

Barrett, Faith. *To Fight Aloud Is Very Brave.* Amherst: University of Massachusetts Press, 2012.

Bates, Samuel P. *History of Pennsylvania Volunteers, 1861–1865.* 5 vols. Harrisburg, PA: B. Singerly, 1869–71.

Bicknell, Thomas W. *History and Genealogy of the Bicknell Family and Some Collateral Lines.* Providence, RI: Thomas Williams Bicknell, 1913.

Billings, John Davis. *Hardtack and Coffee; or, The Unwritten Story of Army Life.* Boston: George M. Smith, 1888.

Biographical Directory of the South Dakota Legislature, 1889–1989. Vol. 1, *A–K.* South Dakota Legislative Research Council, 1989.

Blight, David W. "Decoration Days: The Origins of Memorial Day in North and South." In *The Memory of the Civil War in American Culture,* ed. Alice Fahs and Joan Waugh, 89–119. Chapel Hill: University of North Carolina Press, 2004.

Bonner, Robert E. *The Soldier's Pen: Firsthand Impressions of the Civil War.* New York: Hill and Wang, 2006.

Bourne, William Oland. *Gems from Fable-Land: A Collection of Fables Illustrated by Facts.* New York: Scribner, 1853.

———. *History of the Public School Society of the City of New York.* New York: W. Wood, 1870.

———. *Little Silverstring; or, Tales and Poems for the Young.* New York: Charles Scribner, 1853.

———. *Poems of the Republic.* New York: Edward O. Jenkins, 1864.

Brown, George William. *Baltimore and the Nineteenth of April, 1861: A Study of the War.* Baltimore: N. Murray, 1887.

Bruce, Susannah Ural. *The Harp and the Eagle: Irish-American Volunteers and the Union Army, 1861–1865.* New York: New York University Press, 2006.

Cable, George Washington, ed. *Famous Adventures and Prison Escapes of the Civil War.* New York: Century, 1911.

Carmichael, Peter S. "We Respect a *Good* Soldier, No Matter What Flag He Fought Under." In *The Spotsylvania Campaign,* ed. Gary W. Gallagher, 203–22. Chapel Hill: University of North Carolina Press, 1998.

Carpenter, Amos B. *A Genealogical History of the Rehoboth Branch of the Carpenter Family in America, Brought Down from Their English Ancestor, John Carpenter, 1303, with Many Biographical Notes of Descendants and Allied Families.* Amherst, MA: Carpenter and Morehouse, 1898.

Casey, Silas. *Infantry Tactics for the Instruction, Exercise, and Maneuvers of the Soldier, a Company, Line of Skirmishers, Battalion, Brigade, or Corps d'Armée.* Vol. 1. New York: D. Van Nostrand, 1862.

Catalogue and Circular of the Illinois Soldiers' College. Fulton, IL: Beers & Baton, 1867.

Catalogue of Connecticut Volunteer Organizations. Hartford, CT: Brown & Gross, 1869.

Catalogue of Officers and Students of the Appleton Academy, Mont Vernon, N.H. Milford, NH: Garfield's Fast Rotary Press, 1858.

Catalogue of the Alumni of the Albany Law School, 1851–1908. Schenectady, NY: Union University Department of Law, 1908.

Chisolm, Julian John. *A Manual of Military Surgery.* Richmond: West & Johnson, 1861.

Cimbala, Paul. *Under the Guardianship of the Nation: The Freedmen's Bureau and the Reconstruction of Georgia, 1865–1870.* Athens: University of Georgia Press, 1997.

Clarke, Frances M. *War Stories: Suffering and Sacrifice in the Civil War North.* Chicago: University of Chicago Press, 2011.

Collin, Henry Park. *A Twentieth Century History and Biographical Record of Branch County, Michigan.* New York: Lewis, 1906.

Connecticut Legislative History and Souvenir. Vol. 7. Putnam, CT: William Harrison Taylor, 1910.

Cooper, Benjamin. *Veteran Americans: Literature and Citizenship from Revolution to Reconstruction.* Amherst: University of Massachusetts Press, 2018.

Cunningham, Thomas J. *The Blue Book of the State* of *Wisconsin.* Milwaukee: Milwaukee Litho. & Engr., 1891.

The Daily News Aurora City Directory. Keokuk, IA: W. H. McCoy, 1904.

Dictionary of American Biography. Vol. 2, *Barsotti–Brazer.* New York: Charles Scribner's Sons, 1943.

Documents of the Ninety-Fifth Legislature of the State of New Jersey, and the Twenty-Seventh under the New Constitution. Jersey City, NJ: Pangborn, Dunning, & Dear, 1871.

Doty, Lockwood Richard, ed. *History of Livingston County New York from Its Earliest Traditions to the Present Together with Early Town Sketches.* Jackson, MI: W. J. Van Deusen, 1905.

Edmunds, A. C. *Pen Sketches of Nebraskans.* Lincoln, NE: R. & J. Wilbur, 1871.

Eicher, John, and David Eicher, *Civil War High Commands.* Stanford, CA: Stanford University Press, 2001.

Engel, Stephen D. "Yankee Dutchmen: Germans, the Union, and the Construction of a Wartime Identity." In *Civil War Citizens: Race, Ethnicity, and Identity in America's Bloodiest Conflict,* ed. Susannah J. Ural, 11–56. New York: New York University Press, 2010.

Ettinger, Clara Dare. *Genealogy of the Dare Family.* Chicago: s.n., 1901.

The Every Office Favorite: Seven National Directories, 1886–1887. Des Moines, IA: Johnson Directory, 1886.

Figg, Laurann, and Jane Farrell-Beck. "Amputation in the Civil War: Physical and Social

Dimensions." *Journal of the History of Medicine and Allied Sciences* 48 (October 1993): 454–75.

Galbreath, Charles B. *History of Ohio*. Vol. 3. Chicago: American Historical Society, 1925.

Gannon, Barbara A. *The Won Cause: Black and White Comradeship in the Grand Army of the Republic*. Chapel Hill: University of North Carolina Press, 2011.

Garrison, William Lloyd. "Declaration of Sentiments of the American Anti-Slavery Convention." In *Selections from the Writings and Speeches of William Lloyd Garrison*, 66–71. Boston: R. F. Wallcut, 1852.

Gerber, David A. *Black Ohio and the Color Line, 1860–1915*. Urbana: University of Illinois Press, 1976.

Glasson, William Henry. *Federal Military Pensions in the United States*. New York: Oxford University Press, 1918.

Goodhue, Mary. *Lineage Book*. Washington, DC: National Society of the Daughters of the American Revolution, 1936.

Griffith, George Bancroft. *The Poets of Maine: A Collection of Specimen Poems from over Four Hundred Verse-Makers of the Pine-Tree State*. Portland, ME: Elwell, Pickard, 1888.

Hager, Christopher. *I Remain Yours: Common Lives in Civil War Letters*. Cambridge, MA: Harvard University Press, 2018.

Hall, J. Knox. *History of Stark County, Illinois, and Its People: A Record of Settlement, Organization, Progress, and Achievement*. Vol. 1. Chicago: Pioneer, 1916.

Handley-Cousins, Sarah. *Bodies in Blue: Disability and the American Civil War*. Athens: University of Georgia Press, 2019.

Hanna, Charles W. *African American Recipients of the Medal of Honor: A Biographical Dictionary, Civil War through Vietnam War*. Jefferson, NC: McFarland, 2002.

Hasegawa, Guy R. *Mending Broken Soldiers: The Union and Confederate Programs to Supply Artificial Limbs*. Carbondale: Southern Illinois University Press, 2012.

History of Penobscot County, Maine. Cleveland: Williams, Chase, 1882.

Holbrook, J. *Military Tactics: Adapted to the Different Corps in the United States*. Middletown, CT: E. & H. Clark, 1826.

Hough, Franklin Benjamin. *A History of Lewis County, in the State of New York*. Munsell & Rowland, 1860.

Howard, Henry W. B., ed. *The Eagle and Brooklyn: The Record of the Progress of the Brooklyn Daily Eagle*. New York: Brooklyn Daily Eagle, 1893.

Illustrated Roster of the Department of Illinois Grand Army of the Republic. N.p., 1914.

Johnson, Allison M. *The Scars We Carve: Bodies and Wounds in Civil War Print Culture*. Baton Rouge: Louisiana State University Press, 2019.

Jones, Terry L. *Historical Dictionary of the Civil War* 2 vols. Lanham, MD: Scarecrow, 2011.

Jordan, Brian Matthew. *Marching Home: Union Veterans and Their Unending Civil War*. New York: Liveright, 2014.

Journal of Proceedings of the Forty-First Annual Encampment of the Department of Ohio, Grand Army of the Republic. N.p.: Eagle, 1907.

Journal of the Forty-Fifth Annual Encampment Department of Massachusetts, Grand Army of the Republic. Boston: Wright & Potter, 1911.

Journal of the Twenty-Sixth Annual Session of the Department of Indiana, Grand Army of the Republic, Held at Madison, June 14 and 15, 1905. Indianapolis: Sentinel Printing, 1905.

Keller, Christian B. *Chancellorsville and the Germans: Nativism, Ethnicity, and Civil War Memory.* New York: Fordham University Press, 2007.

Kenilworth Park & Aquatic Gardens. National Park Service, 2020, www.nps.gov/keaq/index.htm.

Kennedy, Frances H., ed. *The Civil War Battlefield Guide.* Boston: Houghton Mifflin, 1990.

Kreiser, Lawrence A., Jr. "A Socioeconomic Study of Veterans of the 103rd Ohio Volunteer Infantry Regiment After the Civil War." *Ohio History* 107 (Summer/Autumn 1998): 171–84.

Ladd, Warren. *The Ladd Family.* New Bedford, MA: Edmund Anthony & Sons, 1890.

Linderman, Gerald. *Embattled Courage: The Experience of Combat in the American Civil War.* New York: Free Press, 1987.

Little, Henry F. W. *The Seventh Regiment New Hampshire Volunteers in the War of the Rebellion.* Concord, NH: Ira C. Evans, 1896.

Logue, Larry M., and Peter Blanck. *Race, Ethnicity, and Disability: Veterans and Benefits in Post–Civil War America.* New York: Cambridge University Press, 2010.

Long, Lisa A. *Rehabilitating Bodies: Health, History, and the American Civil War.* Philadelphia: University of Pennsylvania Press, 2004.

Luebke, Peter C. "'To Transmit and Perpetuate the Fruits of This Victory': Union Regimental Histories and the Great Rebellion in Immediate Retrospect." In *New Perspectives on the Union War,* eds. Gary W. Gallagher and Elizabeth R. Varon, 186–200. New York: Fordham University Press, 2019.

Marquis, Albert Nelson. *Who's Who in New England.* Vol. 2. Chicago: A. N. Marquis, 1916.

Marten, James Alan. *Sing Not War: The Lives of Union and Confederate Veterans in Gilded Age America.* Chapel Hill: University of North Carolina Press, 2011.

Massachusetts Soldiers, Sailors, and Marines in the Civil War. 8 vols. Norwood, MA: Norwood, 1931–35.

McManus, I. C. "The History and Geography of Human Handedness." In *Language Lateralization and Psychosis,* edited by Iris E. C. Sommer and René S. Kahn, 37–57. New York: Cambridge University Press, 2009.

McPherson, James. *Battle Cry of Freedom: The Civil War Era.* New York: Oxford University Press, 1988.

———. *For Cause and Comrades: Why Men Fought in the Civil War.* New York: Oxford University Press, 1997.

The Medical and Surgical History of the War of the Rebellion, 1861–65. Vols. 1–2. Washington, DC: Government Printing Office, 1870–88.

Moak, Jefferson M. *Military Petitions for Naturalization Filed in the Philadelphia [County] District Court, 1862–1874.* Philadelphia: Genealogical Society of Pennsylvania, 2000.

Moore, John William. *Textbook of the Eruptive and Continued Fevers.* New York: William Wood, 1892.

Nason, George W. *History and Complete Roster of the Massachusetts Regiments.* Boston: Smith & McCance, 1910.

Nelson, Megan Kate. *Ruin Nation: Destruction and the American Civil War.* Athens: University of Georgia Press, 2012.

The Northeastern Reporter. Vol. 57. St. Paul, MN: West, 1900.

Norton, C. A. Quincy. "The Lights and Lamps of Early New England." *Connecticut Magazine* 7, no. 5 (1902–3): 501–13.

Nudelman, Franny. *John Brown's Body: Slavery, Violence, and the Culture of War.* Chapel Hill: University of North Carolina Press, 2004.

Official Roster of the Soldiers of the State of Ohio in the War of the Rebellion, 1861–1866. Vols. 1–12. Akron, OH: Werner Printing and Manufacturing, 1886–95.

Padilla, Jalynn Olsen. "Army of 'Cripples': Northern Civil War Amputees, Disability, and Manhood in Victorian America." PhD diss., University of Delaware, 2007. ProQuest (3277826).

Pearson, Henry Greenleaf. *The Life of John A. Andrew.* Vol. 2. Boston: Houghton Mifflin, 1904.

Peck, George B., Jr. *A Recruit before Petersburg.* Providence, RI: N. Bangs Williams, 1890.

Perkins, D. A. W. *History of Osceola County, Iowa, from Its Organization to the Present Time.* Sioux Falls, SD: Brown and Saenger, 1892.

Proceedings of the Forty-First Annual Encampment of the Department of Illinois G.A.R. Chicago: M. Umbdenstock, 1907.

Proceedings of the Thirty-Fifth Annual Encampment of the Department of Ohio, Grand Army of the Republic. Cincinnati: Elm Street Printing, 1901.

Pryce, Samuel D. *Vanishing Footprints: The Twenty-Second Iowa Volunteer Infantry in the Civil War.* Edited by Jeffry C. Burden. Iowa City, IA: Camp Pope Bookshop, 2008.

Quint, Alonzo Hall. *The Record of the Second Massachusetts Infantry, 1861–65.* Boston: James P. Walker, 1867.

Record of Officers and Men of New Jersey in the Civil War, 1861–1865. 2 vols. Trenton, NJ: John L. Murphy, 1876.

Record of Service of Michigan Volunteers in the Civil War, 1861–1865. 46 vols. Kalamazoo, MI: Ihling Bros. & Everard, n.d.

Reed, Thomas J. *The Original Iron Brigade.* Lanham, MD: Fairleigh Dickinson University Press, 2011.

Register of Officers and Agents, Civil, Military, and Naval, in the Service of the United States, on the Thirtieth of September, 1869. Washington, DC: Government Printing Office, 1870.

Register of Officers and Agents, Civil, Military, and Naval, in the Service of the United States, on the Thirtieth of September, 1871. Washington, DC: Government Printing Office, 1872.

Regulations Established for the Organization and Government of the Military Academy, at West Point. New York: Wiley & Putnam, 1839.

Report of the Adjutant General of the State of Illinois. 9 vols. Springfield, IL: Journal, 1900–1902.

Report of the Adjutant General of the State of Indiana. 8 vols. Indianapolis: Alexander H. Conner, 1865–69.

Reports of Committees of the Senate of the United States for the First Session of the Fifty-First Congress. Vol. 2. Washington, DC: Government Printing Office, 1890.

Reports of the Town Officers of Melrose for the Financial Year Ending December 31, 1898. Melrose, MA: Dunton & Potter, Printers, 1899.

Reports to the Legislature of the State of New Hampshire. Manchester, NH: John B. Clarke, 1903.

Revised Register of the Soldiers and Sailors of New Hampshire in the War of the Rebellion, 1861–1866. Concord, NH: Ira C. Evans, 1895.

Revised Roster of Vermont Volunteers and Lists of Vermonters Who Served in the Army and Navy of the United States during the War of the Rebellion, 1861–1866. Montpelier, VT: Watchman, 1892.

Ross, Sam. *The Empty-Sleeve: A Biography of Lucius Fairchild.* Madison: State Historical Society of Wisconsin, 1964.

Roster of Wisconsin Volunteers, War of the Rebellion, 1861–1865. 2 vols. Madison, WI: Democrat Printing, 1886.

Samito, Christian G. *Becoming American under Fire: Irish Americans, African Americans, and the Politics of Citizenship during the Civil War Era.* Ithaca, NY: Cornell University Press, 2009.

Scharf, John Thomas. *History of Saint Louis City and County, from the Earliest Periods to the Present Day: Including Biographical Sketches of Representative Men.* Vol. 2. Philadelphia: Louis H. Everts, 1883.

Smith, John David. *Black Judas: William Hannibal Thomas and the American Negro.* Athens: University of Georgia Press, 2000.

Smith, Sophia. *Mack Genealogy: The Descendants of John Mack of Lyme, Conn.* Rutland, VT: Tuttle, 1903.

The Statutes at Large of the United States of America from March 1911, to March 1913. Vol. 37. Washington, DC, 1913.

Strait, N. A. *Roster of All Regimental Surgeons and Assistant Surgeons in the Late War.* N.p., 1882.

Sweet, Timothy. *Traces of War: Poetry, Photography, and the Crisis of the Union.* Baltimore: Johns Hopkins University Press, 1990.

Thirteenth Annual Report of the State Commissioner of Common Schools to the Governor of Ohio. Columbus: L. D. Myers & Bro., 1867.

Thornton, Tamara Plakins. *Handwriting in America: A Cultural History.* New Haven, CT: Yale University Press, 1996.

The Union Army: A History of Military Affairs in the Loyal States, 1861–65. Vol. 8, *Biographical.* Madison, WI: Federal, 1908.

The United States Biographical Dictionary, Kansas Volume. Chicago: S. Lewis, 1879.

The War of the Rebellion: A Compilation of the Official Records of the Union and Confederate Armies. 70 vols. in 128 pts. Washington, DC: Government Printing Office, 1880–1900.

Washington, D.C., City Directory, 1890. Washington, DC: R. L. Polk, 1890.

Wiley, Bell Irvin. *The Life of Billy Yank: The Common Soldier of the Union.* 1952. Reprint, Baton Rouge: Louisiana State University Press, 2008.

Wiley, Samuel T. *Biographical and Historical Cyclopedia of Delaware County, Pennsylvania.* Richmond, IN: Gresham, 1894.

Winters, John D. *The Civil War in Louisiana.* Baton Rouge: Louisiana State University Press, 1991.

Wittenberg, Eric J. *Holding the Line on the River of Death: Union Mounted Forces at Chickamauga, September 18, 1863.* El Dorado Hills, CA: Savas Beatie, 2018.

INDEX